I0031845

Culture of India

Language, Literaure, Religion, Philosophy, Festivals and Food

Editor

Lita Haggerty

Scribbles

Year of Publication 2018

ISBN : 9789352979738

Book Published by

Scribbles

(An Imprint of Alpha Editions)

email - alphaedis@gmail.com

Produced by: PediaPress GmbH
Limburg an der Lahn
Germany
http://pediapress.com/

The content within this book was generated collaboratively by volunteers.
Please be advised that nothing found here has necessarily been reviewed by
people with the expertise required to provide you with complete, accurate or
reliable information. Some information in this book may be misleading or simply
wrong. Alpha Editions and PediaPress does not guarantee the validity of the
information found here. If you need specific advice (for example, medical, legal,
financial, or risk management) please seek a professional who is licensed or
knowledgeable in that area.
Sources, licenses and contributors of the articles and images are listed in the
section entitled "References". Parts of the books may be licensed under the
GNU Free Documentation License. A copy of this license is included in the
section entitled "GNU Free Documentation License"
The views and characters expressed in the book are those of the contributors and
his/her imagination and do not represent the views of the Publisher.

Contents

Introduction

The culture of India refers collectively to the thousands of distinct and unique cultures of all religions and communities present in India. India's languages, religions, dance, music, architecture, food, and customs differ from place to place within the country. Indian culture, often labeled as an amalgamation of several cultures, spans across the Indian subcontinent and has been influenced by a history that is several millennia old. Many elements of India's diverse cultures, such as Indian religions, philosophy, cuisine, languages, martial arts, dance, music and movies have a profound impact across the Indosphere, Greater India and the world.

Indosphere

Indosphere

Indosphere is a term coined by the linguist James Matisoff for areas of Indian linguistic and cultural influence in Southeast Asia. It is commonly used in areal linguistics in contrast with Sinosphere.

Influence

The Tibeto-Burman family of languages, which extends over a huge geographic range, is characterized by great typological diversity, comprising languages that range from the highly tonal, monosyllabic, analytic type with practically no affixational morphology, like the Loloish languages, to marginally tonal or atonal languages with complex systems of verbal agreement morphology, like the Kiranti group of Nepal. This diversity is partly to be explained in terms of areal influences from Chinese on the one hand and Indo-Aryan languages on the other. Matisoff proposed two large and overlapping areas combining cultural and linguistic features – the "Sinosphere" and the "Indosphere", influenced by China and India respectively.[1,2] A buffer zone between them as a third group was proposed by Kristine A. Hildebrandt, followed by B. Bickel and J. Nichols. The Indosphere is dominated by Indic languages.

Some languages and cultures firmly belong to one or the other. For example, the Munda and Khasi branches of Austroasiatic languages, the Tibeto-Burman languages of Eastern Nepal, and much of the "Kamarupan" group of Tibeto-Burman, which most notably includes the Meitei (Manipuri), are Indospheric; while the Hmong–Mien family, the Kam–Sui branch of Kadai, the Loloish branch of Tibeto-Burman, and Vietnamese (Viet–Muong) are Sinospheric. Some other languages, like Thai and Tibetan, have been influenced by both Chinese and Indian culture at different historical periods. Still other linguistic communities are so remote geographically that they have escaped significant influence from either. For example, the Aslian branch of Mon–Khmer in

Malaya, or the Nicobarese branch of Mon–Khmer in the Nicobar Islands of the Indian Ocean show little influence by Sinosphere or Indosphere. The Bodish languages and Kham languages are characterized by hybrid prosodic properties akin to related Indospheric languages towards the west and also Sinospheric languages towards the east.[3] Some languages of the Kiranti group in the Indosphere rank among the morphologically most complex languages of Asia.[4]

Indian cultural, intellectual, and political influence – especially that of Pallava writing system – began to penetrate both insular and peninsular Southeast Asia about 2000 years ago. Indic writing systems were adopted first by Austronesians, like Javanese and Cham, and Austroasiatics, like Khmer and Mon, then by Tai (Siamese and Lao) and Tibeto-Burmans (Pyu, Burmese, and Karen). Indospheric languages are also found in Mainland Southeast Asia (MSEA), defined as the region encompassing Laos, Cambodia, and Thailand, as well as parts of Burma, Peninsular Malaysia and Vietnam. Related scripts are also found in South East Asian islands ranging from Sumatra, Java, Bali, south Sulawesi and most of the Philippines.[5] The learned components of the vocabularies of Khmer, Mon, Burmese and Thai/Lao consist of words of Pali or Sanskrit origin. Indian influence also spread north to the Himalayan region. Tibetan has used Devanagari writing since 600 AD, but has preferred to calque new religious and technical vocabulary from native morphemes rather than borrowing Indian ones. The Cham empires, known collectively as Champa, which were founded around the end of 2nd century AD, belonged directly to Indosphere of influence, rather than to the Sinosphere which shaped so much of Vietnamese culture and by which Chams were influenced later and indirectly.[6]

Structure

Languages in the "Sinosphere" (roughly Southeast Asia) tend to be analytic, with little morphology, monosyllabic or sesquisyllabic lexical structures, extensive compounding, complex tonal systems, and serial verb constructions. Languages in the "Indosphere" (roughly the Himalayas and South Asia) tend to be more agglutinative, with polysyllabic structures, extensive case and verb morphology, and detailed markings of interpropositional relationships. Manange (like other Tamangic languages) is an interesting case to examine in this regard, as geographically it fits squarely in the "Indospheric" Himalayas, but typologically it shares more features with the "Sinospheric" languages. Tibeto-Burman languages spoken in the Sinosphere tend to be more isolating, while those spoken in the Indosphere tend to be more morphologically complex.[7]

Many languages in the western side of the Sino-Tibetan family, which includes the Tibeto-Burman languages, show significant typological resemblances with other languages of the South Asia, which puts them in the group of Indosphere.

They often have heavier syllables than found in the east, while tone systems, though attested, are not as frequent.[8] Indospheric languages are often toneless and/or highly suffixal.[9] Often there is considerable inflectional morphology, from fully developed case marking systems to extensive pronominal morphology found on the verb. These languages generally mark a number of types of inter-casual relationships and have distinct construction involving verbal auxiliaries. Languages of the Indosphere typically display retroflex stop consonants, postsentential relative clauses and the extended grammaticalization of the verb *say*. In Indospheric languages, such as the Tibeto-Burman languages of Northeast India and Nepal, for example, the development of relative pronouns and correlative structures as well as of retroflex initial consonants is often found.

Further reading

- Language variation: Papers on variation and change in the Sinosphere and in the Indosphere in honor of James A. Matisoff, David Bradley, Randy J. LaPolla and Boyd Michailovsky eds., pp. 113–144. Canberra: Pacific Linguistics.
- Ankerl, Guy (2000) [2000], *Global communication without universal civilization*, INU societal research, Vol.1: Coexisting contemporary civilizations : Arabo-Muslim, Bharati, Chinese, and Western, Geneva: INU Press, ISBN 2-88155-004-5<templatestyles src="Module:Citation/CS1/styles.css"></templatestyles>

External links

- Papers on variation and change in the Sinosphere and in the Indosphere in honour of James A. Matisoff[10]
- Language diversity: Sinosphere vs. Indosphere[11]
- Himalayan Languages Project[12]
- Rethinking Tibeto-Burman – Lessons from Indosphere[13]
- Areal linguistics and Mainland Southeast Asia[14]Wikipedia:Link rot

Greater India

Indian Cultural Sphere

Greater India
Indian cultural extent **Dark orange**: The Indian subcontinent (India, Pakistan, Bangladesh, Sri Lanka, Maldives, Nepal and Bhutan). **Light orange**: Southeast Asia culturally linked to India, notably Burma, Thailand, Cambodia, Laos, Champa (Southern Vietnam), Malaysia, Brunei and Indonesia. **Yellow**: Regions with significant Indian cultural influence, notably China's Yunnan, Tibet, the Philippines and historically Afghanistan.

Southeast Asia	
Indianized kingdoms **Hinduism** **Architecture** **Epigraphy**	Champa, Dvaravati, Funan, Gangga Negara, Chenla, Kalingga, Kutai, Majapahit, Langka-suka, Pagan, Pan Pan, Srivijaya, Tarumanagara Devaraja, Harihara Angkor, Borobodur Sanskrit, Pali, Tamil

South Asia	
Buddhism	Bangladesh, Bhutan, Nepal, Tibet, Sri Lanka
Hinduism	Bangladesh, Bhutan, Nepal, Tibet, Pakistan, Sri Lanka

East Asia	
Buddhism transmitted to East Asia	China, Japan, Korea, Mongolia, Tibet

Central Asia	
Buddhist monasticism	Central Asia (Afghanistan · Uzbekistan)

Indosphere · Hindu texts · Buddhist texts · Folk-lore of India · Ramayana (Versions of Ramayana)

- $\underline{v}$
- $\underline{t}$
- $\underline{e}^{15}$

The term **Greater India** is most commonly used to encompass the historical and geographic extent of all political entities of the Indian subcontinent, and the regions which are culturally linked to India or received significant Indian cultural influence. These countries have to varying degrees been transformed by the acceptance and induction of cultural and institutional elements of India. Since around 500 BCE, Asia's expanding land and maritime trade had resulted in prolonged socio-economic and cultural stimulation and diffusion of Hindu and Buddhist beliefs into the region's cosmology, in particular in Southeast

Asia and Sri Lanka. In Central Asia, transmission of ideas were predominantly of a religious nature.

By the early centuries of the common era most of the principalities of Southeast Asia had effectively absorbed defining aspects of Hindu culture, religion and administration. The notion of divine god-kingship was introduced by the concept of Harihara, Sanskrit and other Indian epigraphic systems were declared official, like those of the south Indian Pallava dynasty and Chalukya dynasty. These Indianized Kingdoms, a term coined by George Cœdès in his work *Histoire ancienne des états hindouisés d'Extrême-Orient*, were characterized by surprising resilience, political integrity and administrative stability.[16]

To the north, Indian religious ideas were accepted into the cosmology of Himalayan peoples, most profoundly in Tibet and Bhutan. Buddhist monasticism extended into Afghanistan, Uzbekistan and other parts of Central Asia, and Buddhist texts and ideas were readily accepted in China and Japan in the east. To the west, Indian culture converged with Greater Persia via the Hindukush and the Pamir Mountains.

Variant utilization & other usage

In the 20th century history, art history, linguistics, and allied fields: consisted of "all the Asian lands including Burma, Java, Cambodia, Bali, and the former Champa and Funan polities of present-day Vietnam,"[17] in which Indian culture left an "imprint in the form of monuments, inscriptions and other traces of the historic 'Indianising' process." In some accounts, many Pacific societies and "most of the Buddhist world including Ceylon, Tibet, central Asia and even Japan were held to fall within this web of Indianising "culture colonies". This particular usage (implying cultural "sphere of influence" of India) does not go back to before the 1920s, and lasted well into the 1970s in history and later in other fields.

European cartography and toponomy

The concept of the *Three Indias* was in common circulation in pre-industrial Europe. *Greater India* was the southern part of South Asia, *Lesser India* was the northern part of South Asia, and *Middle India* was the region near the Middle East. The Portuguese form (Portuguese: *India Maior*) was used at least since the mid-15th century. The term, which seems to have been used with variable precision,[18] sometimes meant only the Indian subcontinent;[19] Europeans used a variety of terms related to South Asia to designate the South Asian peninsula, including *High India*, *Greater India*, *Exterior India* and *India aquosa*.

Figure 1: *The 9th-century Shivaistic temple of Prambanan in Central Java near Yogyakarta, the largest Hindu temple in Indonesia*

However, in some accounts of European nautical voyages, Greater India (or *India Major*) extended from the Malabar Coast (present-day Kerala) to *India extra Gangem*[20] (lit. "India, beyond the Ganges," but usually the East Indies, i.e. present-day Malay Archipelago) and *India Minor*, from Malabar to Sind. *Farther India* was sometimes used to cover all of modern Southeast Asia. Until the fourteenth century, India could also mean areas along the Red Sea, including Somalia, South Arabia, and Ethiopia (e.g., Diodorus of Sicily of the first century BCE says that "the Nile rises in India" and Marco Polo of the fourteenth century says that "Lesser India ... contains ... Abash [Abyssinia]")

In late 19th-century geography, *Greater India* referred to British India, Hindustan (Northwestern Subcontinent) which included the Punjab, the Himalayas, and extended eastwards to Indochina (including Tibet and Burma), parts of Indonesia (namely, the Sunda Islands, Borneo and Celebes), and the Philippines."[21] German atlases distinguished *Vorder-Indien* (Anterior India) as the South Asian peninsula and *Hinter-Indien* as Southeast Asia.

Geology

Greater India, or *Greater India Basin* signifies "the Indian Plate plus a postulated northern extension", the product of the *Indian–Asia collision*. Although its usage in geology pre-dates Plate tectonic theory,[22] the term has seen increased usage since the 1970s.

It is unknown when and where the India–Asia (Indian and Eurasian Plate) convergence occurred, at or before 52 Million years ago. The plates have converged up to 3,600 km (2,200 mi) ± 35 km (22 mi). The upper crustal shortening is documented from geological record of Asia and the Himalaya as up to approximately 2,350 km (1,460 mi) less.

Nationalist movement

Here the use of *Greater India* refers to a popularization by a network of Bengali scholars in the 1920s who were all members of the Calcutta-based *Greater India Society*. The movement's early leaders included the historian R. C. Majumdar (1888–1980), the philologists Suniti Kumar Chatterji (1890–1977) and P. C. Bagchi (1898–1956), and the historians Phanindranath Bose and Kalidas Nag (1891–1966).

The term *Greater India*, whether aligned or separate from the notion of ancient Hindu expansion into Southeast Asia, was linked to both Indian nationalism[23] and Hindu nationalism.[24]

Indianization

The concept of the Indianized kingdoms, a term coined by George Coedès, describes Southeast Asian principalities that flourished since the early common era as a result of centuries of socio-economic interaction having incorporated central aspects of Indian institutions, religion, statecraft, administration, culture, epigraphy, literature and architecture.[25]

Iron Age trade expansion caused regional geostrategic remodeling. Southeast Asia was now situated in the central area of convergence of the Indian and the East Asian maritime trade routes, the basis for economic and cultural growth. The earliest Hindu kingdoms emerged in Sumatra and Java, followed by mainland polities such as Funan and Champa. Adoption of Indian civilization elements and individual adaptation stimulated the emergence of centralized states and the development of highly organized societies. Ambitious local leaders realized the benefits of Hinduism and Indian methods of administration, culture, literature, etc. Rule in accord with universal moral principles, represented in the concept of the *devaraja*, was more appealing than the Chinese concept of intermediaries.

Figure 2: *Ruins of Ayutthaya in Thailand which was named after Ayodhya*

Distinction from colonialism

Indianization is different from traditional colonialismWikipedia:Please clarify as it mostly did not involve strangers conquering an unknown land,Wikipedia:Please clarifyWikipedia:Citation needed with exceptions such as the Chola invasions of mediaeval times. Instead, Indian influence from trade routes and language use slowly permeated through Southeast Asia, making the traditions a part of the region. The interactions between India and Southeast Asia were marked by waves of influence and dominance. At some points the Indian culture solely found its way into the region, and at other points the influence was used to take over. Indianization was seen as total influence of all aspects of Southeast Asian history. Before the take over of the influence of Indian culture, Southeast Asia was seen as a place with no history. The beginning of Indianization marked the start of the cultural commencement in Southeast Asia.

Theories of Indianization

As conclusive evidence is missing numerous Indianization theories of Southeast Asia have emerged since the early 20th century. The central argument usually revolves around the question, who was the main propagator exporting Indian institutional and cultural ideas to Southeast Asia.

One theory of the spread of Indianization that focuses on the caste of Vaishya traders and their role for spreading Indian culture and language into Southeast Asia through trade. There were many trade incentives that brought Vaishya traders to Southeast Asia, the most important of which was gold. During the 4th century C.E., when the first evidence of Indian trader in Southeast Asia, the Indian sub-continent was at a deficiency for gold due to extensive control of overland trade routes by the Roman Empire. This made many Vaishya traders look to the seas to acquire new gold, of which Southeast Asia was abundant. However, the conclusion that Indianization was just spread through trade is insufficient, as Indianization permeated through all classes of Southeast Asian society, not just the merchant classes.

Another theory states that Indianization spread through the warrior class of Kshatriya. This hypothesis effectively explains state formation in Southeast Asia, as these warriors came with the intention of conquering the local peoples and establishing their own political power in the region. However, this theory hasn't attracted much interest from historians as there is very little literary evidence to support it.

The most widely accepted theory for the spread of Indianization into Southeast Asia is through the class of Brahman scholars. These Brahmans brought with them many of the Hindu religious and philosophical traditions and spread them to the elite classes of Southeast Asian polities. Once these traditions were adopted into the elite classes, it disseminated throughout all the lower classes, thus explaining the Indianization present in all classes of Southeast Asian society. Brahmans were also experts in art and architecture, and political affairs, thus explaining the adoption of many Indian style law codes and architecture into Southeast Asian society

Literature

Scripts in Sanskrit discovered during the early centuries of the Common Era are the earliest known forms of writing to have extended all the way to Southeast Asia. Its gradual impact ultimately resulted in its widespread domain as a means of dialect which evident in regions, from Bangladesh to Cambodia, Malaysia and Thailand and additionally a few of the larger Indonesian islands. In addition, alphabets from languages spoken in Burmese, Thai, Laos and Cambodia are a variations formed off of Indian ideals that have localized the language.

The utilization of Sanskrit has been prevalent in all aspects of life including legal purposes. Sanskrit terminology and vernacular appears in ancient courts to establish procedures that have been structured by Indian models such as a system composed of a code of laws. The concept of legislation demonstrated through codes of law and organizations particularly the idea of "God King" was embraced by numerous rulers of Southeast Asia. The rulers amid this time, for example, the Lin-I Dynasty of Vietnam once embraced the Sanskrit dialect and devoted sanctuaries to the Indian divinity Shiva. Many rulers following even viewed themselves as "reincarnations or descendants" of the Hindu Gods. However once Buddhism began entering the nations, this practiced view was eventually altered.

Religion, authority and legitimacy

The pre-Indic political and social systems in Southeast Asia were marked by a relative indifference towards lineage descent. Hindu God kingship enabled rulers to supersede loyalties, forge cosmopolitan polities and the worship of Shiva and Vishnu was combined with ancestor worship, so that Khmer, Javanese, and Cham rulers claimed semi-divine status as descendants of a God. Hindu traditions, especially the relationship to the sacrality of the land and social structures, are inherent in Hinduism's transnational features. The epic traditions of the Mahābhārata and the Rāmāyaṇa further legitimized a ruler identified with a God who battled and defeated the wrong doers that threaten the ethical order of the world.

Hinduism does not have a single historical founder, a centralized imperial authority in India proper nor a bureaucratic structure, thus ensuring relative religious independence for the individual ruler. It also allows for multiple forms of divinity, centered upon the Trimurti the triad of Brahma, Vishnu, and Shiva, the deities responsible for the creation, preservation, and destruction of the universe.

The effects of Hinduism and Buddhism applied a tremendous impact on the many civilizations inhabiting Southeast Asia which significantly provided some structure to the composition of written traditions. An essential factor for the spread and adaptation of these religions originated from trading systems of the third and fourth century. In order to spread the message of these religions Buddhist monks and Hindu priests joined mercantile classes in the quest to share their religious and cultural values and beliefs. Along the Mekong delta, evidence of Indianized religious models can be observed in communities labeled Funan. There can be found the earliest records engraved on a rock in Vocanh. The engravings consist of Buddhist archives and a south Indian scripts written in Sanskrit that have been dated to belong to the early half of the third century. Indian religion was profoundly absorbed by local cultures that formed their own distinctive variations of these structures in order to reflect their own ideals.

Champa, Dvaravati, Funan, Gangga Negara, Kadaram, Kalingga, Kutai, Langkasuka, Pagan, Pan Pan, Po-ni, and Tarumanagara had by the 1st to 4th centuries CE adopted Hinduism's cosmology and rituals, the *devaraja* concept of kingship, and Sanskrit as official writing. Despite the fundamental cultural integration, these kingdoms were autonomous in their own right and functioned independently.

Caste system

The caste system divides Hindus into a hierarchy of groups based on their work (karma) and duty (dharma). The Manusmriti, an ancient authoritative book on Hindu law, maintained that the system is a basis of order and regularity of society. Once born into a group, one can not move to different levels. Lower castes are never able to climb higher within the caste system, limiting the economies progress from growing. The system divides Hindus into four categories – Brahmins (priests and teachers), Kshatriyas (rulers and warriors), Vaishyas (merchants and farmers), and Shudras (craftsmen and labourers).

The Brahmins from the Indian culture spread their religion to Southeast Asia, beginning the Hindu and Buddhist cultures there. They introduced the caste system to the region, especially to Java, Bali, Madura, and Sumatra. The adopted caste system was not as strict as in India, tempered to the local context. There are multiple similarities between the two caste systems such that both state that no one is equal within society and that everyone has their own place. It also promoted the upbringing of highly organized central states. The Brahmins were still able to implement their religion, political ideas, literature, mythology, and art.

Adaption and adoption

It is unknown how immigration, interaction, and settlement took place, whether by key figures from India or through Southeast Asians visiting India who took elements of Indian culture back home. It is likely that Hindu and Buddhist traders, priests, and princes traveled to Southeast Asia from India in the first few centuries of the Common Era and eventually settled there. Strong impulse most certainly came from the region's ruling classes who invited Brahmans to serve at their courts as priests, astrologers and advisers. Divinity and royalty were closely connected in these polities as Hindu rituals validated the powers of the monarch. Brahmans and priests from India proper played a key role in supporting ruling dynasties through exact rituals. Dynastic consolidation was the basis for more centralized kingdoms that emerged in Java, Sumatra, Cambodia, Burma, and along the central and south coasts of Vietnam from the 4th to 8th centuries.

Art, architecture, rituals, and cultural elements such as the Rāmāyaṇa and the Mahābhārata had been adopted and customized increasingly with a regional

Figure 3: *Angkor Wat in Cambodia is the largest Hindu temple in the world*

character. The caste system, although adopted, was never applied universally and reduced to serve for a selected group of nobles only.

States such as Srivijaya, Majapahit and the Khmer empire had territorial continuity, resilient population and surplus economies that rivaled those in India itself. Borobudur in Java and Angkor in Cambodia are, apart from their grandeur, examples of a distinctly developed regional culture, style, and expression.[26]

Southeast Asia is called Suvarnabhumi or Sovannah Phoum - the golden land and Suvarnadvipa - the golden Islands in Sanskrit. It was frequented by traders from eastern India, particularly Kalinga. Cultural and trading relations between the powerful Chola dynasty of South India and the Southeast Asian Hindu kingdoms led the Bay of Bengal to be called "The Chola Lake", and the Chola attacks on Srivijaya in the 10th century CE are the sole example of military attacks by Indian rulers against Southeast Asia. The Pala dynasty of Bengal, which controlled the heartland of Buddhist India, maintained close economic, cultural and religious ties, particularly with Srivijaya.

Mainland kingdoms

- **Funan**: Funan was a polity that encompassed the southernmost part of the Indochinese peninsula during the 1st to 6th centuries. The name *Funan* is not found in any texts of local origin from the period, and so is considered an exonym based on the accounts of two Chinese diplomats, Kang Tai and Zhu Ying who sojourned there in the mid-3rd century CE.[27][:24] It is not known what name the people of Funan gave to their polity. Some scholars believe ancient Chinese scholars transcribed the word Funan from a word related to the Khmer word bnaṃ or vnaṃ (modern: ph-noṃ, meaning "mountain"); while others thought that Funan may not be a transcription at all, rather it meant what it says in Chinese, meaning something like "Pacified South". Centered at the lower Mekong, Funan is noted as the oldest Hindu culture in this region, which suggests prolonged socio-economic interaction with India and maritime trading partners of the Indosphere. Cultural and religious ideas had reached Funan via the Indian Ocean trade route. Trade with India had commenced well before 500 BC as Sanskrit hadn't yet replaced Pali. Funan's language has been determined as to have been an early form of Khmer and its written form was Sanskrit.

- **Chenla** was the successor polity of Funan that existed from around the late 6th century until the early 9th century in Indochina, preceding the Khmer Empire. Like its predecessor, Chenla occupied a strategic position where the maritime trade routes of the Indosphere and the East Asian cultural sphere converged, resulting in prolonged socio-economic and cultural influence, along with the adoption of the Sanskrit epigraphic system of the south Indian Pallava dynasty and Chalukya dynasty.[28] Chenla's first ruler Vīravarman adopted the idea of divine kingship and deployed the concept of Harihara, the syncretistic Hindu "god that embodied multiple conceptions of power". His successors continued this tradition, thus obeying the code of conduct Manusmṛti, the *Laws of Manu* for the Kshatriya warrior caste and conveying the idea of political and religious authority.

- **Langkasuka**: Langkasuka (-*langkha* Sanskrit for "resplendent land" -*sukkha* of "bliss") was an ancient Hindu kingdom located in the Malay Peninsula. The kingdom, along with the Old Kedah settlement, are probably the earliest territorial footholds founded on the Malay Peninsula. According to tradition, the founding of the kingdom happened in the 2nd century; Malay legends claim that Langkasuka was founded at Kedah, and later moved to Pattani.

- **Champa**: The kingdom of Champa (or *Lin-yi* in Chinese) controlled what is now south and central Vietnam since approximately 192 CE. The dominant religion was Hinduism and the culture was heavily influenced by India. By the late fifteenth century, the Vietnamese — proponents of the Sinosphere — had eradicated the last remaining traces of the once powerful maritime kingdom of Champa. The last surviving Chams began their diaspora in 1471, many re-settling in Khmer territory.

- **Kambuja**: The Khmer Empire was established by the early 9th century in a mythical initiation and consecration ceremony by founder Jayavarman II at Mount Kulen (Mount Mahendra) in 802 CE A succession of powerful sovereigns, continuing the Hindu devaraja tradition, reigned over the classical era of Khmer civilization until the 11th century. Buddhism was then introduced temporarily into royal religious practice, with discontinuities and decentralisation resulting in subsequent removal. The royal chronology ended in the 14th century. During this period of the Khmer empire, societal functions of administration, agriculture, architecture, hydrology, logistics, urban planning, literature and the arts saw an unprecedented degree of development, refinement and accomplishment from the distinct expression of Hindu cosmology.
- **Mon kingdoms**: From the 9th century until the abrupt end of the Hanthawaddy Kingdom in 1539, the Mon kingdoms (Hariphunchai, Pegu, Pagan) were notable for facilitating Indianized cultural exchange in lower Burma, in particular by having strong ties with Sri Lanka.
- **Sukhothai**: The first Tai peoples to gain independence from the Khmer Empire and start their own kingdom in the 13th century. Sukhothai was a precursor for the Ayutthaya Kingdom and the Kingdom of Siam. Though ethnically Thai, the Sukhothai kingdom in many ways was a continuation of the Buddhist Mon-Dvaravati civilizations, as well as the neighboring Khmer Empire.Wikipedia:Citation needed

Island kingdoms

- **Salakanagara**: Salakanagara kingdom is the first historically recorded Indianized kingdom in Western Java, established by an Indian trader after marrying a local Sundanese princess. This Kingdom existed between 130-362 CE.
- **Tarumanagara** was an early Sundanese Indianized kingdom, located not far from modern Jakarta, and according to Tugu inscription ruler Purnavarman apparently built a canal that changed the course of the Cakung River, and drained a coastal area for agriculture and settlement. In his inscriptions, Purnavarman associated himself with Vishnu, and Brahmins ritually secured the hydraulic project.
- **Kalingga**: Kalingga (Javanese: Karajan Kalingga) was the 6th century Indianized kingdom on the north coast of Central Java, Indonesia. It was the earliest Hindu-Buddhist kingdom in Central Java, and together with Kutai and Tarumanagara are the oldest kingdoms in Indonesian history.
- **Malayu** was a classical Southeast Asian kingdom. The primary sources for much of the information on the kingdom are the New History of the Tang, and the memoirs of the Chinese Buddhist monk Yijing who visited in 671 CE, and states that it was "absorbed" by Srivijaya by 692 CE, but

Figure 4: *A statue of Hindu goddess Durga Mahisasur-amardini in Prambanan northern cella, dated to the 9th-century Medang I Bhumi Mataram kingdom in Central Java.*

had "broken away" by the end of the eleventh century according to Chao Jukua. The exact location of the kingdom is the subject of studies among historians.

- **Srivijaya**: From the 7th to 13th centuries Srivijaya, a maritime empire centered on the island of Sumatra in Indonesia, had adopted Mahayana and Vajrayana Buddhism under a line of rulers from Dapunta Hyang Sri Jayanasa to the Sailendras. A stronghold of Vajrayana Buddhism, Srivijaya attracted pilgrims and scholars from other parts of Asia. I Ching reports that the kingdom was home to more than a thousand Buddhist scholars. A notable Buddhist scholar of local origin, Dharmakirti, taught Buddhist philosophy in Srivijaya and Nalanda (in India), and was the teacher of Atisha. Most of the time, this Buddhist Malay empire enjoyed cordial relationship with China and the Pala Empire in Bengal, and the 860 CE Nalanda inscription records that Maharaja Balaputra dedicated a monastery at Nalanda university near Pala territory. The Srivijaya kingdom ceased to exist in the 13th century due to various factors, including the expansion of the Javanese, Singhasari, and Majapahit empires.
- **Tambralinga** was an ancient kingdom located on the Malay Peninsula that at one time came under the influence of Srivijaya. The name had

been forgotten until scholars recognized Tambralinga as Nagara Sri Dharmaraja (Nakhon Si Thammarat). Early records are scarce but its duration
is estimated to range from the seventh to the fourteenth century. Tambralinga first sent tribute to the emperor of the Tang dynasty in 616 CE.
In Sanskrit, Tambra means "red" and linga means "symbol", typically
representing the divine energy of Shiva.

* **Medang Mataram**: The Medang i Bhumi Mataram Kingdom flourished
between the 8th and 11th centuries. It was first centered in central Java
before moving later to east Java. This kingdom produced numbers of
Hindu-Buddhist temples in Java, including Borobudur Buddhist mandala
and the Prambanan Trimurti Hindu temple dedicated mainly to Shiva. The
Sailendras were the ruling family of this kingdom at an earlier stage in
central Java, before being replaced by the Isyana Dynasty.

* **Kadiri**: In the 10th century, Mataram challenged the supremacy of Srivijaya, resulting in the destruction of the Mataram capital by Srivijaya
early in the 11th century. Restored by King Airlangga (c. 1020–1050),
the kingdom split on his death; the new state of Kediri, in eastern Java,
became the centre of Javanese culture for the next two centuries, spreading its influence to the eastern parts of Southeast Asia. The spice trade
was now becoming increasingly important, as demand from European
countries grew. Before they learned to keep sheep and cattle alive in
the winter, they had to eat salted meat, made palatable by the addition
of spices. One of the main sources was the Maluku Islands (or "Spice
Islands") in Indonesia, and so Kediri became a strong trading nation.

* **Singhasari**: In the 13th century, however, the Kediri dynasty was overthrown by a revolution, and Singhasari arose in east Java. The domains
of this new state expanded under the rule of its warrior-king Kertanegara.
He was killed by a prince of the previous Kediri dynasty, who then established the last great Hindu-Javanese kingdom, Majapahit. By the middle
of the 14th century Majapahit controlled most of Java, Sumatra and the
Malay peninsula, part of Borneo, the southern Celebes and the Moluccas.
It also exerted considerable influence on the mainland.

* **Majapahit**: The Majapahit empire, centered in East Java, succeeded the
Singhasari empire and flourished in the Indonesian archipelago between
the 13th and 15th centuries. Noted for their naval expansion, the Javanese
spanned west-east from Lamuri in Aceh to Wanin in Papua. Majapahit
was one of the last and greatest Hindu empires in Maritime Southeast
Asia. Most of Balinese Hindu culture, traditions and civilisations were derived from Majapahit legacy. A large number of Majapahit nobles, priests,
and artisans found their home in Bali after the decline of Majapahit to
Demak Sultanate.

- **Galuh** was an ancient Hindu kingdom in the eastern Tatar Pasundan (now west Java province and Banyumasan region of central Java province), Indonesia. It was established following the collapse of the Tarumanagara kingdom around the 7th century. Traditionally the kingdom of Galuh was associated with the eastern Priangan cultural region, around the Citanduy and Cimanuk rivers, with its territory spanning from Citarum river on the west, to the Pamali (present-day Brebes river) and Serayu rivers on the east. Its capital was located in Kawali, near present-day Ciamis city.
- **Sunda**: The Kingdom of Sunda was a Hindu kingdom located in western Java from 669 CE to around 1579 CE, covering the area of present-day Banten, Jakarta, West Java, and the western part of Central Java. According to primary historical records, the Bujangga Manik manuscript, the eastern border of the Sunda Kingdom was the Pamali River (Ci Pamali, the present day Brebes River) and the Serayu River (Ci Sarayu) in Central Java.

Issues with Indianization

Development in Southeast Asia

One of the major issues with Indianization is the common debate whether or not indianization is the reason for the development in South East Asia. Many struggle to date and determine when colonization in Southeast Asia occurred because of the structures and ruins found that were similar to those in India. Several books and anthropologists believe that India is seen as the superior culture that influenced a lot of Southeast Asian countries. However, throughout this time that many began to debate, other anthropologists suggested that Southeast Asia had indigenous civilization and the idea of indianization was just seen as a 'national motivation. These debates continued for some time, until the Pacific War, which led to legitimately ending the debates and reviewing Southeast Asia's response to Indianzation.

Development of caste system

Another main concern for indianization was the understanding and development of caste systems. The debate was often whether or not the caste systems were seen as an elite process or just the process of picking up the Indian culture and calling it their own in each region. This had showed that the Southeast Asian countries were civilized and able to flourish their own interests. For example, Cambodia's caste system is based on people in society. However, in India, the caste system was based on which class they belonged to when they were born. Based on the evidence of the caste system in Southeast Asia, shows that they were applying Indian culture to their own, also known/seen as indianization Similar to the caste systems, the cultures were a huge part of determining the legitimacy of indianization. Many argue that only writing could really date the culture and prove indianization. The lives of rulers, daily lives of people, rituals of funeral, weddings and specific customs were a few that helped anthropologists date the indianization of countries. The religions found in India and Southeast Asian countries was another piece of evidence that led anthropologists to understand where the cultures and customs were adopted from.

Fall of Indianization

Khmer Kingdom

Beginning shortly after the 12th century, the Khmer kingdom, one of the first kingdoms that began the dissipation of Indianization started after Jayavarman VII in which expanded a substantial amount of territory, thus going into war with Champs. Leading into the fall of the Khmer Kingdom, the Khmer political and cultural zones were taken, overthrown, and fallen as well. Not only did Indianization change many cultural and political aspects, but it also changed the spiritual realm as well, creating a type of Northern Culture which began in the early 14th century, prevalent for its rapid decline in the Indian kingdoms. The decline of Hinduism kingdoms and spark of Buddhist kingdoms led to the formation of orthodox Sinhalese Buddhism and is a key factor leading to the decline of Indianization. Sukhothai and Ceylon are the prominent characters who formulated the center of Buddhism and this became more popularized over Hinduism.

Rise of Islam

Not only was the spark of Buddhism the driving force for Indianization coming to an end, but Islamic control took over as well in the midst of the thirteenth century to trump the Hinduist kingdoms. In the process of Islamism coming to the traditional Hinduism kingdoms, trade was heavily practiced and the now Islamic Indians started becoming merchants all over Southeast Asia. Moreover, as trade became more saturated in the Southeast Asian regions wherein Indianization once persisted, the regions had become more Muslim populated. This so-called Islamic control has spanned to many of the trading centers across the regions of Southeast Asia, including one of the most dominant centers, Malacca, and has therefore stressed a widespread rise of Islamization.

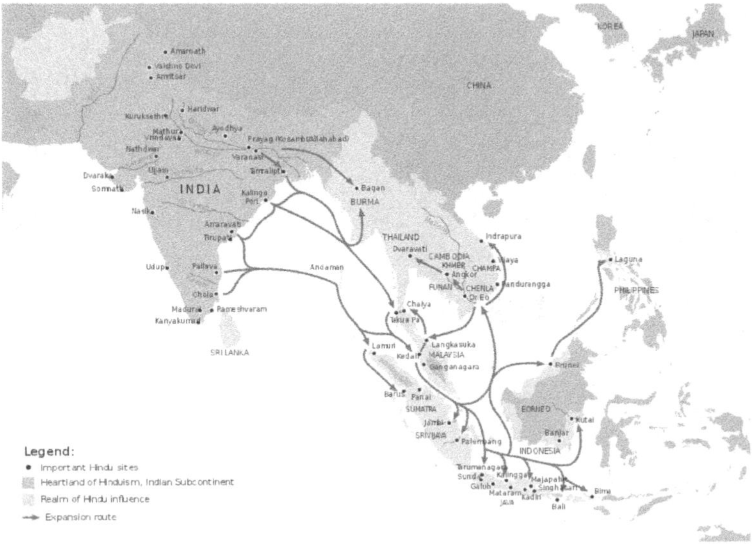

Figure 5: *Expansion of Hinduism in Southeast Asia.*

Indian cultural sphere

The use of *Greater India* to refer to an Indian cultural sphere was popularised by a network of Bengali scholars in the 1920s who were all members of the Calcutta-based Greater India Society. The movement's early leaders included the historian R. C. Majumdar (1888–1980); the philologists Suniti Kumar Chatterji (1890–1977) and P. C. Bagchi (1898–1956), and the historians Phanindranath Bose and Kalidas Nag (1891–1966).[29] Some of their formulations were inspired by concurrent excavations in Angkor by French archaeologists and by the writings of French Indologist Sylvain Lévi. The scholars of the society postulated a benevolent ancient Indian cultural colonisation of Southeast Asia, in stark contrast — in their view — to the Western colonialism of the early 20th century.[30,31]

The term *Greater India* and the notion of an explicit Hindu expansion of ancient Southeast Asia have been linked to both Indian nationalism[32] and Hindu nationalism.[33] However, many Indian nationalists, like Jawaharlal Nehru and Rabindranath Tagore, although receptive to "an idealisation of India as a benign and uncoercive world civiliser and font of global enlightenment,"[34] stayed away from explicit "Greater India" formulations.[35] In addition, some scholars have seen the Hindu/Buddhist acculturation in ancient Southeast Asia as "a single cultural process in which Southeast Asia was the matrix and South Asia

Figure 6: *Candi Bukit Batu Pahat of Bujang Valley. A Hindu-Buddhist kingdom ruled ancient Kedah possibly as early as 110 CE, the earliest evidence of strong Indian influence which was once prevalent among the Kedahan Malays.*

the mediatrix."[36] In the field of art history, especially in American writings, the term survived due to the influence of art theorist Ananda Coomaraswamy. Coomaraswamy's view of pan-Indian art history was influenced by the "Calcutta cultural nationalists."

By some accounts Greater India consists of "lands including Burma, Philippines, Java, Cambodia, Bali, and the former Champa and Funan polities of present-day Vietnam," in which Indian and Hindu culture left an "imprint in the form of monuments, inscriptions and other traces of the historic "Indianizing" process." By some other accounts, many Pacific societies and "most of the Buddhist world including Ceylon, Tibet, Central Asia, and even Japan were held to fall within this web of Indianizing *culture colonies*" This particular usage — implying cultural "sphere of influence" of India — was promoted by the Greater India Society, formed by a group of Bengali men of letters,[37] and is not found before the 1920s. The term *Greater India* was used in historical writing in India into the 1970s.

Figure 7: *Atashgah of Baku, a fire temple in Azerbai-
jan used by both Hindus and Persian Zoroastrians*

Cultural expansion

Culture spread via the trade routes that linked India with southern Burma, central and southern Siam, the Malay peninsula and Sumatra to Java, Philippines, lower Cambodia and Champa. The Pali and Sanskrit languages and the Indian script, together with Theravada and Mahayana Buddhism, Brahmanism and Hinduism, were transmitted from direct contact as well as through sacred texts and Indian literature. Southeast Asia had developed some prosperous and very powerful colonial empires that contributed to Hindu-Buddhist artistic creations and architectural developments. Art and architectural creations that rivaled those built in India, especially in its sheer size, design and aesthetic achievements. The notable examples are Borobudur in Java and Angkor monuments in Cambodia. The Srivijaya Empire to the south and the Khmer Empire to the north competed for influence in the region.

A defining characteristic of the cultural link between Southeast Asia and the Indian subcontinent was the adoption of ancient Indian Vedic/Hindu and Buddhist culture and philosophy into Philippines, Myanmar, Tibet, Thailand, Indonesia, Malaya, Laos and Cambodia. Indian scripts are found in Southeast Asian islands ranging from Sumatra, Java, Bali, South Sulawesi and part of the Philippines.[38] The Ramayana and the Mahabharata have had a large impact on

South Asia and Southeast Asia. One of the most tangible evidence of dharmic Hindu traditions is the widespread use of the *Añjali Mudrā* gesture of greeting and respect. It is seen in the Indian *namasté* and similar gestures known throughout Southeast Asia; its cognates include the Cambodian *sampeah*, the Indonesian *sembah*, the Japanese *gassho* and Thai *wai*.

Cultural commonalities

Religion, mythology and folklore

* Hinduism is practised by the majority of Bali's population.[39] The Cham people of Vietnam still practices Hinduism as well. Though officially Buddhist, many Thai, Khmer, and Burmese people also worship Hindu gods in a form of syncretism. This echoes the beliefs of the past Hindu civilizations such as the Khmer Empire.Wikipedia:Citation needed
* Brahmins have had a large role in spreading Hinduism in Southeast Asia. Even today many monarchies such as the royal court of Thailand still have Hindu rituals performed for the King by Hindu Brahmins.
* Garuda, a Hindu mythological figure, is present in the coats of arms of Indonesia, Thailand and Ulaanbaatar.
* Muay Thai, a fighting art that is the Thai version of the Hindu Musti-yuddha style of martial art.
* Kaharingan, an indigenous religion followed by the Dayak people of Borneo, is categorised as a form of Hinduism in Indonesia.
* Philippine mythology includes the supreme god Bathala and the concept of *Diwata* and the still-current belief in *Karma*—all derived from Hindu-Buddhist concepts.
* Malay folklore contains a rich number of Indian-influenced mythological characters, such as Bidadari, Jentayu, Garuda and Naga.
* Wayang shadow puppets and classical dance-dramas of Indonesia, Cambodia, Malaysia and Thailand took stories from episodes of *Ramayana* and *Mahabharata*.

Architecture and monuments

* The same style of Hindu temple architecture was used in several ancient temples in South East Asia including Angkor Wat, which was dedicated to Hindu god Vishnu and is shown on the flag of Cambodia, also Prambanan in Central Java, the largest Hindu temple in Indonesia, is dedicated to Trimurti — Shiva, Vishnu and Brahma.

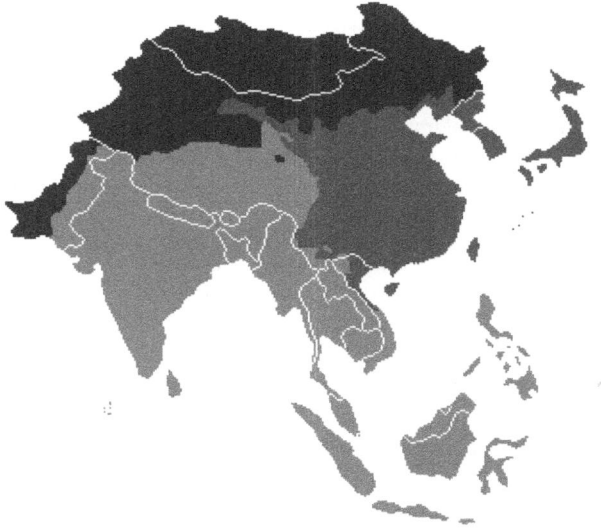

Figure 8: *A map of East, South and Southeast Asia.* **Red** *signifies current and historical (Vietnam) distribution of Chinese characters.* **Green** *signifies current and historical (Malaysia, Pakistan, the Maldives, parts of Indonesia and parts of the Philippines) distribution of Indic scripts.* **Blue** *signifies current use of non-Sinitic or non-Indic scripts.*

- Borobudur in Central Java, Indonesia, is the world's largest Buddhist monument. It took shape of a giant stone mandala crowned with stupas and believed to be the combination of Indian-origin Buddhist ideas with the previous megalithic tradition of native Austronesian step pyramid.
- The minarets of 15th- to 16th-century mosques in Indonesia, such as the Great Mosque of Demak and Kudus mosque resemble those of Majapahit Hindu temples.
- The Batu Caves in Malaysia are one of the most popular Hindu shrines outside India. It is the focal point of the annual Thaipusam festival in Malaysia and attracts over 1.5 million pilgrims, making it one of the largest religious gatherings in history.
- Erawan Shrine, dedicated to Brahma, is one of the most popular religious shrines in Thailand.[40]

Linguistic influence

Scholars like Sheldon Pollock have used the term *Sanskrit Cosmopolis* to describe the region and argued for millennium-long cultural exchanges without necessarily involving migration of peoples or colonisation. Pollock's 2006 book *The Language of the Gods in the World of Men* makes a case for studying the region as comparable with Latin Europe and argues that the Sanskrit language was its unifying element.

Scripts in Sanskrit discovered during the early centuries of the Common Era are the earliest known forms of writing to have extended all the way to Southeast Asia. Its gradual impact ultimately resulted in its widespread domain as a means of dialect which evident in regions, from Bangladesh to Cambodia, Malaysia and Thailand and additionally a few of the larger Indonesian islands. In addition, alphabets from languages spoken in Burmese, Thai, Laos and Cambodia are a variations formed off of Indian ideals that have localized the language.

Sanskrit and related languages have also influenced their Tibeto-Burman-speaking neighbors to the north through the spread of Buddhist texts in translation. The spread of Buddhism to Tibet allowed many Sanskrit texts to survive only in Tibetan translation (in the Tanjur). Buddhism was similarly introduced to China by Mahayanist missionaries sent by the Indian Emperor Ashoka mostly through translations of Buddhist Hybrid Sanskrit and Classical Sanskrit texts, and many terms were transliterated directly and added to the Chinese vocabulary.

In Southeast Asia, languages such as Thai and Lao contain many loan words from Sanskrit, as does Khmer to a lesser extent. For example, in Thai, Rāvaṇa, the legendary emperor of Sri Lanka, is called 'Thosakanth' which is derived from his Sanskrit name 'Daśakaṇṭha' ("having ten necks").

Many Sanskrit loanwords are also found in Austronesian languages, such as Javanese particularly the old form from which nearly half the vocabulary is derived from the language.[41] Other Austronesian languages, such as traditional Malay, modern Indonesian, also derive much of their vocabulary from Sanskrit, albeit to a lesser extent, with a large proportion of words being derived from Arabic. Similarly, Philippine languages such as Tagalog have many Sanskrit loanwords.

A Sanskrit loanword encountered in many Southeast Asian languages is the word *bhāṣā*, or spoken language, which is used to mean language in general, for example *bahasa* in Malay, Indonesian and Tausug, *basa* in Javanese, Sundanese, and Balinese, *phasa* in Thai and Lao, *bhasa* in Burmese, and *phiesa* in Khmer.

The utilization of Sanskrit has been prevalent in all aspects of life including legal purposes. Sanskrit terminology and vernacular appears in ancient courts to establish procedures that have been structured by Indian models such as a system composed of a code of laws. The concept of legislation demonstrated through codes of law and organizations particularly the idea of "God King" was embraced by numerous rulers of Southeast Asia. The rulers amid this time, for example, the Lin-I Dynasty of Vietnam once embraced the Sanskrit dialect and devoted sanctuaries to the Indian divinity Shiva. Many rulers following even viewed themselves as "reincarnations or descendants" of the Hindu gods. However once Buddhism began entering the nations, this practiced view was eventually altered.

Linguistic commonalities

- In the Malay Archipelago: Indonesian, Javanese and Malay have absorbed a large amount of Sanskrit loanwords into their respective lexicons (see: Sanskrit loan words in Indonesian). Many languages of native lowland Filipinos such as Tagalog, Ilocano and Visayan contain numerous Sanskrit loanwords.
- In Mainland Southeast Asia: Thai, Lao, Burmese, and Khmer language have absorbed a significant amount of Sanskrit as well as Pali words.
- Many Indonesian names have Sanskrit origin (e.g. Dewi Sartika, Megawati Sukarnoputri, Susilo Bambang Yudhoyono, Teuku Wisnu).
- Southeast Asian languages are traditionally written with Indic alphabets and therefore have extra letters not pronounced in the local language, so that original Sanskrit spelling can be preserved. An example is how the name of the late King of Thailand, Bhumibol Adulyadej, is spelled in Sanskrit as "Bhumibol"ภูมิพล, yet is pronounced in Thai as "Phumipon" พูมิพน using Thai-Sanskrit pronunciation rules since the original Sanskrit sounds do not exist in Thai.

Toponyms

- Suvarnabhumi is a toponym that has been historically associated with Southeast Asia. In Sanskrit, it means "The Land of Gold". Thailand's Suvarnabhumi Airport is named after this toponym, signifying its intent to be a major transport hub of Southeast Asia.Wikipedia:Citation needed
- Several of Indonesian toponyms have Indian parallel or origin, such as Madura with Mathura, Serayu and Sarayu river, Semeru with Sumeru mountain, Kalingga from Kalinga Kingdom, and Ngayogyakarta from Ayodhya.
- Siamese ancient city of Ayutthaya also derived from Ramayana's Ayodhya.

- Names of places could simply render their Sanskrit origin, such as Singapore, from Singapura (*Singha-pura* the "lion city"), Jakarta from *Jaya* and *kreta* ("complete victory").
- Some of the Indonesian regencies such as Indragiri Hulu and Indragiri Hilir derived from Indragiri River, Indragiri itself means "mountain of Indra".
- Some Thai toponyms also often have Indian parallels or Sanskrit origin, although the spellings are adapted to the Siamese tongue, such as Ratchaburi from *Raja-puri* ("king's city"), and Nakhon Si Thammarat from *Nagara Sri Dharmaraja*.
- The tendency to use Sanskrit for modern neologism also continued to modern day. In 1962 Indonesia changed the colonial name of New Guinean city of Hollandia to Jayapura ("glorious city"), Orange mountain range to Jayawijaya Mountains.
- Malaysia named their new government seat as Putrajaya ("prince of glory") in 1999.

Historiography of Indianization

Indianization of Southeast Asia

The history of South East Asia was mostly always written from the perspective of external civilizations that influenced the region.The prevalent interpretation caused because of the ontological differences, the fundamentally dichotomous histories of Europe and pre-colonial Asia and the conclusion from it was that the despotism, obscurantism, servile equality of Asian societies had caused innovation to become prey to tyranny and had rendered the history of the region cyclical, immobile and non-linear.

The belief in the idea that South East Asia had never engendered its own civilization, and of indigenous incapacity or external benefaction gained additional support, such was the tremendous evidence of Indian architectural and religious influence in South East Asia and we're fundamentally identified as being derivative and thus Indianization was perceived as occurring more so due to the Indian initiatives rather than the indigenous initiatives of South East Asia.[42]

Caste systems

Another main concern for Indianization was the understanding and development of caste systems. The debate was often whether or not the caste systems were seen as an elite process or just the process of picking up the Indian culture and calling it their own in each region. This had showed that the Southeast

Asian countries were civilized and able to flourish their own interests. For example, Cambodia's caste system is based on people in society. However, in India, the caste system was based on which class they belonged to when they were born. Based on the evidence of the caste system in Southeast Asia, shows that they were applying Indian culture to their own, also known/seen as Indianization

References

- Ali, Jason R.; Aitchison, Jonathan C. (2005), "Greater India", *Earth-Science Reviews*, **72** (3–4): 169–188, doi: 10.1016/j.earscirev.2005.07.005[43]<templatestyles src="Module:Citation/CS1/styles.css"></templatestyles>.
- Azurara, Gomes Eannes de (1446), *Chronica do Discobrimento e Conquista de Guiné (eds. Carreira and Pantarem, 1841)*, Paris<templatestyles src="Module:Citation/CS1/styles.css"></templatestyles>.
- Bayley, Susan (2004), "Imagining 'Greater India': French and Indian Visions of Colonialism in the Indic Mode", *Modern Asian Studies*, **38** (3): 703–744, doi: 10.1017/S0026749X04001246[44]<templatestyles src="Module:Citation/CS1/styles.css"></templatestyles>.
- Beazley, Raymond (December 1910), "Prince Henry of Portugal and the Progress of Exploration", *The Geographical Journal*, **36** (6): 703–716, doi: 10.2307/1776846[45], JSTOR 1776846[46]<templatestyles src="Module:Citation/CS1/styles.css"></templatestyles>.
- Caverhill, John (1767), "Some Attempts to Ascertain the Utmost Extent of the Knowledge of the Ancients in the East Indies", *Philosophical Transactions*, **57**: 155–178, doi: 10.1098/rstl.1767.0018[47]<templatestyles src="Module:Citation/CS1/styles.css"></templatestyles>
- Guha-Thakurta, Tapati (1992), *The making of a new 'Indian' art. Artists, aesthetics and nationalism in Bengal, c. 1850–1920*, Cambridge, UK: Cambridge University Press<templatestyles src="Module:Citation/CS1/styles.css"></templatestyles>.
- Handy, E. S. Craighill (1930), "The Renaissance of East Indian Culture: Its Significance for the Pacific and the World", *Pacific Affairs*, University of British Columbia, **3** (4): 362–369, doi: 10.2307/2750560[48], JSTOR 2750560[49]<templatestyles src="Module:Citation/CS1/styles.css"></templatestyles>.
- Keenleyside, T. A. (Summer 1982), "Nationalist Indian Attitudes Towards Asia: A Troublesome Legacy for Post-Independence Indian Foreign Policy", *Pacific Affairs*, University of British Columbia, **55** (2):

210–230, doi: 10.2307/2757594[50], JSTOR 2757594[51]<templatestyles
src="Module:Citation/CS1/styles.css"></templatestyles>.

- Majumdar, R. C., H. C. Raychaudhuri, and Kalikinkar
  Datta (1960), *An Advanced History of India*, London: Macmillan and Co., 1122 pages<templatestyles
  src="Module:Citation/CS1/styles.css"></templatestyles>.
- Narasimhaiah, C. D. (1986), "The cross-cultural dimensions of English in religion, politics and literature", *World Englishes*, **5** (2–3):
  221–230, doi: 10.1111/j.1467-971X.1986.tb00728.x[52]<templatestyles
  src="Module:Citation/CS1/styles.css"></templatestyles>.
- Thapar, Romila (1968), "Interpretations of Ancient Indian History", *History and Theory*, Wesleyan University, **7** (3): 318–335,
  doi: 10.2307/2504471[53], JSTOR 2504471[54]<templatestyles
  src="Module:Citation/CS1/styles.css"></templatestyles>.
- Wheatley, Paul (November 1982), "Presidential Address: India Beyond the Ganges—Desultory Reflections on the Origins of Civilisation in Southeast Asia", *The Journal of Asian
  Studies*, Association for Asian Studies, **42** (1): 13–28, doi:
  10.2307/2055365[55], JSTOR 2055365[56]<templatestyles
  src="Module:Citation/CS1/styles.css"></templatestyles>

Further reading

- Language variation: Papers on variation and change in the Sinosphere and
  in the Indosphere in honour of James A. Matisoff, David Bradley, Randy
  J. LaPolla and Boyd Michailovsky eds., pp. 113–144. Canberra: Pacific
  Linguistics.
- Bijan Raj Chatterjee (1964). *Indian Cultural Influence
  in Cambodia*[57]. University of Calcutta.<templatestyles
  src="Module:Citation/CS1/styles.css"></templatestyles>
- Ankerl, Guy (2000). *Global communication without universal
  civilisation*. INU societal research. Vol.1: Coexisting contemporary civilisations : Arabo-Muslim, Bharati, Chinese, and Western. Geneva: INU Press. ISBN 2-88155-004-5.<templatestyles
  src="Module:Citation/CS1/styles.css"></templatestyles>
- Cœdès, George (1968). Walter F. Vella, ed. *The Indianized
  States of Southeast Asia*. trans.Susan Brown Cowing. University of Hawaii Press. ISBN 978-0-8248-0368-1.<templatestyles
  src="Module:Citation/CS1/styles.css"></templatestyles>
- Lokesh, Chandra, & International Academy of Indian Culture. (2000).
  Society and culture of Southeast Asia: Continuities and changes. New
  Delhi: International Academy of Indian Culture and Aditya Prakashan.

- R. C. Majumdar, Study of Sanskrit in South-East Asia
- R. C. Majumdar, *India and South-East Asia*, I.S.P.Q.S. History and Archaeology Series Vol. 6, 1979, <templatestyles src="Module:Citation/CS1/styles.css" />ISBN 81-7018-046-5.
- R. C. Majumdar, *Champa, Ancient Indian Colonies in the Far East*, Vol.I, Lahore, 1927. <templatestyles src="Module:Citation/CS1/styles.css" />ISBN 0-8364-2802-1
- R. C. Majumdar, *Suvarnadvipa, Ancient Indian Colonies in the Far East*, Vol.II, Calcutta,
- R. C. Majumdar, *Kambuja Desa Or An Ancient Hindu Colony In Cambodia*, Madras, 1944
- Daigorō Chihara (1996). *Hindu-Buddhist Architecture in Southeast Asia*[58]. BRILL. ISBN 90-04-10512-3.<templatestyles src="Module:Citation/CS1/styles.css"></templatestyles>
- Hoadley, M. C. (1991). Sanskritic continuity in Southeast Asia: The ṣaḍātatāyī and aṣṭacora in Javanese law. Delhi: Aditya Prakashan.

External links

- Rethinking Tibeto-Burman – Lessons from Indosphere[59]
- THEORIES OF INDIANISATION[60] Exemplified by Selected Case Studies from Indonesia (Insular Southeast Asia), by Dr. Helmut Lukas

Philosophy

Indian philosophy

Part of a series on
Eastern philosophy

- Aryadeva and Nagarjuna
- Adi Shankara
- Laozi and Confucius

- $\underline{v}$
- $\underline{t}$
- $\underline{e}^{61}$

Part of a series on

Philosophy

- Plato
- Kant
- Nietzsche
- Buddha
- Confucius
- Averroes

Philosophers

- Aestheticians
- Epistemologists
- Ethicists
- Logicians
- Metaphysicians
- Social and political philosophers

Traditions

- African
- Analytic
- Aristotelian
- Buddhist
- Chinese
- Christian
- Continental
- Existentialism
- Hindu
- Jain
- Jewish
- Pragmatism
- Eastern
- Islamic
- Platonic
- Western

Periods

• Ancient • Medieval • Modern • Contemporary
Literature
• Aesthetics • Epistemology • Ethics • Logic • Metaphysics • Political philosophy
Branches
• Aesthetics • Epistemology • Ethics • Legal philosophy • Logic • Metaphysics • Political philosophy • Social philosophy
Lists
• Index • Outline • Years • Problems • Publications • Theories • Glossary • Philosophers
Miscellaneous
• Philosopher • Philomath • Philalethes • Women in philosophy
🏛 **Philosophy portal**
• $\underline{v}$ • $\underline{t}$ • $\underline{e}$[62]

Indian philosophy refers to ancient philosophical traditions of the Indian sub-continent. The principal schools are classified as either orthodox or heterodox – āstika or nāstika – depending on one of three alternate criteria: whether it believes the Vedas are a valid source of knowledge; whether the school believes in the premises of Brahman and Atman; and whether the school believes in afterlife and Devas.[63]

There are six major schools of orthodox Indian Hindu philosophy—Nyaya, Vaisheshika, Samkhya, Yoga, Mīmāṃsā and Vedanta, and five major heterodox schools—Jain, Buddhist, Ajivika, Ajñana, and Cārvāka. However, there are other methods of classification; Vidyaranya for instance identifies sixteen schools of Indian philosophy by including those that belong to the Śaiva and Raseśvara traditions.[64,65]

The main schools of Indian philosophy were formalised chiefly between 1000 BCE to the early centuries of the Common Era. Competition and integration between the various schools was intense during their formative years, especially between 800 BCE and 200 CE. Some schools like Jainism, Buddhism, Yoga, Śaiva and Vedanta survived, but others, like Ajñana, Charvaka and Ājīvika did not.

Ancient and medieval era texts of Indian philosophies include extensive discussions on Ontology (metaphysics, Brahman-Atman, Sunyata-Anatta), reliable means of knowledge (epistemology, Pramanas), value system (axiology) and other topics.

Common themes

Earliest Hindu philosophy were arranged and codified by Hindu Vedic sages, such as Yajnavalkya (c. 8th century BCE), who is considered one of the earliest philosophers in recorded history, after Aruni (c. 8th century BCE).[66]

Jain philosophy was propagated by Tirthankaras, notably Parshvanatha (c. 872 – c. 772 BCE) and Mahavira (c. 549–477 BCE).

Buddhist philosophy was founded by Gautama Buddha (c. 563–483 BCE).

Sikh philosophy was crystalised in Guru Granth Sahib enshrined by Guru Gobind Singh (c. 1666–1708 CE).

Figure 9: *Hindu philosophy has a diversity of traditions and numerous saints and scholars, such as Adi Shankara of Advaita Vedanta school.*

Indian philosophies share many concepts such as dharma, karma, samsara, reincarnation, dukkha, renunciation, meditation, with almost all of them focussing on the ultimate goal of liberation of the individual through diverse range of spiritual practices (moksha, nirvana). They differ in their assumptions about the nature of existence as well as the specifics of the path to the ultimate liberation, resulting in numerous schools that disagreed with each other. Their ancient doctrines span the diverse range of philosophies found in other ancient cultures.

Orthodox schools

Many Hindu intellectual traditions were classified during the medieval period of Brahmanic-Sanskritic scholasticism into a standard list of six orthodox (Astika) schools (darshanas), the "Six Philosophies" (*ṣaḍ-darśana*), all of which accept the testimony of the Vedas.[67,68,69]

- Samkhya, the rationalism school with dualism and atheistic themes[70,71]
- Yoga, a school similar to Samkhya but accepts personally defined theistic themes[72]

- Nyaya, the realism school emphasizing analytics and logic[73,74]
- Vaisheshika, the naturalism school with atomistic themes and related to the Nyaya school[75,76]
- Purva Mimamsa (or simply Mimamsa), the ritualism school with Vedic exegesis and philology emphasis,[77,78] and
- Vedanta (also called Uttara Mimamsa), the Upanishadic tradition, with many sub-schools ranging from dualism to nondualism.[79,80]

These are often coupled into three groups for both historical and conceptual reasons: Nyaya-Vaishesika, Samkhya-Yoga, and Mimamsa-Vedanta. The Vedanta school is further divided into six sub-schools: Advaita (monism/nondualism), also includes the concept of Ajativada, Visishtadvaita (monism of the qualified whole), Dvaita (dualism), Dvaitadvaita (dualism-nondualism), Suddhadvaita, and Achintya Bheda Abheda schools.

Besides these schools Mādhava Vidyāraṇya also includes the following of the aforementioned theistic philosophies based on the Agamas and Tantras:

- Pasupata, school of Shaivism by Nakulisa
- Saiva, the theistic Sankhya school
- Pratyabhijña, the recognitive school
- Raseśvara, the mercurial school
- Pāṇini Darśana, the grammarian school (which clarifies the theory of Sphoṭa)

The systems mentioned here are not the only orthodox systems, they are the chief ones, and there are other orthodox schools. These systems, accept the authority of Vedas and are regarded as orthodox (astika) schools of Hindu philosophy; besides these, schools that do not accept the authority of the Vedas are heterodox (nastika) systems such as Buddhism, Jainism, Ajivika and Cārvāka.[81,82,83] This orthodox-heterodox terminology is a construct of Western languages, and lacks scholarly roots in Sanskrit. According to Andrew Nicholson, there have been various heresiological translations of Āstika and Nāstika in 20th century literature on Indian philosophies, but quite many are unsophisticated and flawed.[84]

- Cārvāka / Charvaka is a materialistic and atheistic school of thought and, is noteworthy as evidence of a materialistic movement within Hinduism.[85]

Heterodox (Śramaṇic schools)

Several Śramaṇic movements have existed before the 6th century BCE, and these influenced both the āstika and nāstika traditions of Indian philosophy.[86] The Śramaṇa movement gave rise to diverse range of heterodox beliefs, ranging from accepting or denying the concept of soul, atomism, antinomian ethics,

Figure 10: *Rishabhanatha, believed to have lived over a million years ago, is considered the founder of Jain philosophy.*

materialism, atheism, agnosticism, fatalism to free will, idealization of extreme asceticism to that of family life, strict ahimsa (non-violence) and vegetarianism to permissibility of violence and meat-eating.[87] Notable philosophies that arose from Śramaṇic movement were Jainism, early Buddhism, Cārvāka, Ajñana and Ājīvika.[88]

Ajñana philosophy

Ajñana was one of the nāstika or "heterodox" schools of ancient Indian philosophy, and the ancient school of radical Indian skepticism. It was a Śramaṇa movement and a major rival of early Buddhism and Jainism. They have been recorded in Buddhist and Jain texts. They held that it was impossible to obtain knowledge of metaphysical nature or ascertain the truth value of philosophical propositions; and even if knowledge was possible, it was useless and disadvantageous for final salvation. They were sophists who specialised in refutation without propagating any positive doctrine of their own.

Jain philosophy

Jain philosophy is the oldest Indian philosophy that separates body (matter) from the soul (consciousness) completely. Jainism was revived and re-established after Mahavira, the last and the 24th *Tirthankara*, synthesised and

Figure 11: *The Buddhist philosophy is based on the teachings of the Buddha.*

revived the philosophies and promulgations of the ancient Śramaṇic traditions laid down by the first Jain tirthankara Rishabhanatha millions of years ago.[89] According to Dundas, outside of the Jain tradition, historians date the Mahavira as about contemporaneous with the Buddha in the 5th-century BC, and accordingly the historical Parshvanatha, based on the c. 250-year gap, is placed in 8th or 7th century BC.[90]

Jainism is a Śramaṇic religion and rejected the authority of the Vedas. However, like all Indian religions, it shares the core concepts such as karma, ethical living, rebirth, samsara and moksha. Jainism places strong emphasis on asceticism, ahimsa (non-violence) and anekantavada (relativity of viewpoints) as a means of spiritual liberation, ideas that influenced other Indian traditions. Jainism strongly upholds the individualistic nature of soul and personal responsibility for one's decisions; and that self-reliance and individual efforts alone are responsible for one's liberation. According to the Jain philosophy, the world (*Saṃsāra*) is full of *hiṃsā* (violence). Therefore, one should direct all his efforts in attainment of Ratnatraya, that are Samyak Darshan, Samyak Gnana, and Samyak Chàritra which are the key requisites to attain liberation.[91]

Buddhist philosophy

Buddhist philosophy is a system of thought which started with the teachings of Siddhartha Gautama, the Buddha, or "awakened one". Buddhism is founded

Figure 12: *Monastic life has been a part of all Indian philosophy traditions. Mendicant caves of extinct Ājīvikas in Bihar.*

on elements of the Śramaṇa movement, which flowered in the first half of the 1st millennium BCE, but its foundations contain novel ideas not found or accepted by other Sramana movements. Buddhism and Hinduism mutually influenced each other and shared many concepts, states Paul Williams, however it is now difficult to identify and describe these influences. Buddhism rejected the Vedic concepts of Brahman (ultimate reality) and Atman (soul, self) at the foundation of Hindu philosophies.[92,93,94]

Buddhism shares many philosophical views with other Indian systems, such as belief in *karma* – a cause-and-effect relationship, samsara – ideas about cyclic afterlife and rebirth, dharma – ideas about ethics, duties and values, impermanence of all material things and of body, and possibility of spiritual liberation (nirvana or moksha). A major departure from Hindu and Jain philosophy is the Buddhist rejection of an eternal soul (*atman*) in favour of *anatta* (non-Self).[95]

Ājīvika philosophy

The philosophy of Ājīvika was founded by Makkhali Gosala, it was a Śramaṇa movement and a major rival of early Buddhism and Jainism.[96] Ājīvikas were organised renunciates who formed discrete monastic communities prone to an ascetic and simple lifestyle.[97]

Original scriptures of the Ājīvika school of philosophy may once have existed, but these are currently unavailable and probably lost. Their theories are extracted from mentions of Ajivikas in the secondary sources of ancient Indian literature, particularly those of Jainism and Buddhism which polemically criticized the Ajivikas.[98] The Ājīvika school is known for its *Niyati* doctrine of absolute determinism (fate), the premise that there is no free will, that everything that has happened, is happening and will happen is entirely preordained and a function of cosmic principles.[98] Ājīvika considered the karma doctrine as a fallacy. Ājīvikas were atheists[99] and rejected the authority of the Vedas, but they believed that in every living being is an *ātman* – a central premise of Hinduism and Jainism.[100,101]

Cārvāka philosophy

Cārvāka or Lokāyata was a philosophy of scepticism and materialism, founded in the Mauryan period. They were extremely critical of other schools of philosophy of the time. Cārvāka deemed Vedas to be tainted by the three faults of untruth, self-contradiction, and tautology.[102] Likewise they faulted Buddhists and Jains, mocking the concept of liberation, reincarnation and accumulation of merit or demerit through karma.[103] They believed that, the viewpoint of relinquishing pleasure to avoid pain was the "reasoning of fools".

Comparison of Indian philosophies

The Indian traditions subscribed to diverse philosophies, significantly disagreeing with each other as well as orthodox Hinduism and its six schools of Hindu philosophy. The differences ranged from a belief that every individual has a soul (self, atman) to asserting that there is no soul, from axiological merit in a frugal ascetic life to that of a hedonistic life, from a belief in rebirth to asserting that there is no rebirth.

Comparison of ancient Indian philosophies

	Ājīvika	Early Buddhism	Cārvāka	Jainism	Orthodox schools of Hinduism (Non-Śramaṇic)
Karma	Denies[104,105]	Affirms	Denies	Affirms	Affirms
Samsara, Rebirth	Affirms	Affirms[106]	Denies[107]	Affirms	Some school affirm, some not[108]
Ascetic life	Affirms	Affirms	Affirms	Affirms	Affirms as Sannyasa[109]

Rituals, Bhakti	Affirms	Affirms, optional[110] (Pali: *Bhatti*)	Denies	Affirms, optional[111]	Theistic school: Affirms, optional[112] Others: Deny[113,114]
Ahimsa and Vegetarianism	Affirms	Affirms, Unclear on meat as food[115]		Strongest proponent of non-violence; Vegetarianism to avoid violence against animals[116]	Affirms as highest virtue, but Just War affirmed Vegetarianism encouraged, but choice left to the Hindu[117,118]
Free will	Denies[119]	Affirms[120]	Affirms	Affirms	Affirms[121]
Maya	Affirms[122]	Affirms (*prapañca*)[123]	Denies	Affirms	Affirms[124,125]
Atman (Soul, Self)	Affirms	Denies[126]	Denies[127]	Affirms:[119]	Affirms[128]
Creator God	Denies	Denies	Denies	Denies	Theistic schools: Affirm[129] Others: Deny[130,131]
Epistemology (Pramana)	Pratyakṣa, Anumāna, Śabda	Pratyakṣa, Anumāna[132]	Pratyakṣa[133]	Pratyakṣa, Anumāna, Śabda	Various, Vaisheshika (two) to Vedanta (six):[134,135] Pratyakṣa (perception), Anumāna (inference), Upamāna (comparison and analogy), Arthāpatti (postulation, derivation), Anupalabdi (non-perception, negative/-cognitive proof), Śabda (Reliable testimony)
Epistemic authority	Denies: Vedas	Affirms: Buddha text[136] Denies: Vedas	Denies: Vedas	Affirms: Jain Agamas Denies: Vedas	Affirm: Vedas and Upanishads,[137] (Note: This differentiation between epistemic and deontic authority is true for all Indian religions.)</ref> Affirm: other texts[138]
Salvation (Soteriology)	Samsdra-suddhi[139]	Nirvana (realize Śūnyatā)[140]		Siddha[141]	Moksha, Nirvana, Kaivalya Advaita, Yoga, others: Jivanmukti[142] Dvaita, theistic: Videhamukti

Meta-physics (Ulti-mate Reality)		Śūny-atā[143,144]		Anekān-tavāda[145]	Brahman[146,147]

Political philosophy

The Arthashastra, attributed to the Mauryan minister Chanakya, is one of the early Indian texts devoted to political philosophy. It is dated to 4th century BCE and discusses ideas of statecraft and economic policy.

The political philosophy most closely associated with India is the one of ahimsa (non-violence) and Satyagraha, popularised by Mahatma Gandhi during the Indian struggle for independence. In turn it influenced the later movements for independence and civil rights, especially those led by Martin Luther King, Jr. and Nelson Mandela.

Influence

In appreciation of complexity of the Indian philosophy, T S Eliot wrote that the great philosophers of India "make most of the great European philosophers look like schoolboys". Arthur Schopenhauer used Indian philosophy to improve upon Kantian thought. In the preface to his book *The World As Will And Representation*, Schopenhauer writes that one who "has also received and assimilated the sacred primitive Indian wisdom, then he is the best of all prepared to hear what I have to say to him" The 19th century American philosophical movement Transcendentalism was also influenced by Indian thought[148]

References

Sources

<templatestyles src="Refbegin/styles.css" />
- Dundas, Paul (2002) [1992], *The Jains*[149] (Second ed.), Routledge, ISBN 0-415-26605-X<templatestyles src="Module:Citation/CS1/styles.css"></templatestyles>
- Nicholson, Andrew J. (2010), *Unifying Hinduism: Philosophy and Identity in Indian Intellectual History*, Columbia University Press<templatestyles src="Module:Citation/CS1/styles.css"></templatestyles>

Further reading

- Apte, Vaman Shivram (1965). *The Practical Sanskrit-English Dictionary* (Fourth Revised and Enlarged ed.). Delhi: Motilal Banarsidass Publishers. ISBN 81-208-0567-4.<templatestyles src="Module:Citation/CS1/styles.css"></templatestyles>
- Basham, A.L. (1951). *History and Doctrines of the Ājīvikas*[150] (2nd ed.). Delhi, India: Moltilal Banarsidass (Reprint: 2002). ISBN 81-208-1204-2.<templatestyles src="Module:Citation/CS1/styles.css"></templatestyles> originally published by Luzac & Company Ltd., London, 1951.
- Balcerowicz, Piotr (2015). *Early Asceticism in India: Ājīvikism and Jainism*[151] (1st ed.). Routledge. p. 368. ISBN 9781317538530.<templatestyles src="Module:Citation/CS1/styles.css"></templatestyles>
- Cowell, E. B.; Gough, A. E. (2001). *The Sarva-Darsana-Samgraha or Review of the Different Systems of Hindu Philosophy: Trubner's Oriental Series*[152]. Taylor & Francis. ISBN 978-0-415-24517-3.<templatestyles src="Module:Citation/CS1/styles.css"></templatestyles>
- Flood, Gavin (1996), *An Introduction to Hinduism*, Cambridge: Cambridge University Press, ISBN 0-521-43878-0<templatestyles src="Module:Citation/CS1/styles.css"></templatestyles>
- Gandhi, M.K. (1961). *Non-Violent Resistance (Satyagraha)*. New York: Schocken Books.<templatestyles src="Module:Citation/CS1/styles.css"></templatestyles>
- Jain, Dulichand (1998). *Thus Spake Lord Mahavir*. Chennai: Sri Ramakrishna Math. ISBN 81-7120-825-8.<templatestyles src="Module:Citation/CS1/styles.css"></templatestyles>
- Michaels, Axel (2004). *Hinduism: Past and Present*. New York: Princeton University Press. ISBN 0-691-08953-1.<templatestyles src="Module:Citation/CS1/styles.css"></templatestyles>
- Radhakrishnan, S (1929). *Indian Philosophy, Volume 1*[153]. Muirhead library of philosophy (2nd ed.). London: George Allen and Unwin Ltd.<templatestyles src="Module:Citation/CS1/styles.css"></templatestyles>
- Radhakrishnan, S.; Moore, CA (1967). *A Sourcebook in Indian Philosophy*. Princeton. ISBN 0-691-01958-4.<templatestyles src="Module:Citation/CS1/styles.css"></templatestyles>
- Stevenson, Leslie (2004). *Ten theories of human nature*. Oxford University Press.<templatestyles src="Module:Citation/CS1/styles.css"></templatestyles> 4th edition.

- Hiriyanna, M. (1995). *Essentials of Indian Philosophy*. Motilal Banarsidas. ISBN 978-81-208-1304-5.<templatestyles src="Module:Citation/CS1/styles.css"></templatestyles>

External links

Wikimedia Commons has media related to *Indian philosophy*.

- A History of Indian Philosophy I HTML ebook (vol. 1)[154] I (vol. 2)[155] I (vol. 3)[156] I (vol. 4)[157] I (vol. 5)[158]
- A recommended reading guide from the philosophy department of University College, London: London Philosophy Study Guide — Indian Philosophy[159]
- Articles at the Internet Encyclopedia of Philosophy[160]
- Indian Psychology Institute[161] The application of Indian Philosophy to contemporary issues in Psychology
- A History of Indian Philosophy by Surendranath Dasgupta (5 Volumes)[162] at archive.org
- Indian Idealism by Surendranath Dasgupta[163] at archive.org
- The Essentials of Indian Philosophy by Prof. Mysore Hiriyanna[164] at archive.org
- Outlines of Indian Philosophy by Prof. Mysore Hiriyanna[165] at archive.org
- Indian Philosophy by Dr. Sarvepalli Radhakrishnan (2 Volumes)[153] at archive.org
- History of Philosophy – Eastern and Western Edited by Dr. Sarvepalli Radhakrishnan (2 Volumes)[166] at archive.org
- Indian Schools of Philosophy and Theology[167] (Jiva Institute)

Wildlife

Wildlife of India

Part of a series on the

Wildlife of India

- **Portal**
- v
- t
- e[168]

India is home to a variety of animal life.[169] Apart from a handful of domesticated animals, such as cows, water buffaloes, goats, chickens, and both Bactrian and Dromedary camels, India has a wide variety of animals native to the country. It is home to Bengal and Indochinese tigers, Asiatic lions, Indian and White Girrafe and Indochinese leopards, snow leopards, clouded leopards, various species of Deer, including Chital, Hangul, Barasingha; the Indian Elephant, the Great Indian Rhinoceros, and many others. The region's diverse wildlife is preserved in more than 120 national parks, 18 Bio-reserves and more than 500 wildlife sanctuaries across the country. India has some of the most biodiverse regions of the world and contains four of the world's 36 biodiversity hotspots – the Western Ghats, the Eastern Himalayas, Indo-Burma and Sunda Land.[170] Wildlife management is essential to preserve the rare and endangered endemic species.[171] India is one of the seventeen megadiverse countries. According to one study, India along with the other 16 megadiverse countries is home to about 60-70% of the world's biodiversity.[172] India, lying within the Indomalaya ecozone, is home to about 7.6% of all mammalian, 12.6% of avian (bird), 6.2% of reptilian, and 6.0% of flowering plant species.[173]

Many Indian species are descendants of taxa originating in Gondwana, of which India originally was a part. Peninsular India's subsequent movement towards, and collision with, the Laurasian landmass set off a mass exchange of species. However, volcanism and climatic change 20 million years ago caused the extinction of many endemic Indian forms.[174] Soon thereafter, mammals entered India from Asia through two zoogeographical passes on either side of the emerging Himalaya. As a result, among Indian species, only 12.6% of mammals and 4.5% of birds are endemic, contrasting with 45.8% of reptiles and 55.8% of amphibians. Notable endemics are the Nilgiri leaf monkey and the brown and carmine Beddome's toad of the Western Ghats. India contains 172, or 2.9%, of IUCN-designated threatened species.[175] These include the Asian elephant, the Asiatic lion, Bengal tiger, Indian rhinoceros, mugger crocodile, and Indian white-rumped vulture, which suffered a near-extinction from ingesting the carrion of diclofenac-treated cattle.Wikipedia:Citation needed

In recent decades, human encroachment has posed a threat to India's wildlife; in response, the system of national parks and protected areas, first established in 1935, was substantially expanded. In 1972, India enacted the Wildlife Protection Act and Project Tiger to safeguard crucial habitat; further federal protections were promulgated in the 1980s. Along with over 515 wildlife sanctuaries, India now hosts 18 biosphere reserves, 10 of which are part of the World Network of Biosphere Reserves; 26 wetlands are registered under the Ramsar Convention.

The peepul tree, shown on the seals of Mohenjo-daro, shaded Gautama Buddha as he sought enlightenment. The varied and rich wildlife of India has had a profound impact on the region's popular culture. The wildlife has also been made famous in *The Jungle Book* by Rudyard Kipling. India's wildlife has been the subject of numerous other tales and fables such as the *Panchatantra*.

Figure 13: *A female Indian elephant in Nagerhole National Park. India has the largest population of this subspecies of Asian elephants.*

Fauna

India is home to several well-known large mammals, including the Asian elephants, Bengal and Indochinese Tigers,[176] Asiatic lions, Snow leopards, Clouded leopards, Indian leopards, Indian sloth bear and Indian rhinoceros. Some other well-known large Indian mammals are: ungulates such as the rare wild Asian water buffalo, common domestic Asian water buffalo, gail, gaur, and several species of deer and antelope. Some members of the dog family, such as the Indian wolf, Bengal fox and golden jackal, and the dhole or wild dogs are also widely distributed. However, the dhole, also known as *the whistling hunter,* is the most endangered top Indian carnivore, and the Himalayan wolf is now a critically endangered species endemic to India.Wikipedia:Citation needed It is also home to the striped hyena, macaques, langur and mongoose species.

Flora

There are about 17500 taxa of flowering plants from India. The Indian Forest Act, 1927 helped to improve protection of the natural habitat. Many ecoregions, such as the *shola* forests, also exhibit extremely high rates of endemism; overall, 33% of Indian plant species are endemic.[177,178]

Figure 14: *The Valley of Flowers National Park in Uttarakhand*

India's forest cover ranges from the tropical rainforest of the Andaman Islands, Western Ghats, and Northeast India to the coniferous forest of the Himalaya. Between these extremes lie the sal-dominated moist deciduous forest of eastern India; teak-dominated dry deciduous forest of central and southern India; and the babul-dominated thorn forest of the central Deccan and western Gangetic plain.[179] Important Indian trees include the medicinal neem, widely used in rural Indian herbal remedies.

Fungi

The diversity of fungi[180] and their natural beauty occupy a prime place in the biological world and India has been a cradle for such organisms. Only a fraction of the total fungal wealth of India has been subjected to scientific scrutiny and mycologists have to unravel this unexplored and hidden wealth. One-third of fungal diversity of the globe exists in India. The country has an array of 10 diverse biomes including Trans-Himalayan zone, Himalaya, Desert, Semi-Arid zone, Western Ghats, Deccan Peninsula, Gangetic Plain, North-Eastern India, Coasts and Islands where varied dominating regimes manifest. This enables the survival of manifold fungal flora in these regions which include hot spot areas like the Himalayan ranges, Western Ghats, hill stations, mangroves, sea coasts, fresh water bodies etc. Many fungi have been recorded

Figure 15: *Valley of Flowers National Park, Ut-trakhand, is part of the Nanda Devi Bio-reserve*

from these regions and from the country in general comprising thermophiles, psychrophiles, mesophiles, aquatic forms, marine forms, plant and animal pathogens, edible fungi and beneficial fungi and so on. The number of fungi recorded in India exceeds 27,000 species, the largest biotic community after insects. The true fungi belong to the Kingdom[181] Fungi which has four phyla, 103 orders, 484 families and 4979 genera. About 205 new genera have been described from India, of which 32% were discovered by C. V. Subramanian of the University of Madras.[182,183] These features indicate a ten-fold increase in the last 80 years.

Conservation

The need for conservation of wildlife in India is often questioned because of the apparently incorrect priority in the face of direct poverty of the people. However, Article 48 of the Constitution of India specifies that, "The state shall endeavor to protect and improve the environment and to safeguard the forests and wildlife of the country" and Article 51-A states that "it shall be the duty of every citizen of India to protect and improve the natural environment including forests, lakes, rivers, and wildlife and to have compassion for living creatures."[184] The committee in the Indian Board for Wildlife, in their report, defines wildlife as "the entire natural uncultivated flora and fauna of the country" while the Wildlife (protection) Act 1972 defines it as "any animal, bees, butterflies, crustacea, fish, moths and aquatic or land vegetation which forms part of any habitat."

Despite the various environmental issues faced, the country still has a rich and varied wildlife compared to Europe. Large and charismatic mammals are important for wildlife tourism in India, and several national parks and wildlife sanctuaries cater to these needs. Project Tiger, started in 1972, is a major effort to conserve the tiger and its habitats.[185] At the turn of the 20th century, one estimate of the tiger population in India placed the figure at 40,000, yet an Indian tiger census conducted in 2008 revealed the existence of only 1,411 tigers. 2010 tiger census revealed that there are 1700 tigers left in India.[186] As per the latest tiger census (2015), there are around 2226 tigers in India. By far, there is an overall 30% increase in tiger population.[187] Various pressures in the later part of the 20th century led to the progressive decline of wilderness resulting in the disturbance of viable tiger habitats. At the International Union for the Conservation of Nature and Natural Resources (IUCN) General Assembly meeting in Delhi in 1969, serious concern was voiced about the threat to several species of wildlife and the shrinkage of wilderness in India. In 1970, a national ban on tiger hunting was imposed, and in 1972 the Wildlife Protection Act came into force. The framework was then set up to formulate a project for tiger conservation with an ecological approach. However, there is not much optimism about this framework's ability to save the peacock, which is the national bird of India. George Schaller wrote about tiger conservation:[188]

Recent extinctions

The exploitation of land and forest resources by humans along with capturing and trapping for food and sport has led to the extinction of many species in India in recent times. These species include mammals such as the Asiatic cheetah, wild zebu, Indian Javan rhinoceros, and Northern Sumatran rhinoceros. While some of these large mammal species are confirmed extinct, there have been many smaller animal and plant species whose status is harder to determine. Many species have not been seen since their description. Gir forest in India has the only surviving population of Asiatic lions in the world.

Some species of birds have gone extinct in recent times, including the pink-headed duck (*Rhodonessa caryophyllacea*) and the Himalayan quail (*Ophrysia superciliosa*). A species of warbler, *Acrocephalus orinus*, known earlier from a single specimen collected by Allan Octavian Hume from near Rampur in Himachal Pradesh, was rediscovered after 139 years in Thailand.[189,190]

MALACORTYX SUPERCILIARIS

Figure 16: *Illustration of a Himalayan quail from A. O. Hume's work. Last seen in 1876.*

National animals

- National animal: Royal Bengal tiger
- National heritage animal of India: Elephant
- National mammal: Hanuman langur
- National aquatic animal: Ganges river dolphin[191]
- National bird: Peacock

Biosphere reserves

The Indian government has established eighteen biosphere reserves of India which protect larger areas of natural habitat and often include one or more national parks and/or preserves, along buffer zones that are open to some economic uses. Protection is granted not only to the flora and fauna of the protected region, but also to the human communities who inhabit these regions, and their ways of life.

The bio-reserves are:

- Achanakmar-Amarkantak
- Agasthyamalai
- Dibru Saikhowa
- Dihang Dibang

Figure 17: *The peacock*

Figure 18: *The Sundarbans in the Bengal*

Figure 19: *Gulf of Mannar from Rameshwaram, Tamil Nadu*

- Great Nicobar
- Gulf of Mannar
- Kachchh
- Khangchendzonga
- Manas
- Nanda Devi
- The Nilgiris
- Nokrek
- Pachmarhi
- Simlipal
- Sundarbans
- Cold Desert
- Seshachalam hills
- Panna

Eleven of the eighteen biosphere reserves are a part of the World Network of Biosphere Reserves, based on the UNESCO Man and the Biosphere Programme (MAB) list.[192]

- Gulf of Mannar Biosphere Reserve
- Nanda Devi Biosphere Reserve
- Nilgiri Biosphere Reserve

- Nokrek National Park
- Pachmarhi Biosphere Reserve
- Simlipal National Park
- Sundarbans Biosphere Reserve
- Achanakmar-Amarkantak Biosphere Reserve
- Nicobar Islands
- Agasthyamala Biosphere Reserve
- Khangchendzonga

Examples of Wildlife

Figure 20: *The Indian rhinoceros in the Kaziranga National Park. Kaziranga in the state of Assam is home to two-thirds of the one-horned rhinoceros population.*

Figure 21: *Indian wild ass*

Figure 22: *Gaur*

Figure 23: *Yak (Bos grunniens and Bos mutus)*

Figure 24: *Sambar deer*

Figure 25: *Chital*

Figure 26: *Nilgai (Boselaphus tragocamelus)*

Figure 27: *Chinkara (Indian gazelle)*

Figure 28: *Royal Bengal tiger*

Figure 29: *A couple of Asiatic lions at Gir Forest National Park*

Figure 30: *Indian leopard in Karnataka. Found across the Indian subcontinent, poaching for its skin is a threat to it.*

Figure 31: *Snow leopard*

Figure 32: *Striped hyena (Hyaena hyaena)*

Figure 33: *Indian wolf*

Figure 34: *Golden jackal*

Figure 35: *Indian wild dog (dhole)*

Figure 36: *Bengal fox*

Figure 37: *Sloth bear*

Figure 38: *Asian black bear*

Figure 39: *Red panda*

Figure 40: *Rhesus macaque*

Figure 41: *Hanuman langur with a newborn. At least seven species of grey langurs are found in India, out of which five are endemic.*

Figure 42: *The Gee's golden langur, one of the world's rarest monkeys, typifies the precarious survival of much of India's megafauna*

Figure 43: *Gray langur*

Figure 44: *Lion-tailed macaque*

Figure 45: *Indian crested porcupine*

Figure 46: *Himalayan Marmot*

Figure 47: *Indian flying fox*

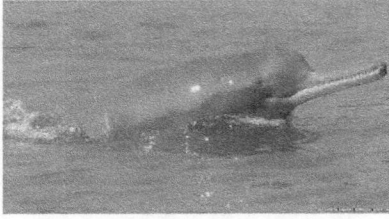

Figure 48: *South Asian river dolphin*

Figure 49: *Greater Flamingo*

Figure 50: *Nicobar pigeon*

Figure 51: *Brahminy kite*

Figure 52: *Brown fish-owl*

Figure 53: *Great hornbill*

Figure 54: *Rose-ringed parakeet*

Figure 55: *Red avadavat*

Figure 56: *Saltwater crocodile*

Figure 57: *Indian cobra*

Figure 58: *Indian chameleon*

Figure 59: *Draco dussumieri (southern flying lizard)*

Figure 60: *Indian black turtle*

Figure 61: *Purple frog*

Figure 62: *Green chromide*

Figure 63: *Pearse's mudskipper*

Figure 64: *Papilio polymnestor*

References

- SPECIES CHECKLIST: Species Diversity in India[193]; ENVIS Centre: Wildlife & Protected Areas (Secondary Database); Wildlife Institute of India (WII)
- ENVIS Centre: Wildlife & Protected Areas (Secondary Database)[194]; Wildlife Institute of India (WII)
- Free EBOOK: Special Habitats and Threatened Plants of India[195]; Wildlife Institute of India (WII)
- ENVIS Centre on Conservation of Ecological Heritage and Sacred Sights of India[196]; ENVIS; C.P.R. Environmental Education Centre is a Centre of Excellence of the Ministry of Environment and Forests, Government of India. Home page[196]
- Conservation of wetlands of India – a review[197] by S.N. PRASAD1, T.V. RAMACHANDRA2, N. AHALYA2, T. SENGUPTA1, ALOK KUMAR1, A.K. TIWARI3, V.S. VIJAYAN1 & LALITHA VIJAYAN1; 1Salim Ali Centre for Ornithology and Natural History, Coimbatore 641108, 2Centre for Ecological Sciences, Indian Institute Of Science, Bangalore 560012, 3Regional Remote Sensing Service Centre, Dehradun, Uttaranchal 248001; Tropical Ecology 43(1): 173-186, 2002 <templatestyles src="Module:Citation/CS1/styles.css" />ISSN 0564-3295[198]; © International Society for Tropical Ecology. PDF[199]
- [200];Fungal biodiversity: Distribution, conservation and prospecting of fungi from India. By: C. Manoharachary, K. Sridhar, Reena Singh, Alok Adholeya, T. S. Suryanarayanan, Seema Rawat and B. N. Johri. CURRENT SCIENCE, VOL. 89, NO. 1, 10 JULY 2005. PDF
- [201];Fungi of India 1989-2001. By: Jamaluddin, M.G. Goswami and B.M. Ojha, Scientific Publishers, 2004, vii, 326 p, <templatestyles src="Module:Citation/CS1/styles.css" />ISBN 8172333544.

External links

Wikimedia Commons has media related to *Wildlife of India*.

- Official website of: Government of India, Ministry of Environment & Forests[202]
- "Legislations on Environment, Forests, and Wildlife" from the Official website of: Government of India, Ministry of Environment & Forests[203]
- "India's Forest Conservation Legislation: Acts, Rules, Guidelines", from the official website of the Government of India, Ministry of Environment & Forests[204]

- Wildlife Legislations, including - "The Indian Wildlife (Protection) Act" from the Official website of: Government of India, Ministry of Environment & Forests[205]
- Eight lions, 15 tigers, and a whole lot of elephants — an Indian wildlife safari[206]

Indian cuisine

Indian cuisine

This article is part of the series
Indian cuisine
• ⚏ India portal • ◎ Food portal
• $\underline{v}$ • $\underline{t}$ • $\underline{e}^{207}$

Part of a series on the
Culture of India
History
People

Cuisine
Religion
Sport
• ⚞ **India portal**
• $\frac{v}{}$
• $\frac{t}{}$
• $\frac{e}{}$[208]

Indian cuisine consists of a wide variety of regional and traditional cuisines native to the Indian subcontinent. Given the range of diversity in soil type, climate, culture, ethnic groups, and occupations, these cuisines vary substantially from each other and use locally available spices, herbs, vegetables, and fruits. Indian food is also heavily influenced by religion, in particular Hindu, cultural choices and traditions. The cuisine is also influenced by centuries of Islamic rule, particularly the Mughal rule. Samosas and pilafs can be regarded as examples.

Historical events such as foreign invasions, trade relations, and colonialism have played a role in introducing certain foods to this country. For instance, potato, a staple of the diet in some regions of India, was brought to India by the Portuguese, who also introduced chillies and breadfruit. Indian cuisine has shaped the history of international relations; the spice trade between India and Europe was the primary catalyst for Europe's Age of Discovery. Spices were bought from India and traded around Europe and Asia. Indian cuisine has influenced other cuisines across the world, especially those from Europe, the Middle East, North Africa, sub-Saharan Africa, Southeast Asia, the British Isles, Fiji, and the Caribbean.

History

Indian cuisine reflects an 8,000-year history of various groups and cultures interacting with the Indian subcontinent, leading to diversity of flavours and regional cuisines found in modern-day India. Later, trade with British and Portuguese influence added to the already diverse Indian cuisine.

Figure 65: *Spices at a grocery shop in India*

Antiquity

Early diet in India mainly consisted of legumes, vegetables, fruits, grains, dairy products, and honey.Wikipedia:Citation needed Staple foods eaten today include a variety of lentils (*dal*), whole-wheat flour (*atta*), rice, and pearl millet (*bājra*), which has been cultivated in the Indian subcontinent since 6200 BCE. Over time, segments of the population embraced vegetarianism during Śramaṇa movement[209],[210] while an equitable climate permitted a variety of fruits, vegetables, and grains to be grown throughout the year. A food classification system that categorised any item as *saatvic*, *raajsic*, or *taamsic* developed in Yoga tradition.[211],[212] The *Bhagavad Gita* proscribes certain dietary practices (chapter 17, verses 8–10). Consumption of beef is taboo, due to cows being considered sacred in Hinduism. Beef is generally not eaten by Hindus in India except for Kerala and the north east.

Middle Ages to the 16th centuries

During the Middle Ages, several Indian dynasties were predominant, including the Gupta dynasty. Travel to India during this time introduced new cooking methods and products to the region, including tea. India was later invaded by tribes from Central Asian cultures, which led to the emergence of Mughlai cuisine, a mix of Indian and Central Asian cuisine. Hallmarks include seasonings such as saffron.

Figure 66: *Lentils are a staple ingredient in Indian cuisine.*

Ingredients

Staple foods of Indian cuisine include pearl millet (*bājra*), rice, whole-wheat flour (*atta*), and a variety of lentils, such as *masoor* (most often red lentils), *tuer* (pigeon peas), *urad* (black gram), and *moong* (mung beans). Lentils may be used whole, dehusked—for example, *dhuli moong* or *dhuli urad*—or split. Split lentils, or *dal*, are used extensively. Some pulses, such as *channa* or *cholae* (chickpeas), *rajma* (kidney beans), and *lobiya* (black-eyed peas) are very common, especially in the northern regions. *Channa* and *moong* are also processed into flour (*besan*).

Many Indian dishes are cooked in vegetable oil, but peanut oil is popular in northern and western India, mustard oil in eastern India, and coconut oil along the western coast, especially in Kerala. *Gingelly* (sesame) oil is common in the south since it imparts a fragrant, nutty aroma. In recent decades, sunflower, safflower, cottonseed, and soybean oils have become popular across India. Hydrogenated vegetable oil, known as *Vanaspati ghee*, is another popular cooking medium. Butter-based ghee, or *deshi ghee*, is used frequently, though less than in the past.Wikipedia:Citation needed Many types of meat are used for Indian cooking, but chicken and mutton tend to be the most commonly consumed meats. Fish and beef consumption are prevalent in some parts of India, but they are not widely consumed except for coastal areas, as well as the north east.Wikipedia:Citation needed

The most important and frequently used spices and flavourings in Indian cuisine are whole or powdered chilli pepper (*mirch*, introduced by the Portuguese from Mexico in the 16th century), black mustard seed (*sarso*), cardamom (*elaichi*), cumin (*jeera*), turmeric (*haldi*), asafoetida (*hing*), ginger (*adrak*), coriander (*dhania*), and garlic (*lasoon*). One popular spice mix is *garam masala*, a powder that typically includes seven dried spices in a particular ratio, including black cardamom, cinnamon (*dalchini*), clove (*laung),* cumin (jeera), black peppercorns, coriander seeds and anise star. Each culinary region has a distinctive *garam masala* blend—individual chefs may also have their own. *Goda masala* is a comparable, though sweet, spice mix popular in Maharashtra. Some leaves commonly used for flavouring include bay leaves (*tejpat*), coriander leaves, fenugreek leaves, and mint leaves. The use of curry leaves and roots for flavouring is typical of Gujarati and South Indian cuisine. Sweet dishes are often seasoned with cardamom, saffron, nutmeg, and rose petal essences.

Regional cuisines

Cuisine differs across India's diverse regions as a result of variation in local culture, geographical location (proximity to sea, desert, or mountains), and economics. It also varies seasonally, depending on which fruits and vegetables are ripe.

Andaman and Nicobar Islands

Seafood plays a major role in the cuisine of the Andaman and Nicobar Islands. Staples of the diet of the Indigenous Andamanese traditionally included roots, honey, fruits, meat, and fish, which were obtained by hunting and gathering. Some insects were also eaten as delicacies. Immigration from mainland of India, however, has resulted in variations in the cuisine.

Andhra Pradesh

The cuisine of Andhra Pradesh belongs to the two Telugu-speaking regions of Rayalaseema and Coastal Andhra and is part of Telugu cuisine. The food of Andhra Pradesh is known for its heavy use of spices, and the use of tamarind. Seafood is common in the coastal region of the state. Rice is the staple food (as is with all South Indian states) eaten with lentil preparations such as *pappu* (lentils) and *pulusu* (stew) and spicy vegetables or curries. In Andhra, leafy greens or vegetables such as bottle-gourd and eggplant are usually added to *dal*. Pickles are an essential part of the local cuisine; popular among those are mango-based pickles such as *avakaya* and *maagaya*, *gongura* (a pickle made from Kenaf leaves), *usirikaya* (gooseberry or *amla*), *nimmakaya* (lime), and tomato pickle. Dahi (yogurt) is a common addition to meals, as a way of tempering spiciness. Breakfast items include *dosa, pesarattu* (mung bean *dosa*), *vada*, and *idli*.

Figure 67: *A vegetarian Andhra meal served on important occasions*

Arunachal Pradesh

The staple food of Arunachal Pradesh is rice, along with fish, meat, and leaf vegetables. Many varieties of rice are used. Lettuce is the most common vegetable, usually prepared by boiling with ginger, coriander, and green chillies. Boiled rice cakes wrapped in leaves are a popular snack. *Thukpa* is a kind of noodle soup common among the Monpa tribe of the region. Native tribes of Arunachal are meat eaters and use fish, eggs, beef, chicken, pork, and mutton to make their dishes. *Apong* or rice beer made from fermented rice or millet is a popular beverage in Arunachal Pradesh and is consumed as a refreshing drink.

Assam

Assamese cuisine is a mixture of different indigenous styles, with considerable regional variation and some external influences. Although it is known for its limited use of spices, Assamese cuisine has strong flavours from its use of endemic herbs, fruits, and vegetables served fresh, dried, or fermented. Rice is the staple food item and a huge variety of endemic rice varieties, including several varieties of sticky rice are a part of the cuisine in Assam. Fish, generally freshwater varieties, are widely eaten. Other nonvegetarian items include chicken, duck, squab, snails, silkworms, insects, goat, pork, venison, turtle, monitor lizard, etc. The region's cuisine involves simple cooking processes, mostly barbecuing, steaming, or boiling. *Bhuna*, the gentle frying of

Figure 68: *Assamese Thali*

spices before the addition of the main ingredients, generally common in Indian cooking, is absent in the cuisine of Assam. A traditional meal in Assam begins with a *khar*, a class of dishes named after the main ingredient and ends with a *tenga*, a sour dish. Homebrewed rice beer or rice wine is served before a meal. The food is usually served in bell metal utensils. *Paan*, the practice of chewing betel nut, generally concludes a meal.

Bihar

Bihari cuisine is wholesome and simple. *Litti chokha*, a baked salted wheat-flour cake filled with *sattu* (baked chickpea flour) and some special spices, is well known among the middle-class families served with *baigan bharta*, made of roasted eggplant (brinjal) and tomatoes. Among meat dishes, meat *saalan* is a popular dish made of mutton or goat curry with cubed potatoes in *garam masala*. *Dalpuri* is another popular dish in Bihar. It is salted wheat-flour bread, filled with boiled, crushed, and fried gram pulses. *Malpua* is a popular sweet dish of Bihar, prepared by a mixture of *maida*, milk, bananas, cashew nuts, peanuts, raisins, sugar, water, and green cardamom. Another notable sweet dish of Bihar is *balushahi*, which is prepared by a specially treated combination of *maida* and sugar along with *ghee*, and the other worldwide famous sweet, *khaja*, also very popular, is made from flour, vegetable fat, and sugar, which is mainly used in weddings and other occasions. Silav near Nalanda is famous

Figure 69: *Palak paneer, a dish made from spinach and paneer (cottage cheese)*

for its production. During the festival of Chhath, *thekua*, a sweet dish made of *ghee*, jaggery, and whole-meal flour, flavoured with aniseed, is made.

Chandigarh

Chandigarh, the capital of Punjab and Haryana is a city of 20th century origin with a cosmopolitan food culture mainly involving North Indian cuisine.

People enjoy home-made recipes such as *parantha*, especially at breakfast, and other Punjabi foods like *roti* which is made from wheat, corn, or other glutenous flour with cooked vegetables or beans. *Sarson da saag* and *dal makhani* are well-known dishes among others.[213] Popular snacks include *gol gappa* (known as *panipuri* in other places). It consists of a round, hollow *puri*, fried crisp and filled with a mixture of flavoured water, boiled and cubed potatoes, bengal gram beans, etc.

Chhattisgarh

Chhattisgarh cuisine is unique in nature and not found in the rest of India, although the staple food is rice, like in much of the country. Many Chhattisgarhi people drink liquor brewed from the mahuwa flower palm wine (*tadi* in rural areas). The tribal people of the Bastar region of Chhattisgarh eat ancestral dishes such as mushrooms, bamboo pickle, bamboo vegetables, etc.

Figure 70: *Roti with Baigan (Brinjal) subji and curd*

Dadra and Nagar Haveli

The local cuisine resembles the cuisine of Gujarat. *Ubadiyu* is a local delicacy made of vegetables and beans with herbs. The common foods include rice, *roti*, vegetables, river fish, and crab. People also enjoy buttermilk and chutney made of different fruits and herbs.

Daman and Diu

Daman and Diu is a union territory of India which, like Goa, was a former colonial possession of Portugal. Consequently, both native Gujarati food and traditional Portuguese food are common. Being a coastal region, the communities are mainly dependent on seafood. Normally, *rotli* and tea are taken for breakfast, *rotla* and *saak* for lunch, and *chokha* along with *saak* and curry are taken for dinner. Some of the dishes prepared on festive occasions include *puri*, *lapsee*, *potaya*, *dudh-plag*, and *dhakanu*. While alcohol is prohibited in the neighbouring state of Gujarat, drinking is common in Daman and Diu. Better known as the "pub" of Gujarat. All popular brands of alcohol are readily available.

Figure 71: *Rajma-chawal, curried red kidney beans with steamed rice*

Delhi

Delhi was once the capital of the Mughal empire, and it became the birthplace of Mughlai cuisine. Delhi is noted for its street food. The Paranthewali Gali in Chandani Chowk is just one of the culinary landmarks for stuffed flatbread (*paranthas*). Delhi has people from different parts of India, thus the city has different types of food traditions; its cuisine is influenced by the various cultures. Punjabi cuisine is common, due to the dominance of Punjabi communities. Delhi cuisine is actually an amalgam of different Indian cuisines modified in unique ways. This is apparent in the different types of street food available. *Kababs, kachauri, chaat,* Indian sweets, Indian ice cream (commonly called *kulfi*), and even western food items like sandwiches and patties, are prepared in a style unique to Delhi and are quite popular.

Goa

The area has a tropical climate, which means the spices and flavours are intense. Use of *kokum* is a distinct feature of the region's cuisine. Goan cuisine is mostly seafood and meat-based; the staple foods are rice and fish. Kingfish (*vison* or *visvan*) is the most common delicacy, and others include pomfret, shark, tuna, and mackerel; these are often served with coconut milk. Shellfish, including crabs, prawns, tiger prawns, lobster, squid, and mussels, are

Figure 72: *Pork vindaloo (pictured) is a popular curry dish in Goa and around the world.*

commonly eaten. The cuisine of Goa is influenced by its Hindu origins, 400 years of Portuguese colonialism, and modern techniques. Bread, introduced by the Portuguese, is very popular, and is an important part of goan breakfast. Frequent tourism in the area gives Goan food an international aspect. Vegetarianism is equally popular.

Gujarat

Gujarati cuisine is primarily vegetarian. The typical Gujarati *thali* consists of *roti* (*rotlii* in Gujarati), *daal* or *kadhi*, rice, *sabzi/shaak*, *papad* and *chaas* (buttermilk). The *sabzi* is a dish of different combinations of vegetables and spices which may be stir fried, spicy or sweet. Gujarati cuisine can vary widely in flavour and heat based on personal and regional tastes. North Gujarat, Kathiawad, Kachchh, and South Gujarat are the four major regions of Gujarati cuisine. Many Gujarati dishes are simultaneously sweet, salty (like vegetable Handvo), and spicy. In mango season, *keri no ras* (fresh mango pulp) is often an integral part of the meal. Spices also vary seasonally. For example, garam masala is used much less in summer. Few of Gujarati Snacks like Sev Khamani, Khakhra, Dal Vada, Methi na Bhajiya, Khaman, Bhakharwadi etc. Regular fasting, with diets limited to milk, dried fruit, and nuts, is a common practice.

Figure 73: *Khaman is a popular Gujarati snack.*

Figure 74: *Vegetable Handva is a savory Gujarati dinner dish.*

Figure 75: *Rogan josh is a popular Kashmiri dish.*

Haryana

Cattle being common in Haryana, dairy products are a common component of its cuisine. Specific dishes include *kadhi*, *pakora*, *besan masala roti*, *bajra aloo roti*, *churma*, *kheer*, *bathua raita*, *methi gajar*, *singri ki sabzi*, and *tamatar* chutney. In the olden days, its staple diet included, bajra khichdi, rabdi, onion chutney, milet roti and bajra roti. In the non-veg cuisine it includes kukad kadhai and masala gravy chicken. *Lassi*, *sharbat*, *nimbu pani* and "labsi(which is a mixture of bajra flour and lassi) are three popular nonalcoholic beverages in Haryana. Liquor stores are common there, which cater to a large number of truck drivers.

Himachal Pradesh

The daily diet of Himachal people is similar to that of the rest of North India, including lentils, broth, rice, vegetables, and bread, although nonvegetarian cuisine is preferred. Some of the specialities of Himachal include *sidu*, *patande*, *chukh*, *rajmah*, and *til* chutney.

Jammu and Kashmir

The cuisine of Jammu and Kashmir is from three regions of the state: Jammu, Kashmir, and Ladakh. Kashmiri cuisine has evolved over hundreds of years. Its first major influence was the food of the Kashmiri Hindus and Buddhists.

The cuisine was later influenced by the cultures which arrived with the invasion of Kashmir by Timur from the area of modern Uzbekistan. Subsequent influences have included the cuisines of Central Asia and the North Indian plains. The most notable ingredient in Kashmiri cuisine is mutton, of which over 30 varieties are known. *Wazwan* is a multicourse meal in the Kashmiri tradition, the preparation of which is considered an art.

Kashmiri Pandit food is elaborate, and an important part of the Pandits' ethnic identity. Kashmiri Pandit cuisine usually uses dahi (yogurt), oil, and spices such as turmeric, red chilli, cumin, ginger, and fennel, though they do not use onion and garlic. Also, *birayanis* are quite popular here. They are the speciality of Kashmir.

The Jammu region is famous for its Sund Panjeeri, Patisa, Rajma (Kidney Beans) with rice and Kalari cheese. Dogri food includes ambal (sour pumpkin dish), khatta meat, Kulthein (Macrotyloma uniflorum) di dal, dal chawal, maa da madra and Uriya. Many types of pickles are made including mango, kasrod, girgle, etc. Street food is also famous which include various types of chaats, specially Gol Gappas, Gulgule, Chole Bhature, Rajma Kulcha and Dahi Bhalla.

Jharkhand

Traditional Jharkhand dishes are not available at restaurants, as they have not been commercialised.Wikipedia:Citation needed Prepared exclusively in tribal regions, this cuisine uses oil and spices infrequently, except for pickle production and special occasions. *Baiganee chop*, a snack made of *brinjal* slices or eggplant, is popular in Jharkhand. *Thekua* is a sweet dish made of sugar, wheat, flour, and chopped coconuts. *Hadia*, which is made of paddy rice, is a refreshing drink. A wide variety of recipes is prepared with different types of rice in Jharkhand, including *dhuska, pittha*, and different kinds of *rotis* prepared with rice.

Karnataka

A number of dishes, such as *idli, rava idli*, Mysore *masala dosa*, etc. were invented here and have become popular beyond the state of KarnatakaWikipedia:Citation needed. Equally, varieties in the cuisine of Karnataka have similarities with its three neighbouring South Indian states, as well as the states of Maharashtra and Goa to its north. It is very common for the food to be served on a banana leaf, especially during festivals and functions.

Karnataka cuisine can be very broadly divided into: 1) Mysore/Bangalore cuisine, 2) North Karnataka cuisine, 3) Udupi cuisine, 4) Kodagu/Coorg cuisine, and 5) Karavali/coastal cuisine. The cuisine covers a wide spectrum of food from pure vegetarian and vegan to meats like pork, and from savouries to

Figure 76: *Staple vegetarian meal of Karnataka jolada rotti, palya, and anna-saaru*

Figure 77: *Bisi bele bath, a delicacy in Karnataka made of rice, lentils, spices, and vegetables*

Figure 78: *A full-course Sadya is the ceremonial meal of Kerala eaten usually on celebrations (like Onam, Vishu, etc.) and is served on a plantain leaf.*

sweets. Typical dishes include *bisi bele bath, jolada rotti, badanekai yennegai, Holige, Kadubu, chapati, idli vada, ragi rotti, akki rotti, saaru, huli, kootu, vangibath, khara bath, kesari bhath, sajjige, neer dosa, mysoore, haal bai, chiroti, benne dose, ragi mudde*, and *uppittu*.

The Kodagu district is known for spicy pork curries, while coastal Karnataka specialises in seafood. Although the ingredients differ regionally, a typical *Kannadiga oota* (Kannadiga meal) is served on a banana leaf. The coastal districts of Dakshina Kannada and Udupi have slightly varying cuisines, which make extensive use of coconut in curries and frequently include seafood.

Kerala

Traditional food of Kerala Hindus is vegetarianWikipedia:Citation needed, with regional exceptions such as the food of the Malabar area. It includes Kerala *sadhya*, which is an elaborate vegetarian banquet prepared for festivals and ceremonies. Contemporary Kerala food also includes nonvegetarian dishes. A full-course *sadya*, which consists of rice with about 20 different accompaniments and desserts is the ceremonial meal, eaten usually on celebrations such as marriages, Onam, Vishu, etc. and is served on a plantain leaf.

Fish and seafood play a major role in Kerala cuisine, as Kerala is a coastal state. An everyday Kerala meal in most households consists of rice with fish curry made of sardines, mackerel, *seer* fish, king fish, pomfret, prawns, shrimp, sole, anchovy, parrotfish, etc. (mussels, oysters, crabs, squid, scallops etc. are not rare), vegetable curry and stir-fried vegetables with or without coconut

Figure 79: *Spicy fish from Kerala*

Figure 80: *Fish moilee Kerala style (KeralaFish Molly)*

traditionally known as *thoran* or *mizhukkupiratti*. As Kerala has large inland water bodies, freshwater fish are abundant, and constitute regular meals.

It is common in Kerala to have a breakfast with nonvegetarian dishes in restaurants, in contrast to other states in India. Chicken/mutton stews, lamb/chicken/beef/pork/egg curry, fish curry with tapioca for breakfast are common. A wide range of breakfast with non-vegetarian is common in Malabar and in Central Kerala.

Kerala cuisine reflects its rich trading heritage. Over time, various cuisines have blended with indigenous dishes, while foreign ones have been adapted to local tastes. Significant Arab, Syrian, Portuguese, Dutch, Jewish, and Middle Eastern influences exist in this region's cuisine, through ancient trade routes via the Arabian Sea and through Arab traders who settled here, contributed to the evolution of *kozhikodan halwa* along with other dishes like *Thalassery biryani*.

Coconuts grow in abundance in Kerala, so grated coconut and coconut milk are commonly used for thickening and flavouring. Kerala's long coastline and numerous rivers have led to a strong fishing industry in the region, making seafood a common part of the meal. Rice is grown in abundance, along with tapioca. It is the main starch ingredient used in Kerala's food.

Having been a major production area of spices for thousands of years, the region makes frequent use of black pepper, cardamom, clove, ginger, and cinnamon. Most of Kerala's Hindus, except its Brahmin community, eat fish, chicken, beef, pork, eggs, and mutton. The Brahmin is famed for its vegan cuisine, especially varieties of *sambar* and *rasam*. A thick vegetable stew popular in South and Central India called *avial* is believed to have originated in southern Kerala. *Avial* is a widely eaten vegetarian dish in the state and plays a major role in *sadya*.

In most Kerala households, a typical meal consists of rice and vegetables. Kerala also has a variety of breakfast dishes like *idli*, *dosa*, *appam*, *idiyappam*, *puttu*, and *pathiri*. The Muslim community of Kerala blend Arabian, North Indian, and indigenous Malabari cuisines, using chicken, eggs, beef, and mutton.*Thalassery biryani* is the only *biryani* variant, which is of Kerala origin having originated in Talassery, in Malabar region. The dish is significantly different from other biryani variants.

The Pathanamthitta region is known for *raalan* and fish curries. *Appam* along with wine and curries of cured beef and pork are popular among Syrian Christians in Central Kerala.

Popular desserts are *payasam* and *halwa*. The Hindu community's *payasams*, especially those made at temples, like the Ambalappuzha temple, are famous for their rich taste. *Halva* is one of the most commonly found or easily recognised sweets in bakeries throughout Kerala, and Kozhikode is famous for its unique and exotic *haluva*, which is popularly known as *Kozhikodan haluva*. Europeans used to call the dish "sweetmeat" due to its texture, and a street in Kozhikode where became named Sweet Meat Street during colonial rule. *Kozhikodan haluva* is mostly made from *maida* (highly refined wheat), and comes in various flavours, such as banana, *ghee* or coconut. However, *karutha haluva* (black *haluva*) made from rice is also very popular. Many Muslim families in the region are famed for their traditional *karutha haluva*.

Lakshadweep

The cuisine of Lakshadweep prominently features seafood and coconut. Local food consists of spicy nonvegetarian and vegetarian dishes. The culinary influence of Kerala is quite evident in the cuisines of Lakshadweep, since the island lies in close proximity to Kerala. Coconut and sea fish serve as the foundations of most of the meals. The people of Lakshadweep drink large amounts of coconut water, which is the most abundant aerated drink on the island. Coconut milk is the base for most of the curries. All the sweet or savory dishes have a touch of famous Malabar spices. Local people also prefer to have *dosa, idlis,* and various rice dishes.

Madhya Pradesh

The cuisine in Madhya Pradesh varies regionally. Wheat and meat are common in the north and west of the state, while the wetter south and east are dominated by rice and fish. Milk is a common ingredient in Gwalior and Indore. The street food of Indore is renowned, with shops that have been active for generations. Bhopal is known for meat and fish dishes such as *rogan josh*, *korma, qeema, biryani, pilaf*, and *kebabs*. On a street named Chatori Gali in old Bhopal, one can find traditional Muslim nonvegetarian fare such as *paya* soup, *bun kabab*, and *nalli-nihari* as some of the specialties.

Dal bafla is a common meal in the region and can be easily found in Indore and other nearby regions, consisting of a steamed and grilled wheat cake dunked in rich *ghee*, which is eaten with *daal* and *ladoos*. The culinary specialty of the Malwa and Indore regions of central Madhya Pradesh is *poha* (flattened rice); usually eaten at breakfast with *jalebi*. Beverages in the region include *lassi*, beer, rum and sugarcane juice. A local liquor is distilled from the flowers of the mahua tree. Date palm *toddy* is also popular. In tribal regions, a popular drink is the sap of the *sulfi* tree, which may be alcoholic if it has fermented.

Figure 81: *Daal bafla, a popular dish in Madhya Pradesh, Rajasthan, and Gujarat*

Maharashtra

Maharashtrian cuisine is an extensive balance of many different tastes. It includes a range of dishes from mild to very spicy tastes. *Bajri*, wheat, rice, *jowar*, vegetables, lentils, and fruit form important components of the Maharashtrian diet. Popular dishes include *puran poli, ukdiche modak, batata wada, sabudana khichdi, masala bhat, pav bhaji,* and *wada pav. Poha* or flattened rice is also usually eaten at breakfast. Kanda poha and aloo poha are some of the dishes cooked for breakfast and snacking in evenings. Popular spicy meat dishes include those that originated in the Kolhapur region. These are the Kolhapuri Sukka mutton, *pandhra rassa,* and *tabmda rassa. Shrikhand*, a sweet dish made from strained yogurt, is a main dessert of Maharashtrian cuisine. The cuisine of Maharashtra can be divided into two major sections—the coastal and the interior. The Konkan, on the coast of the Arabian Sea, has its own type of cuisine, a homogeneous combination of Malvani, Goud Saraswat Brahmin, and Goan cuisine. In the interior of Maharashtra, the Paschim Maharashtra, Khandesh, Vidarbha and Marathwada areas have their own distinct cuisines. The cuisine of Vidarbha uses groundnuts, poppy seeds, jaggery, wheat, *jowar*, and *bajra* extensively. A typical meal consists of rice, *roti, poli,* or *bhakar*, along with *varan* and *aamtee*—lentils and spiced vegetables. Cooking is common with different types of oil. Savji food from Vidarbha

Figure 82: *Pav bhaji, a popular fast food originating in Maharashtra*

is well known all over Maharashtra. Savji dishes are very spicy and oily. Savji mutton curries are very famous.

Like other coastal states, an enormous variety of vegetables, fish, and coconuts exists, where they are common ingredients. Peanuts and cashews are often served with vegetables. Grated coconuts are used to flavour many types of dishes, but coconut oil is not widely used; peanut oil is preferred. Kokum, most commonly served chilled, in an appetiser-digestive called *sol kadhi*, is prevalent. During summer, Maharashtrians consume *panha*, a drink made from raw mango.

Malwani

Malwani cuisine is a specialty of the tropical area which spans from the shore of Deogad Malwan to the southern Maharashtrian border with Goa. The unique taste and flavor of Malwani cuisine comes from Malwani *masala* and use of coconut and *kokam*. The staple foods are rice and fish. Various kinds of red and green fish, prawns, crab, and shellfish curries (also called *mashacha sar* in the Malwani language) are well known, along with *kombadi* (chicken) *wade* and mutton prepared Malwani style. *Mohari* mutton is also one of the distinct delicacies of Malwani cuisine.

Figure 83: *Poha, a popular Maharashtrian breakfast dish*

A large variety of fish is available in the region, which include *surmai, karali, bangada, bombil*(Bombay duck), *paplet* (pompret), *halwa, tarali, suandale, kolambi* (prawns), *tisari* (shell fish), *kalwa* (stone fish) and *kurli* (crab).

All these fish are available in dried form, including prawns, which are known as *sode*. Local curries and *chatanis* are also prepared with dried fish.

Different types of rice breads and pancakes add to the variety of Malwani cuisine and include *tandlachi bhakari, ghawane, amboli, patole, appe, tandalachi* and *shavai* (rice noodles). These rice breads can be eaten specially flavored with coconut milk, fish curries, and chicken or mutton curries.

Sole kadi made from *kokam* and coconut milk is a signature appetizer drink . For vegetarians, Malwani delicacies include *alloochi bhaji, alloochi gathaya, kalaya watanyacha*, and *sambara*(black gram stew).

The sweets and desserts include *ukadiche modak, Malawani khaje, khadakahde kundiche ladu, shegdanyache ladu, tandalchi kheer*, and *tandalachi shavai ani ras* (specially flavored with coconut milk).

Manipur

Manipuri cuisine is represented by the cuisine of the Meitei people who form the majority population in the central plain. Meitei food are simple, tasty, organic and healthy. Rice with local seasonal vegetables and fish form the main diet. Most of the dishes are cooked like vegetable stew, flavored with either fermented fish called ngari, or dried and smoked fish. The most popular manipuri dish is the Eromba; it's a preparation of boiled and mashed vegetables, often including potatoes or beans, mixed with chilli and roasted fermented fish. Another popular dish is the savory cake called Paknam, made of a base of lentil flour stuffed with various ingredients such as banana inflorescence, mushrooms, fish, vegetables etc., and baked covered in turmeric leaves. Along with spicy dishes, a mild side dish of steamed or boiled sweet vegetables are often served in the daily meals. The manipuri salad dish called singju, made of finely julienned cabbage, green papaya, and other vegetables, and garnished with local herbs, toasted sesame powder and lentil flour is extremely popular locally, and often found sold in small street side vendors. Singju is often served with bora which are fritters of various kinds, and also kanghou, or oil fried spicy veggies. Cooked and fermented soybean is a popular condiment in all manipuri kitchens. The staple diet of Manipur consists of rice, fish, large varieties of leafy vegetables (of both aquatic and terrestrial). Manipuris typically raise vegetables in a kitchen garden and rear fishes in small ponds around their house. Since the vegetables are either grown at home or obtained from local market, the cuisines are very seasonal, each season having its own special vegetables and preparations. The taste is very different from mainland Indian cuisines because of the use of various aromatic herbs and roots that are peculiar to the region. They are however very similar to the cuisines of Southeast/East/Central Asia, Siberia, Micronesia and Polynesia.

Meghalaya

Meghalayan cuisine is unique and different from other Northeastern Indian states. Spiced meat is common, from goats, pigs, fowl, ducks, chickens, and cows. In the Khasi and Jaintia Hills districts, common foods include *jadoh*, *ki kpu*, *tung-rymbai*, and pickled bamboo shoots. Other common foods in Meghalaya include *minil songa* (steamed sticky rice), *sakkin gata*, and *momo* dumplings. Like other tribes in the northeast, the Garos ferment rice beer, which they consume in religious rites and secular celebrations.

Mizoram

The cuisine of Mizoram differs from that of most of India, though it shares characteristics to other regions of Northeast India and North India. Rice is the staple food of Mizoram, while Mizos love to add non-vegetarian ingredients in every dish. Fish, chicken, pork and beef are popular meats among Mizos. Dishes are served on fresh banana leaves. Most of the dishes are cooked in mustard oil. Meals tend to be less spicy than in most of India. Mizos love eating boiled vegetables along with rice. A popular dish is *bai*, made from boiling vegetables (spinach, eggplant, beans, and other leafy vegetables) with

Figure 84: *Dried fish, prawns, ghost chili, and preserved colocasia leaves are common ingredients in Naga cuisine*

bekang fermented soya beans or Sa-um, a fermented pork and served with rice. *Sawhchiar* is another common dish, made of rice and cooked with pork or chicken.

Nagaland

The cuisine of Nagaland reflects that of the Naga people. It is known for exotic pork meats cooked with simple and flavourful ingredients, like the extremely hot Bhut jolokia pepper, fermented bamboo shoots and akhuni or fermented soya beans. Another unique and strong ingredient used by the Naga people, is the fermented fish known as ngari. Fresh herbs and other local greens also feature prominently in the Naga cuisine. The Naga use oil sparingly, preferring to ferment, dry, and smoke their meats and fish. Traditional homes in Nagaland have external kitchens that serve as smokehouses.

A typical meal consists of rice, meat, a chutney, a couple of stewed or steamed vegetable dishes – flavored with ngari or akhuni. Desserts usually consist of fresh fruits.

Figure 85: *Oriya mutton curry (mansha tarkari).*

Odisha

The cuisine of Odisha relies heavily on local ingredients. Flavours are usually subtle and delicately spiced, unlike the spicy curries typically associated with Indian cuisine.Wikipedia:Citation needed Fish and other seafood, such as crab and shrimp, are very popular, and chicken and mutton are also consumed. *Panch phutana*, a mix of cumin, mustard, fennel, fenugreek and *kalonji* (nigella), is widely used for flavouring vegetables and *dals*, while *garam masala* and turmeric are commonly used for meat-based curries. *Pakhala*, a dish made of rice, water, and dahi (yogurt), that is fermented overnight, is very popular in summer in rural areas. Oriyas are very fond of sweets, so dessert follows most meals.

Few popular Oriya cuisines, Anna, Kanika, Dalma, Khata (Tamato & Oou), Dali (Different types of lentils, i.e. Harada (Red Gram), known as *Arhar* in Hindi), Muga (Moong), Kolatha (Horsegram), etc. And many more varieties both in Veg. (Niramisha) & Non-Veg. (Aamisha). Saga (spinach and other green leaves) and Alu-bharta(mashed potato) along with Pakhala are popular dishes(lunch) in rural Odisha.

Odisha is well known for its milk-based sweets. Among the many Rasagula which originated in Odisha, Chhena poda, Chhena gaja, Chhena jhili, and Rasabali are very famous.

Figure 86: *Tandoori chicken is a popular grilled dish.*

Puducherry

The union territory of Puducherry was a French colony for around 200 years, making French cuisine a strong influence on the area. Tamil cuisine is eaten by the territory's Tamil majority. The influence of the neighbouring areas, such as Andhra Pradesh and Kerala, is also visible on the territory's cuisine. Some favourite dishes include coconut curry, *tandoori* potato, *soya dosa*, *podanlangkai*, curried vegetables, stuffed cabbage, and baked beans.

Punjab

The cuisine of Punjab is known for its diverse range of dishes which are most similar to Pakistani cuisine. The state, being an agriculture center, is abundant with whole grains, vegetables, and fruits. Home-cooked and restaurant Punjabi cuisine can vary significantly. Restaurant-style Punjabi cooking puts emphasis on creamy textured foods by using *ghee*, butter and cream to accustom various kinds of guest taste preferences; while, home-cooked equivalents center around whole wheat, rice, and other ingredients flavored with various kinds of masalas. Common dishes cooked at home are roti with daal and dahi (yogurt) with a side chutney and salad that includes raw onion, tomato, cucumber, etc. The meals are also abundant of local and seasonal vegetables usually sautéed with spices such as cumin, dried coriander, red chili powder, turmeric, black cloves, etc. Masala Chai is a favorite drink and is consumed in everyday life and at special occasions. Many regional differences exist in the Punjabi cuisine based on traditional variations in cooking similar dishes, food combinations, preference of spice combination, etc. Is it apparent that "the food is simple, robust, and closely linked to the land." Certain dishes exclusive to Punjab, such as makki di roti and *sarson da saag*, dal makhani, etc. are a favorite of many. The *masala* in a Punjabi dish traditionally consists of onion, garlic, ginger, cumin, garam masala, salt, turmeric, tomatoes sauteed in mustard oil. *Tandoori* food is a Punjabi specialty. Common meat dishes in this region are Bhakra curry (Goat) and fish dishes Dairy products are commonly consumed and usually accompany main meals in the form of dahi, milk, and milk derived products such as lassi, paneer, etc. Punjab consists of a high number of people following the Sikh religion who traditionally follow a vegetarian diet (which includes plant derived foods, milk, and milk by-products. See diet in Sikhism) in accordance to their beliefs.

No description of Punjabi cuisine is complete without the myriad of famous desserts, such as kheer, gajar ka halwa, sooji (cream of wheat) halwa, rasmalai, gulab jamun and jalebi. Most desserts are ghee or dairy-based, use nuts such as almonds, walnuts, pistachios, cashews, and, raisins.

Many of the most popular elements of Anglo-Indian cuisine, such as *tandoori* foods, *naan*, *pakoras* and vegetable dishes with *paneer*, are derived from Punjabi styles. Punjabi food is well liked in the world for its flavors, spices, and, versatile use of produce; and hence it is one of the most popular cuisine's from the sub continent. And last but not least is the Chhole Bhature and Chhole Kulche which are famous all over the north India.

Rajasthan

Cooking in Rajasthan, an arid region, has been strongly shaped by the availability of ingredients. Food is generally cooked in milk or *ghee*, making it quite rich. Gram flour is a mainstay of Marwari food mainly due to the scarcity of vegetables in the area.

Historically, food that could last for several days and be eaten without heating was preferred. Major dishes of a Rajasthani meal may include *daal-baati*, *tarfini*, *raabdi*, *Ghevar*, *bail-gatte*, *panchkoota*, *chaavadi*, *laapsi*, *kadhi* and *boondi*. Typical snacks include *bikaneri bhujia*, *mirchi bada*, *Pyaaj Kachori*, and *Dal Kachori*.

Daal-baati is the most popular dish prepared in the state. It is usually supplemented with *choorma*, a mixture of finely ground baked *rotis*, sugar and ghee.

Figure 87: *Rajasthani thali*

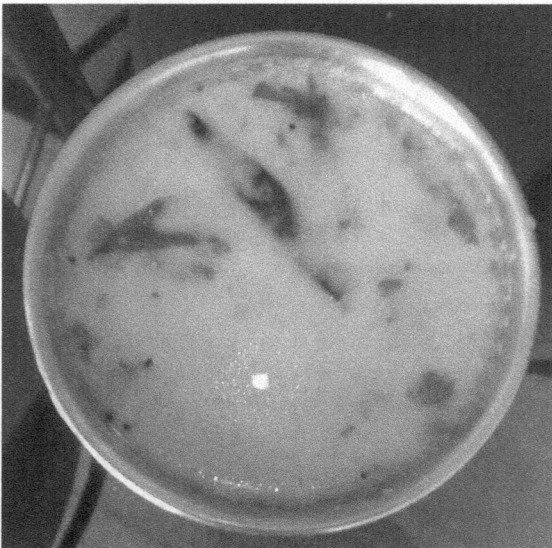

Figure 88: *Kadhi, a spicy North Indian dish*

Rajasthan is also influenced by the Rajput community who have liking for meat dishes. Their diet consisted of game meat and gave birth to dishes like laal maas, safed maas, khad khargosh and jungli maas.[214]

Sikkim

In Sikkim, various ethnic groups such as the Nepalese, Bhutias, and Lepchas have their own distinct cuisines. Nepalese cuisine is very popular in this area. Rice is the staple food of the area, and meat and dairy products are also widely consumed. For centuries, traditional fermented foods and beverages have constituted about 20 percent of the local diet. Depending on altitudinal variation, finger millet, wheat, buckwheat, barley, vegetables, potatoes, and soybeans are grown. *Dhindo, Daal bhat, Gundruk, Momo, gya thuk, ningro, phagshapa,* and *sel roti* are some of the local dishes. Alcoholic drinks are consumed by both men and women. Beef is eaten by the Bhutias.

Sindh

Sindhi cuisine refers to the native cuisine of the Sindhi people from the Sindh region, now in Pakistan. While Sindh is not geographically a part of modern India, its culinary traditions persist, due to the sizeable number of Hindu Sindhis who migrated to India following the independence of Pakistan in 1947, especially in Sindhi enclaves such as Ulhasnagar and Gandhidam. A typical meal in most Sindhi households consists of wheat-based flatbread (*phulka*) and rice accompanied by two dishes, one with gravy and one dry. Lotus stem (known as *kamal kakri*) is also used in Sindhi dishes. Cooking vegetables by deep frying is a common practice that is followed. Some common Sindhi dishes are Sindhi Kadhi, Sai Bhaji, Koki and Besan Bhaji. Some common ingredients used are mango powder, tamarind, *kokum* flowers, and dried pomegranate seeds.

Tamil Nadu

Tamil Nadu is noted for its deep belief that serving food to others is a service to humanity, as is common in many regions of India. The region has a rich cuisine involving both traditional non-vegetarian and vegetarian dishes. Tamil food is characterised by its use of rice, legumes, and lentils, along with distinct aromas and flavours achieved by the blending of spices such as mustard, curry leaves, tamarind, coriander, ginger, garlic, chili pepper, cinnamon, clove, cardamom, cumin, nutmeg, coconut and rose water. The traditional way of eating a meal involves being seated on the floor, having the food served on a plantain leaf, and using the right hand to eat. After the meal the plantain leaf is discarded but becomes food for free-ranging cattle and goats. A meal (called *Saapadu*)

Figure 89: *Vegetarian meals in Tamil Nadu traditionally served on a plantain leaf*

Figure 90: *Dosa served with sambar and chutney*

consists of rice with other typical Tamil dishes on a plantain leaf. A typical Tamilian would eat on a plantain leaf as it is believed to give a different flavour and taste to food. Also growing in popularity are stainless steel trays – plates with a selection of different dishes in small bowls.

Tamil food is characterized by *tiffin*, which is a light food taken for breakfast or dinner, and *meals* which are usually taken during lunch. The word "curry" is derived from the Tamil *kari*, meaning something similar to "sauce". The southern regions such as Tirunelveli, Madurai, Paramakudi, *Karaikudi*, and *Chettinad,Kongu Nadu* are noted for their spicy non-vegetarian dishes. *Dosa*, *idli*, *pongal* and Biryani are some of the popular dishes that are eaten with *chutney* and *sambar*. Fish and other seafoods are also very popular, because the state is located on the coast. Chicken and goat meat are the predominantly consumed meats in Tamil Nadu.

Many Tamilians are vegetarian, however, and the typical meal is heavily dependent on rice, vegetables and lentil preparations such as *rasam* and *sambar*. There are further variations of Tamil vegetarian dishes. They have some influences from Kerala as well in their Kootu, Arachi vitta sambhar and mola-gootals. As mentioned above, the Chettinad variety of food uses lots of strong spices, such as pepper, garlic, fennel seeds and onions. Tamil food tends to be spicy compared to other parts of India so there is a tradition of finishing the meal with dahi (yogurt) is considered a soothing end to the meal.

Notably, Tamil Brahmin cuisine, the food of the Iyers and Iyengar community, is characterized by slightly different meal times and meal structures compared to other communities within the state. Historically vegetarian, the cuisine is renown for its milder flavor and avoidance of onion and garlic (although this practice appears to be disappearing with time). After a light morning meal of filter coffee and different varieties of porridges (oatmeal and *janata kanji* are immensely popular), the main meal of the day, lunch/brunch is usually at 11 am and typically follows a two-three course meal structure. Steamed rice is the main dish, and is always accompanied by a seasonally steamed/sauteed vegetable (poriyal), and two or three types of tamarind stews, the most popular being sambhar and rasam. The meal typically ends with *thair sadham* (rice with yogurt), usually served with pickled mangoes or lemons. *Tiffin* is the second meal of the day and features several breakfast favorites such as idli, rava idli, upma, dosa varieties, vada and is usually accompanied by *chai*. Dinner is the simplest meal of the day, typically involving leftovers from either lunch or tiffin. Fresh seasonal fruit consumed in the state include bananas, papaya, honeydew and canteloupe melons, jackfruit, mangos, apples, *kasturi* oranges, pomegranates, and *nongu* (hearts of palm).

Figure 91: *Hyderabadi Biryani from the city of Hyderabad*

Telangana

The cuisine of Telangana consists of the Telugu cuisine, of Telangana's Telugu people as well as Hyderabadi cuisine (also known as Nizami cuisine), of Telangana's Hyderabadi Muslim community. Hyderabadi food is based heavily on non-vegetarian ingredients, while Telugu food is a mix of both vegetarian and non-vegetarian ingredients. Telugu food is rich in spices and chillies are abundantly used. The food also generally tends to be more on the tangy side with tamarind and lime juice both used liberally as souring agents. Rice is the staple food of Telugu people. Starch is consumed with a variety of curries and lentil soups or broths. Vegetarian and non-vegetarian foods are both popular. Hyderabadi cuisine includes popular delicacies such as *Biryani, Haleem, Baghara baingan* and *Kheema,* while Hyderabadi day to day dishes see some commonalities with Telanganite Telugu food, with its use of tamarind, rice, and lentils, along with meat. Dahi (yogurt) is a common addition to meals, as a way of tempering spiciness.

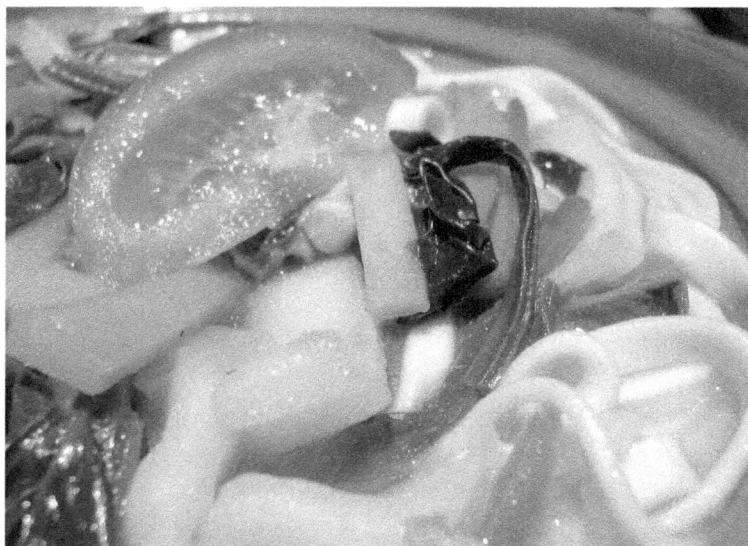

Figure 92: *A bowl of thukpa*

Tripura

The Tripuri people are the original inhabitants of the state of Tripura in north-east India. Today, they comprise the communities of Tipra, Reang, Jamatia, Noatia, and Uchoi, among others. The Tripuri are non-vegetarian, although they have a minority of Vaishnavite vegetarians. The major ingredients of Tripuri cuisine include vegetables, herbs, pork, chicken, mutton, fishes, turtle, shrimps, crabs, freshwater mussels, periwinkles, edible freshwater snails and frogs.

Uttar Pradesh

Traditionally, Uttar Pradeshi cuisine consists of Awadhi and Mughlai cuisine, though a vast majorityWikipedia:Citation needed of the state is vegetarian, preferring *dal*, *roti*, *sabzi*, and rice. *Pooris* and *kachoris* are eaten on special occasions. *Chaat*, *samosa*, and *pakora*, among the most popular snacks in India, originate from Uttar Pradesh. Well known dishes include *kebabs*, *dum biryani*, and various mutton recipes. *Sheer Qorma*, *Ghevar*, *Gulab jamun*, *Kheer*, and *Ras malai* are some of the popular desserts in this region.

Awadhi cuisine (Hindi: अवधी खाना) is from the city of Lucknow, which is the capital of the state of Uttar Pradesh in Central-South Asia and Northern India, and the cooking patterns of the city are similar to those of Central Asia,

Figure 93: *Uttar Pradeshi thali (platter)*
with naan, daal, raita, gul paneer, and salad

the Middle East, and other parts of Northern India. The cuisine consists of both vegetarian and non-vegetarian dishes. Awadh has been greatly influenced by Mughal cooking techniques, and the cuisine of Lucknow bears similarities to those of Central Asia, Kashmir, Punjab and Hyderabad. The city is also known for its Nawabi foods. The bawarchis and rakabdars of Awadh gave birth to the dum style of cooking or the art of cooking over a slow fire, which has become synonymous with Lucknow today.[215] Their spread consisted of elaborate dishes like kebabs, kormas, biryani, kaliya, nahari-kulchas, zarda, sheermal, roomali rotis, and warqi parathas. The richness of Awadh cuisine lies not only in the variety of cuisine but also in the ingredients used like mutton, paneer, and rich spices, including cardamom and saffron.

Mughlai cuisine is a style of cooking developed in the Indian subcontinent by the imperial kitchens of the Mughal Empire. It represents the cooking styles used in North India (especially Uttar Pradesh). The cuisine is strongly influenced by the Central Asian cuisine, the region where the Chagatai-Turkic Mughal rulers originally hailed from, and it has in turn strongly influenced the regional cuisines of Kashmir and the Punjab region. The tastes of Mughlai cuisine vary from extremely mild to spicy, and is often associated with a distinctive aroma and the taste of ground and whole spices. A Mughlai course is an elaborate buffet of main course dishes with a variety of accompaniments.

Figure 94: *Saag, a popular Kumauni dish from Uttarakhand, is made from any of the various green vegetables like spinach and fenugreek.*

Uttarakhand

The food from Uttrakhand is known to be healthy and wholesome to suit the high-energy necessities of the cold, mountainous region. It is a high protein diet that makes heavy use of pulses and vegetables. Traditionally it is cooked over wood or charcoal fire mostly in iron utensils. While also making use of condiments such as *jeera, haldi* and *rai* common in other Indian cuisines, Uttarakhand cuisine uses some exotic condiments like *jambu, timmer, ghandhraini* and *bhangira*. Similarly, although the people in Uttarakhand also prepare the dishes common in other parts of northern India, several preparations are unique to Uttarakhand tradition such as *rus, chudkani, dubuk, chadanji, jholi, kapa*, etc. Among dressed salads and sauces, *kheere ka raita, nimbu mooli ka raita, daarim ki khatai* and *aam ka fajitha* necessarily deserve a mention. The cuisine mainly consists of food from two different sub regions—Garhwal and Kumaon—though their basic ingredients are the same. Both the Kumaoni and Garhwali styles make liberal use of *ghee*, lentils or pulses, vegetables and *bhaat* (rice). They also use *Badi* (sun-dried *Urad Dal* balls) and *Mungodi* (sun-dried *Moong Dal* balls) as substitutes for vegetables at times. During festivals and other celebrations, the people of Uttarakhand prepare special refreshments which include both salty preparations such as *bada* and sweet preparations such as *pua* and *singal*. Uttarakhand also has several sweets (*mithai*) such as *singodi, bal-mithai, malai laddu*, etc. native to its tradition.

Figure 95: *Bengali authentic full meal*

West Bengal

During the 19th century, many Odia-speaking cooks were employed in BengalWikipedia:Citation needed, which led to the transfer of several food items between the two regions. Bengali cuisine is the only traditionally developed multi-course tradition from the Indian subcontinent that is analogous in structure to the modern service à la russe style of French cuisine, with food served course-wise rather than all at onceWikipedia:Citation needed. Bengali cuisine differs according to regional tastes, such as the emphasis on the use of chilli pepper in the Chittagong district of Bangladesh However, across all its varieties, there is predominant use of mustard oil along with large amounts of spices. The cuisine is known for subtle flavours with an emphasis on fish, meat, vegetables, lentils, and rice. Bread is not a common dish in Bengali cuisine, but a deep fried version called *luchi* is popular. Fresh sweetwater fish is one of its most distinctive features; Bengalis prepare fish in many ways, such as steaming, braising, or stewing in vegetables and sauces based on coconut milk or mustard. East Bengali food, which has a high presence in West Bengal and Bangladesh, is much spicier than the West Bengali cuisine, and tends to use high amounts of chilli, and is one of the spiciest cuisines in India and the World. *Shondesh* and *Rasgulla* are popular sweet dishes made of sweetened, finely ground fresh cheese. The "Jaggery Rasgullas" are even more famous. The rasgulla originated in Bengal. and later became popular in erstwhile Odisha. The government of west Bengal has recently acquired the GI status of rasgulla after citing proof in court.

The cuisine is also found in the state of Tripura and the Barak Valley of Assam.

Diaspora and fusion cuisines

The interaction of various Indian diaspora communities with the native cultures of their domiciles have resulted in the creation of many fusion cuisines, which blend aspects of Indian and foreign cuisines. These cuisines tend to adapt Indian seasoning and cooking techniques to foreign dishes.

Indian Chinese cuisine

Indian Chinese cuisine, also known as Indo-Chinese cuisine originated in the 19th century among the Chinese community of Calcutta, during the immigration of Hakka Chinese from Canton (present-day Guangzhou) seeking to escape the First and Second Opium Wars and political instability in the region. Upon exposure to local Indian cuisine, they incorporated many spices and cooking techniques into their own cuisine, thus creating a unique fusion of Indian and Chinese cuisine. After 1947, many Cantonese immigrants fleeing political repression under Mao Zedong, opened their own restaurants in Calcutta, whose dishes combined aspects of Indian cuisine with Cantonese cuisine. While Indian Chinese cuisine is heavily derived from traditional Chinese cuisine, it bears little resemblance to its Chinese counterpart. The dishes tend to be flavoured with cumin, coriander seeds, and turmeric, which with a few regional exceptions, are not traditionally associated with Chinese cuisine. Chilli, ginger, garlic and dahi (yogurt) are also frequently used in dishes.

Popular dishes include Chicken Manchurian, Chicken lollipop, Chilli chicken, Hakka noodles, Hunan chicken, Chow mein, and Szechwan fried rice. Soups such as Manchow soup and Sweet corn soup are very popular, whereas desserts include ice cream on honey-fried noodles and date pancakes. Chow mein is now known as one of the most favorite Chinese dishes in India. Especially in West Bengal, it is one of the most loved street foods.

Indian Singaporean cuisine

Indian Singaporean cuisine refers to foods and beverages produced and consumed in Singapore that are derived, wholly or in part, from South Asian culinary traditions. The great variety of Singaporean food includes Indian food, which tends to be Tamil cuisine, especially local Tamil Muslim cuisine, although North Indian food has become more visible recently. Indian dishes have become modified to different degrees, after years of contact with other Singaporean cultures, and in response to locally available ingredients, as well as changing local tastes.

Anglo-Indian cuisine

Anglo-Indian cuisine is the cuisine that developed during the British Raj in India, as the British wives interacted with their Indian cooks. Well-known Anglo-Indian dishes include chutneys, salted beef tongue, kedgeree, ball curry, fish rissoles, and mulligatawny soup.

Desserts

<templatestyles src="Multiple_image/styles.css" />

Kheer

Phirni

Phirni and Kheer are two of the most popular rice puddings in India.

Many Indian desserts, or *mithai*, are fried foods made with sugar, milk or condensed milk. Ingredients and preferred types of dessert vary by region. In the eastern part of India, for example, most are based on milk products. Many are flavoured with almonds and pistachios, spiced with cardamon, nutmeg, cloves and black pepper, and decorated with nuts, or with gold or silver leaf. Popular Indian desserts include Rasogolla, gulab jamun, jalebi, laddu, peda etc.

Beverages

Non-alcoholic beverages

Non-alcoholic beverages

Figure 96: *Indian filter coffee is popular in Southern India. UNIQ-ref-0-9c34fa5f9dcb4f28-QINU*

Figure 97: *Badam milk*

Figure 98: *A cup of Darjeeling tea.*

Figure 99: *Lassi served at an Indian restaurant.*

Tea is a staple beverage throughout India, since the country is one of the largest producers of tea in the world. The most popular varieties of tea grown in India include Assam tea, Darjeeling tea and Nilgiri tea. It is prepared by boiling the tea leaves in a mix of water, milk, and spices such as cardamom, cloves, cinnamon, and ginger. In India, tea is often enjoyed with snacks like biscuits and pakoda.

Coffee is another popular beverage, but more popular in South India. Coffee is also cultivated in some parts of India. There are two varieties of coffee popular in India, which include Indian filter coffee and instant coffee.

Lassi is a traditional dahi (yogurt)-based drink in India. It is made by blending yogurt with water or milk and spices. Salted *lassi* is more common in villages of Punjab and in Porbandar, Gujarat. Traditional *lassi* is sometimes flavoured with ground roasted cumin. *Lassi* can also be flavoured with ingredients such as sugar, rose water, mango, lemon, strawberry, and saffron.

Sharbat is a sweet cold beverage prepared from fruits or flower petals. It can be served in concentrate form and eaten with a spoon, or diluted with water to create a drink. Popular *sharbats* are made from plants such as rose, sandalwood, *bel*, *gurhal* (hibiscus), lemon, orange, pineapple, sarasaparilla and *falsa* (*Grewia asiatica*). In Ayurveda, *sharbats* are believed to hold medicinal value.

Other beverages include *nimbu pani* (lemonade), *chaas*, *badam doodh* (almond milk with nuts and cardamom), and coconut water. Cold drinks unique to southern India include beverages, such as "Panner Soda" or "Gholi Soda", which is a mixture of carbonated water, rose water, rose milk, and sugar. "*Narenga Soda*", a mixture of carbonated water, salt and lemon juice and "*Soda Nannari Sharbat*", a mixture of sarasaparilla Sharbat with carbonated water are most popular non alcoholic beverages in Kerala and Tamil Nadu. Street shops in Central Kerala and Madurai region of Tamil Nadu are most popular for these drinks which are also called 'Kulukki Sharbats' in Kerala

Alcoholic beverages

Beer

Most beers in India are either lagers (4.8 percent alcohol) or strong lagers (8.9 percent). The Indian beer industry has witnessed steady growth of 10–17 percent per year over the last ten years. Production exceeded 170 million cases during the 2008–2009 financial year. With the average age of the population decreasing and income levels on the rise, the popularity of beer in the country continues to increase.

Others

Other popular alcoholic drinks in India include *fenny*, a Goan liquor made from either coconut or the juice of the cashew apple. The state of Goa has registered for a geographical indicator to allow its *fenny* distilleries to claim exclusive rights to production of liquor under the name "*fenny*."

Figure 100: *Bastar Beer prepared from Sulfi*

Hadia is a rice beer, created by mixing herbs with boiled rice and leaving the mixture to ferment for around a week. It is served cold and is less alcoholic than other Indian liquors. *Chuak* is a similar drink from Tripura. Palm wine, locally known as *Neera*, is a sap extracted from inflorescences of various species of toddy palms. *Chhaang* is consumed by the people of Sikkim and the Darjeeling Himalayan hill region of West Bengal. It is drunk cold or at room temperature in summer, and often hot during cold weather. *Chhaang* is similar to traditional beer, brewed from barley, millet, or rice. Kallu(Chetthu Kallu) is a popular natural alcohol extracted from coconut and pine trees in Kerala. It is sold in local Kallu shops and is consumed with fried fish and chicken. Its alcoholic content is increased by addition of alcoholic additives.

Eating habits

Indians consider a healthy breakfast important. They generally prefer to drink tea or coffee with breakfast, though food preferences vary regionally. North Indian people prefer *roti*, *parathas*, and a vegetable dish accompanied by *achar* (a pickle) and some curd. Various types of packaged pickles are available in the market. One of the oldest pickle-making companies in India is Harnarains, which had started in the 1860s in Old Delhi. People of Gujarat prefer *dhokla*

Figure 101: *Paan is often eaten after a meal.*

and milk, while south Indians prefer idli and dosa, generally accompanied by sambhar or sagu and various *chutneys*.

Traditional lunch in India usually consists of a main dish of rice in the south and the east, and whole wheat rotis in the north. It typically includes two or three kinds of vegetables, and sometimes items such as *kulcha, naan,* or *parathas. Paan* (stuffed, spiced and folded betel leaves) which aids digestion is often eaten after lunch and dinner in many parts of India. Apart from that, many households, specially those in north and central India, prefer having sweets after the dinner (similar like the western concept of dessert after meals).

Indian families often gather for "evening snack time", similar to tea time to talk and have tea and snacks. Dinner is considered the main meal of the day.

Dietary restrictions

In India people often follow dietary restrictions based on their religion or faith:

- Hindu communities consider beef taboo since it is believed that Hindu scriptures condemn cow slaughter. Cow slaughter has been banned in many states of India.
- Vaishnavism followers generally do not eat garlic and onions because they are advised against it in the Bhagavad Gita.

- Jains follow a strict form of vegetarianism, known as Jain vegetarianism, which in addition to being completely vegetarian, also excludes potatoes and other root vegetables because when the root is pulled up, organisms that live around the root also die.
- Muslims do not eat pork or pork products.

Etiquette

Traditionally, meals in India were eaten while seated either on the floor or on very low stools or mattress. Food is most often eaten with the hands rather than cutlery. Often *roti* is used to scoop curry without allowing it to touch the hand. In the wheat-producing north, a piece of *roti* is gripped with the thumb and middle finger and ripped off while holding the *roti* down with the index finger. A somewhat different method is used in the south for the dosai, the adai, and the uththappam, where the middle finger is pressed down to hold the crepe down and the forefinger and thumb used to grip and separate a small part. Traditional serving styles vary regionally throughout India.

Contact with other cultures has affected Indian dining etiquette. For example, the Anglo-Indian middle class commonly uses spoons and forks, as is traditional in Western culture.

In South India, cleaned banana leaves, which can be disposed of after meals, are used for serving food. When hot food is served on banana leaves, the leaves add distinctive aromas and taste to the food. Leaf plates are less common today, except on special occasions.

Outside India

Indian migration has spread the culinary traditions of the subcontinent throughout the world. These cuisines have been adapted to local tastes, and have also affected local cuisines. Curry's international appeal has been compared to that of pizza. Indian tandoor dishes such as *chicken tikka* enjoy widespread popularity.

Canada

As in the United Kingdom and the United States, Indian cuisine is widely available in Canada, especially in the cities of Toronto and Vancouver, where the majority of Canadians of South Asian heritage live.

China

Indian food is gaining popularity in China, where there are many Indian restaurants in Beijing, Shanghai, and Shenzhen. Hong Kong alone has more than 50 Indian restaurants, some of which date back to the 1980s. Most of the Indian restaurants in Hong Kong are in Tsim Sha Tsui.

Middle East

The Indian culinary scene in the Middle East has been influenced greatly by the large Indian diaspora in these countries. Centuries of trade relations and cultural exchange resulted in a significant influence on each region's cuisines. The use of the *tandoor*, which originated in northwestern India, is an example. The large influx of Indian expatriates into the Middle Eastern countries during the 1970s and 1980s led to the booming of Indian restaurants to cater to this population and was also widely influenced by the local and international cuisines.

Nepal

Indian cuisine is available in the streets of Nepalese cities, including Kathmandu and Janakpur.

Southeast Asia

Indian cuisine is very popular in Southeast Asia, due to the strong Hindu and Buddhist cultural influence in the region. Indian cuisine has had considerable influence on Malaysian cooking styles and also enjoys popularity in Singapore. There are numerous North and South Indian restaurants in Singapore, mostly in Little India. Singapore is also known for fusion cuisine combining traditional Singaporean cuisine with Indian influences. Fish head curry, for example, is a local creation. Indian influence on Malay cuisine dates to the 19th century. Other cuisines which borrow inspiration from Indian cooking styles include Filipino, Vietnamese, Indonesian, Thai, and Burmese cuisines. The spread of vegetarianism in other parts of Asia is often credited to Hindu and Buddhist practices.

Figure 102: *An Indian restaurant in Singapore*

Figure 103: *Chicken tikka masala, a modified version of Indian chicken tikka, has been called "a true British national dish."*

United Kingdom

The UK's first Indian restaurant, the Hindoostanee Coffee House, opened in 1810. By 2003, there were as many as 10,000 restaurants serving Indian cuisine in England and Wales alone. According to Britain's Food Standards Agency, the Indian food industry in the United Kingdom is worth 3.2 billion pounds, accounts for two-thirds of all eating out and serves about 2.5 million customers every week.

One of the best known examples of British Indian restaurant cuisine is *Chicken tikka masala*, which has also been called "a true British national dish."

Ireland

Ireland's first Indian restaurant, the Indian Restaurant and Tea Rooms, opened in 1908 on Sackville Street, now O'Connell Street, in Dublin. Today, Indian restaurants are commonplace in most Irish cities and towns. Southeast Asians are the fastest growing ethnic group in Ireland.

United States

A survey by *The Washington Post* in 2007 stated that more than 1,200 Indian food products had been introduced into the United States since 2000. There are numerous Indian restaurants across the US, which vary based on regional culture and climate. North Indian and South Indian cuisines are especially well represented. Most Indian restaurants in the United States serve Americanized versions of North Indian food, which is generally less spicy than its Indian equivalents.

At sit-down restaurants with North Indian cuisine (the most common), complimentary papadum is served with three dipping sauces – typically hari chutney (mint and cilantro), imli chutney (taramind), and a spicy red chili or onion chutney – in place of European-style bread before the meal.

References

<templatestyles src="Refbegin/styles.css" />

Bibliography

- Pat Chapman. *India: Food & Cooking*, New Holland, London — <templatestyles src="Module:Citation/CS1/styles.css" />ISBN 978-1-84537-619-2 (2007)

External links

Wikimedia Commonshas media related to:
Cuisine of India(category)

Wikibooks Cookbookhas a recipe/module on
* *Cuisine of India*

- Indian cuisine[216] at Curlie (based on DMOZ)
- Indian Cuisine in Hindi[217]

Clothing in India

Clothing in India

Part of a series on the
Culture of India
History
People
Cuisine
Religion
Sport
• ⚓ **India portal**
• $\frac{v}{t}$ • $\underline{e}^{218}$

Clothing in India varies depending on the different ethnicity, geography, climate and cultural traditions of the people of each region of India. Historically, male and female clothing has evolved from simple kaupinam, langota, dhoti,

Figure 104: *The Didarganj Yakshi depicting the dhoti wrap.*

lungi, saree, gamucha, and loincloths to cover the body to elaborate costumes
not only used in daily wear but also on festive occasions as well as rituals and
dance performances. In urban areas, western clothing is common and uni-
formly worn by people of all social levels. India also has a great diversity[219] in
terms of weaves, fibers, colours and material of clothing. Sometimes, color
codes are followed in clothing based on the religion and ritual concerned.
The clothing in India also encompasses the wide variety of Indian embroidery, prints, handwork, embellishment, styles of wearing cloths. A wide mix
of Indian traditional clothing and western styles can be seen in India.

History

India's recorded history of clothing goes back to the 5th millennium BC in
the Indus Valley civilization where cotton was spun, woven and dyed. Bone
needles and wooden spindles have been unearthed in excavations at the site.
The cotton industry in ancient India was well developed, and several of the
methods survive until today. Herodotus, an ancient Greek historian described
Indian cotton as "a wool exceeding in beauty and goodness that of sheep".
Indian cotton clothing was well adapted to the dry, hot summers of the subcontinent. The grand epic Mahabharata, composed by about 400 BC, tells of
the god Krishna staving off Draupadi's disrobing by bestowing an unending

Figure 105: *Lady wearing saree, painting by Raja Ravi Varma.*

cheera upon her.WP:NOTRS Most of the present knowledge of ancient Indian clothing comes from rock sculptures and paintings in cave monuments such as Ellora. These images show dancers and goddesses wearing what appears to be a dhoti wrap, a predecessor to the modern sari.The upper castes dressed themselves in fine muslin and wore gold ornaments The Indus civilisation also knew the process of silk production. Recent analysis of Harappan silk fibres in beads have shown that silk was made by the process of reeling, a process known only to China until the early centuries AD.

According to the Greek historian Arrian:

'The Indians use linen clothing, as says Nearchus, made from the flax taken from the trees, about which I have already spoken. And this flax is either whiter in colour than any other flax, or the people being black make the flax appear whiter. They have a linen frock reaching down halfway between the knee and the ankle, and a garment which is partly thrown round the shoulders and partly rolled round the head. The Indians who are very well-off wear earrings of ivory; for they do not all wear them. Nearchus says that the Indians dye their beards various colours; some that they may appear white as the whitest, others dark blue; others have them red, others purple, and others green. Those who are of any rank have umbrellas held over them in the summer. They wear shoes of white

Figure 106: *The Buddha, in Greco-Buddhist style, 1st–2nd century CE, Gandhara (modern Eastern Afghanistan).*

leather, elaborately worked, and the soles of their shoes are many-coloured and raised high, in order that they may appear taller. "

Evidence from the 1st century AD shows some cultural exchanges with the Greeks. Indo-Greek influence is seen in the Greco-Buddhist art of the time. The Buddhas were portrayed as wearing the Greek himation, which is the forerunner of the modern saṃghāti that forms a part of the Kasaya of Buddhist monks. During the Maurya and Gupta period, the people continued to wear the three piece unstitched clothing as in Vedic times. The main items of clothing were the Antariya made of white cotton or muslin, tied to the waist by a sash called *Kayabandh* and a scarf called the Uttariya used to drape the top half of the body.Wikipedia:Citation needed

New trade routes, both overland and overseas, created a cultural exchange with Central Asia and Europe. Romans bought indigo for dyeing and cotton cloth as articles of clothing. Trade with China via the Silk road introduced silk textiles into India. The Chinese had a monopoly in the silk trade and kept its production process a trade secret. However, this monopoly ended when, according to legend, a Chinese princess smuggled mulberry seeds and silkworms in her headdress when she was sent to marry the king of Khotan (present day Xinjiang). From there, the production of silk spread throughout Asia, and by

Figure 107: *Painting on wooden panel discovered by Aurel Stein in Dandan Oilik, depicting the legend of the princess who hid silk worm eggs in her headdress to smuggle them out of China to the Kingdom of Khotan.*

AD 140, the practise had been established in India. Chanakya's treatise on public administration, the Arthashastra written around 3rd century BC, briefly describes the norms followed in silk weaving.

A variety of weaving techniques were employed in ancient India, many of which survive to the present day. Silk and cotton were woven into various designs and motifs, each region developing its distinct style and technique. Famous among these weaving styles were the Jamdani, *Kasika vastra* of Varanasi, *butidar* and the Ilkal saree.Wikipedia:Citation needed Brocades of silk were woven with gold and silver threads and were deeply influenced by Persian designs. The Mughals played a vital role in the enhancement of the art, and the paisley and *Latifa Buti* are fine examples of Mughal influence

Dyeing of clothes in ancient India was practised as an art form. Five primary colours (*Suddha-varnas*) were identified and complex colours (*Misra – varnas*) were categorised by their many hues. Sensitivity was shown to the most subtlest of shades; the ancient treatise, Vishnudharmottara states five tones of white, namely Ivory, Jasmine, August moon, August clouds after the rain and the conch shell. The commonly used dyes were indigo(*Nila*), madder red and safflower.[220] The technique of mordant dyeing was prevalent in India since the second millennium BC. Resist dyeing and Kalamkari techniques were hugely popular and such textiles were the chief exports.

Integral to the history of Indian clothing is the Kashmiri shawl. Kashmiri shawl varieties include the Shahtoosh, popularly known as the 'ring shawl' and the pashmina wool shawls, historically called *pashm*. Textiles of wool finds mention as long back as the Vedic times in association with Kashmir; the Rig Veda refers to the Valley of Sindh as being abundant in sheep,Wikipedia:Citation needed[221] and the god Pushan has been addressed as the 'weaver of garments', which evolved into the term *pashm* for the wool of the area. Woolen shawls have been mentioned in Afghan texts of the 3rd century BC, but reference to the Kashmir work is done in the 16th century AD. The sultan of Kashmir, Zain-ul-Abidin is generally credited with the founding of the industry. A story says that the Roman emperor Aurelian received a purple pallium from a Persian king, made of Asian wool of the finest quality.Wikipedia:Citation needed The shawls were dyed red or purple, red dye procured from cochineal insects and purple obtained by a mixture of red and blue from indigo The most prized kashmiri shawls were the Jamavar and the *Kanika Jamavar*, woven using weaving spools with coloured thread called *kani* and a single shawl taking more than a year for completion and requiring 100 to 1500 *kanis* depending on the degree of elaboration.

Indian textiles were traded from ancient times with China, Southeast Asia and the Roman Empire. The Periplus of the Erythraean Sea mentions mallow cloth, muslins and coarse cottons.[222] Port towns like Masulipatnam and Barygaza won fame for its production of muslins and fine cloth. Trade with the Arabs who were middlemen in the spice trade between India and Europe brought Indian textiles into Europe, where it was favored by royalty in the 17th–18th century. The Dutch, French and British East India Companies competed for monopoly of the spice trade in the Indian Ocean, but were posed with the problem of payment for spices, which was in gold or silver. To counter this problem, bullion was sent to India to trade for the textiles, a major portion of which were subsequently traded for spices in other trade posts, which then were traded along with the remaining textiles in London. Printed Indian calicos, chintz, muslins and patterned silk flooded the English market and in time the designs were copied onto imitation prints by English textile manufacturers, reducing the dependence on India.

The British rule in India and the subsequent oppression following the Bengal Partition sparked a nationwide Swadeshi movement. One of the integral aims of the movement was to attain self-sufficiency, and to promote Indian goods while boycotting British goods in the market. This was idealised in the production of Khadi. Khadi and its products were encouraged by the nationalist leaders over British goods, while also being seen as a means to empower the rural artisans.

Female clothing

In India, women's clothing varies widely and is closely associated with the local culture, religion and climate.

Traditional Indian clothing for women in the north and east are saris worn with choli tops; a long skirt called a lehenga or pavada worn with choli and a dupatta scarf to create an ensemble called a gagra choli; or salwar kameez suits, while many south Indian women traditionally wear sari and children wear

Figure 108: *Indo-Western outfit based on salwar kameez, worn by Bhavana Balsavar, and traditional sari and choli, worn by Shubha Khote. (2012)*

*pattu langa.*Wikipedia:Citation needed Saris made out of silk are considered the most elegant. Mumbai, formerly known as Bombay, is one of India's fashion capitals.Wikipedia:Citation needed In many rural parts of India, traditional clothing is worn. Women wear a sari, a long sheet of colourful cloth, draped over a simple or fancy blouse. Little girls wear a *pavada*. Both are often patterned. Bindi is a part of women's make-up.Wikipedia:Citation needed Indo-western clothing is the fusion of Western and Subcontinental fashion. Other clothing includes the churidar, gamucha, kurti and kurta, and sherwani.

The traditional style of clothing in India varies with male or female distinctions. This is still followed in the rural areas, though is changing in the urban areas. Girls before puberty wear a long skirt (called langa/paawada in Andhra) and a short blouse, called a choli, above it.

Figure 109: *Purple silk sari worn by Vidya Balan.*

Traditional clothing

Sari and wrapped garments

A *saree* or *sari* is a female garment in the Indian subcontinent.[223] A sari is a strip of unstitched cloth, ranging from four to nine meters in length, that is draped over the body in various styles. These include: Sambalpuri Saree from East, Mysore silk and Ilkal of Karnataka and, Kanchipuram of Tamil Nadu from South, Paithani from West and Banarasi from North among others.[224] The most common style is for the sari to be wrapped around the waist, with one end then draped over the shoulder baring the midriff. The sari is usually worn over a petticoat. Blouse may be "backless" or of a halter neck style. These are usually more dressy with a lot of embellishments such as mirrors or embroidery and may be worn on special occasions. Women in the armed forces, when wearing a sari uniform, don a half-sleeve shirt tucked in at the waist. Teenage girls wear half-sarees, a three piece set consisting of a langa, a choli and a stole wrapped over it like a saree. Women usually wear full sarees. Indian wedding saris are typically red or pink, a tradition that goes back to India's pre-modern history.

Saris are usually known with different names in different places. In Kerala, white saris with golden border, are known as *kavanis* and are worn on special occasions. A simple white sari, worn as a daily wear, is called a *mundu*. Saris

Figure 110: *Malayalee lady wearing mundum ner-iyathum. Painted by Raja Ravi Varma, c.1900*

are called *pudavai* in Tamil Nadu. In Karnataka, saris are called *Seere*. The traditional production of handloom sarees is important to economic development in rural communities.

Mundum Neriyathum

Mundum Neriyathum is the oldest remnant of the ancient form of the saree which covered only the lower part of the body, a traditional dress of women in Kerala, South India.[225,226] The basic traditional piece is the *mundu* or lower garment which is the ancient form of the saree denoted in Malayalam as 'Thuni' (meaning cloth), while the *neriyathu* forms the upper garment the mundu.

Mekhela Sador

Mekhela Sador (Assamese: মেখেলা চাদৰ) is the traditional Assamese dress worn by women. It is worn by women of all ages.

There are three main pieces of cloth that are draped around the body.

The bottom portion, draped from the waist downwards is called the *Mekhela* (Assamese: মেখেলা). It is in the form of a sarong—very wide cylinder of cloth—that is folded into pleats to fit around the waist and tucked in. The folds are to the right, as opposed to the pleats in the Nivi style of the saree, which are

Figure 111: *An Assamese girl wearing mekhela sador, 2010*

folded to the left. Strings are never used to tie the mekhela around the waist, though an underskirt with a string is often used.

The top portion of the three-piece dress, called the *Sador* (Assamese: চাদৰ), is a long length of cloth that has one end tucked into the upper portion of the Mekhela and the rest draped over and around the rest of the body. The Sador is tucked in triangular folds. A fitted blouse is worn to cover the breasts.

The third piece is called a *Riha*, which is worn under the Sador. It is narrow in width. This traditional dress of the Assamese women are very famous for their exclusive patterns on the body and the border. Women wear them during important religious and ceremonious occasions of marriage. Riha is worn exactly like a Sador and is used as *Orni*.

Salwaar Kameez

Salwar is a generic description of the lower garment incorporating the Punjabi salwar, Sindhi suthan, Dogri pajamma (also called suthan) and the Kashmiri suthan.

The *salwar kameez* is the traditional wear of women in Punjab, Haryana and Himachal Pradesh and is called the *Punjabi suit* which is most common in the northwestern part of India (Punjab region). The Punjabi suit also includes

Figure 112: *Four women wearing salwar kameez, Puducherry, 2006*

the "churidaar" and "kurta" ensemble which is also popular in Southern India where it is known as the "churidaar".

The salwar kameez has become the most popular dress for females. It consists of loose trousers (the salwar) narrow at the ankles, topped by a tunic top (the kameez). Women generally wear a *dupatta* or *odani* (Veil) with *salwar kameez* to cover their head and shoulders. It is always worn with a scarf called a *dupatta*, which is used to cover the head and drawn over the bosom.

The material for the *dupatta* usually depends upon that of the suit, and is generally of cotton, georgette, silk, chiffon among others. Wikipedia:Citation needed This dress is worn by almost every teenage girl in lieu of western clothes. Many actresses wear the salwar kameez in Bollywood movies.

The suthan, similar to the salwar is common in Sindh where it is worn with the cholo and Kashmir where it is worn with the Phiran.[227] The Kashmiri phiran is similar to the Dogri pajamma. The patiala salwar is an exaggeratedly wide version of the salwar, its loose pleats stitched together at the bottom.

Churidaar

Churidaar is a variation on the salwar, loose above the knees and tightly fitted to the calf below. While the salwar is baggy and caught in at the ankle, the churidar fits below the knees with horizontal gathers near the ankles. The

Figure 113: *Ancient form of Churidar worn during the Gupta period.*

churidaar can be worn with any upper garment such as a long *kurta*, which goes below the knees, or as part of the anarkali suit.

Anarkali Suit

The anarkali suit is made up of a long, frock-style top and features a slim fitted bottom.The anarkali is an extremely desirable style that is adorned by women located in Northern India, Pakistan and The Middle East. The anarkali suit varies in many different lengths and embroideries including floor length anarkali styles. Many women will also opt for heavier embroidered anarkali suits on wedding functions and events. Indian women wear anarkali suits on various other occasions as well such as traditional festivals, casual lunch, anniversary celebrations etc. The kameez of the anarkali can be sleevelesss or with sleeves ranging from cap- to wrist-length.[228]

Lehenga Choli (skirt and blouse)

A *Ghagra Choli* or a *Lehenga Choli* is the traditional clothing of women in Rajasthan and Gujarat.Wikipedia:Citation needed Punjabis also wear them and they are used in some of their folk dances. It is a combination of *lehenga*, a tight *choli* and an *odhani*. A *lehenga* is a form of a long skirt which is pleated. It is usually embroidered or has a thick border at the bottom. A *choli* is a blouse

Figure 114: *A lady wearing a lehenga and choli.*

shell garment, which is cut to fit to the body and has short sleeves and a low neck.

Different styles of *ghagra cholis* are worn by the women, ranging from a simple cotton lehenga choli as a daily wear, a traditional ghagra with mirrors embellished usually worn during navratri for the *garba* dance or a fully embroidered lehenga worn during marriage ceremonies by the bride.

Popular among unmarried women other than salwar kameez are Gagra choli and Langa voni.

Pattu Pavadai/Reshme Langa

Pattu Pavadai or *Langa davani* is a traditional dress in south India and Rajasthan, usually worn by teenage and small girls. The *pavada* is a cone-shaped skirt, usually of silk, that hangs down from the waist to the toes. It normally has a golden border at the bottom.

Girls in south India often wear *pattu pavadai* or *Langa davani* during traditional functions. Girls in Rajasthan wear this dress before marriage (and after marriage with sight modification in certain section of society.)

Figure 115: *Two girls wearing Pattu Pavadai.*

Langa - Voni/Dhavani

This is a type of South Indian dress mainly worn in Karnataka, Andhra Pradesh, and Tamil Nadu, as well as in some parts of Kerala. This dress is a three-piece garment where the langa or lehanga is the cone shaped long flowing skirt.

Male clothing

Traditional clothing

For men, traditional clothes are the Achkan/Sherwani, Bandhgala, Lungi, Kurta, Angarkha, Jama and Dhoti or Pajama. Additionally, recently pants and shirts have been accepted as traditional Indian dress by the Government of India.

Undergarments

Kaupin is unsewn and langota is sewn loincloth worn as underwear in dangal held in akharas especially wrestling, to prevent hernias and hydrocele.

It is mandatory for Sikhs to wear kacchera.

Figure 116: *Mahatma Gandhi in traditional dhoti, 1937*

Dhoti

<templatestyles src="Multiple_image/styles.css" />

A *Chakravartin* wearing a *pancha*. Amaravathi, 1st century BCE/CE. (Musee Guimet)

A man wearing a dhoti.

Dhoti is the national dress of India. A *dhoti* is from four to six feet long white or colour strip of cotton. This traditional attire is mainly worn by men in villages. It is held in place by a style of wrapping and sometimes with the help of a belt, ornamental and embroidered or a flat and simple one, around the waist.

In India men also wear long, white sarong like sheets of cloth known as Mundu. It's called dhotar in Marathi. In north and central Indian languages like Hindi, and Odia these are called "Mundu", In Gujarati it's known as "Dhotiyu", while in Telugu they are called *Pancha*, in Tamil they are called *veshti* and in Kannada it is called *Panche/Lungi*. Over the dhoti, men wear shirts.

Panche or Lungi

A *Lungi*, also known as sarong, is a traditional garment of India. A *Mundu* is a lungi, except that it is always white. It is either tucked in, over the waist, up to knee-length or is allowed to lie over and reach up to the ankle. It is usually tucked in when the person is working, in fields or workshops, and left open usually as a mark of respect, in worship places or when the person is around dignitaries.

Lungis, generally, are of two types: the open lungi and the stitched lungi. The open lungi is a plain sheet of cotton or silk, whereas the stitched one has both of its open ends stitched together to form a tube like structure.

Though mostly worn by men, elderly women also prefer lungi to other garments owing to its good aeration. It is mostly popular in south India, though people of Bangladesh, Brunei, Indonesia, Malaysia, Myanmar and Somalia also can be seen in lungis, because of the heat and humidity, which create an unpleasant climate for trousers, though trousers have now become common outside the house.

Figure 117: *Achkan worn by men during a wedding in Rajasthan, India.*

Achkan/Sherwani

An Achkan or a Sherwani is a long coat / jacket that usually sports exposed buttons through the length of the jacket. The length is usually just below the knees and the jacket ends just below the knee. The jacket has a Nehru collar, which is a collar that stands up.Wikipedia:Citation needed The Achkan is worn with tight fitting pants or trousers called churidars. Churidars are trousers that are loose around the hips and thighs, but are tight and gathered around the ankle. Achkan is usually worn during the wedding ceremonies by the groom and is usually cream, light ivory, or gold coloured. It may be embroidered with gold or silver. A scarf called a dupatta is sometimes added to the achkan.

Bandhgala

A *Jodhpuri* or a *Bandhgala* is a formal evening suit from India. It originated in the Jodhpur State, and was popularized during the British Raj in India. Also known as *Jodhpuri Suit*, it is a western style suit product, with a coat and a trouser, at times accompanied by a vest. It brings together the western cut with Indian hand-embroidery escorted by the Waist coat. It is suitable for occasions such as weddings and formal gatherings.

The material can be silk or any other suiting material. Normally, the material is lined at the collar and at the buttons with embroidery. This can be plain,

Figure 118: *Garba dancers, Ahmedabad. On the left, a male dancer in a Gujarati Angarakha*

jacquard or jamewari material. Normally, the trousers match that of the coat. There is also a trend now to wear contrasting trousers to match the coat colour. Bandhgala quickly became a popular formal and semi-formal uniform across Rajasthan and eventually throughout India.

Angarkha

The term angarkha is derived from the Sanskrit word *Aṅgarakṣaka*, which means protection of the body.[229] The angarkha was worn in various parts of the Indian Subcontinent, but while the basic cut remained the same, styles and lengths varied from region to region. Angarakha is a traditional upper garment worn in the Indian Subcontinent which overlap and are tied to the left or right shoulder. Historically, the Angrakha was a court outfit that a person could wrap around himself, offering flexible ease with the knots and ties appropriate for wearing in the various principalities of ancient India.[230]

Sari jama The jama is a long coat which was popular during the Mughal period. There are many types of jama costumes which were worn in various regions of South Asia, the use of which began to wane by the end of the 19th century A.D.[231] However, men in parts of Kutch still wear the jama also known as the angarkha[232] which has an asymmetric opening with the skirt flaring out to around the hips.[233] However, some styles fall to below the knees.

Figure 119: *A Sikh wearing dastar*

Headgear

The Indian turban or the *pagri* is worn in many regions in the country, incorporating various styles and designs depending on the place. Other types of headgear such as the Taqiyah and Gandhi cap are worn by different communities within the country to signify a common ideology or interest.

Dastar

The Dastar, also known as a pagri, is a turban worn by the Sikh community of India. Is a symbol of faith representing values such as valour, honour and spirituality among others. It is worn to protect the Sikh's long, uncut hair, the Kesh which is one of the Five Ks of Sikhism. Over the years, the dastar has evolved into different styles pertaining to the various sects of Sikhism such as the Nihang and the Namdhari.

Pheta

Pheta is the Marathi name for turbans worn in the state of Maharashtra. Its usually worn during traditional ceremonies and occasions. It was a mandatory part of clothing in the past and have evolved into various styles in different regions. The main types are the Puneri Pagadi, Kolhapuri and Mawali *pheta*.

Figure 120: *Traditional Mysore Peta on a bust of M. Visvesvaraya*

Mysore Peta

Originally worn by the kings of Mysore during formal meeting in durbar and in ceremonial processions during festivals, and meeting with foreign dignitaries, the Mysore peta has come to signify the cultural tradition of the Mysore and Kodagu district. The Mysore University replaced the conventional mortarboard used in graduation ceremonies with the traditional *peta*.

Rajasthani safa

Turbans in Rajasthan are called *pagari* or "safa". They are distinctive in style and colour, and indicate the caste, social class and region of the wearer. In the hot and dry regions, turbans are large and loose. The *paggar* is traditional in Mewar while the *safa* is to Marwar. The colour of the *pagaris* have special importance and so does the *pagari* itself. In the past, saffron stood for valour and chivalry. A white turban stood for mourning. The exchange of a turban meant undying friendship.

Gandhi cap

The Gandhi cap, a white coloured cap made of khadi was popularised by Mahatma Gandhi during the Indian independence movement. The practice of wearing a Gandhi cap was carried on even after independence and became a

Figure 121: *Jawaharlal Nehru wearing the Gandhi cap, 1946*

symbolic tradition for politicians and social activists. The cap has been worn throughout history in many states such as Gujarat, Maharashtra, Uttar Pradesh and West Bengal and is still worn by many people without political signif-icance. In 2013, the cap regained its political symbolism through the Aam Aadmi Party, which flaunted Gandhi caps with "I am a Common Man" written over it. This was partly influenced by the "I Am Anna" caps used during Anna Hazare's Lokpal movement. During the Delhi Legislative Assembly election, 2013, these caps led to a scuffle between Aam Aadmi Party and Congress workers, based on the reasoning that Gandhi caps were being used for politi-cal benefits.

Contemporary clothing

During the 1960s and 1970s, at the same time as Western fashion was absorb-ing elements of Indian dress, Indian fashion also began to actively absorb ele-ments of Western dress. Throughout the 1980s and 1990s, Western designers enthusiastically incorporated traditional Indian crafts, textiles and techniques in their work at the same time as Indian designers allowed the West to influ-ence their work. By the turn of the 21st century, both Western and Indian clothing had intermingled creating a unique style of clothing for the typical urban Indian population. Women started wearing more comfortable clothing

Figure 122: *Actress Gul Panag wearing a modern kameez top having low neckline and with dupatta draped over the neck*

and exposure to international fashion led to a fusion of western and Indian styles of clothing. Following the economic liberalisation, more jobs opened up, and created a demand for formal wear. While women have the choice to wear either Western or traditional dress to work, most Indian multinational companies insist that male employees wear Western dress.

Women's clothing in India nowadays consist of both formal and casual wear such as gowns, pants, shirts and tops. Traditional Indian clothing such as the *kurti* have been combined with jeans to form part of casual attire. Fashion designers in India have blended several elements of Indian traditional designs into conventional western wear to create a unique style of contemporary Indian fashion.

Bibliography

- J.Forbes Watson (1866). *The Textile Manufactures and the Costumes of the People of India*[234]. India Office by George Edward Eyre and William Spottiswoode, London.<templatestyles src="Module:Citation/CS1/styles.css"></templatestyles>

- *Illustrations of the Textile Manufactures of India*[235]. Victoria & Albert Museum, London. 1881.<templatestyles src="Module:Citation/CS1/styles.css"></templatestyles>
- Albert Buell Lewis (1924). *Block Prints from India for Textiles*[236]. Field Museum for Natural History, Chicago.<templatestyles src="Module:Citation/CS1/styles.css"></templatestyles>

Further reading

- Boroian, Michael; Poix, Alix de. (2008). *India by Design: The Pursuit of Luxury and Fashion*[237]. <templatestyles src="Module:Citation/CS1/styles.css" />ISBN 0-470-82396-8.
- Russell, Rebecca Ross (2010). Ownership Case Study: Indian Wife/Widow Jewelry, in: *Gender and Jewelry: A Feminist Analysis*[238]. CreateSpace. <templatestyles src="Module:Citation/CS1/styles.css" />ISBN 1-4528-8253-3.

Indian literature

Indian literature

Part of a series on the
Culture of India
History
People
Cuisine
Religion
Sport
• 🚉 India portal
• v
• t
• e[239]

Indian literature

- Assamese
- Bengali
- Bhojpuri
- English
- Gujarati
- Hindi
- Kannada
- Kashmiri
- Konkani
- Malayalam
- Meitei
- Marathi
- Mizo
- Nepali
- Odia
- Punjabi
- Rajasthani
- Sanskrit
- Sindhi
- Tamil
- Telugu
- Urdu
- $\underline{v}$
- $\underline{t}$
- $\underline{e}^{240}$

History of literature <templatestyles src="Nobold/styles.css"/>by era

Bronze Age

- Ancient Egyptian
- Akkadian
- Sumerian

Classical

- Avestan
- Chinese
- Greek
- Hebrew
- Latin
- Pali
- Prakrit
- Sanskrit

- Syriac
- Tamil

Early Medieval

- Matter of Rome
- Matter of France
- Matter of Britain
- Armenian
- Byzantine
- Georgian
- Japanese
- Kannada
- Middle Persian
- Turkish

Medieval

- Old Bulgarian
- Old English
- Middle English
- Arabic
- Persian
- Armenian
- Byzantine
- Castilian
- Catalan
- Dutch
- French
- Georgian
- German
- Bengali
- Indian
- Old Irish
- Italian
- Korean
- Nepal Bhasa
- Norse
- Russian
- Telugu
- Serbian
- Turkish
- Welsh

Early Modern

- Renaissance
- Baroque

Modern by century

- 18th
- 19th
- 20th
- 21st

Literature portal

- <u>v</u>
- <u>t</u>
- <u>e</u>[241]

Indian literature refers to the literature produced on the Indian subcontinent until 1947 and in the Republic of India thereafter. The Republic of India has 22 officially recognized languages.

The earliest works of Indian literature were orally transmitted. Sanskrit literature begins with the oral literature of the Rig Veda a collection of sacred hymns dating to the period 1500–1200 BCE. The Sanskrit epics *Ramayana* and *Mahabharata* appeared towards the end of the 2nd millennium BCE. Classical Sanskrit literature developed rapidly during the first few centuries of the first millennium BCE, as did the Tamil Sangam literature, and the Pāli Canon. In the medieval period, literature in Kannada and Telugu appeared in the 9th and 11th centuries respectively.[242] Later, literature in Marathi, Odia and Bengali appeared. Thereafter literature in various dialects of Hindi, Persian and Urdu began to appear as well. Early in the 20th century, Bengali poet Rabindranath Tagore became India's first Nobel laureate. In contemporary Indian literature, there are two major literary awards; these are the Sahitya Akademi Fellowship and the Jnanpith Award. Eight Jnanpith Awards each have been awarded in Hindi and Kannada, followed by five in Bengali and Malayalam, four in Odia, three in Gujarati, Marathi, Telugu and Urdu,[243] two each in Assamese and Tamil, and one in Sanskrit.

In archaic Indian languages

History of literature
<templatestyles src="Nobold/-styles.css"/>by region or country

General topics

- Basic topics
- Literary terms
- Criticism
- Theory

Types

- Epic
- Novel
- Poetry
- Prose
- Romance

Lists

- Books
- Authors

Middle Eastern

- Ancient
- Sumerian
- Babylonian
- Egyptian
  - Ancient Egyptian
- Hebrew
- Pahlavi
- Persian
- Arabic
- Israeli

European

- Greek
- Latin
- Early Medieval
  - Matter of Rome
  - Matter of France
  - Matter of Britain
- Medieval
- Renaissance

Modern

- Structuralism
- Poststructuralism
- Deconstruction
- Modernism
- Postmodernism
- Post-colonialism
- Hypertexts

North and South American

- American
- Canadian
- Mexican
- Jamaican

Latin American

- Argentine
- Brazilian
- Colombian
- Cuban
- Peruvian

Australasian

| • Australian |
| • New Zealand |

Asian

East / Southeast
• Chinese • Japanese • Korean • Vietnamese • Thai
South
• Sanskrit • Indian • Pakistani • Assamese • Bengali • Gujurati • Hindi • Kannada • Kashmiri • Malayalam • Marathi • Nepali • Rajasthani • Sindhi • Tamil • Telugu • Urdu • Indian writing in English

African
• Moroccan • Nigerian • South African • Swahili

Related topics
• History of science fiction
• List of years in literature
• Literature by country
• History of theatre
• History of ideas
• Intellectual history

🛍 **Literature portal**
• v • t • e[244]

Vedic literature

Examples of early works written in Vedic Sanskrit include the holy Hindu texts, such as the core Vedas. Other examples include the Sulba Sutras, which are some of the earliest texts on geometry..

Epic Sanskrit literature

Ved Vyasa's *Mahabharata* and Valmiki's *Ramayana*, written in Epic Sanskrit, are regarded as the greatest Sanskrit epics.

Classical Sanskrit literature

The famous poet and playwright Kālidāsa wrote one epic: *Raghuvamsha (Dynasty of Raghu)* ; it was written in Classical Sanskrit rather than Epic Sanskrit. Other examples of works written in Classical Sanskrit include the Pāṇini's *Ashtadhyayi* which standardized the grammar and phonetics of Classical Sanskrit. The *Laws of Manu* is a controversial text in Hinduism. Kālidāsa is often considered to be the greatest playwright in Sanskrit literature, and one of the greatest poets in Sanskrit literature, whose *Recognition of Shakuntala* and *Meghaduuta* are the most famous Sanskrit plays. Some other famous plays were *Mricchakatika* by Shudraka, *Svapna Vasavadattam* by Bhasa, and *Ratnavali* by Sri Harsha. Later poetic works include *Geeta Govinda* by Jayadeva. Some other famous works are Chanakya's *Arthashastra* and Vatsyayana's *Kamasutra*.

Prakrit literature

The most notable Prakrit languages were the Jain Prakrit (Ardhamagadhi), Pali, Maharashtri and Shauraseni.

One of the earliest extant Prakrit works is Hāla's anthology of poems in Maharashtri, the Gāhā Sattasaī, dating to the 3rd to 5th century CE. Kālidāsa and Harsha also used Maharashtri in some of their plays and poetry. In Jainism, many Svetambara works were written in Maharashtri.

Many of Aśvaghoṣa's plays were written in Shauraseni as were a sizable number of Jain works and Rajasekhara's *Karpuramanjari*. Canto 13 of the Bhaṭṭikāvya[245] is written in what is called "like the vernacular" (*bhāṣāsama*), that is, it can be read in two languages simultaneously: Prakrit and Sanskrit.[246]

Pali literature

The Pali Canon is mostly of Indian origin. Later Pali literature however was mostly produced outside of the mainland Indian subcontinent, particularly in Sri Lanka and Southeast Asia.

Pali literature includes Buddhist philosophical works, poetry and some grammatical works. Major works in Pali are *Jataka tales*, *Dhammapada*, *Atthakatha*, and *Mahavamsa*. Some of the major Pali grammarians were Kaccayana, Moggallana and Vararuci (who wrote *Prakrit Prakash*).

Figure 123:
Sahityarathi Lakshminath Bezbaroa

In common Indian languages

Assamese literature

The Charyapadas are often cited as the earliest example of Assamese literature. The Charyapadas are Buddhist songs composed in the 8th to 12th centuries. These writings bear similarities to Oriya and Bengali languages as well. The phonological and morphological traits of these songs bear very strong resemblance to Assamese some of which are extant.

After the Charyapadas, the period may again be split into (a) Pre-Vaishnavite and (b) Vaishnavite sub-periods. The earliest known Assamese writer is Hema Saraswati, who wrote a small poem "Prahlada Charita". In the time of the King Indranarayana (1350–1365) of Kamatapur the two poets Harihara Vipra and Kaviratna Saraswati composed Asvamedha Parva and Jayadratha Vadha respectively. Another poet named Rudra Kandali translated Drona Parva into Assamese. But the most well-known poet of the Pre-Vaishnavite sub period is Madhav Kandali, who rendered Valmiki's Ramayana into Assamese verse (Kotha Ramayana, 11th century) under the patronage of Mahamanikya, a Kachari king of Jayantapura.

Assamese writers of Vaishnavite periods had been Srimanta Sankardev, Madhabdev, Damodardev, Haridevand Bhattadev. Among these, Srimanta Sankardev has been widely acknowledged as the top Assamese littérateur of all-time, and generally acknowledged as the one who introduced drama, poetry, classical dance form called Satriya, classical music form called Borgeet, art and painting, stage enactment of drama called Bhaona and Satra tradition of monastic lifestyle. His main disciples Madhabdev and Damodardev followed in his footsteps, and enriched Assamese literary world with their own contributions. Damodardev's disciple Bhattadev is acknowledged as the first Indian prose writer, who introduced the unique prose writing style in Assamese.

Of the post-Vaishnavite age of Assamese literature, notable modern Assamese writers are Lakshminath Bezbaruah, Padmanath Gohain Baruah, Hemchandra Goswami, Hem Chandra Barua, Atul Chandra Hazarika, Nalini Bala Devi, Birendra Kumar Bhattacharya, Amulya Barua, Navakanta Barua, Syed Abdul Malik, Bhabananda Deka, Jogesh Das, Homen Borgohain, Bhabendra Nath Saikia, Lakshmi Nandan Bora, Nirmal Prabha Bordoloi, Mahim Bora, Hiren Gohain, Arun Sharma, Hiren Bhattacharyya, Mamoni Raisom Goswami, Nalini Prava Deka, Nilamani Phukan, Arupa Kalita Patangia, Dhrubajyoti Bora, Arnab Jan Deka, Rita Chowdhury, Anuradha Sharma Pujari, Manikuntala Bhattacharya and several others.

A comprehensive introductory book *Assamese Language-Literature & Sahityarathi Lakshminath Bezbaroa* originally authored by leading Assamese littérateur of *Awahon-Ramdhenu Era* and pioneer Assam economist Bhabananda Deka together with his three deputies, Parikshit Hazarika, Upendra Nath Goswami and Prabhat Chandra Sarma, was published in 1968. This book was officially released in New Delhi on 24 Nov 1968 by then President of India Dr Zakir Hussain in commemoration of the birth centenary celebration of doyen of Assamese literature Lakshminath Bezbaroa. After almost half a century, this historic book has been recovered and re-edited by Assamese award-winning short-story writer & novelist Arnab Jan Deka, which was published by Assam Foundation-India in 2014. This second enlarged edition was officially released on 4 December 2014 on the occasion of 150th birth anniversary of Lakshminath Bezbaroa and 8th Death Anniversary of Bhabananda Deka by Great Britain-based bilingual magazine *Luit to Thames* (*Luitor Pora Thamsoloi*) editor Dr Karuna Sagar Das.

Bengali literature

The first evidence of Bengali literature is known as Charyapada or Charyageeti, which were Buddhist hymns from the 8th century. Charyapada is in the oldest known written form of Bengali. The famous Bengali linguist Harprashad Shastri discovered the palm leaf Charyapada manuscript in the Nepal Royal

Figure 124: *Rabindranath Tagore, the author of many works, including Gitanjali and India's national anthem 'Jana Gana Mana'. He was awarded the Noble Prize in Literature in 1913 for "his profoundly sensitive, fresh and beautiful verse, by which, with consummate skill, he has made his poetic thought, expressed in his own English words, a part of the literature of the West." He was the first person of non-European lineage to win a Nobel Prize.*

Court Library in 1907. The most internationally famous Bengali writer is Nobel laureate Rabindranath Tagore, who received the Nobel Prize for Literature in 1913 for his work "Gitanjali". He wrote the national anthem of India and Bangladesh namely, "Jana Gana Mana" and "Amar Sonar Bangla", respectively. He was the first Asian who won the Nobel Prize. Rabindranath has written enormous amount of poems, songs, essays, novels, plays and short stories. His songs remain popular and are still widely sung in Bengal.

Kazi Nazrul Islam, who is one generation younger than Tagore, is also equally popular, valuable, and influential in socio-cultural context of the Bengal, though virtually unknown in foreign countries. And among later generation poets, Jibanananda Das is considered the most important figure. Other famous Indian Bengali writers were Sharat Chandra Chattopadhyay, Bankim Chandra Chattopadhyay, Michael Madhusudan Dutt, Sunil Gangopadhyay etc.

Sukanta Bhattacharya (15 August 1926 – 13 May 1947) was a Bengali poet and playwright. Along with Rabindranath Tagore and Kazi Nazrul Islam, he

Figure 125: *The author of India's National Song 'Vande Mataram'.*

was one of the key figures of modern Bengali poetry, despite the fact that most of his works had been in publication posthumously. During his life, his poems were not widely circulated, but after his death his reputation grew to the extent that he became one of the most popular Bengali poet of the 20th century.

Bengali is the second most commonly spoken language in India (after Hindi). As a result of the Bengal Renaissance in the 19th and 20th centuries, many of India's most famous, and relatively recent, literature, poetry, and songs are in Bengali.

In the history of Bengali literature there has been only one pathbreaking literary movement by a group of poets and artists who called themselves Hungryalists.

Chhattisgarhi literature

Literature in Chhattisgarh reflects the regional consciousness and the evolution of an identity distinct from others in Central India. The social problems of the lower castes/untouchables were highlighted in the writings of Khub Chand Baghel through his plays *Jarnail Singh* and *Unch Neech*.

English literature

In the 20th century, several Indian writers have distinguished themselves not only in traditional Indian languages but also in English, a language inherited from the British. As a result of British colonisation, India has developed its own unique dialect of English known as Indian English. Indian English typically follows British spelling and pronunciation as opposed to American, and books published in India reflect this phenomenon. Indian English literature, however, tends to utilise more internationally recognisable vocabulary then does colloquial Indian English, in the same way that American English literature does so as compared to American slang.

India's only Nobel laureate in literature was the Bengali writer Rabindranath Tagore, who wrote some of his work originally in English, and did some of his own English translations from Bengali. India's best selling English-language novelists of all-time are the contemporary writers like Chetan Bhagat, Manjiri Prabhu and Ashok Banker. More recent major writers in English who are either Indian or of Indian origin and derive much inspiration from Indian themes are R. K. Narayan, Vikram Seth, Salman Rushdie, Arundhati Roy, Raja Rao, Amitav Ghosh, Rohinton Mistry, Vikram Chandra, Mukul Kesavan, Raj Kamal Jha, Vikas Swarup, Khushwant Singh, Shashi Tharoor, Nayantara Sehgal, Anita Desai, Kiran Desai, Ashok Banker, Shashi Deshpande, Arnab Jan Deka, Jhumpa Lahiri, Kamala Markandaya, Gita Mehta, Manil Suri, Manjiri Prabhu, Ruskin Bond, Chitra Banerjee Divakaruni and Bharati Mukherjee.

In category of Indian writing in English is poetry. Rabindranath Tagore wrote in Bengali and English and was responsible for the translations of his own work into English. Other early notable poets in English include Derozio, Michael Madhusudan Dutt, Toru Dutt, Romesh Chunder Dutt, Sri Aurobindo, Sarojini Naidu, and her brother Harindranath Chattopadhyay.

In the 1950s, the Writers Workshop collective in Calcutta was founded by the poet and essayist P. Lal to advocate and publish Indian writing in English. The press was the first to publish Pritish Nandy, Sasthi Brata, and others; it continues to this day to provide a forum for English writing in India. In modern times, Indian poetry in English was typified by two very different poets. Dom Moraes, winner of the Hawthornden Prize at the age of 19 for his first book of poems *A Beginning* went on to occupy a pre-eminent position among Indian poets writing in English. Nissim Ezekiel, who came from India's tiny Bene Israel Jewish community, created a voice and place for Indian poets writing in English and championed their work.

Their contemporaries in English poetry in India were Jayanta Mahapatra, Gieve Patel, A. K. Ramanujan, Arun Kolatkar, Dilip Chitre, Arvind Krishna

Mehrotra, Eunice De Souza, Kersi Katrak, P. Lal and Kamala Das among several others.

Younger generations of poets writing in English include G. S. Sharat Chandra, Hoshang Merchant, Makarand Paranjape, Anuradha Bhattacharyya, Nandini Sahu, Arundhathi Subramaniam, Jeet Thayil, Ranjit Hoskote, Sudeep Sen, Abhay K, Jerry Pinto, K Srilata, Gopi Kottoor, Tapan Kumar Pradhan, Arnab Jan Deka, Anju Makhija, Robin Ngangom, Rukmini Bhaya Nair, Smita Agarwal, Vihang A. Naik and Vivekanand Jha among others.

A generation of exiles also sprang from the Indian diaspora. Among these are names like Agha Shahid Ali, Sujata Bhatt, Richard Crasta, Yuyutsu Sharma, Shampa Sinha, Tabish Khair and Vikram Seth.

In recent years, English-language writers of Indian origin are being published in the West at an increasing rate.

Salman Rushdie, Arundhati Roy, Kiran Desai and Arvind Adiga have won the prestigious Man Booker Prize, with Salman Rushdie going on to win the Booker of Bookers.

Hindi literature

Hindi literature started as religious and philosophical poetry in medieval periods in dialects like Avadhi and Brij. The most famous figures from this period are Kabir and Tulsidas. In modern times, the *Khariboli dialect* became more prominent than Sanskrit.

Chandrakanta, written by Devaki Nandan Khatri, is considered to be the first work of prose in Hindi. Munshi Premchand was the most famous Hindi novelist. The *chhayavadi* poets include Suryakant Tripathi 'Nirala', Prem Bajpai, Jaishankar Prasad, Sumitranandan Pant, and Mahadevi Varma. Other renowned poets include Ramdhari Singh 'Dinkar', Maithili Sharan Gupt, Agyeya, Harivansh Rai Bachchan, and Dharmveer Bharti.

Gujarati literature

Gujarati literature's history may be traced to 1000 AD. Since then literature has flourished till date. Well known laureates of Gujarati literature are Hemchandracharya, Narsinh Mehta, Mirabai, Akho, Premanand Bhatt, Shamal Bhatt, Dayaram, Dalpatram, Narmad, Govardhanram Tripathi, Gandhi, K. M. Munshi, Umashankar Joshi, Suresh Joshi, Pannalal Patel and Rajendra Keshavlal Shah.

Gujarat Vidhya Sabha, Gujarat Sahitya Sabha, and Gujarati Sahitya Parishad are Ahmedabad based literary institutions promoting the spread of Gujarati literature. Umashankar Joshi, Pannalal Patel, Rajendra Keshavlal Shah and Raghuveer Chaudhary have won the Jnanpith Award, the highest literary award in India.

Figure 126: *Gandhi extensively wrote in Gujarati*

Kannada literature

The oldest existing record of Kannada prose is the Halmidi inscription of 450 CE, and poetry in *tripadi* metre is the Kappe Arabhatta record of 700 CE. The folk form of literature began earlier than any other literature in Kannada. *Gajashtaka* (800 CE) by King Shivamara II, *Chudamani* (650 CE) by Thumbalacharya are examples of early literature now considered extinct. *Kavirajamarga* by King Nripatunga Amoghavarsha I (850 CE) is the earliest existing literary work in Kannada. It is a writing on literary criticism and poetics meant to standardize various written Kannada dialects used in literature in previous centuries. The book makes reference to Kannada works by early writers such as King Durvinita of the 6th century and Ravikirti, the author of the Aihole record of 636 CE. An early extant prose work, the *Vaddaradhane* by Shivakotiacharya of 900 CE provides an elaborate description of the life of Bhadrabahu of Shravanabelagola. Since the earliest available Kannada work is one on grammar and a guide of sorts to unify existing variants of Kannada grammar and literary styles, it can be safely assumed that literature in Kannada must have started several centuries earlier. Pampa who popularised Champu style which is unique to Kannada wrote the epic "Vikramarjuna Vijaya". He also wrote "Adipurana". Other famous poets like Ponna wrote "shantinatapurana", "Bhuvanaikaramabhyudaya", "Jinaksharamale",and "gatapratyagata".Ranna wrote "Shantipurana" and "Gha-

Figure 127: *Kannada writer and Jnanpith Award winner for the year 1994, U. R. Ananthamurthy*

dayudha".The jain poet Nagavarma 2 wrote "Kavyavalokana", "Karnatab-hashabhushana" and "Vardhamanapurana" . Janna was the author of "Yashod-hara Charitha". Rudhrabhatta and Durgashima wrote "Jagannatha Vijaya" and "Panchatantra" respectively. The works of the medieval period are based on Jain and Hindu principles. The Vachana Sahitya tradition of the 12th century is purely native and unique in world literature. It is the sum of contributions by all sections of society. Vachanas were pithy comments on that period's social, religious and economic conditions. More importantly, they held a mirror to the seed of social revolution, which caused a radical re-examination of the ideas of caste, creed and religion. Some of the important writers of Vachana literature include Basavanna, Allama Prabhu and Akka Mahadevi. Kumara Vyasa, who wrote the *Karnata Bharata Katamanjari*, has arguably been the most famous and most influential Kannada writer of the 15th century. The Bhakti move-ment gave rise to Dasa Sahitya around the 15th century which significantly contributed to the evolution of Carnatic music in its present form. This pe-riod witnessed great Haridasas like Purandara Dasa who has been aptly called the *Pioneer of Carnatic music*, Kanaka Dasa, Vyasathirtha and Vijaya Dasa. Modern Kannada in the 20th century has been influenced by many movements, notably *Navodaya*, *Navya*, *Navyottara*, *Dalita* and *Bandaya*. Contemporary Kannada literature has been highly successful in reaching people of all classes in society. Works of Kannada literature have received Eight Jnanpith awards, which is the highest number awarded for the literature in any Indian language. It has also received forty-seven Sahitya Academy awards.

Malayalam literature

Even up to 500 years since the start of the Malayalam calendar which commenced in 825 AD, Malayalam literature remained in preliminary stage. During this time, Malayalam literature consisted mainly of various genres of songs. *Ramacharitham* written by *Cheeramakavi* is a collection of poems written at the end of preliminary stage in Malayalam literature's evolution, and is the oldest Malayalam book available. Thunchaththu Ramanujan Ezhuthachan (17th century) is considered as the Father of the Malayalam language, because of his influence on the acceptance of the Malayalam alphabet and his extremely popular poetic works like Adhyathmaramayanam. Several noted works were written during the 19th century, but it was in the 20th century the Malayalam literary movement came to prominence. Malayalam literature flourished under various genres and today it is a fully developed part of Indian literature.

Meitei literature

Meitei literature is literature written in the Meitei language (Manipuri, Meiteilon), including literature composed in Meitei by writers from Manipur, Assam, Tripura, Myanmar and Bangladesh. The history of Meitei literature can be traced back to thousands of years with the flourish of Meitei civilization. Despite massive devastation and the burning of Meitei scriptures, such as the Puya Meithaba, Meitei literature survived. The resilience that Meiteis would demonstrate in the event of devastation proves their ability to survive throughout history. Most of the early literary works found in Meitei literature were in poetry and prose or a combination of both. One of the most famous Meitei writers of the twentieth century is M. K. Binodini Devi.

Marathi literature

Marathi literature began with saint-poets like Dnyaneshwar, Tukaram, Ramdas, and Eknath. Modern Marathi literature was marked by a theme of social reform. Well-known figures from this phase include Mahatma Jyotiba Phule, Lokhitwadi, and others. Prominent modern literary figures include Jnanpith Award winners Vishnu Sakharam Khandekar, Vishnu Vaman Shirvadakar (*Kavi Kusumagraj*) and Govind Vinayak Karandikar. Though the earliest known Marathi inscription found at the foot of the statue at Shravanabelgola in Karnataka is dated c. 983 CE, the Marathi literature actually started with the religious writings by the saint-poets belonging to Mahanubhava and Warkari sects. Mahanubhava saints used prose as their main medium, while Warkari saints preferred poetry as the medium. The early saint-poets were Mukundaraj who wrote Vivekasindhu, Dnyaneshwar (1275–1296) (who wrote Amrutanubhav and Bhawarthadeepika, which is popularly known as Dnyaneshwari, a 9000-couplets long commentary on the Bhagavad Gita) and Namdev. They were followed by the Warkari saint-poet Eknath (1528–1599). Mukteswar translated the great epic Mahabharata into Marathi. Social reformers like saint-poet Tukaram transformed Marathi into an enriched literary language. Ramdas's (1608–1681) Dasbodh and Manache Shlok are well-known products of this tradition.

In the 18th century, some well-known works like Yatharthadeepika (by Vaman Pandit), Naladamayanti Swayamvara (by Raghunath Pandit), Pandava Pratap, Harivijay, Ramvijay (by Shridhar Pandit) and Mahabharata (by Moropant) were produced. However, the most versatile and voluminous writer among the poets was Moropanta (1729–1794) whose Mahabharata was the first epic poem in Marathi. The historical section of the old Marathi literature was unique as it contained both prose and poetry. The prose section contained the Bakhars that were written after the foundation of the Maratha kingdom by Shivaji. The poetry section contained the Povadas and the Katavas composed by the Shahirs. The period from 1794 to 1818 is regarded as the closing period of the Old Marathi literature and the beginning of the Modern Marathi literature.

Modern period (after 1800)

The period of the late 19th century in Maharashtra is the period of colonial modernity. Like the corresponding periods in the other Indian languages, this was the period dominated by the English educated intellectuals. It was the age of prose and reason. It was the period of reformist didacticism and a great intellectual ferment.

The first English book was translated in Marathi in 1817. The first Marathi newspaper started in 1835. Many books on social reforms were written by Baba Padamji (Yamuna Paryatana, 1857), Mahatma Jyotiba Phule, Lokhitwadi, Justice Mahadev Govind Ranade, Hari Narayan Apte (1864–1919) etc. Lokmanya Tilak's newspaper Kesari, set up in 1880, provided a platform for sharing literary views. Marathi at this time was efficiently aided by Marathi Drama. Here, there also was a different genre called 'Sangit Natya' or musicals. The first play was V.A. Bhave's *Sita Swayamvar* in 1843. Later Kirioskar (1843–85) and G.B. Deval (1854-1916) brought a romantic aroma and social content. But Krishnaji Prabhakar Khadilkar (1872~1948) with his banned play *Kichaka-Vadh* (1910) set the trend of political playwriting. Later on this "stage" was ably served by stalwarts like Ram Ganesh Gadkari and Prahlad Keshav Atre. The drama flourished in the 1960s and 70s with few of the best

Indian actors available to take on a variety of protagonists. Mohan Agashe, Sri-
ram Lagoo, Kashinath Ghanekar, Prabhakar Panshikar playing many immortal characters penned by greats like Vasant Kanetkar, Kusumagraj, vijay Tendulkar to name a few. This drama movement was ably supported by Marathi
films which did not enjoy a continuous success. Starting with V.Shantaram
and before him the pioneer DadaSaheb Phalke, Marathi cinema went on to influence contemporary Hindi cinema. Director Raja Paranjape, Music director
Sudhir Phadke, lyricist G.Madgulkar and actor Raja Gosavi came together to
give quite a few hits in later period. Marathi language as spoken by people
here was throughout influenced by drama and cinema along with contemporary literature. Modern Marathi poetry began with Mahatma Jyotiba Phule's
compositions. The later poets like Keshavsuta, Balakavi, Govindagraj, and
the poets of Ravi Kiran Mandal like Madhav Julian wrote poetry which was
influenced by the Romantic and Victorian English poetry. It was largely sen-
timental and lyrical. Prahlad Keshav Atre, the renowned satirist and a politician wrote a parody of this sort of poetry in his collection Jhenduchi Phule.
Sane Guruji (1899–1950) contributed to the children's literature in Marathi.
His major works are *Shyamchi Aai* (Shyam's Mother), *Astik* (Believer), *Gode
Shevat* (The Sweet Ending) etc. He translated and simplified many Western
classics and published them in a book of stories titled *Gode Goshti* (Sweet
Stories).

Mizo literature

Mizo literature is the literature written in Mizo ṭtawng, the principal language
of the Mizo peoples, which has both written and oral traditions. It has un-
dergone a considerable change in the 20th century. The language developed
mainly from the Lushai language, with significant influence from Pawi language, Paite language and Hmar language, especially at the literary level.[247]
All Mizo languages such as Pawi language, Paite language etc. remained unwritten until the beginning of the 20th century. However, there was unwritten
secular literature in the form of folktales, war chants etc. passed down from
one generation to another. And there was rich religious literature in the form
of sacerdotal chants. These are the chants used by the two types of priests,
namely *Bawlpu* and *Sadâwt*. This article is about the written literature.

Odia literature

Odia language literary history started with the charyapadas written in the 8th
century AD. Odia has a rich literary heritage, the medieval period dating back
to the 13th century. Sarala Dasa who lived in the 14th century is known as the
Vyasa of Odisha. He translated the Mahabharata into Odia. In fact the language was initially standardized through a process of translation of classical

Sanskrit texts like the Mahabharata, the Ramayana and the Srimad Bhagabatam. Jagannatha Das translated the Srimad Bhagabatam into Odia and his translation standardized the written form of the language. Odia has had a strong tradition of poetry, especially that of devotional poetry. Some other eminent ancient Odia Poets include Kabi Samrat Upendra Bhanja and Kavisurya Baladev Rath.

Odia language is replete in classisicm. Various forms of poetry like champu, chhanda, bhajan, janan, poi, chautisha etc. were written during the medieval ages.

In the 19th century, Swabhab Kavi Gangadhar Meher (1862-1924), Fakir Mohan Senapati (1843–1918), Gouri Shankar Ray, Gopal Chandra Praharaj, Pandit Nilmani Vidyaratna, Kabibar Radhanath Ray were few of the prominent figures in prose and poetry writings of Odia literature. In the 20th century Godabarish Mohapatra, Kalindi Charana Panigrahi, Kanhu Charan Mohanty (1906–1994), Godabarish Mishra, Gopinath Mohanty (1914–1991), Sachidananda Routray (1916–2004), Sitakant Mahapatra (born 17 September 1937), Surendra Mohanty, Manoj Das, Kishori Charan Das, Ramakanta Rath (born 13 December 1934), Binapani Mohanty, Jagadish Mohanty, Sarojini Sahoo, Rajendra Kishore Panda, Padmaj Pal, Ramchandra Behera, Pratibha Satpathy, Nandini Sahu, Debaraj Samantray are few names who created Odia literature. RecentlyWikipedia:Manual of Style/Dates and numbers#Chronological items the Government of India accorded classical status to Odia.

Punjabi literature

The history of Punjabi literature starts with advent of Aryan in Punjab. Punjab provided them the perfect environment in which to compose the ancient texts. The Rig-Veda is first example in which references are made to the rivers, flora and fauna of Punjab. The Punjabi literary tradition is generally conceived to commence with Fariduddin Ganjshakar (1173–1266).[2]. Farid's mostly spiritual and devotional verse were compiled after his death in the Adi Granth.

The Janamsakhis, stories on the life and legend of Guru Nanak (1469–1539), are early examples of Punjabi prose literature. Nanak himself composed Punjabi verse incorporating vocabulary from Sanskrit, Arabic, Persian, and other Indic languages as characteristic of the Gurbani tradition. Sufi poetry developed under Shah Hussain (1538–1599), Sultan Bahu (1628–1691), Shah Sharaf (1640–1724), Ali Haider (1690–1785), and Bulleh Shah (1680–1757). In contrast to Persian poets who had preferred the ghazal for poetic expression, Punjabi Sufi poets tended to compose in the Kafi.[3].

Punjabi Sufi poetry also influenced other Punjabi literary traditions particularly the Punjabi Qissa, a genre of romantic tragedy which also derived inspiration from Indic, Persian and Qur'anic sources. The Qissa of Heer Ranjha by Waris Shah (1706–1798) is among the most popular of Punjabi qisse. Other popular stories include Sohni Mahiwal by Fazal Shah, Mirza Sahiba by Hafiz Barkhudar (1658–1707), Sassi Punnun by Hashim Shah (1735?-1843?), and Qissa Puran Bhagat by Qadaryar (1802–1892).

The Victorian novel, Elizabethan drama, free verse and Modernism entered Punjabi literature through the introduction of British education during colonial rule. The setting up of a Christian mission at Ludhiana in 1835 (where a printing press was installed for using Gurmukhi fonts, and which also issued the first Punjabi grammar in 1838), the publication of a Punjabi dictionary by Reverend J. Newton in 1854 and the ripple-down effect of the strengthening and modernizing the education system under the patronage of the Singh Sabha Movement in the 1860s, were some of the developments that made it possible for 'modernism' to emerge in Punjabi literary culture. It needs to be pointed out here that 'modernism' is being used here as an umbrella term to cover a whole range of developments in the Punjabi literary culture, starting with the break from tradition or the past to a commitment to progressive ideology, from the experimental nature of the avant-garde to the newness of the forward-looking.

Tamil literature

Tamil literature has a rich and long literary tradition spanning more than 2000 years(5th century BC-3rd century CE.) Tolkaappiyam has been credited as the oldest work in Tamil available today. The history of Tamil literature follows the history of Tamil Nadu, closely following the social and political trends of various periods. The secular nature of the early Sangam poetry gave way to works of religious and didactic nature during the Middle Ages. Tirukkural is a fine example of such work on human behaviour and political morals. A wave of religious revival helped generate a great volume of literary output by Saivite and Vaishnavite authors. Jain and Buddhist authors during the medieval period and Muslim and EuropeanWikipedia:Citation needed authors later also contributed to the growth of Tamil literature.

A revival of Tamil literature took place from the late 19th century when works of religious and philosophical nature were written in a style that made it easier for the common people to enjoy. Nationalist poets began to utilise the power of poetry in influencing the masses. Short stories and novels began to appear. The popularity of Tamil Cinema has also provided opportunities for modern Tamil poets to emerge.

Telugu literature

Telugu, the Indian language with the third largest number of speakers (after Hindi & Bengali), is rich in literary traditions. The earliest written literature dates back to the 7th century. The epic literary tradition started with Nannayya who is acclaimed as Telugu's *Aadikavi* meaning the first poet. He belongs to the 10th or 11th century.

Vemana was a prince, also called Pedakomati or Vemaa Reddy, who lived in the 14th century and wrote poems in the language of the common man. He questioned the prevailing values and conventions and religious practices in his poems. His philosophy made him a unique poet of the masses.

Viswanadha Satyanarayana (*Veyipadagalu*) (1895–1976), a doyen of conventional yet creative literature, was the first to receive the Jnanpith Award for Telugu followed by C. Narayana Reddy and Ravuri Bharadwaja.

Srirangam Srinivasarao or **Sri Sri** (born 1910) was a popular 20th century poet and lyricist. Srisri took the "Telugu literary band wagon that travelled in roads of kings and queens in to that of muddy roads of common man".

Literary movements

Old Era

Telugu literature has been enriched by many literary movements, like the Veera Shaiva movement which gave birth to dwipada kavitvam (couplets). The Bhakti movement gave rise to compilations by Annamayya, Kshetrayya and Tyagaraja and kancharla Gopanna (Ramadasu). The renaissance movement heralded by Vemana stands for the old Telugu literary movements.

New Era

The Romantic Movement (led by Krishnasashtri, Rayaprolu, Vedula), Progressive Writers Movement, Digambara Kavitvam (Nagnamuni, Cherabanda Raju, Jwalamukhi, Nikhileswar, Bhairavayya and Mahaswapna Revolutionary Writers' Movement, Streevada Kavitvam and Dalita Kavitvam all flourished in Telugu literature. Telugu literature has been the standard bearer of Indian literature in these respects.

Fiction and prose literature:

Kandukuri Veeresalingam is said to be the father of Modern Telugu fiction. Kodavatiganti Kutumba Rao laid the foundation for the realistic modern Telugu novel and short story, and Rachakonda and Kalipatnam carried the flag in to excellency.

Annamaya, Gurajada Appa Rao, Kandukuri, Devulapalli, Jashuva, Unnava Laxminarayana (*Malapalli*), Bucchi Babu, Tripuraneni Gopichand and many more had a profound impact on Telugu literature.

Urdu literature

Among other traditions, Urdu poetry is a fine example of linguistic and cul-tural synthesis. Arab and Persian vocabulary based on the Hindi language resulted in a vast and extremely beloved class of ghazal literature, usually writ-ten by Muslims in contexts ranging from romance and society to philosophy and Tassawuf(Sufism). Urdu soon became the court language of the Mughals and in its higher forms was once called the "Kohinoor" of Indian languages. Its surely most refined, enriched, sophisticated and ripended language and lit-erature, producing poets like, Meer Ghalib, Iqbal and Faiz. The poetry of Mohammed Iqbal invoked a spirit of freedom among the Muslims of India, thus contributing a pivotal role in the making of Pakistan.

In Urdu literature fiction has also flourished well. Umrao Jaan Ada of Mirza Hadi Ruswa is first significant Urdu novel. Premchand is treated as father of modern Urdu fiction with his novel Godan and short stories like Kafan. The art of short story was further taken ahead by Manto, Bedi, Krishn Chander and a host of highly acclaimed writers. Urdu novel reached further heights in the 1960s with novels of Qurratulain Haider and Abdullah Hussain. Towards the end of the 20th century Urdu novel entered into a new phase with trend setter novel MAKAAN of Paigham Afaqui. Urdu ghazal has also recently changed its colour with more and more penetration in and synchronization with modern and contemporary issues of life.

In foreign languages

Indian Persian literature

During the early Muslim period, Persian became the official language of the northern part of Indian subcontinent, used by most of the educated and the government. The language had, from its earliest days in the 11th century AD, been imported to the subcontinent by various culturally Persianised Central Asian Turkic and Afghan dynasties.[248] Several Indians became major Persian poets later on, the most notable being Amir Khusro and, in more modern times, Muhammad Iqbal. Much of the older Sanskrit literature was also translated into Persian. For a time, it remained the court language of the Mughals, soon to be replaced by Urdu. Persian still held its status, despite the spread of Urdu, well into the early years of the British rule in India. Most British officials had to learn Persian on coming to India and concluded their conversations in Persian. In 1837, however, the British, in an effort to expand their influence, made a government ruling to discontinue the use of Persian and commence the use of English instead. Thus started the decline of Persian as most of the subcontinent's official governmental language, a position to be taken up by the new language of the British Raj, English. Many modern Indian languages still show signs of relatively heavy Persian influence, most notably Urdu and Hindi.

English literature from North East India

English literature from North East India refers to the body of work by English-language writers from North-East India. North-East India is an under-represented region in many ways. The troubled political climate, the beautiful landscape and the confluence of various ethnic groups perhaps have given rise to a body of writing that is completely different from Indian English Literature.

Journalism in India

The first printing press arrived in India in the year 1556, through the efforts of Jesuit missionaries. It was brought from Portugal and installed at the college of St. Paul in Goa. It was used mainly for printing religious literature like tracts, hymn books etc.[249]

The first printed newspaper of India was in English, and was called Hicky's Bengal Gazette. It was edited and published by James Augustus Hicky, an ex-employee of the East India Company. The first issue of this newspaper came out in 1780 and carried only classified advertisements on its front page. It was a weekly newspaper and generally dealt with the arrival and departure of Europeans, timings of steamers, fashionable news from London, Paris and Vienna, and personal news. It attended to the needs of the small European community of Calcutta. Many other Anglo-Indian newspapers emerged after Hicky's pattern- such as John Bull, Calcutta Journal, Bengal Harkaru. In the year 1781, Hicky's Bengal Gazette was forced to close down after Hicky published a scandalous story about Warren Hastings, the then Governor-General and his wife.

Later on, another type of newspaper emerged- Indo-Anglian papers. They were English newspapers run by Indians primarily for English educated elite Indians. The first newspaper of this type was *Bengal Gazette*, started in 1816 by Gangadhar Bhattacharya, a disciple of Raja Rammohan Roy. Rammohan Roy also began his famous Brahmanical Magazine, English fortnightly.

The early Indo-Anglian papers concentrated on drawing the attention of the British to the cultural and philosophical history of India. They did not openly attack social and political evils.

The first war of independence was fought from 1857 to 1859 in various parts of the country. Between 1860 and 1899, hundreds of newspapers came up demanding freedom of expression and criticizing the repressive measures taken by the British. Journalism played an important role in making educated Indians aware of their rights. Some newspapers of this period are *The Hindu* of Madras and *Amrit Bazaar Patrika* of Calcutta. Another significant factor was that during this period a large number of colleges imparting science and liberal arts education sprang up in the major towns of India.

Digdarshan (World Vision) was the first Indian language newspaper, a Bengali religious weekly started in Sehrampur by Christian missionaries. Based on the pattern of *Digdarshan*, Raja Rammohan Roy brought out Bengali and Urdu weeklies like *Bangadoota* and *Mirat-ul-Akhbar*. The newspaper with the greatest longevity in India is the first Gujarati newspaper- *Mumbai Samachar*, established in 1822. Some of the early Hindi publications were Oodunt Martand, Banaras Akhbar, Shimla Akhbar and Samayadant Martand, the first Hindi daily. Mangaloora Samachar, published from Mangalore, was the first Kannada journal. Malayala Manorama, the second oldest newspaper in Kerala was started in 1890, and was the first newspaper to be published by a joint stock company formed solely for the purpose of publishing a newspaper. The first Marathi newspaper was Darpan- a bilingual fortnightly in Englisha and Marathi, started by a professor of the Elphinstone College of Bombay. The first all Marathi journal was Mumbai Akhbar. During the early part of the 20th century, Marathi journalism played an important role in the freedom movement. Bal Gangadhar Tilak, a renowned freedom fighter started two powerful journals- Kesari and Maratha.

Despite the numerous columns and articles demanding political and social reforms, journalism during the 19th century had little impact on the Indian masses, due to widespread illiteracy and poverty.

In 1947, the major English newspaper in India were the Times of India (Bombay), Statesman (Calcutta), Hindu (Madras), Hindustan Times (New Delhi), Indian Express (Bombay & Madras) Amrita Bazaar Patrika (Calcutta). Of these, the Times of India, Statesman & Pioneer were under British ownership till 1964, when it came under a group of Indian business.

During the long struggle for India's Independence, the major English newspaper that served the national cause were the Hindu (1878), Amrita Bazaar Patrika (1868), & Hindustan Times (1924). Among the Indian language newspapers, the prominent ones were, Ananda bazaar Patrika (1922), Sakal (1931), Mumbai Samachar (1822), Malayala Manorama (1890) & Mathrubhumi (1930).

During the 1950s 214 daily newspapers were published in the country. Out of these, 44 were English language dailies while the rest were published in various regional languages. This number rose to 2,856 dailies in 1990 with 209 English dailies.

There are four major publishing groups in India, each of which controls national and regional English-language and vernacular publications. They are the Times of India Group, the Indian Express Group, the Hindustan Times Group, and the Anandabazar Patrika Group. The Times of India is India's largest English-language daily, with a circulation of 656,000 published in six cities. The Indian Express, with a daily circulation of 519,000, is published in seventeen cities. There also are seven other daily newspapers with circulations of between 134,000 and 477,000, all in English and all competitive with one another. Indian-language newspapers also enjoy large circulations but usually on a statewide or citywide basis. For example, the Malayalam-language daily Malayala Manorama circulates 673,000 copies in Kerala; the Hindi-language Dainik Jagran circulates widely in Uttar Pradesh and New Delhi, with 580,000 copies per day; Punjab Kesari, also published in Hindi and available throughout Punjab and New Delhi, has a daily circulation of 562,000; and the Anandabazar Patrika, published in Calcutta in Bengali, has a daily circulation of 435,000. There are also numerous smaller publications throughout the nation. The combined circulation of India's newspapers and periodicals is in the order of 60 million, published daily in more than ninety languages.

Journalism during the Emergency Period

During the summer of 1975, as Indira Gandhi became increasingly threatened by the mounting criticisms of her government, she declared a state of emergency. The declaration of a national emergency lasted for about 19 months. The emergency was declared as a result of mounting political pressure exerted upon the government from opposing political parties which were striving to fight corruption, inflation and economic chaos in the country. Indira Gandhi's government, rather than taking this as a political challenge, resorted to declaring a national emergency and imprisoning the opposition party leaders, including all dissenting voices from the media.

Immediately she took control of the press, prohibiting their reporting of all domestic and international news. The government expelled several foreign correspondents (mainly American and British) and withdrew accreditation from more than 40 Indian reporters who normally covered the capital.

The fundamental rights of the Indian people were suspended, and strict controls were imposed on freedom of speech and press. According to the Right of Freedom-Article 19(1) of the Indian Constitution, Indians have the right (a) to freedom of speech and expression, (b) to assemble peacefully and without arms, (c) to form associations or unions, (d) to move freely across the length and breadth of the country, (e) to reside or settle in any part of India, (f) to own or dispose of property, and (g) to carry on any lawful trade of occupation.'

Unlike the American Constitution or others In which freedom of the press is mentioned as one of the fundamental rights, the Indian Constitution doesn't specifically mention freedom of the press. However, the fundamental Rights Clause of the Indian Constitution treats freedom of the press as an integral part of the larger "freedom of expression."

Indira Gandhi's government used the "security of the state" and "promotion of disaffection" as its defense for imposing strict control on the press. And with the airwaves already under government ownership, Indira Gandhi successfully controlled the mass communication system in India for over a year and a half.

During censorship, most of the nation's domestic dailies gave up the battle for press freedom. Their pages were "filled with fawning accounts of national events, flattering pictures of Gandhi and her ambitious son, and not coincidentally, lucrative government advertising." But two tough, prominent publishers of English language dailies, The Indian Express and The Statesman, fought courageously against Indira Gandhi's opposition of the Indian press. Despite some bold fights and stubborn stands taken up by these publishers, it was quite clear that Indira Gandhi had as strong a grip on the Indian press as she had on Indian politics, at least during the government-imposed emergency.

Methods of press control

Like other dictators in history, Indira Gandhi's first attempt was to impose "thought control" on the populace. For her, this was to be effectuated not merely by controlling the Indian mass media but also by moulding the media to her own purpose. It has now become a well-known fact that during the emergency Indira Gandhi had a firm grip on the Indian mass media. This was especially true since radio and television in India are government owned and operated; for Indira, there was the simple matter of controlling the newspapers in order to achieve a total control of the mass media. She used at least three methods in manipulating the newspapers:

1. allocation of government advertising;
2. shotgun merger of the news agencies; and
3. use of fear-arousal techniques on newspaper publishers, journalists and individual shareholders.

The Indian newspapers depend a great deal on governmental advertising; without such revenues, it would be difficult for many Indian newspapers to stay in business. Unfortunately, this has kept many of them vulnerable to government manipulation. The large-scale possibility of such manipulation, however, was not fully demonstrated until Indira Gandhi's government decided to take advantage of this unique circumstance. In the beginning of censorship, when a few leading newspapers such as The Indian Express and The Statesman refused to abide the governmental censorship, the government withdrew its advertising support from these newspapers. Later on, this type of financial castigation was used on several other rebellious newspapers.

The second and perhaps more profound way of manipulating the news flow resulted from the governmental decision to bring about a shot-gun merger of the four privately owned Indian news agencies; the main purpose behind this merger was to alter the management and control of the Indian news agencies and thus to control much of the content of the leading newspapers. Since these agencies had been acting as the gatekeepers of information, it was essential for Indira Gandhi and her Information and Broadcasting Minister, Mr. V.C. Shukla, to control the gatekeepers. To effect such a merger, the government carried through various successful tactics. First of all, pressure was put on the members of boards of these agencies. Then the financial squeeze was applied to the agencies themselves by withholding governmental subsidy. Thirdly, the government introduced the threat of cutting-off the teleprinter services, the lifelines of a news agency. For example, the government-owned Post and Telegraph Department was ordered to impose a suspension of services to the United News of India if it resisted the merger. The manipulation of these four news agencies was so effective that hardly a voice was raised to resist the governmental perfidy. Soon after this, Shukla reported to the Indian parliament that these four news agencies accepted the merger "voluntarily."

A third and an equally effective method applied by Indira Gandhi was to use fear-arousal techniques on the newspaper publishers, editors, reporters and shareholders. Such techniques were imposed by making false charges with regard to tax arrears, possible reductions in newsprint quotas, imprisonment of publishers

Awards

- Sahitya Akademi Fellowship
- Jnanpith Award
- Sahitya Akademi Award
- Vyas Samman
- Saraswati Samman

External links

Wikimedia Commons has media related to *Literature of India*.

- Indian Literature on Indohistory[250]
- Indian Literature, Fiction and Poetry Magazine[251]
- South Asian Canonical Texts[252]Wikipedia:Link rot
- Bhas - Longest Poem on Indian Constitution set World Record[253]
- Literature in India[254]

Dance in India

Dance in India

Part of a series on the
Culture of India
History
People
Cuisine
Religion
Sport
• ⚖ **India portal**
• v • t • e[255]

Dance in India comprises numerous styles of dances, generally classified as classical or folk. As with other aspects of Indian culture, different forms of

Figure 128: *Dance in India include classical (above), semiclassical, folk and tribal.*

dances originated in different parts of India, developed according to the local traditions and also imbibed elements from other parts of the country.

Sangeet Natya Academy, the national academy for performing arts in India, recognizes eight traditional dances as Indian classical dances, while other sources and scholars recognize more.[256] These have roots in the Sanskrit text *Natya Shastra*,[257] and the religious performance arts of Hinduism.[258,259,260]

Folk dances are numerous in number and style and vary according to the local tradition of the respective state, ethnic or geographic regions. Contemporary dances include refined and experimental fusions of classical, folk and Western forms. Dancing traditions of India have influence not only over the dances in the whole of South Asia, but on the dancing forms of South East Asia as well. Dances in Indian films like Bollywood Dance for Hindi films, are often noted for freeform expression of dance and hold a significant presence in popular culture of the Indian subcontinent.

Nomenclature

A classical dance is one whose these theory, cultyre.training, means and rationale for expressive practice is documented and Pragathi traceable to ancient classical texts, particularly the *Natya Shastra*. Classical Indian dances have

Figure 129: *Shiva as Nataraja (Lord of Dance).*

historically involved a school or *guru-shishya parampara* (teacher-disciple tradition) and require studies of the classical texts, physical exercises and extensive training to systematically synchronize the dance repertoire with underlying play or composition, vocalists and the orchestra.

A folk Indian dance is one which is largely an oral tradition, whose traditions have been historically learnt and mostly passed down from one generation to the next through word of mouth and casual joint practice. A semi-classical Indian dance is one that contains a classical imprint but has become a folk dance and lost its texts or schools. A tribal dance is a more local form of folk dance, typically found in one tribal population; typically tribal dances evolve into folk dances over a historic period.

Origin of Dance in India

The origins of dance in India go back into the ancient times. The earliest paleolithic and neolithic cave paintings such at the UNESCO world heritage site at Bhimbetka rock shelters in Madhya Pradesh shows dance scenes. Several sculptures found at Indus Valley Civilization archaeological sites, now distributed between Pakistan and India, show dance figures. For example, the Dancing Girl sculpture is dated to about 2500 BCE, shows a 10.5 centimetres (4.1 in) high figurine in a dance pose.

The Vedas integrate rituals with performance arts, such as a dramatic play, where not only praises to gods were recited or sung, but the dialogues were part of a dramatic representation and discussion of spiritual themes.[261] The Sanskrit verses in chapter 13.2 of Shatapatha Brahmana (~800–700 BCE), for example, are written in the form of a play between two actors.[262]

<templatestyles src="Template:Quote/styles.css"/>

> *The Vedic sacrifice (yajna) is presented as a kind of fight, with its actors, its dialogues, its portion to be set to music, its interludes, and its climaxes.*
>
> —*Louis Renou, Vedic India*[263]

The evidence of earliest dance related texts are in *Natasutras*, which are mentioned in the text of Panini, the sage who wrote the classic on Sanskrit grammar, and who is dated to about 500 BCE.[264] This performance arts related Sutra text is mentioned in other late Vedic texts, as are two scholars names Shilalin (IAST: Śilālin) and Krishashva (Kṛśaśva), credited to be pioneers in the studies of ancient drama, singing, dance and Sanskrit compositions for these arts.[265] Richmond et al. estimate the *Natasutras* to have been composed around 600 BCE, whose complete manuscript has not survived into the modern age.[264]

The classic text of dance and performance arts that has survived is the Hindu text *Natya Shastra*, attributed to sage Bharata. He credits the art his text systematically presents to times before him, ultimately to Brahma who created Natya-veda by taking the word from the Rigveda, melody from the Samaveda, mime from the Yajurveda, and emotion from the Atharvaveda. The first complete compilation of *Natya Shastra* is dated to between 200 BCE and 200 CE,[266,267] but estimates vary between 500 BCE and 500 CE.[268] The most studied version of the Natya Shastra text consists of about 6000 verses structured into 36 chapters.[266,269] The classical dances are rooted in *Natya Shastra*.

India has a number of classical Indian dance forms, each of which can be traced to different parts of the country. Classical and folk dance forms also emerged from Indian traditions, epics and mythology.

Classical dance

Classical dance of India has developed a type of dance-drama that is a form of a total theater. The dancer acts out a story almost exclusively through gestures. Most of the classical dances of India enact stories from Hindu mythology. Each form represents the culture and ethos of a particular region or a group of people.

Figure 130: *Bharatanatyam*

The criteria for being considered as classical is the style's adherence to the guidelines laid down in Natyashastra, which explains the Indian art of acting. The Sangeet Natak Akademi currently confers classical status on eight Indian classical dance styles: Bharatanatyam (Tamil Nadu), Kathak (North, West and Central India), Kathakali (Kerala), Kuchipudi (Andhra Pradesh), Odissi (Odisha), Manipuri (Manipur), Mohiniyattam (Kerala), and Sattriya (Assam). All classical dances of India have roots in Hindu arts and religious practices.

The tradition of dance has been codified in the Natyashastra and a performance is considered accomplished if it manages to evoke a *rasa* (emotion) among the audience by invoking a particular *bhava*(gesture or facial expression). Classical dance is distinguished from folk dance because it has been regulated by the rules of the Natyashastra and all classical dances are performed only in accordance with them.

Bharatanatyam

Dating back to 1000 BC, *barathanatyam* is a classical dance from the South Indian state of Tamil Nadu, practiced predominantly in modern times by women. The dance is usually accompanied by classical Carnatic music. Bharatnatyam is a major genre of Indian classical dance that originated in the Hindu temples of Tamil Nadu and neighboring regions.[270,271] Traditionally, Bharatanatyam

Figure 131: *Kathakali*

has been a solo dance that was performed exclusively by women, and expressed Hindu religious themes and spiritual ideas, particularly of Shaivism, but also of Vaishnavism and Shaktism.[272]

Bharatanatyam and other classical dances in India were ridiculed and suppressed during the colonial British Raj era. In the post-colonial period, it has grown to become the most popular classical Indian dance style in India and abroad, and is considered to be synonymous with Indian dance by many foreigners unaware of the diversity of dances and performance arts in Indian culture.

Kathakali

Kathakali (*katha*, "story"; *kali*, "performance") is a highly stylized classical dance-drama form which originated from Kerala in the 17th century. This classical dance form is another "story play" genre of art, but one distinguished by its elaborately colorful make-up, costumes and face masks wearing actor-dancers, who have traditionally been all males.

Kathakali primarily developed as a Hindu performance art, performing plays and mythical legends related to Hinduism. While its origin are more recent, its roots are in temple and folk arts such as *Kutiyattam* and religious drama traceable to at least the 1st millennium CE. A Kathakali performance incorporates

Figure 132: *Kathak*

movements from the ancient martial arts and athletic traditions of south India. While linked to the temple dancing traditions such as *Krishnanattam*, *Kutiyattam* and others, *Kathakali* is different from these because unlike the older arts where the dancer-actor also had to be the vocal artist, *Kathakali* separated these roles allowing the dancer-actor to excel in and focus on choreography while the vocal artists focused on delivering their lines.

Kathak

Kathak is traditionally attributed to the traveling bards of ancient northern India, known as Kathakars or storytellers. The term Kathak is derived from the Vedic Sanskrit word *Katha* meaning "story", and *kathaka* in Sanskrit means "he who tells a story", or "to do with stories".[273] Kathak evolved during the Bhakti movement, particularly by incorporating childhood and amorous stories of Hindu god Krishna, as well as independently in the courts of north Indian kingdoms. It transitioned, adapted and integrated the tastes and Persian arts influence in the Mughal courts of the 16th and 17th century, was ridiculed and declined in the colonial British era, then was reborn as India gained independence.

Kathak is found in three distinct forms, named after the cities where the Kathak dance tradition evolved – Jaipur, Benares and Lucknow.[274] Stylistically, the

Figure 133: *Kuchipudi*

Kathak dance form emphasizes rhythmic foot movements, adorned with small bells (*Ghungroo*), the movement harmonized to the music, the legs and torso are generally straight, and the story is told through a developed vocabulary based on the gestures of arms and upper body movement, facial expressions, stage movements, bends and turns.

Kuchipudi

Kuchipudi classical dance originated in a village of Krishna district in modern era Indian state of Andhra Pradesh.[275,276] It has roots in antiquity and developed as a religious art linked to traveling bards, temples and spiritual beliefs, like all major classical dances of India.[277,278] In its history, the Kuchipudi dancers were all males, typically Brahmins, who would play the roles of men and women in the story after dressing appropriately.

Modern Kuchipudi tradition believes that Tirtha Narayana Yati and his disciple an orphan named Siddhendra Yogi founded and systematized the art in the 17th century.[279,280] Kuchipudi largely developed as a Hindu god Krishna-oriented Vaishnavism tradition,[281] and it is most closely related to Bhagavata Mela performance art found in Tamil Nadu,[277] which itself has originated from Andhra Pradesh. The Kuchipudi performance includes pure dance (*nritta*),[282] and expressive part of the performance (*nritya*), where rhythmic gestures as

Figure 134: *Odissi*

a sign language mime the play.[282] Vocalists and musicians accompany the artist, and the *tala* and *raga* set to (Carnatic music).[283] In modern productions, Kuchipudi dancers include men and women.[284]

Odissi

Odissi originated in the Hindu temples of Odisha – an eastern coastal state of India.[285,286] Odissi, in its history, was performed predominantly by women, and expressed religious stories and spiritual ideas, particularly of Vaishnavism (Vishnu as Jagannath), but also of other traditions such as those related to Hindu gods Shiva and Surya, as well as Hindu goddesses (Shaktism).[287] Odissi is traditionally a dance-drama genre of performance art, where the artist(s) and musicians play out a mythical story, a spiritual message or devotional poem from the Hindu texts, using symbolic costumes, body movement, *abhinaya* (expressions) and *mudras* (gestures and sign language) set out in ancient Sanskrit literature.

Figure 135: *Sattriya*

Sattriya

Sattriya is a classical dance-drama performance art with origins in the Kr-
ishna-centered Vaishnavism monasteries of Assam, and attributed to the 15th
century Bhakti movement scholar and saint named Srimanta Sankardev.[288]
One-act plays of *Sattriya* are called *Ankiya Nat*, which combine the aesthetic
and the religious through a ballad, dance and drama.[289] The plays are usually performed in the dance community halls (*namghar*) of monastery temples
(*sattras*). The themes played relate to Krishna and Radha, sometimes other
Vishnu avatars such as Rama and Sita.

Manipuri

Manipuri, also known as Jagoi,[290] is named after the region of its origin –
Manipur, a state in northeastern India bordering with Myanmar (Burma).[291]
It is particularly known for its Hindu Vaishnavism themes, and performances
of love-inspired dance drama of Radha-Krishna called Rass Lila.[290,292] However, the dance is also performed to themes related to Shaivism, Shaktism
and regional deities such as Umang Lai during Lai Haraoba.[293] The Manipuri
dance is a team performance, with its own unique costumes notably the *Ku-
mil* (a barrel shaped, elegantly decorated skirt), aesthetics, conventions and

Figure 136: *Manipuri*

repertoire.[294] The Manipuri dance drama is, for most part, marked by a performance that is graceful, fluid, sinuous with greater emphasis on hand and upper body gestures.[295,296]

Mohiniyattam

Mohiniyattam developed in the state of Kerala, gets its name from Mohini – the seductress avatar of Vishnu, who in Hindu mythology uses her charms to help the good prevail in a battle between good and evil.[297] Mohiniyattam follows the Lasya style described in *Natya Shastra*, that is a dance which is delicate, with soft movements and feminine. It is traditionally a solo dance performed by women after extensive training. The repertoire of Mohiniyattam includes pure and expressive dance-drama performance, timed to sopana (slower melody) styled music, with recitation. The songs are typically in Malayalam-Sanskrit hybrid called Manipravala.

Folk and tribal dance forms

Folk dances and plays in India retain significance in rural areas as the expression of the daily work and rituals of village communities.

Figure 137: *Mohiniyattam.*

Figure 138: *Gujarati Navaratri Garba at Ambaji Temple*

Figure 139: *Bhangra, folk dance form from dancers Punjab, India.*

Sanskrit literature of medieval times describes several forms of group dances such as Hallisaka, Rasaka, Dand Rasaka and Charchari. The Natya Shastra includes group dances of women as a preliminary dance performed in prelude to a drama.

India has numerous folk dances. Every state has its own folk dance forms like Bedara Vesha, Dollu Kunitha in Karnataka, Thirayattam and Theyyam in Kerala, Garba, Gagari (dance), Ghodakhund & Dandiya in Gujarat, Kalbelia, Ghoomar, Rasiya in Rajasthan, Neyopa, Bacha Nagma in Jammu and Kashmir, Bhangra & Giddha in Punjab, Perini Dance in Telangana, Chholiya dance in Uttarakhand, Bihu and Bagurumba dance in Assam, Sambalpuri Dance in Western Odisha and likewise for each state and smaller regions in it. Lavani, and Lezim, and Koli dance are among the most popular dances of Maharashtra. Thirayattam is a ritual performing ethnic art of Kerala state. This vibrant art form is performed in courtyards of sacred groves and village shrines, during the Thirayattam Festival. This art form combines dance, music, drama, instrumental music, facial and body makeup, martial art and ritualistic functions, composed in a harmonizing manner.[298]

Tribal Dances in India are inspired by the tribal folklore. Each ethnic group has its own distinct combination of myths, legends, tales, proverbs, riddles, ballads, folk songs, folk dance, and folk music.

The dancers do not necessarily fall rigidly into the category of "tribal". However, these forms of dance closely depict their life, social relationships, work and religious affiliations. They represent the rich culture and customs of their native lands through intricate movements of their bodies. A wide variation can be observed in the intensity of these dances. Some involve very slight movement with a more groovy edge to it, while others involve elevated and vigorous involvement of limbs.

These dances are composed mostly on locally made instruments. Percussion instruments feature in most of these dances. Music is produced through indigenous instruments. Music too has its own diversity in these tribal dances with the aesthetics ranging from mild and soothing to strong and weighted rhythms. A few of them also have songs, either sung by themselves or by onlookers. The costumes vary from traditional saris of a particular pattern to skirts and blouses with mirror work for women and corresponding dhotis and upper-wear for men. They celebrate contemporary events, victories and are often performed as a mode of appeasing the tribal deities.

A lot of the dance styles depend upon the regional positioning of the ethnic group. Factors as small as east or west of a river result in a change of dance form even though the over-reaching look of it may seem the same. The religious affiliation affects the content of the songs and hence the actions in a dance sequence. Another major factor affecting their content are the festivals, mostly harvest.

For example, the ethnic groups from the plain land rabhas from the hilly forested areas of Assam make use of baroyat (plate-like instrument), handa (a type of sword), boushi (adze-like instrument), boumshi (bamboo flute), sum (heavy wooden instrument), dhansi. kalbansi, kalhurang, chingbakak. Traditionally, their dances are called basili. Through their dance, they express their labours, rejoicings and sorrows. Handur Basu their pseudo-war dance expresses their strength and solidarity.

From a broader point of view, the different tribal dance forms, as they would be classified in the context of territory are:

Andhra Pradesh

Siddi, Tappeta Gundlu, Urumulu (thunder dance), Butta Bommalata, Goravayyalu, Garaka (Vessel Dance), Vira Ntyam (Heroic Dance), Kolatam, Chiratala Bhajana, Dappu, Puli V esham (Tiger Dance), Gobbi, Karuva, and Veedhi Bhagavatam.

Arunachal Pradesh

Ponung, Sadinuktso, Khampti, Ka Fifai, Idu Mishmi (ritual) and Wancho.

Assam

Dhuliya and Bhawariya, Deodhani, Zikirs, Apsara-Sabah.

Figure 140: *Thirayattam, an ethnic dance form from Kerala, India.*

Goa

Mussoll, Dulpod or Durpod, Kunnbi-Geet, Amon, Shigmo, Foogddi, and Dhalo.

Haryana

Rasleela, Phag Dance, Phalgun, Daph Dance, Dhamaal, Loor, Guga, Jhomar, Ghomar, Khoria, Holi, Sapela.

Himachal Pradesh

Chamba, Dalshone and Cholamba, Jataru Kayang, Nuala, Jhoori, Ji, Swang Tegi, Rasa.

Jharkhand

Jhumair, Janani Jhumar, Mardana Jhumar, Domkach, Fagua, Jhumta, Painki, Karma Naach, Chhau.

Karnataka

veeragase, Nandi Dhwaja, Beesu Kamshaley, Pata Kunitha, Bana Debara Kunitha, Pooja kunitha, Karaga, Gorawa Mela, Bhuta Nrutya, Naga Nrutya, Batte Kola, Chennu Kunitha, Maaragalu Kunitha, Kolata, Simha Nrutya, Yakshagana

Kerala

Thirayattam, Padayani, Ayyappanvilakku, Vattakkali, Theyyam,

Madhya Pradesh

Gaur, Muriya, Saila, Kaksar, Sugga, Banjaara (Lehangi), Matki Dance, Phul Patti Dance, Grida Dance.

Manipur

Lie Haraoba Dance, Chanlam, Toonaga Lomna Dance

Meghalaya

Wiking, Pombalang Nongkrem

Maharashtra Lavani, Koli, Tamasha, Bala Dindi & Dhangari Gaja

Odisha

Chau, Naga, Ghumri

Punjab

Kikri, Sammi, Jhumar, Karthi

Rajasthan

Banjaara, Fire dance, Tera tali, Kachhi Ghori, Geedar

Sikkim

Pang Toed Chaam (Chaam means dance) performed during the Pang Lhabsol festival in honour of the Guardian deity Khang-Chen-Dzonga, Maruni (Nepali Dance) and Tamak.

Tamil Nadu

Karakam, Puravai Attam, Ariyar Natanam, Podikazhi Attam, Kummi, Kavadi, Kolattam, Navasandhi, Kuravaik Koothu, Mayilaattam, Oyil Kummi, Pavakkuthu

West Bengal

Chau, Santari, Jatra, Gazan

Tribal Gypsies

Lozen, Gouyen

Figure 141: *Dance accompanied by Rabindra Sangeet,*
a music genre started by Rabindranath Tagore.

Contemporary dance

Contemporary dance in India encompasses a wide range of dance activities currently performed in India. It includes choreography for Indian cinema, modern Indian ballet and experiments with existing classical and folk forms of dance by various artists.

Uday Shankar and Shobana Jeyasingh have led modern Indian ballet which combined classical Indian dance and music with Western stage techniques. Their productions have included themes related to Shiva-Parvati, Lanka Dahan, Panchatantra, Ramayana among others.

Dance in films- Bollywood Dance

The presentation of Indian dance styles in film, Hindi Cinema, has exposed the range of dance in India to a global audience.

Dance and song sequences have been an integral component of films across the country. With the introduction of sound to cinema in the film Alam Ara in 1931, choreographed dance sequences became ubiquitous in Hindi and other Indian films.

Dance in early Hindi films was primarily modelled on classical Indian dance styles such as Kathak, or folk dancers. Modern films often blend this earlier

Figure 142: *A Bollywood dance performance in Bristol.*

style with Western dance styles (MTV or in Broadway musicals), though it is
not unusual to see western choreography and adapted classical dance numbers
side by side in the same film. Typically, the hero or heroine performs with a
troupe of supporting dancers. Many song-and-dance routines in Indian films
feature dramatic shifts of location and/or changes of costume between verses
of a song. It is popular for a hero and heroine to dance and sing a pas de deux (a
French ballet term, meaning "dance of two") in beautiful natural surroundings
or architecturally grand settings, referred to as a "picturisation". Indian films
have often used what are now called "item numbers" where a glamorous female
figure performs a cameo. The choreography for such item numbers varies
depending on the film's genre and situation. The film actress and dancer Helen
was famous for her cabaret numbers.

Often in movies, the actors don't sing the songs themselves that they dance
too, but have another artist sing in the background. For an actor to sing in the
song is unlikely but not rare. The dances in Bollywood can range from slow
dancing, to a more upbeat hip hop style dance. The dancing itself is a fusion of
all dance forms. It could be Indian classical, Indian folk dance, belly dancing,
jazz, hip hop and everything else you can imagine.[299]

Dance education

Since India's independence from colonial rule, numerous schools have opened to further education, training and socialization through dance classes, or simply a means to exercise and fitness.

Major cities in India now have numerous schools that offer lessons in dances such as *Odissi*, *Bharatanatyam*, and these cities host hundreds of shows every year. Dances which were exclusive to one gender, now have participation by both males and females. Many innovations and developments in modern practice of classical Indian dances, states Anne-Marie Geston, are of a quasi-religious type.

Geographic spread

Some traditions of the Indian classical dance are practiced in the whole Indian subcontinent, including Pakistan and Bangladesh, with which India shares several other cultural traits. Indian mythologies play significant part in dance forms of countries in South East Asia, an example being the performances based on Ramayana in Javanese dances.

Festivals

Sangeet Natak Akademi organizes dance festivals around India.

Notes

- Massey, Reginald (2004), *"India's Dances: Their History, Technique, and Repertoire"*, Abhinav Publications<templatestyles src="Module:Citation/CS1/styles.css"></templatestyles>
- Narayan, Shovanna (2005). " The Sterling Book :Indian Classical Dance", Nepalian Dawn Press Group, New Delhi, India.
- "Revealing the Art of surya-namasjarnatyasastra" by Narayanan Chittoor Namboodiripad <templatestyles src="Module:Citation/CS1/styles.css" />ISBN 9788121512183□□□
- Ragini Devi (1990). *Dance Dialects of India*[300]. Motilal Banarsidass. ISBN 978-81-208-0674-0.<templatestyles src="Module:Citation/CS1/styles.css"></templatestyles>
- Saryu Doshi (1989). *Dances of Manipur: The Classical Tradition*[301]. Marg Publications. ISBN 978-81-85026-09-1.<templatestyles src="Module:Citation/CS1/styles.css"></templatestyles>

- Sunil Kothari; Avinash Pasricha (2001). *Kuchipudi*[302]. Abhinav Publications. ISBN 978-81-7017-359-5.<templatestyles src="Module:Citation/CS1/styles.css"></templatestyles>
- Natalia Lidova (2014). "Natyashastra". Oxford University Press. doi: 10.1093/obo/9780195399318-0071[303].<templatestyles src="Module:Citation/CS1/styles.css"></templatestyles>
- Natalia Lidova (1994). *Drama and Ritual of Early Hinduism*[304]. Motilal Banarsidass. ISBN 978-81-208-1234-5.<templatestyles src="Module:Citation/CS1/styles.css"></templatestyles>
- Massey, Reginald (1999). *India's Kathak Dance - Past, Present, Future*[305]. Abhinav Publications. ISBN 81-7017-374-4.<templatestyles src="Module:Citation/CS1/styles.css"></templatestyles>
- Tarla Mehta (1995). *Sanskrit Play Production in Ancient India*[306]. Motilal Banarsidass. ISBN 978-81-208-1057-0.<templatestyles src="Module:Citation/CS1/styles.css"></templatestyles>
- Emmie Te Nijenhuis (1974). *Indian Music: History and Structure*[307]. BRILL Academic. ISBN 90-04-03978-3.<templatestyles src="Module:Citation/CS1/styles.css"></templatestyles>
- Williams, Drid (2004). "In the Shadow of Hollywood Orientalism: Authentic East Indian Dancing"[308] (PDF). *Visual Anthropology*. Routledge. **17** (1): 69–98. doi: 10.1080/08949460490274013[309].<templatestyles src="Module:Citation/CS1/styles.css"></templatestyles>
- Farley P. Richmond; Darius L. Swann; Phillip B. Zarrilli (1993). *Indian Theatre: Traditions of Performance*[310]. Motilal Banarsidass Publ. ISBN 978-81-208-0981-9.<templatestyles src="Module:Citation/CS1/styles.css"></templatestyles>
- Wallace Dace (1963). "The Concept of "Rasa" in Sanskrit Dramatic Theory". *Educational Theatre Journal*. **15** (3): 249. doi: 10.2307/3204783[311]. JSTOR 3204783[312].<templatestyles src="Module:Citation/CS1/styles.css"></templatestyles>
- Maurice Winternitz (2008). *History of Indian Literature Vol 3 (Original in German published in 1922, translated into English by VS Sarma, 1981)*. New Delhi: Motilal Banarsidass. ISBN 978-8120800564.<templatestyles src="Module:Citation/CS1/styles.css"></templatestyles>

External links

> Wikimedia Commons has media related to *Dance of India*.

- Dance - Indian performing arts[313], National Centre for the Performing Arts, Mumbai
- Center for the Performance Arts in India[314], University of Pittsburgh
- Dance and Theatre in India[315], Goethe Institut
- Center for India Studies, Performance Art Series: Classical Dances[316], Stony Brook University
- Dance in India college exchange programs[317], City University of New York
- [318], Darpana Academy of Performing Arts, Ahmedabad
- Dance in India Study Abroad Programs in the USA[319], Schools for International Training
- The Anthropology of Theater and Spectacle[320] William Beeman (1993)

Theatre in India

Theatre of India

Theatre of India

Part of a series on the
Culture of India
History
People
Cuisine
Religion
Sport
• ⚒ India portal
• v
• t
• e[321]

Indian theatre is one of the most ancient forms of Indo-European and Asian theatre and it features a detailed textual, sculptural, and dramatic effects. Like in the areas of music and dance, the Indian theatre is also defined by the dramatic performance defined by the concept of *Natya*, which is a Sanskrit word for drama but encompasses dramatic narrative, virtuostic dance, and music. Indian theatre exerted influence beyond its borders, reaching ancient China and other countries in the Far East.

The earliest form of **classical theatre of India** was the Sanskrit theatre which came into existence after the development of Greek and Roman theatres in the west.[322] One theory describes this development as an offshoot of Alexander the Great's Indian conquest. The invading army staged Greek-style plays and Indians picked up the performance art. While some scholars argue that traditional Indian theatre predated it, there is a recognition that classical Greek theatre has helped transformed it.

With the Islamic conquests that began in the 10th and 11th centuries, theatre was discouraged or forbidden entirely.[323] Later, in an attempt to re-assert indigenous values and ideas, village theatre was encouraged across the subcontinent, developing in a large number of regional languages from the 15th to the 19th centuries.[324] Modern Indian theatre developed during the period of colonial rule under the British Empire, from the mid-19th century until the mid-20th.[325]

From the last half of the 19th century, theatres in India experienced a boost in numbers and practice. After Indian independence in 1947, theatres spread throughout India as one of the means of entertainment. As a diverse, multicultural nation, the theatre of India cannot be reduced to a single, homogenous trend.

In contemporary India, the major competition with its theatre is that represented by growing television industry and the spread of films produced in the Indian film industry based in Mumbai (formerly Bombay), known as "Bollywood". Lack of finance is another major obstacle.

History of Indian theatre

Sanskrit theatre

Sanskrit theatre emerged in the 2nd century BCE and flourished between the 1st century CE and the 10th, which was a period of relative peace in the history of India during which hundreds of plays were written.[326] Despite its name, Sanskrit theatre was not exclusively in Sanskrit language. Other Indic languages collectively called as Prakrit were also used in addition to Sanskrit.[327]

The earliest-surviving fragments of Sanskrit drama date from the 1st century CE.[328] The wealth of archeological evidence from earlier periods offers no indication of the existence of a tradition of theatre.[329] The *Vedas* (the earliest Indian literature, from between 1500 and 600 BCE) contain no hint of it; although a small number of hymns are composed in a form of dialogue), the rituals of the Vedic period do not appear to have developed into theatre. The *Mahābhāṣya* by Patañjali contains the earliest reference to what may have been the seeds of Sanskrit drama.[330] This treatise on grammar from 140 BCE provides a feasible date for the beginnings of theatre in India.

However, although there are no surviving fragments of any drama prior to this date, it is possible that early Buddhist literature provides the earliest evidence for the existence of Indian theater. The Pali suttas (ranging in date from the 5th to 3rd centuries BCE) refer to the existence of troupes of actors (led by a chief actor), who performed dramas on a stage. It is indicated that these dramas incorporated dance, but were listed as a distinct form of performance, alongside dancing, singing, and story recitations.[331,332]</ref>

The major source of evidence for Sanskrit theatre is *A Treatise on Theatre* (*Nātyaśāstra*), a compendium whose date of composition is uncertain (estimates range from 200 BCE to 200 CE) and whose authorship is attributed to Bharata Muni. The *Treatise* is the most complete work of dramaturgy in the ancient world. It addresses acting, dance, music, dramatic construction, architecture, costuming, make-up, props, the organisation of companies, the audience, competitions, and offers a mythological account of the origin of theatre. In doing so, it provides indications about the nature of actual theatrical practices. Sanskrit theatre was performed on sacred ground by priests who had been trained in the necessary skills (dance, music, and recitation) in a [hereditary process]. Its aim was both to educate and to entertain.

An appreciation for the stagecraft and classic Sanskrit drama was seen as an essential part of a sophisticated world view, by the end of the seventh century. Under the patronage of royal courts, performers belonged to professional companies that were directed by a stage manager (*sutradhara*), who may also have acted.[333] This task was thought of as being analogous to that

Figure 143: *Performer playing Sugriva in
the Koodiyattam form of Sanskrit theatre.*

of a puppeteer—the literal meaning of *"sutradhara"* is "holder of the strings
or threads". The performers were trained rigorously in vocal and physical
technique.[334] There were no prohibitions against female performers; companies were all-male, all-female, and of mixed gender. Certain sentiments were
considered inappropriate for men to enact, however, and were thought better
suited to women. Some performers played characters their own age, while
others played ages different from their own (whether younger or older). Of
all the elements of theatre, the *Treatise* gives most attention to acting (*abhinaya*), which consists of two styles: realistic (*lokadharmi*) and conventional
(*natyadharmi*), though the major focus is on the latter.[335]

Its drama is regarded as the highest achievement of Sanskrit literature.[336] It
utilised stock characters, such as the hero (*nayaka*), heroine (*nayika*), or clown
(*vidusaka*). Actors may have specialised in a particular type. Kālidāsa is arguably considered to be India's greatest Sanskrit dramatist, writing in the ca.
4th century CE-ca. 5th century CE. Three famous romantic plays written by
Kālidāsa are the *Mālavikāgnimitram* (*Mālavikā and Agnimitra*), *Vikramuur-
vashiiya* (*Pertaining to Vikrama and Urvashi*), and *Abhijñānaśākuntala* (*The
Recognition of Shakuntala*). The last was inspired by a story in the *Mahabharata* and is the most famous. It was the first to be translated into English

and German. *Śakuntalā* (in English translation) influenced Goethe's *Faust* (1808–1832).

The next great Indian dramatist was Bhavabhuti (c. 7th century CE). He is said to have written the following three plays: *Malati-Madhava, Mahaviracharita* and *Uttar Ramacharita.* Among these three, the last two cover between them the entire epic of *Ramayana.* The powerful Indian emperor Harsha (606-648) is credited with having written three plays: the comedy *Ratnavali, Priyadarsika,* and the Buddhist drama *Nagananda.*

Theatre in medieval India

Mid twelfth century - eighteenth century

India's artistic identity is deeply routed within its social, economical, cultural, and religious views. For this reason it is essential to understand Indian cultural practices as they relate directly to performers and performances of this time. Performances including dance, music, and text are an expression of devotion for the Indian culture, so when looking at 'theatre' of this time a broader definition must be ascribed to the word.

Based on the understanding that performing arts are audience-oriented and must continuously adapt to the socio-cultural landscape of their patronage. Northern India managed to retain their cultural traditions in spite of the new Turko-Persian influences. The early thirteenth century marked this change for the Indian culture, where Sanskrit dramas and stage craft had been previously revered by the elites, it was now no longer relevant. This was due to the invading cultures that began to dominate and did not appreciate or understand, and since they did not understand the Sanskrit language it could no longer be held in such a high regard, and as a consequence many theatre artist suffered from neglect.

The commonplace to find performers was in urban centers, because it was there they were able to find work to support themselves. Large temples where home to musical and theatrical shows.

A Bharata Natyshatra also known as the śāstra was written to list costumes, gestures, positions of the body, and make up. It also lists plots that were wieghed unsuitable and it also the most completed document. Most of Indian theatre had no scenery. There was usually a few props like a brass lamp.

When the concept of "Theatrical Art" was introduced medieval India was narrating poems. Bhakti poetry became popular.

During medieval India Bhavabhuti was a famous dramatist, he had three portent plays Malati-Madhava, Magviracharita and the Uttar Ramacharita.

Theatre in India under British

Under British colonial rule, modern Indian theatre began when a theatre was started in Belgachia. One of the earliest plays composed and staged during this period was Buro Shalikher Ghaare Roa (1860) by Michael Madhusudan Dutt, both in Bengali. Around the same time, Nil Darpan (1858–59, first commercial production in 1872, by Girish Chandra Ghosh at the national theatre in Calcutta) a Bengali play by Dinabandhu Mitra garnered both accolades and controversy for depicting the horror and tragedy of indigo cultivation in rural Bengal, and played a major role in the indigo revolt. Rabindranath Tagore was a pioneering modern playwright who wrote plays noted for their exploration and questioning of nationalism, identity, spiritualism and material greed.[337] His plays are written in Bengali and include *Chitra* (*Chitrangada*, 1892), *The King of the Dark Chamber* (*Raja*, 1910), *The Post Office* (*Dakghar*, 1913), and *Red Oleander* (*Raktakarabi*, 1924).

Kalyanam Raghuramaiah, a recipient of the Sangeet Natak Akademi Award, and the Padmashri, was known for the roles of Krishna or Dushyantha, Bhavanisankar, Narada etc. in Telugu theatre. He performed those roles for about 60 years. He indulged in elaborate raga alapana, based on different ragas while rendering padyams. One of the finest method actors, He had the ability to sing padyams and songs through whistle, by putting his finger in mouth and producing the whistle or flute sound (meaning Eela in Telugu). He has acted in various dramas and gave more than 20,000 stage performances. He was called the "Nightingale of the Stage" by Rabindranath Tagore[338]

The British believed that the Indian actors were mystical creatures. They believed they brought them luck and prosperity. The emergent modern Indian theater, which is also referred to as Native theater, features a theatrical approach that has been viewed as an intersection of Indian social space with Western theater formats and conventions. The resulting theatrical space is described to be existing at the material, symbolic, and discursive levels. In order to resist its use by Indians as an instrument of protest against colonial rule, the British Government imposed the Dramatic Performances Act in 1876.

Indian theatre after Independence (1947-1992)

Contemporary (post-1992) Indian theatre

Mrityunjay Prabhakar is one of the major young Hindi theatre director and playwright who emerged on Indian Theatre Scene in the last decade of the 20th century and established himself as a significant theatre activist in first decade of the 21st century. He started his theatre career from Patna during his graduation days. He has worked with several theatre groups like Abhiyan, Prerna, Mach Art group and Prangan in Patna. Later, he co-founded the group Abhiyan along with his friends. When he arrived Delhi for his further studies in Jawaharlal Nehru University, New Delhi. Here he worked with famous groups like Rang Saptak, Bahroop and Dastak. Later he founded his own group named SEHAR in 2005 and started working rigorously. He has got trained under leading figures of Indian Drama and Theatre world through different workshops he attended like Habib Tanvir, B.V. Karanth, Prasanna, Ratan Thiyam, D.R. Ankur and many more. He has worked with directors like D.R. Ankur, Lokendra Arambam, H.S. Shiva Prakash, Surendra Sharma, Parvez Akhtar, Vijay Kumar, Javed Akhtar Khan, Suman Kumar and others. He has worked as an actor, director, set designer, light designer and organiser in theatre. Presently, Mrityunjay Prabhakar works primarily as a Theatre Director and Playwright with his group SEHAR. He is the founder-director of theatre troupe, SEHAR (Society of Education, Harmony, Art, Culture and Media Reproduction) (Registered under Society Act) in 2007. He has directed more than two dozens plays among them 'Sabse Udas Kavita', 'Khwahishen', 'Jee Humen To Natak Karna Hai', 'Dhruvswamini', 'Vithalala' and 'Suicide' have got special attention from the larger section of the society. His plays has been performed in different cities and theatre centres of the country apart from Delhi. His plays were part of some of the important theatre festivals of the country. Mrityunjay Prabhakar's originally written play 'Sadho Dekho Jag Baudana' was published by InkLit Publication. He has also written famous plays like 'Aao Natak Natak Khelen', 'Khwahishen', 'Jee Humen To Natak Karna Hai', 'Suicide', 'Hey Ram', 'Teri Meri Kahani Hai', 'Karnav' and others, which has been performed by different groups and directors in various theatre centres of the country. He has adopted famous Keniyan playwright Ngugi Wa Thiong's play 'The Black Hermit' as 'Jayen To Jayen Kahan'. The adaptation was first performed by NSD Graduate Randhir Kumar in 2005 in Patna. Later he reproduced the play in 2010 with SEHAR in Delhi. He has adopted H.S. Shivaprakash famous Kannad play 'Mochi Madaiah' in Hindi which was directed by Lokendra Arambam and published by Yash Publication, Delhi. An anthology on Contemporary Indian Theatre titled 'Samkaleen Rangkarm' is also credited on his name published by InkLit Publication. His

Hindi Poetry Collection 'Jo Mere Bheetar Hain' was published by Akademi of Letters (Sahitya Akademi), India.

Saurabh Srivastava is another versatile theatre worker who has been active in different parts of country since 1980, acting and directing in plays in Allahabad, Varanasi, Lucknow, Kanpur, Delhi, Vadodara, Hyderabad, Jodhpur and Jaipur.[339] Working with Campus Theatre, Creative Arts, Apurva Society etc., Saurabh Srivastava has directed more than two dozen Hindi plays and presented hundreds of shows in different cities. Literary interpretation, mature insight, penetrating vision and an ability to successfully communicate the essence to the audience are some of the strengths of Saurabh's style and vision of theatrical presentation. He is currently active in Jaipur.

Improvisation

Improvisational (also known as improv or impro) is a form of theatre in which the actors use improvisational acting techniques to perform spontaneously. Improvisers typically use audience suggestions to guide the performance as they create dialogue, setting, and plot extemporaneously.

Many improvisational actors also work as scripted actors and "improv" techniques are often taught in standard acting classes. The basic skills of listening, clarity, confidence, and performing instinctively and spontaneously are considered important skills for actors to develop.

Improvisational Theatre in India is largely used for educational, interventional and entertainment purposes. The traces of Improvisational theatre in India dates back to the 1990s with the advent of Forum theatre with Janasanskriti under the leadership of Sanjoy Ganguly. After that in 1999, a team from the US with Bev Hoskins and Mary Good introduced Playback theatre to India. Thus Playback theatre and Forum theatre began to take its shape in the remotest parts of India, such as Karur, Chennai, West Bengal, as well as Bangalore too. Yours Truly Theatre, a Bangalore-based group, developed "complete the story", an indigenous format of improvisational theatre developed under the leadership of Ranji David and Nandini Rao in 2006. In 2009, they also developed another form of improvisational theatre called "mushyara theatre".

In the late 1960s Badal Sircar introduced a new form of political theatre called the Third Theatre. Badal Sarkar's anti-establishment experimental theatre created a new genre of social enlightenment. He formed his first Third Theatre Group satabdi,in the year 1967. They used to perform Drama written by Badal Sircar in Anganmancha (theatre in the courtyard) in the Third Theatre form that break away from the tradition of One point view of the Proscenium and urged on the taking theatre to the people.

Improvisational Theatre groups in India:

- Yours Truly Theatre

Improvisational Theatre forms practiced in India:

- Playback theatre
- Theatre of the Oppressed
- Forum theatre

Notable theatres in India in different Indian languages and regions

- Marathi theatre
- Bengali Theatre
- Hindi theatre
- Telugu drama
- Bhojpuri

Notable people

Ancient Indian playwrights

- Bharata Muni
- Kalidasa
- Bhāsa
- bhavabhuti

Playwrights working under British rule

- Bankim Chandra Chatterjee
- Dinabandhu Mitra
- Jaishankar Bhojak 'Sundari'
- Jaishankar Prasad
- Girish Chandra Ghosh
- Bhartendu Harishchandra
- Rabindranath Tagore

Post-Independence theatre-makers

Notable theatre directors:

- Ebrahim Alkazi
- K.V. Akshara
- Nadira Babbar
- Ram Gopal Bajaj
- Suresh Bhardwaj
- Bijon Bhattacharya
- Raj Bisaria
- Manish Joshi Bismil
- Chandradasan
- Neelam Mansingh Chowdhry
- Satyadev Dubey
- Utpal Dutta
- Arvind Gaur
- Sachin Gupta
- Safdar Hashmi
- Rohini Hattangadi
- Shafi Inamdar
- Prithviraj Kapoor
- Shashi Kapoor
- B.V. Karanth
- Bansi Kaul
- Kader Khan
- Mohan Maharishi
- Ramesh Mehta
- Shaoli Mitra
- Sombhu Mitra
- Shankar Nag
- Kavalam Narayana Panicker
- Mrityunjay Prabhakar
- Prasanna
- Rathna Shekar Reddy
- Rudraprasad Sengupta
- B.M. Shah
- Naseeruddin Shah
- Gursharan Singh
- Badal Sircar
- Deepan Sivaraman
- Anjan Srivastav
- K.V. Subbanna

- Habib Tanvir Bhopal
- Ratan Thiyam
- Kumara Varma
- Sankar Venkateswaran
- Shyamanand Jalan
- Nemi Chandra Jain
- Ajitesh Bandopadhyay

Notable playwrights

- Gurazada Apparao (Telugu)
- Abhimanyu (Malayalam)
- Satish Alekar (Marathi)
- Rambriksh Benipuri (Hindi)
- Datta Bhagat (Marathi)
- Dharamvir Bharati (Hindi)
- Anupama Chandrasekhar (English)
- Asif Currimbhoy (English)
- Gurcharan Das (English)
- Mahesh Dattani (English)
- Swadesh Deepak (Hindi)
- Govind Purushottam Deshpande (Marathi)
- Utpal Datta (Bangla)
- Mahesh Elkunchwar (Marathi)
- Sachin Gupta (Hindi)
- Rajesh Joshi (Hindi)
- Sharad Joshi (Hindi)
- T. P. Kailasam (Kannada, English)
- Chandrashekhara Kambara (Kannada)
- Prithviraj Kapoor (Hindi), (Urdu), (Pashto), (Bangla)
- Girish Karnad (Kannada)
- Kader Khan (Urdu)
- Ramesh Mehta (Urdu)
- Piyush Mishra (Hindi)
- Torit Mitra (Bengali)
- Narendra Mohan (Hindi)
- Arun Mukherjee (Bangla)
- Manjula Padmanabhan (English)
- Mrityunjay Prabhakar (Hindi)
- Mohan Rakesh (Hindi)
- Bhisham Sahni (Hindi)
- Badal Sarkar (Bengali)
- Sarveshwar Dayal Saxena (Hindi)

- B. M. Shah (Urdu)
- Partap Sharma (English)
- Gopal Sharman (English)
- Javed Siddiqui (Urdu)
- Harcharan Singh (Punjabi)
- Hrishikesh Sulabh
- Rajesh Talwar (English)
- Habib Tanvir (Hindi)
- Habib Tanvir (Urdu)
- Vijay Tendulkar (Marathi)
- Shreekumar Varma (English)
- Surendra Verma (Hindi)
- Asghar Wajahat (Urdu)
- Naren Weiss (English)

Forms of Indian theatre

Traditional Indian theatre

Kutiyattam is the only surviving specimen of the ancient Sanskrit theatre, thought to have originated around the beginning of the Common Era, and is officially recognised by UNESCO as a Masterpiece of the Oral and Intangible Heritage of Humanity. In addition, many forms of Indian folk theatre abound. Bhavai (strolling players) is a popular folk theatre form of Gujarat, said to have arisen in the 14th century AD. Bhaona and Ankiya Nats have been practicing in Assam since the early 16th century which were created and initiated by Mahapurusha Srimanta Sankardeva. Jatra has been popular in Bengal and its origin is traced to the Bhakti movement in the 16th century. Another folk theatre form popular in Haryana, Uttar Pradesh and Malwa region of Madhya Pradesh is Swang, which is dialogue-oriented rather than movement-oriented and is considered to have arisen in its present form in the late 18th – early 19th centuries. Yakshagana is a very popular theatre art in Karnataka and has existed under different names at least since the 16th century. It is semi-classical in nature and involves music and songs based on carnatic music, rich costumes, storylines based on the *Mahabharata* and *Ramayana*. It also employs spoken dialogue in-between its songs that gives it a folk art flavour. Kathakali is a form of dance-drama, characteristic of Kerala, that arose in the 17th century, developing from the temple-art plays Krishnanattam and Ramanattam.

Urdu/Hindustani Theatre

Urdu Drama evolved from the prevailing dramatic traditions of North India shaping Rahas or Raas as practiced by exponents like Nawab Wajid Ali Shah of Awadh. His dramatic experiments led to the famous Inder Sabha of Amanat and later this tradition took the shape of Parsi Theatre. Agha Hashr Kashmiri is culmination of this tradition.

In some way or other, Urdu theatre tradition has greatly influenced modern Indian theatre. Among all the languages Urdu(which was called Hindi by early writers), along with Gujrati,Marathi and Bengali theatres have kept flourishing and demand for its writers and artists has not subsided by the drama aficionados. For Urdu drama, no place is better than Bombay Film industry otherwise known as Hindi film industry. All the early gems of Urdu Theatre (performed by Parsi Companies) were made into films. Urdu Dramatic tradition has been a spectator's delight since 100 years and counting.

Drama as a theme is made up of several elements. It focuses on life and different aspects of it. The thing to be noticed here is that drama on stage imitates drama in life. It has been said that, there has always been a mutual relationship between theatre and real life. Great historical personalities like Shakespeare have influenced Modern Urdu tradition to a large extent when Indian, Iranian, Turkish stories and folk was adapted for stage with heavy doses of Urdu Poetry. In modern times writers like Imtiaz Ali Taj, Rafi Peer, Krishan Chander,

Manto, Upender Nath Ashk, Ghulam Rabbani, Prof. Mujeeb and many others shaped this tradition.

While Prof Hasan, Ghulam Jeelani, J.N. Kaushal, Shameem Hanfi, Jameel Shaidayi etc. belong to the old generation, contemporary writers like Mujeeb Khan, Javed Siddiqui, [Sayeed Alam], Danish Iqbal, Anis Azmi, Aftab Hasnain, Aslam Parvez, Anis Javed, Iqbal Niyazi and Zaheer Anwar are few post modern playwrights actively contributing in the field of Urdu Drama.

Danish Iqbal's 'Dara Shikoh' directed by M.S. Sathyu is considered a modern classic for the use of newer theatre techniques and contemporary perspective. His other Plays are 'Sahir' on the famous lyricist and revolutionary poet. 'Kuchh Ishq kiya Kuchh Kaam' is another Play written by Danish which is basically a Celebration of the Faiz's Poetry, featuring events from the early part of his life, particularly the events and incidents of pre-partition days which shaped his life and ideals. 'Chand Roz Aur Meri Jaan' - another Play inspired from Faiz's letters written from various jails during the Rawalpindi Conspiracy days. He has written 14 other Plays including 'Dilli Jo Ek Shehr Thaa' and 'Main Gaya Waqt Nahin hoon'.

Zaheer Anwar has kept the flag of Urdu Theatre flying in Kolkata. Unlike the writers of previous generation, Danish iqbal and Zaheer do not write bookish Plays but their work is a product of vigorous performing tradition. Iqbal Niyazi of Mumbai has written several plays in Urdu. His play, "Aur Kitne Jalyanwala BaughU??" won National award other awards. Hence this is the only generation after Amanat and Agha Hashr who actually write for stage and not for libraries.

Indian puppet theatre

Yakshagana is a popular semi-classical theatre art from coastal Karnataka. It uses rich costumes, music, dance, and dialogue. Puppet shows in parts of Karnataka uses all these elements of yakshagana to depict stories from the *Ramayana* and *Mahabharata*.

Indian street theatre

• Jan Natya Manch (JANAM)

Figure 144: *A street play (nukkad natak) in Dharavi slums in Mumbai.*

Mobile theatre

Mobile theatres are a kind of popular theatre form that exist only in Assam. For staging their plays, theatre groups travel different places with their casts, singers, musicians, dancers and entire crew. Even the tent and chairs for the audience are carried with them. Mobile theatre was first staged on 2 October 1963 in Pathshala, Assam. Achyut Lahkar is known as the father of mobile theatre.

Mobile theatre in Salempur Deoria Eastern Uttar Pradesh is over 500 years played on stage within eight years. sanskritiksangam.com is a leading cultural organisation that has been promoting rich Indian culture through regional artists based in Eastern Uttar Pradesh. Since its establishment in 2005, One of its most popular classical-Musical-Dance Drama creation Sanskritik Sangam Salempur, Meghdoot Ki Puravanchal Yatra[340] in Bhojpuri an adaptation of Kalidasa's Meghdootam has done a record 96 shows in cities like Mumbai, Delhi, Rishikesh, Agra, Varanasi, Patna, Sonpur Mela Gorakhpur, near by areas in eastern UP among others. The creations has won many awards and recognitions for its team through leading organisations Its creations revolve around famous mythological and historical personalities and stories like, Ramayana (7 to 9 days play) 26 places, Bhagwata (7 days play) two places, Kabir (23 places), Harishchandra Taramati, (27 Places), Utho Ahilya (26 places) and

Sri Krishna (Three places). And also perform popular plays from Hindi literature including Kaptan Sahab (31), Court Marshall (1), Saiyyan Bhaye Kotwal
(22), Muvaavaje (2), Bakari (2), Bade Bhai Saheb (63), Kafan(12), Bholaram
ka jeev (17), Satgati (2), Boodhi kaaki (3), kakha ga kaa chakkar (7), Jago gra-
hak jaago (3) etc. among other presentations based on famous literary geniuses
like Munshi Premchand, Bhikaari Thakur, etc.

Notable awards and festivals

Awards

- Sangeet Natak Akademi Award
- Theatre Pasta Theatre Awards
- Kalidas Samman
- Karmaveer Puraskaar Nobel Laureates, Artistes for Change

Festivals of theatre in India

- Prithvi Theatre Festival (Prithvi Festival), held every year since its in-
  ception on 3 November, the birth anniversary of its legendary founder
  Prithviraj Kapoor
- Bharat Rang Mahotsav, NSD, New Delhi
- Jairangam- Jaipur Theatre Festival, Jaipur
- Nandikar's National Theatre Festival
- Purple Umbrella Theater Festival, New Delhi

Notable groups and companies

- Chilsag Chillies Theatre Company
- Dramanon
- Indian People's Theatre Association
- Kerala People's Arts Club
- Mandap
- Manch Theatre
- Madras Players
- Nandikar
- Ninasam
- Platform for Action in Creative Theater
- Prithvi Theatre
- Rangayana
- Ranga Shankara
- Samahaara
- Theatre Arts Workshop (TAW)

- Theatre Formation Paribartak
- WeMove Theatre
- Asmita Theatre Group
- Pravara art studio[341]

Notable theatres

- Academy of Fine Arts, Calcutta (Ranu Mukherjee Mancha)
- Girish Mancha
- Kalidasa Kalakendram
- Rabindra Sadan
- Star Theatre
- Surabhi (theatre group)

Notable practitioners who have moved from theatre to films

- Shabana Azmi
- Raj Babbar
- Manoj Bajpai
- Suresh Bhardwaj
- Seema Biswas
- Deepak Dobriyal
- Neena Gupta
- Shafi Inamdar
- Pankaj Kapoor
- Shahid Kapoor
- Prithviraj Kapoor
- Raj Kapoor
- Shammi Kapoor
- Shashi Kapoor
- Girish Karnad
- Kader Khan
- Shahrukh Khan
- Kulbhushan Kharbanda
- Satish Kaushik
- Anupam Kher
- Swanand Kirkire
- Sohrab Modi

- Ananth Nag
- Shankar Nag

- Alok Nath
- Rajkumar
- Kangana Ranaut
- Paresh Rawal
- Rathna Shekar Reddy
- Naseeruddin Shah
- Ratna Pathak Shah
- Om Shivpuri
- Sudha Shivpuri
- Shilpa Shukla
- Ashish Vidyarthi
- Rajpal Yadav
- Rajendra Gupta
- Nawazuddin Siddiqui
- Nana Patekar
- Balraj Sahni
- A. K. Hangal
- Pankaj Tripathi
- Piyush Mishra
- Sadashiv Amrapurkar
- Om Puri
- Brijendra Kala

Training

- Bhartendu Academy of Dramatic Arts
- National School of Drama

Sources

<templatestyles src="Refbegin/styles.css" />

- Banham, Martin, ed. 1998. *The Cambridge Guide to Theatre*. Cambridge: Cambridge UP. <templatestyles src="Module:Citation/CS1/styles.css" />ISBN 0-521-43437-8.
- Brandon, James R. 1981. Introduction. In Baumer and Brandon (1981, xvii-xx).
- —, ed. 1997. *The Cambridge Guide to Asian Theatre.'* 2nd, rev. ed. Cambridge: Cambridge UP. <templatestyles src="Module:Citation/CS1/styles.css" />ISBN 978-0-521-58822-5.
- Brockett, Oscar G. and Franklin J. Hildy. 2003. *History of the Theatre*. Ninth edition, International edition. Boston: Allyn and Bacon. <templatestyles src="Module:Citation/CS1/styles.css" />ISBN 0-205-41050-2.

- Baumer, Rachel Van M., and James R. Brandon, eds. 1981. *Sanskrit Theatre in Performance.* Delhi: Motilal Banarsidass, 1993. <templatestyles src="Module:Citation/CS1/styles.css" />ISBN 978-81-208-0772-3.
- Richmond, Farley. 1998. "India." In Banham (1998, 516-525).
- Richmond, Farley P., Darius L. Swann, and Phillip B. Zarrilli, eds. 1993. *Indian Theatre: Traditions of Performance.* U of Hawaii P. <templatestyles src="Module:Citation/CS1/styles.css" />ISBN 978-0-8248-1322-2.
- Sharma, Shrikrishna, ed. 1996. *Rangkarmi.* Cultural Societies of Rajasthan. (1996, 139)

Further reading

> Wikimedia Commons has media related to *Theater of India*.

- Wilson, Horace Hayman (tr. from the Original Sanskrit) (1827). *Select Specimens of the Theatre of the Hindus*[342]. V.Holcroft at The Asiatic Press, Calcutta.<templatestyles src="Module:Citation/CS1/styles.css"></templatestyles>
- ., Dhanamjaya; Haas, George C.O.(tr. from Sanskrit by) (1912). *The Dasarupa or Treatise on Ten Forms of Drama - A Treatise on Hindu Dramaturgy*[343]. Columbia University.<templatestyles src="Module:Citation/CS1/styles.css"></templatestyles>
- ., Nandikeśvara; Coomaraswamy, Ananda Kentish (tr by); Duggirala, Gopala Kristnayya (tr by) (1917). *The Mirror of Gesture - Being the Abhinaya Darpana of Nandikeśvara*[344]. Harvard University Press.<templatestyles src="Module:Citation/CS1/styles.css"></templatestyles>
- *The Indian theatre*, by Mulk Raj Bansal, Published by D. Dobson, 1950.
- *Theatre in India*, by Balwant Gargi. Published by Theatre Arts Books, 1962.
- *A panorama of theatre in India*, by Som Benegal. Published by Popular Prakashan [for] Indian Council for Cultural Relations (ICCR), 1968.
- Roy, Pinaki. "Bratya Basu's *Boma: Bombing the Coloniser-supervised Chronicle*". *Postcolonial Indian Drama in English and English Translation: Reading Themes and Techniques* (<templatestyles src="Module:Citation/CS1/styles.css" />ISBN 978-93-5207-560-7). Eds. Sarkar, J., and U. De. New Delhi: Authors Press, 2017. pp. 287–300.
- *Indian Theatre: Traditions of Performance*, by Farley P. Richmond, Darius L. Swann, Phillip B. Zarrilli. Motilal Banarsidass Publ., 1993.

<templatestyles src="Module:Citation/CS1/styles.css" />ISBN 81-208-0981-5.

* *Indian theatre: theatre of origin, theatre of freedom*, by Ralph Yarrow. Routledge, 2001. <templatestyles src="Module:Citation/CS1/styles.css" />ISBN 0-7007-1412-X.
* *The Oxford companion to Indian theatre*, by Ananda Lal. Oxford University Press, 2004. <templatestyles src="Module:Citation/CS1/styles.css" />ISBN 0-19-564446-8.
* *jagrancityplus*[345]
* *A History of the Jana Natya Manch: Plays for the People" by Arjun Ghosh; Published by SAGE Publications India, New Delhi; 2012*

Music of India

Music of India

<indicator name="pp-default"> 🔒 </indicator>

Music of India
A Lady Playing the Tanpura, c. 1735 (Rajasthan)
Genres
Traditional

- Classical
  - Carnatic
  - Hindustani
- Folk
- Baul
- Bhajan
- Odissi
- Rabindra Sangeet
- Thumri
- Dadra
- Chaiti
- Kajari
- Sufi
  - Ghazal
  - Qawwali

Modern

- Bhangra
  - Bhangragga
- Blues
- Filmi
  - Bollywood
  - Ghazal
  - Qawwali
- Goa trance
- Dance
- Indi-pop
  - Asian Underground
- Jazz
- Rock
  - Bengali
  - Raga

Media and performance	
Music awards	• Filmfare Awards • Sangeet Natak Akademi Award
Music festivals	• Saptak Festival of Music • Chennai Music Season • Dover Lane music festival • Tyagaraja Aradhana • Harivallabh Sangeet Sammelan
Music media	• *Sruti* • *The Record*
Nationalistic and patriotic songs	
National anthem	Jana Gana Mana
Regional music	

- Andaman and Nicobar Islands
- Andhra Pradesh
- Arunachal Pradesh
- Assam
- Bihar
- Chhattisgarh
- Goa
- Gujarat
- Haryana
- Himachal Pradesh
- Kashmir, Jammu and Ladakh
- Jharkhand
- Karnataka
- Kerala
- Madhya Pradesh
- Maharashtra
- Manipur
- Meghalaya
- Mizoram

- Nagaland
- Odisha
- Punjab
- Rajasthan
- Sikkim
- Tamil Nadu
  - Ancient
- Tripura
- Uttar Pradesh
- Uttarakhand
- West Bengal

- $\underline{v}$
- $\underline{t}$
- $\underline{e}$[346]

Part of a series on the
Culture of India
History
People
Cuisine
Religion
Sport
• ⚙ **India portal**

- $\underline{v}$
- $\underline{t}$
- $\underline{e}$[347]

The **music of India** includes multiple varieties of classical music, folk music, filmi, Indian rock and Indian pop. India's classical music tradition, including

Figure 145: *Dancing Girl sculpture from the Indus Valley Civilization (c. 4,500 years ago)*

Hindustani music and Carnatic, has a history spanning millennia and developed over several areas. Music in India began as an integral part of socio-religious life.

History

The 30,000 years old paleolithic and neolithic cave paintings at the UNESCO world heritage site at Bhimbetka rock shelters in Madhya Pradesh shows music instruments and dance.

Dancing Girl sculpture (2500 BCE) was found from the Indus Valley Civilization (IVC) site. There are IVC-era paintings on pottery of a man with a dhol hanging from his neck and a woman holding a drum under her left arm.[348]

Vedas (c. 1500 – c. 800 BCE Vedic period)[349,350,351] document rituals with performing arts and play.[352] For example, Shatapatha Brahmana (~800–700 BCE) has verses in chapter 13.2 written in the form of a play between two actors.[353] *Tala* or *taal* is an ancient music concept traceable to Vedic era texts of Hinduism, such as the *Samaveda* and methods for singing the Vedic hymns.[354] Smriti (500 BCE to 100 BCE) post-vedic Hindu texts[355,356,357] include Valmiki's Ramayana (500 BCE to 100 BCE) which mentions dance and music (dance by Apsaras such as Urvashi, Rambha, Menaka, Tilottama Panchāpsaras, and Ravana's wives excelling in *nrityageeta* or "singing and dancing" and *nritavaditra* or "playing musical instruments"), music and singing by Gandharvas, several string instruments (vina, tantri, vipanci and *vallaki* similar to *veena*), wind instruments (shankha, venu and *venugana* - likely a mouth organ made by tying several flutes together), raga (including *kaushika* such as *raag kaushik dhwani*), vocal registers (seven *svara* or *sur*, *ana* or *ekashurti* drag note, *murchana* the regulated rise and fall of voice in *matra* and *tripramana* three-fold *teen taal laya* such as *drut* or quick, *madhya* or middle, and *vilambit* or slow), poetry recitation in Bala Kanda and also in Uttara Kanda by Luv and Kusha in *marga* style.[358]

Under the Khiljis, there were concerts and competitions between Hindustani and Carnatic musicians.[359] Madhava Kandali, 14th century Assamese poet and writer of Saptakanda Ramayana, lists several instruments in his version of *"Ramayana"*, such as mardala, khumuchi, bhemachi, dagar, gratal, ramtal, tabal, jhajhar, jinjiri, bheri mahari, tokari, dosari, kendara, dotara, vina, rudravipanchi, etc. (meaning that these instruments existed since his time in 14th century or earlier).[360] The Indian system of notation is perhaps the world's oldest and most elaborate.[361]

Classical music

The two main traditions of Indian classical music are Carnatic music, which is found predominantly in the peninsular regions, and Hindustani music, which is found in the northern, eastern and central regions. The basic concepts of this music includes *shruti* (microtones), *swaras* (notes), *alankar* (ornamentations), *raga* (melodies improvised from basic grammars), and *tala* (rhythmic patterns used in percussion). Its tonal system divides the octave into 22 segments called Shrutis, not all equal but each roughly equal to a quarter of a whole tone of the Western music.

Hindustani music

The tradition of Hindustani music dates back to Vedic times where the hymns in the Sama Veda, an ancient religious text, were sung as Samagana and not chanted. It diverged from Carnatic music around the 13th-14th centuries CE, primarily due to Islamic influences.Wikipedia:Citation needed Developing a strong and diverse tradition over several centuries, it has contemporary traditions established primarily in India but also in Pakistan and Bangladesh. In contrast to Carnatic music, the other main Indian classical music tradition originating from the South, Hindustani music was not only influenced by ancient Hindu musical traditions, historical Vedic philosophy and native Indian sounds but also enriched by the Persian performance practices of the Mughals. Classical genres are dhrupad, dhamar, khyal, tarana and sadra, and there are also several semi-classical forms.

Carnatic music

Carnatic music can be traced to the 14th - 15th centuries AD and thereafter. It originated in South India during the rule of Vijayanagar Empire. Like Hindustani music, it is melodic, with improvised variations, but tends to have more fixed compositions. It consists of a composition with improvised embellishments added to the piece in the forms of *Raga Alapana, Kalpanaswaram, Neraval* and, in the case of more advanced students, Raga, Tala, Pallavi. The main emphasis is on the vocals as most compositions are written to be sung, and even when played on instruments, they are meant to be performed in a singing style (known as *gāyaki*). Around 300 ragams are in use today. Annamayya is the first known composer in Carnatic music. He is widely regarded as the Andhra Pada kavitā Pitāmaha (Godfather of Telugu song-writing). Purandara Dasa is considered the father of Carnatic music, while the later musicians Tyagaraja, Shyama Shastry and Muthuswami Dikshitar are considered the trinity of Carnatic music.Wikipedia:Citation needed

Noted artists of Carnatic music include Ariyakudi Ramanuja Iyengar (the father of the current concert format), Semmangudi Srinivasa Iyer, Alathur Brothers, MS Subbulakshmi, Lalgudi Jayaraman and more recently Balamuralikrishna, TN Seshagopalan, K J Yesudas, N. Ramani, Umayalpuram K. Sivaraman, Sanjay Subrahmanyan, TM Krishna, Bombay Jayashri, T S Nandakumar, Aruna Sairam, and Mysore Manjunath.

Every December, the city of Chennai in India has its eight-week-long Music Season, which is the world's largest cultural event.Wikipedia:Citation needed

Carnatic music has served as the foundation for most music in South India, including folk music, festival music and has also extended its influence to film music in the past 100–150 years or so.

Light classical music

There are many types of music which comes under the category of light classical or semi-classical. Some of the forms are Thumri, Dadra, Ghazal, Chaiti, Kajri, Tappa, Natya Sangeet and Qawwali. These forms place emphasis on explicitly seeking emotion from the audience, as opposed to the classical forms.

Figure 146: *Hira Devi Waiba, pioneer of Nepali folk songs in India*

Folk music

Tamang Selo

This is a genre of Nepali folk song of the Tamang people and popular amongst the Nepali speaking community in West Bengal, Sikkim and around the world. It is accompanied by Tamang instruments, the Madal, Damphu and Tungna, although nowadays musicians have taken to modern instruments. A Tamang Selo can be catchy and lively or slow and melodious, and is usually sung to convey sorrow, love, happiness or day-to-day incidents and stories of folklore.

Hira Devi Waiba is hailed as the pioneer of Nepali folk songs and Tamang Selo. Her song 'Chura ta Hoina Astura' (चुरा त होइन अस्तुरा) is said to be the first Tamang Selo ever recorded. She has sung nearly 300 songs through her musical career spanning 40 years. After Waiba's death in 2011, her son Satya Waiba (producer) and Navneet Aditya Waiba (singer) collaborated and re-recorded her most iconic songs and released an album titled *Ama Lai Shraddhanjali* (आमालाई श्रद्धाञ्जली-Tribute to Mother).

Figure 147: *Group of Dharohar folk musicians performing in Mehrangarh Fort, Jodhpur, India*

Rabindra Sangeet (music of Bengal)

Rabindra Sangeet (Bengali: রবীন্দ্রসঙ্গীত *Robindro Shonggit*, Bengali pronunciation: [robindro ʃoŋgit]), also known as Tagore songs, are songs written and composed by Rabindranath Tagore. They have distinctive characteristics in the music of Bengal, popular in India and Bangladesh.[362] "Sangeet" means music, "Rabindra Sangeet" means music (or more aptly songs) of Rabindra.

Tagore wrote some 2,230 songs in Bengali, now known as *Rabindra Sangeet*, using classical music and traditional folk music as sources.[363]

Bihu of Assam

Bihu (Assamese: বিহু) is the festival of New Year of Assam falling on mid-April. This is a festival of nature and mother earth where the first day is for the cows and buffaloes. The second day of the festival is for the man. Bihu dances and songs accompanied by traditional drums and wind instruments are an essential part of this festival. Bihu songs are energetic and with beats to welcome the festive spring. Assamese drums (dhol), Pepa(usually made from buffalo horn), Gogona are major instruments used.

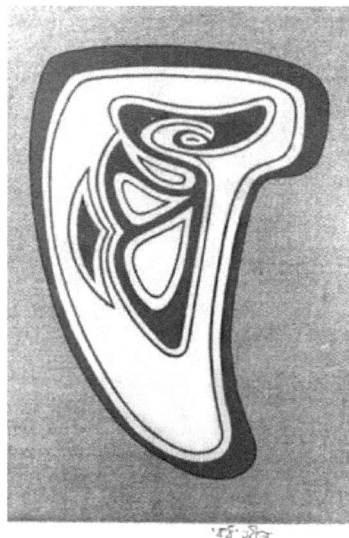

Figure 148: *Rabindranath Tagore's Bengali-language initials are worked into this "Ro-Tho" wooden seal, stylistically similar to designs used in traditional Haida carvings. Tagore embellished his manuscripts with such art.*

Figure 149: *Dance accompanied by Rabindra Sangeet*

Figure 150: *N. Ramani and N Rajam accompanied by T S Nandakumar*

Figure 151: *Jeng Bihu dancers at Rongali Bihu celebration in Bangalore*

Sufi folk rock / Sufi rock

Sufi folk rock contains elements of modern hard rock and traditional folk music with Sufi poetry. While it was pioneered by bands like Junoon in Pakistan it became very popular, especially in north India. In 2005, Rabbi Shergill released a Sufi rock song called "Bulla Ki Jaana", which became a chart-topper in India and Pakistan. More recently, the sufi folk rock song "Bulleya" from the 2016 film *Ae Dil Hai Mushkil* became a mammoth hit.Wikipedia:Citation needed

Dandiya

Dandiya or Raas is a form of Gujarati cultural dance that is performed with sticks. The present musical style is derived from the traditional musical accompaniment to the folk dance. It is practiced mainly in the state of Gujarat. There is also another type of dance and music associated with Dandiya/Raas called Garba.

Uttarakhandi music

Uttarakhandi folk music had its root in the lap of nature and the hilly terrain of the region. Common themes in the folk music of Uttarakhand are the beauty of nature, various seasons, festivals, religious traditions, cultural practices, folk stories, historical characters, and the bravery of ancestors. The folk songs of Uttarakhand are a reflection of the cultural heritage and the way people live their lives in the Himalayas. Musical instruments used in Uttarakhand music include the Dhol, Damoun, Turri, Ransingha, Dholki, Daur, Thali, Bhankora and Masakbhaja. Tabla and Harmonium are also sometimes used, especially in recorded folk music from the 1960s onwards. Generic Indian and global musical instruments have been incorporated in modern popular folks by singers like Narendra Singh Negi, Mohan Upreti, Gopal Babu Goswami, and Chandra Singh Rahi.

Lavani

Lavani comes from the word *Lavanya* which means "beauty". This is one of the most popular forms of dance and music that is practiced all over Maharashtra. It has, in fact, become a necessary part of the Maharashtrian folk dance performances. Traditionally, the songs are sung by female artists, but male artists may occasionally sing Lavanis. The dance format associated with Lavani is known as Tamasha. Lavani is a combination of traditional song and dance, which particularly performed to the enchanting beats of 'Dholaki', a drum-like instrument. The dance is performed by attractive women wearing nine-yard saris. They are sung in a quick tempo. Lavani originated in the arid region of Maharashtra and Madhya Pradesh.

Rajasthan

Rajasthan has a very diverse cultural collection of musician castes, including Langas, Sapera, Bhopa, Jogi and Manganiyar (lit. "the ones who ask/beg"). *Rajasthan Diary* quotes it as a soulful, full-throated music with harmonious diversity. The melodies of Rajasthan come from a variety of instruments. The stringed variety includes the Sarangi, Ravanahatha, Kamayacha, Morsing and Ektara. Percussion instruments come in all shapes and sizes from the huge Nagaras and Dhols to the tiny Damrus. The Daf and Chang are a favorite of Holi (the festival of colours) revelers. Flutes and bagpipers come in local flavors such as Shehnai, Poongi, Algoza, Tarpi, Been and Bankia.

Rajasthani music is derived from a combination of string instruments, percussion instruments and wind instruments accompanied by renditions of folk singers.   It enjoys a respectable presence in Bollywood music as well.Wikipedia:Citation needed

Popular music

Filmi music

The biggest form of Indian popular music is filmi, or songs from Indian films, it makes up 72% of the music sales in India. The film industry of India supported music by according reverence to classical music while utilising the western orchestration to support Indian melodies. Music composers, like R. D. Burman, Shankar Jaikishan, S. D. Burman, Madan Mohan, Bhupen Hazarika, Naushad Ali, O. P. Nayyar, Hemant Kumar, C. Ramchandra, Salil Chowdhury, Kalyanji Anandji, Ilaiyaraaja, A. R. Rahman, Jatin Lalit, Anu Malik, Nadeem-Shravan, Harris Jayaraj, Himesh Reshammiya, Vidyasagar, Shankar Ehsaan Loy, Salim-Sulaiman, Pritam, M.S. Viswanathan, K. V. Mahadevan, Ghantasala and S. D. Batish employed the principles of harmony while retaining classical and folk flavor. Reputed names in the domain of Indian classical music like Ravi Shankar, Vilayat Khan, Ali Akbar Khan and Ram Narayan have also composed music for films. Traditionally, in Indian films, the voice for the songs is not provided by the actors, they are provided by the professional playback singers, to sound more developed, melodious and soulful, while actors lipsynch on the screen. In the past, only a handful of singers provided the voice in Hindi films. These include Kishore Kumar,K. J. Yesudas, Mohammed Rafi, Mukesh, S.P. Balasubrahmanyam, T.M. Soundararajan, Hemant Kumar, Manna Dey, P. Susheela, Lata Mangeshkar, Asha Bhonsle, K.S. Chitra, Geeta Dutt, S. Janaki, Shamshad Begum, Suraiya, Noorjahan and Suman Kalyanpur. Recent playback singers include Udit Narayan, Kumar Sanu, Kailash Kher, Alisha Chinai, KK, Shaan, Madhushree, Shreya Ghoshal, Nihira Joshi, Kavita

Krishnamurthy, Hariharan (singer), Ilaiyaraaja, A.R. Rahman, Sonu Nigam, Sukhwinder Singh, Kunal Ganjawala, Anu Malik, Sunidhi Chauhan, Anushka Manchanda, Raja Hasan, Arijit Singh and Alka Yagnik. Rock bands like Indus Creed, Indian Ocean, Silk Route and Euphoria have gained mass appeal with the advent of cable music television.

Interaction with non-Indian music

In the late 1970s and early 1980s, rock and roll fusions with Indian music were well known throughout Europe and North America. Ali Akbar Khan's 1955 performance in the United States was perhaps the beginning of this trend.

Jazz pioneers such as John Coltrane—who recorded a composition entitled 'India' during the November 1961 sessions for his album *Live At The Village Vanguard* (the track was not released until 1963 on Coltrane's album *Impressions*)—also embraced this fusion. George Harrison (of the Beatles) played the sitar on the song "Norwegian Wood (This Bird Has Flown)" in 1965, which sparked interest from Shankar, who subsequently took Harrison as his apprentice. Jazz innovator Miles Davis recorded and performed with musicians like Khalil Balakrishna, Bihari Sharma, and Badal Roy in his post-1968 electric ensembles. Virtuoso jazz guitarist John McLaughlin spent several years in Madurai learning Carnatic music and incorporated it into many of his acts including Shakti which featured prominent Indian musicians. Other Western artists such as the Grateful Dead, Incredible String Band, the Rolling Stones, the Move and Traffic soon incorporated Indian influences and instruments, and added Indian performers. Legendary Grateful Dead frontman Jerry Garcia joined guitarist Sanjay Mishra on his classic CD "Blue Incantation" (1995). Mishra also wrote an original score for French Director Eric Heumann for his film *Port Djema* (1996) which won best score at Hamptons film festival and The Golden Bear at Berlin. in 2000 he recorded *Rescue* with drummer Dennis Chambers (Carlos Santana, John McLaughlin et al.) and in 2006 Chateau Benares with guests DJ Logic and Keller Williams (guitar and bass).

Though the Indian music craze soon died down among mainstream audiences, die-hard fans and immigrants continued the fusion. In 1985, a beat-oriented, Raga Rock hybrid called Sitar Power by Ashwin Batish reintroduced sitar in western nations. Sitar Power drew the attention of a number of record labels and was snapped up by Shanachie Records of New Jersey to head their World Beat Ethno Pop division.

In the late 1980s, Indian-British artists fused Indian and Western traditions to make the Asian Underground. Since the 1990s, Canadian born musician Nadaka who has spent most of his life in India, has been creating music that is an acoustic fusion of Indian classical music with western styles. One such singer who has merged the Bhakti sangeet tradition of India with the western non-Indian music is Krishna Das and sells music records of his musical sadhana. Another example is the Indo-Canadian musician Vandana Vishwas who has experimented with western music in her 2013 album *Monologues*.

In the new millennium, American hip-hop has featured Indian filmi and bhangra. Mainstream hip-hop artists have sampled songs from Bollywood movies and have collaborated with Indian artists. Examples include Timbaland's "Indian Flute", Erick Sermon and Redman's "React", Slum Village's "Disco", and Truth Hurts' hit song "Addictive", which sampled a Lata Mangeshkar song, and The Black Eyed Peas sampled Asha Bhosle's song "Yeh Mera Dil" in their hit single "Don't Phunk With My Heart". In 1997, the British band Cornershop paid tribute to Asha Bhosle with their song *Brimful of Asha*, which became an international hit. British-born Indian artist Panjabi MC also had a Bhangra hit in the U.S. with "Mundian To Bach Ke" which featured rapper Jay-Z. Asian Dub Foundation are not huge mainstream stars, but their politically charged rap and punk rock influenced sound has a multiracial audience in their native UK. In 2008, international star Snoop Dogg appeared in a song in the film Singh Is Kinng. In 2007, hip-hop producer Madlib released Beat Konducta Vol 3–4: Beat Konducta in India; an album which heavily samples and is inspired by the music of India.

Sometimes, the music of India will fuse with the traditional music of other countries. For example, Delhi 2 Dublin, a band based in Canada, is known for fusing Indian and Irish music, and Bhangraton is a fusion of Bhangra music with reggaeton, which itself is a fusion of hip hop, reggae, and traditional Latin American music.[364]

In a more recent example of Indian-British fusion, Laura Marling along with Mumford and Sons collaborated in 2010 with the Dharohar Project on a four-song EP. The British band Bombay Bicycle Club also sampled the song "Man Dole Mera Tan Dole" for their single "Feel".

Indian pop music

Indian pop music is based on an amalgamation of Indian folk and classical music, and modern beats from different parts of the world. Pop music really started in the South Asian region with the playback singer Ahmed Rushdi's song '*Ko Ko Korina*' in 1966, followed initially by Mohammad Rafi in the late 1960s and then by Kishore Kumar in the early 1970s.

After that, much of Indian Pop music comes from the Indian Film Industry, and until the 1990s, few singers like Usha Uthup, Sharon Prabhakar, and Peenaz Masani outside it were popular. Since then, pop singers in the latter group have included Daler Mehndi, Baba Sehgal, Alisha Chinai, KK, Shantanu Mukherjee a.k.a. Shaan, Sagarika, Colonial Cousins (Hariharan, Lesle Lewis), Lucky Ali, and Sonu Nigam, and music composers like Zila Khan or Jawahar Wattal, who made top selling albums with, Daler Mehndi, Shubha Mudgal, Baba Sehgal, Shweta Shetty and Hans Raj Hans.

Besides those listed above, popular Indi-pop singers include Sanam (Band), Gurdas Maan, Sukhwinder Singh, Papon, Zubeen Garg, Raghav Sachar Rageshwari, Vandana Vishwas, Devika Chawla, Bombay Vikings, Asha Bhosle, Sunidhi Chauhan, Anushka Manchanda, Bombay Rockers, Anu Malik, Jazzy B, Malkit Singh, Raghav, Jay Sean, Juggy D, Rishi Rich, Sheila Chandra, Bally Sagoo, Punjabi MC, Bhangra Knights, Mehnaz, Sanober and Vaishali Samant.Wikipedia:Citation needed

Recently, Indian pop has taken an interesting turn with the "remixing" of songs from past Indian movie songs, new beats being added to them.

Rock and metal music

Raga rock

Raga rock is rock or pop music with a heavy Indian influence, either in its construction, its timbre, or its use of instrumentation, such as the sitar and tabla. Raga and other forms of classical Indian music began to influence many rock groups during the 1960s; most famously the Beatles. The first traces of "raga rock" can be heard on songs such as "See My Friends" by the Kinks and the Yardbirds' "Heart Full of Soul", released the previous month, featured a sitar-like riff by guitarist Jeff Beck. The Beatles song "Norwegian Wood (This Bird Has Flown)", which first appeared on the band's 1965 album Rubber Soul, was the first western pop song to actually incorporate the sitar (played by lead guitarist George Harrison). The Byrds' March 1966 single "Eight Miles High" and its B-side "Why" were also influential in originating the musical subgenre. Indeed, the term "raga rock" was coined by The Byrds' publicist in the press releases for the single and was first used in print by journalist Sally Kempton in her review of "Eight Miles High" for The Village Voice. George Harrison's interest in Indian music, popularised the genre in the mid-1960s with songs such as "Love You To", "Tomorrow Never Knows" (credited to Lennon-McCartney), "Within You Without You" and "The Inner Light". The rock acts of the sixties both in turn influenced British and American groups and Indian acts to develop a later form of Indian rock.

Figure 152: *Nicotine playing at 'Pedal To The Metal', TDS, Indore, India in 2014. The band is known for being the pioneer of metal music in Central India.*

Indian rock

The rock music "scene" in India is small compared to the filmi or fusion musicality "scenes" but as of recent years has come into its own, achieving a cult status of sorts. Rock music in India has its origins in the 1960s when international stars such as the Beatles visited India and brought their music with them. These artists' collaboration with Indian musicians such as Ravi Shankar and Zakir Hussain have led to the development of raga rock. International shortwave radio stations such as The Voice of America, BBC, and Radio Ceylon played a major part in bringing Western pop, folk, and rock music to the masses. Indian rock bands began to gain prominence only much later, around the late 1980s.

It was around this time that the rock band Indus Creed formerly known as The Rock Machine got itself noticed on the international stage with hits like *Rock N Roll Renegade*. Other bands quickly followed. As of now, the rock music scene in India is quietly growing day by day and gathering more support. With the introduction of MTV in the early 1990s, Indians began to be exposed to various forms of rock such as grunge and speed metal. This influence can be clearly seen in many Indian bands today. The cities of the North Eastern Region, mainly Guwahati and Shillong, Kolkata, Delhi, Mumbai and Bangalore have emerged as major melting pots for rock and metal enthusiasts. Bangalore has been the hub for rock and metal movement in India. Some prominent bands include Nicotine, Voodoo Child, Indian Ocean, Kryptos, Thermal and a Quarter, Demonic Resurrection, Motherjane, Avial, and Parikrama. The future looks encouraging thanks to entities such as DogmaTone Records and Eastern Fare Music Foundation that are dedicated to promoting and supporting Indian rock.

From Central India, Nicotine, an Indore-based metal band, is widely credited of being the pioneer of metal music in the region.

Western classical music

The spread and following of Western classical music in India is almost entirely non-existent. It is mainly patronised by the Indian Zoroastrian community and small esoteric groups with historical exposure to Western classical music. Another esoteric group with significant patronage is the Protestant Christian community in Chennai and Bangalore.Wikipedia:Citation needed Western Music education is also severely neglected and pretty rare in India. Western keyboard, drums and guitar instruction being an exception as it has found some interest; mainly in an effort to create musicians to service contemporary popular Indian music. Many reasons have been cited for the obscurity of Western classical music in India, a country rich in its musical heritage by its own right, however, the two main reasons are an utter lack of exposure and a passive disinterest in what is considered esoteric at best. The difficulty in importing Western musical instruments and their rarity have also contributed to the obscurity of classical Western music.Wikipedia:Citation needed

Despite more than a century of exposure to Western classical music and two centuries of British colonialism, classical music in India has never gained more than 'fringe' popularity. Many attempts to popularise Western classical music in India have failed in the past due to disinterest and lack of sustained efforts.Wikipedia:Citation needed Today, Western classical music education has improved with the help of numerous institutions in India. Institutions like KM Music Conservatory (founded by Oscar-winning Composer A.R.Rahman), Calcutta School of Music, Eastern Fare Music Foundation, Delhi School of Music, Delhi Music Academy, Guitarmonk and many others are dedicated to contributing to the progress or growth and supporting Western classical music. In 1930, Mehli Mehta set up the Bombay Symphony Orchestra.

The Bombay Chamber Orchestra (BCO) was founded in 1962.

In 2006, the Symphony Orchestra of India was founded, housed at the NCPA in Mumbai. It is today the only professional symphony orchestra in India and

presents two concert seasons per year, with world-renowned conductors and
soloists.

Some prominent Indians in Western classical music are:

- Andre de Quadros, conductor and music educator
- Zubin Mehta, conductor
- Mehli Mehta, father of Zubin, violinist and founding conductor of the
  Bombay Symphony Orchestra
- Anil Srinivasan, pianist
- Ilaiyaraaja, the first Indian to compose a full symphony performed by the
  Royal Philharmonic Orchestra in London's Walthamstow Town Hall
- Naresh Sohal, British Indian-born composer
- Param Vir, British Indian-born composer

Patriotism and music

Patriotic feelings have been instigated within Indians through music since the
era of the freedom struggle. Jana Gana Mana, the national anthem of India by
Rabindranath Tagore, is largely credited for uniting India through music and
Vande Mataram by Bankim Chandra Chattopadhyay as the national song of
India. Patriotic songs were also written in many regional languages such as
Biswo Bizoyi No Zuwan in Assamese. Post-independence songs such as Aye
mere watan ke logo, Mile Sur Mera Tumhara, Ab Tumhare Hawale Watan
Saathiyo, Maa Tujhe Salaam by A.R.Rahman have been responsible for con-
solidating feelings of national integration and unity in diversity.

Further reading

- Day; Joshi, O. P. (1982). "The changing social structure of music in India". *International Social Science Journal*. **34** (94): 625.<templatestyles
  src="Module:Citation/CS1/styles.css"></templatestyles>
- Day, Charles Russell (1891). *The Music and Musical instruments of Southern India and the Deccan*[365]. Adam Charles Black, London.<templatestyles
  src="Module:Citation/CS1/styles.css"></templatestyles>
- Clements, Sir Ernest (1913). *Introduction to the Study of Indian Music*[366]. Longmans, Green & Co., London.<templatestyles
  src="Module:Citation/CS1/styles.css"></templatestyles>
- Strangways, A.H. Fox (1914). *The Music of Hindostan*[367].
  Oxford at The Clarendon Press, London.<templatestyles
  src="Module:Citation/CS1/styles.css"></templatestyles>

- Popley, Herbert Arthur (1921). *The Music of India*[368]. Association Press, Calcutta.<templatestyles src="Module:Citation/CS1/styles.css"></templatestyles>
- Killius, Rolf. *Ritual Music and Hindu Rituals of Kerala. New Delhi: B.R. Rhythms, 2006*.<templatestyles src="Module:Citation/CS1/styles.css"></templatestyles>
- Moutal, Patrick (2012). *Hindustāni Gata-s Compilation: Instrumental themes in north Indian classical music*. Rouen: Patrick Moutal Publisher. ISBN 978-2-9541244-1-4.<templatestyles src="Module:Citation/CS1/styles.css"></templatestyles>
- Moutal, Patrick (1991). *A Comparative Study of Selected Hindustāni Rāga-s*. New Delhi: Munshiram Manoharlal Publishers Pvt Ltd. ISBN 81-215-0526-7.<templatestyles src="Module:Citation/CS1/styles.css"></templatestyles>
- Moutal, Patrick (1991). *Hindustāni Rāga-s Index*. New Delhi: Munshiram Manoharlal Publishers Pvt Ltd.<templatestyles src="Module:Citation/CS1/styles.css"></templatestyles>
- Manuel, Peter. *Thumri in Historical and Stylistic Perspectives. New Delhi: Motilal Banarsidass, 1989*.<templatestyles src="Module:Citation/CS1/styles.css"></templatestyles>
- Manuel, Peter. *Cassette Culture: Popular Music and Technology in North India. University of Chicago Press, 1993*. ISBN 0-226-50401-8.<templatestyles src="Module:Citation/CS1/styles.css"></templatestyles>
- Wade, Bonnie C. (1987). *Music in India: the Classical Traditions*. New Dehi, India: Manohar, 1987, t.p. 1994. xix, [1], 252 p., amply ill., including with examples in musical notation. <templatestyles src="Module:Citation/CS1/styles.css" />ISBN 81-85054-25-8
- Maycock, Robert and Hunt, Ken. "How to Listen - a Routemap of India". 2000. In Broughton, Simon and Ellingham, Mark with McConnachie, James and Duane, Orla (Ed.), *World Music, Vol. 2: Latin & North America, Caribbean, India, Asia and Pacific*, pp 63–69. Rough Guides Ltd, Penguin Books. <templatestyles src="Module:Citation/CS1/styles.css" />ISBN 1-85828-636-0
- Hunt, Ken. "Ragas and Riches". 2000. In Broughton, Simon and Ellingham, Mark with McConnachie, James and Duane, Orla (Ed.), *World Music, Vol. 2: Latin & North America, Caribbean, India, Asia and Pacific*, pp 70–78. Rough Guides Ltd, Penguin Books. <templatestyles src="Module:Citation/CS1/styles.css" />ISBN 1-85828-636-0.
- "Hindu music." (2011). Columbia Electronic Encyclopedia, 6th Edition, 1.

- Emmie te Nijenhuis (1977), *A History of Indian Literature: Musi-cological Literature*[369], Otto Harrassowitz Verlag, <templatestyles src="Module:Citation/CS1/styles.css" />ISBN 978-3447018319, <templatestyles src="Module:Citation/CS1/styles.css" />OCLC 299648131[370]
- Natya Sastra[371] *Ancient Indian Theory and Practice of Music* (translated by M. Ghosh)

External links

Wikimedia Commons has media related to *Music of India*.

- BBC Radio 3 Audio (45 minutes): The Nizamuddin shrine in Delhi.[372] Accessed November 25, 2010.
- BBC Radio 3 Audio (45 minutes): A mahfil Sufi gathering in Karachi.[373] Accessed November 25, 2010.
- BBC Radio 3 Audio (60 minutes): The Misra brothers perform Vedic chant.[374] Accessed November 25, 2010.
- BBC Radio 3 Audio (60 minutes): Rikhi Ram and sons, Nizami brothers.[375] Accessed November 25, 2010.
- BBC Radio 3 Audio (60 minutes): Rajasthan, Bombay and Trilok Gurtu.[376] Accessed November 25, 2010.
- BBC Radio 3 Audio (45 minutes): Gujarat - Praful Dave.[377] Accessed November 25, 2010.
- BBC Radio 3 Audio (45 minutes): Courtesan songs and music of the Bauls.[378] Accessed November 25, 2010.
- BBC Radio 3 Audio (60 minutes): Music from the Golden Temple of Amritsar.[379] Accessed November 25, 2010.
- (in English) (in French) Hindustani Rag Sangeet Online - A rare collection of more than 800 audio and video archives from 1902[380]

Indian painting

Indian painting

Indian paintings

Figure 153: *Raja Ravi Varma Shakuntala (1870); oil on canvas.*

Figure 154: *Hindu iconography are shown in Pattachitra.*

Figure 155: *Painting of Radha, the companion of the Hindu god Krishna.*

Figure 156: *Fresco from Ajanta caves, c. 450–500 CE.*

Part of a series on the
Culture of India
History
People
Cuisine
Religion
Sport
• India portal

- v
- t
- e[381]

Indian painting has a very long tradition and history in Indian art. The earliest Indian paintings were the rock paintings of pre-historic times, the petroglyphs as found in places like Bhimbetka rock shelters, some of the Stone Age rock paintings found among the Bhimbetka rock shelters are approximately 30,000 years old. India's Buddhist literature is replete with examples of texts which describe palaces of the army and the aristocratic class embellished with paintings, but the paintings of the Ajanta Caves are the most significant of the few survivals. Smaller scale painting in manuscripts was probably also practised in this period, though the earliest survivals are from the medieval period. Mughal painting represented a fusion of the Persian miniature with older Indian traditions, and from the 17th century its style was diffused across Indian princely courts of all religions, each developing a local style. Company paintings were made for British clients under the British raj, which from the 19th century also introduced art schools along Western lines, leading to modern Indian painting, which is increasingly returning to its Indian roots.

Indian paintings provide an aesthetic continuum that extends from the early civilisation to the present day. From being essentially religious in purpose in the beginning, Indian painting has evolved over the years to become a fusion of various cultures and traditions.

Shadanga of Indian painting

Around the 1st century BC the *Shadanga* or Six Limbs of Indian Painting, were evolved, a series of canons laying down the main principles of the art. Vatsyayana, who lived during the third century A.D., enumerates these in his Kamasutra having extracted them from still more ancient works.

These 'Six Limbs' have been translated as follows:

1. *Rupabheda* The knowledge of appearances.
2. *Pramanam* Correct perception, measure and structure.
3. *Bhava* Action of feelings on forms.
4. *Lavanya Yojanam* Infusion of grace, artistic representation.
5. *Sadrisyam* Similitude.
6. *Varnikabhanga* Artistic manner of using the brush and colours. (Tagore.)

The subsequent development of painting by the Buddhists indicates that these ' Six Limbs ' were put into practice by Indian artists, and are the basic principles on which their art was founded.

Figure 157: *Painting of Mysore style during Tippu Sultan period*

Genres of Indian painting

Indian paintings can be broadly classified as murals and miniatures. Murals are large works executed on the walls of solid structures, as in the Ajanta Caves and the Kailashnath temple. Miniature paintings are executed on a very small scale for books or albums on perishable material such as paper and cloth. The Palas of Bengal were the pioneers of miniature painting in India. The art of miniature painting reached its glory during the Mughal period. The tradition of miniature paintings was carried forward by the painters of different Rajasthani schools of painting like the Bundi, Kishangarh, Jaipur, Marwar and Mewar. The Ragamala paintings also belong to this

school, as does the Company painting produced for British clients under the British Raj.

Ancient Indian art has seen the rise of the Bengal School of art in 1930s followed by many forms of experimentations in European and Indian styles. In the aftermath of India's independence, many new genres of art developed by important artists like Jamini Roy, M. F. Husain, Francis Newton Souza, and Vasudeo S. Gaitonde. With the progress of the economy the forms and styles of art also underwent many changes. In the 1990s, Indian economy was liberalised and integrated to the world economy leading to the free flow of cultural information within and without. Artists include Subodh Gupta, Atul Dodiya,

Figure 158: *A mural painting depicting a scene from Mahajanaka Jataka, Cave 1, Ajanta*

Devajyoti Ray, Bose Krishnamachari and Jitish Kahllat whose works went for auction in international markets. Bharti Dayal has chosen to handle the traditional Mithila painting in most contemporary way and created her own style through the exercises of her own imagination, they appear fresh and unusual.

Murals

The history of Indian murals starts in ancient and early medieval times, from the 2nd century BC to 8th – 10th century AD. There are known more than 20 locations around India containing murals from this period, mainly natural caves and rock-cut chambers. The highest achievements of this time are the caves of Ajanta, Bagh, Sittanavasal, Armamalai Cave (Tamil Nadu), Ravan Chhaya rock shelter, Kailasanatha temple in Ellora Caves.

Murals from this period depict mainly religious themes of Buddhist, Jain and Hindu religions. There are though also locations where paintings were made to adorn mundane premises, like the ancient theatre room in Jogimara Cave and possible royal hunting lodge circa 7th-century AD – Ravan Chhaya rock shelter.

The pattern of large scale wall painting which had dominated the scene, witnessed the advent of miniature paintings during the 11th and 12th centuries. This new style figured first in the form of illustrations etched on palm-leaf manuscripts. The contents of these manuscripts included literature on Buddhism and Jainism. In eastern India, the principal centres of artistic and intellectual activities of the Buddhist religion were Nalanda, Odantapuri, Vikramshila and Somarpura situated in the Pala kingdom (Bengal and Bihar).

Eastern India painting

In eastern India miniature painting developed in the 10th century. These miniatures, depicting Buddhist divinities and scenes from the life of Buddha were painted on the leaves (about 2.25 by 3 inches) of the palm-leaf manuscripts as well as their wooden covers. Most common Buddhist illustrated manuscripts include the texts *Astasahasrika Prajnaparamita*,[382] *Pancharaksa*, *Karandavyuha* and *Kalachakra Tantra*. The earliest extant miniatures are found in a manuscript of the *Astasahasrika Prajnaparamita* dated in the sixth regnal year of Mahipala (c. 993), presently the possession of The Asiatic Society, Kolkata. This style disappeared from India in the late 12th century.

Influences in foreign arts

The influence of eastern Indian paintings can be seen in various Buddhist temples in Bagan, Myanmar particularly Abeyadana temple which was named after Queen consort of Myanmar, Abeyadana who herself had Indian roots and Gubyaukgyi Temple. The influences of eastern Indian paintings can also be clearly observed in Tibetan Thangka paintings.

Western Indian Miniature Painting

Miniature paintings are beautiful handmade paintings, which are quite colorful but small in size. The highlight of these paintings is the intricate and delicate brushwork, which lends them a unique identity. The colors are handmade, from minerals, vegetables, precious stones, indigo, conch shells, pure gold and silver. The evolution of Indian Miniatures paintings started in the Western Himalayas, around the 17th century

The subjects of these miniature paintings are in relation to the subjects of the manuscripts mostly religious and literary. Many paintings are from Sanskrit and folk literature. It is on the subject of love stories. Some paintings from Vaishnav sect of Hindu religion and some are from Jain sect. The Paintings of Vaishnav sect are regarding various occasions of the life of Lord Krishna and

Gopies. Vaishnav paintings of "Gita Govinda" is about Lord Krishna. The paintings of Jain sect is concerning to Jain Lords and religious subjects.

These paintings were created on "Taadpatra" that means the leaf of the palm tree, and Paper. During that period earlier manuscripts were created from the leaf of the palm tree and later on from the paper.

In these paintings there are very few human characters with front face are seen. Most of the human characters are seen with side profile. Big eyes, pointed nose and slim waist are the features of these paintings. The skin colours of human being are Brown and fair. The skin colour of the Lord Krishna is Blue. The colour of the hair and eyes is black. Women characters have long hair. Human characters have worn jewellery on the hand, nose, neck, hair, waist and ankles. Men and women wear the traditional Indian dress, slippers and shoes. Men wear turbans on their head. In these paintings trees, rivers, flowers, birds, the land, the sky, houses, traditional chairs, cushions, curtains, lamps, and human characters have been painted.

Mostly Natural colours have been used in these paintings. Black, red, white, brown, blue, and yellow colours are used to decorate the paintings.

The Kings, Courtiers of the kings, wealthy businessmen, and religious leaders of the time were the promoters of these miniature paintings.

Painters of these pictures were from the local society." Vaachhak " was the famous painter of the time.Painters tried to make the subject of the manuscript live by these pictures so that the readers of the manuscript can enjoy reading.

Malwa, Deccan and Jaunpur schools of painting

A new trend in manuscript illustration was set by a manuscript of the *Nimat-nama* painted at Mandu, during the reign of Nasir Shah (1500–1510). This represent a synthesis of the indigenous and the patronized Persian style, though it was the latter which dominated the Mandu manuscripts.Wikipedia:Citation needed There was another style of painting known as Lodi Khuladar that flourished in the Sultanate's dominion of North India extending from Delhi to Jaunpur.Wikipedia:Citation needed

The miniature painting style, which flourished initially in the Bahmani court and later in the courts of Ahmadnagar, Bijapur and Golkonda is popularly known as the Deccan school of Painting.Wikipedia:Citation needed One of the earliest surviving paintings are found as the illustrations of a manuscript *Tarif-i-Hussain Shahi* (c.1565), which is now in Bharata Itihasa Samshodhaka Mandala, Pune. About 400 miniature paintings are found in the manuscript of Nujum-ul-Ulum (Stars of Science) (1570), kept in Chester Beatty Library, Dublin.

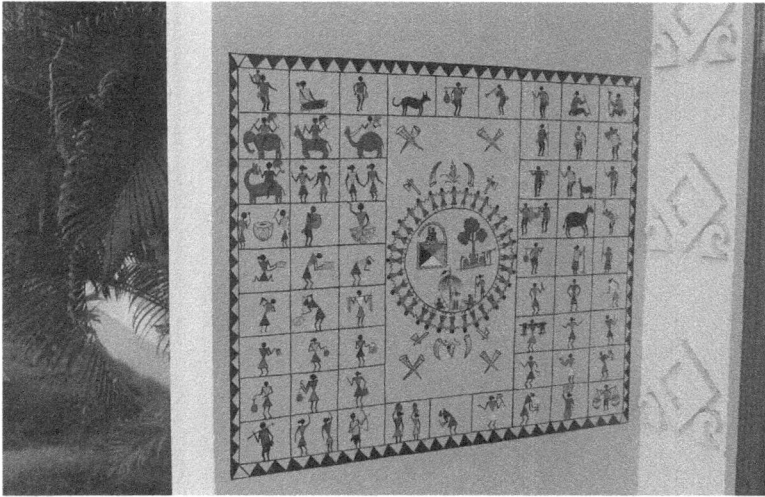

Figure 159: *Wall painting at AP Museum in Amaravathi*

Mughal painting

Mughal painting is a particular style of Indian painting, generally confined to illustrations on the book and done in miniatures, and which emerged, developed and took shape during the period of the Mughal Empire 16th –19th centuries.

Mughal paintings were a unique blend of Indian, Persian and Islamic styles. Because the Mughal kings wanted visual records of their deeds as hunters and conquerors, their artists accompanied them on military expeditions or missions of state, or recorded their prowess as animal slayers, or depicted them in the great dynastic ceremonies of marriages.

Akbar's reign (1556–1605) ushered a new era in Indian miniature painting. After he had consolidated his political power, he built a new capital at Fatehpur Sikri where he collected artists from India and Persia. He was the first monarch who established in India an atelier under the supervision of two Persian master artists, Mir Sayyed Ali and Abdus Samad. Earlier, both of them had served under the patronage of Humayun in Kabul and accompanied him to India when he regained his throne in 1555. More than a hundred painters were employed, most of whom were Hindus from Gujarat, Gwalior and Kashmir, who gave a birth to a new school of painting, popularly known as the Mughal School of miniature Paintings.

One of the first productions of that school of miniature painting was the Hamzanama series, which according to the court historian, Badayuni, was

Figure 160: *A 17th-century Mughal painting*

Figure 161: *A folio from the Hamzanama*

Figure 162: *An 18th-century Rajput painting by the artist Nihâl Chand*

started in 1567 and completed in 1582. The Hamzanama, stories of Amir Hamza, an uncle of the Prophet, were illustrated by Mir Sayyid Ali. The paintings of the Hamzanama are of large size, 20 x 27" and were painted on cloth. They are in the Persian safavi style. Brilliant red, blue and green colours predominate; the pink, eroded rocks and the vegetation, planes and blossoming plum and peach trees are reminiscent of Persia. However, Indian tones appear in later work, when Indian artists were employed.

After him, Jahangir encouraged artists to paint portraits and durbar scenes. His most talented portrait painters were Ustad Mansur, Abul Hasan and Bishandas.

Shah Jahan (1627–1658) continued the patronage of painting. Some of the famous artists of the period were Mohammad Faqirullah Khan, Mir Hashim, Muhammad Nadir, Bichitr, Chitarman, Anupchhatar, Manohar and Honhar.

Aurangzeb had no taste for fine arts. Due to lack of patronage artists migrated to Hyderabad in the Deccan and to the Hindu states of Rajasthan in search of new patrons.

Rajput painting

Rajput painting, a style of Indian painting, evolved and flourished, during the 18th century, in the royal courts of Rajputana, India. Each Rajput kingdom evolved a distinct style, but with certain common features. Rajput paintings depict a number of themes, events of epics like the Ramayana and the Mahabharata, Krishna's life, beautiful landscapes, and humans. Miniatures were the preferred medium of Rajput painting, but several manuscripts also contain Rajput paintings, and paintings were even done on the walls of palaces, inner chambers of the forts, havelies, particularly, the havelis of Shekhawati.

The colours extracted from certain minerals, plant sources, conch shells, and were even derived by processing precious stones, gold and silver were used. The preparation of desired colours was a lengthy process, sometimes taking weeks. Brushes used were very fine.

Mysore painting

Mysore painting is an important form of classical South Indian painting that originated in the town of Mysore in Karnataka. These paintings are known for their elegance, muted colours and attention to detail. The themes for most of these paintings are Hindu Gods and Goddesses and scenes from Hindu mythology. In modern times, these paintings have become a much sought-after souvenir during festive occasions in South India.

The process of making a Mysore painting involves many stages. The first stage involves the making of the preliminary sketch of the image on the base. The base consists of cartridge paper pasted on a wooden base. A paste made of zinc oxide and arabic gum is made called "gesso paste". With the help of a thin brush all the jewellery and parts of throne or the arch which have some relief are painted over to give a slightly raised effect of carving. This is allowed to dry. On this thin gold foil is pasted. The rest of the drawing is then painted using watercolours. Only muted colours are used.

Tanjore painting

Tanjore painting is an important form of classical South Indian painting native to the town of Tanjore in Tamil Nadu. The art form dates back to the early 9th century, a period dominated by the Chola rulers, who encouraged art and literature. These paintings are known for their elegance, rich colours, and attention to detail. The themes for most of these paintings are Hindu Gods and Goddesses and scenes from Hindu mythology. In modern times, these paintings have become a much sought-after souvenir during festive occasions in South India.

The process of making a Tanjore painting involves many stages. The first stage involves the making of the preliminary sketch of the image on the base. The base consists of a cloth pasted over a wooden base. Then chalk powder or zinc oxide is mixed with water-soluble adhesive and apply it on the base. To make

Figure 163: *Tanjore style painting depicting the ten Sikh Gurus with Bhai Bala and Bhai Mardana.*

the base smoother, a mild abrasive is sometimes used. After the drawing is made, decoration of the jewelry and the apparels in the image is done with semi-precious stones. Laces or threads are also used to decorate the jewelry. On top of this, the gold foils are pasted. Finally, dyes are used to add colours to the figures in the paintings.

Kangra painting

This style originated in Guler State, in the first half of the 18th century and reached its zenith during the reign of Maharaja Sansar Chand Katoch.

Madhubani painting

Madhubani painting is a style of painting, practised in the Mithila region of Bihar state. Themes revolve around Hindu Gods and mythology, along with scenes from the royal court and social events like weddings. Generally no space is left empty; the gaps are filled by paintings of flowers, animals, birds, and even geometric designs.In this paintings, artists use leaves, herbs, and flowers to make the colour which is used to draw the paintings.

Pattachitra

Pattachitra refers to the Classical painting of West Bengal and Odisha, in the eastern region of India.'Patta' in Sanskrit means 'Vastra' or 'clothings' and 'chitra' means paintings.

<templatestyles src="Multiple_image/styles.css" />

Patachitra of Naya village

Patachitra of Naya village

Goddess Durga and his family in Medinipur Patachitra

Manasa in Kalighat Patachitra

The Bengal Patachitra

The Bengal Patachitra refers to the painting of West Bengal. It is a traditional and mythological heritage of West Bengal. The Bengal Patachitra is divided into some different aspects like **Durga Pat**, *Chalchitra*, *Tribal Patachitra*, *Medinipur Patachitra*, Kalighat Patachitra etc. The subject matter of Bengal Patachitra is mostly mythological, religious stories, folk lore and social. The Kalighat Patachitra, the last tradition of Bengal Patachitra is developed by Jamini Roy. The artist of the Bengal Patachitra is called Patua.[383]

The tradition of Orisha Pattachitra is closely linked with the worship of Lord Jagannath. Apart from the fragmentary evidence of paintings on the caves

Figure 164: *Gita Govinda depicted in Pattachitra*

of Khandagiri and Udayagiri and Sitabhinji murals of the Sixth century A.D., the earliest indigenous paintings from Odisha are the Pattachitra done by the Chitrakars (the painters are called Chitrakars). The theme of Oriya painting centres round the Vaishnava sect. Since beginning of Pattachitra culture Lord Jagannath who was an incarnation of Lord Krishna was the major source of inspiration. The subject matter of Patta Chitra is mostly mythological, religious stories and folk lore. Themes are chiefly on Lord Jagannath and Radha-Krishna, different "Vesas" of Jagannath, Balabhadra and Subhadra, temple activities, the ten incarnations of Vishnu basing on the 'Gita Govinda' of Jayadev, Kama Kujara Naba Gunjara, Ramayana, Mahabharata. The individual paintings of gods and goddesses are also being painted.The painters use vegetable and mineral colours without going for factory made poster colours. They prepare their own colours. White colour is made from the conch-shells by powdering, boiling and filtering in a very hazardous process. It requires a lot of patience. But this process gives brilliance and premanence to the hue. 'Hingula', a mineral colour, is used for red. 'Haritala', king of stone ingredients for yellow, 'Ramaraja' a sort of indigo for blue are being used. Pure lamp-black or black prepared from the burning of cocoanut shells are used.The brushes that are used by these 'Chitrakaras' are also indigenous and are made of hair of domestic animals. A bunch of hair tied to the end of a bamboo stick make the brush. It is really a matter of wonder as to how these painters bring out lines of such precision and finish with the help of these crude brushes. That

Figure 165: *Bharat Mata by Abanindranath Tagore (1871–1951), a nephew of the poet Rabindranath Tagore, and a pioneer of the movement*

old tradition of Oriya painting still survives to-day in the skilled hands of Chitrakaras (traditional painters) in Puri, Raghurajpur, Paralakhemundi, Chikiti and Sonepur.

Bengal school

The Bengal School of Art was an influential style of art that flourished in India during the British Raj in the early 20th century. It was associated with Indian nationalism, but was also promoted and supported by many British arts administrators.

The Bengal school arose as an avant garde and nationalist movement reacting against the academic art styles previously promoted in India, both by Indian artists such as Ravi Varma and in British art schools. Following the widespread influence of Indian spiritual ideas in the West, the British art teacher Ernest Binfield Havel attempted to reform the teaching methods at the Calcutta School of Art by encouraging students to imitate Mughal miniatures. This caused immense controversy, leading to a strike by students and complaints from the local press, including from nationalists who considered it to be a retrogressive move. Havel was supported by the artist Abanindranath Tagore, a nephew

Figure 166: *Bengal Women, painted around 1950 by Manishi Dey*

of the poet Rabindranath Tagore. Tagore painted a number of works influenced by Mughal art, a style that he and Havel believed to be expressive of India's distinct spiritual qualities, as opposed to the "materialism" of the West. Abanindranath Tagore's best-known painting, *Bharat Mata* (Mother India), depicted a young woman, portrayed with four arms in the manner of Hindu deities, holding objects symbolic of India's national aspirations. Tagore later attempted to develop links with Far-Eastern artists as part of an aspiration to construct a pan-Asianist model of art. Those associated with this Indo-FarEastern model included Nandalal Bose, Mukul Dey, Kalipada Ghoshal, Benode Behari Mukherjee, Vinayak Shivaram Masoji, B.C. Sanyal, Beohar Rammanohar Sinha, and subsequently their students A. Ramachandran, Tan Yuan Chameli, Ramananda Bandopadhyay and a few others.

The Bengal school's influence on Indian art scene gradually started alleviating with the spread of modernist ideas post-independence.K. G. Subramanyan's role in this movement is significant.

Contextual Modernism

The term Contextual Modernism that Siva Kumar used in the catalogue of the exhibition has emerged as a postcolonial critical tool in the understanding of the art the Santiniketan artists had practised.

Several terms including Paul Gilroy's *counter culture of modernity* and Tani Barlow's *Colonial modernity* have been used to describe the kind of alternative modernity that emerged in non-European contexts. Professor Gall argues that 'Contextual Modernism' is a more suited term because "the colonial in *colonial modernity* does not accommodate the refusal of many in colonised situations to internalise inferiority. Santiniketan's artist teachers' refusal of subordination incorporated a counter vision of modernity, which sought to correct the racial and cultural essentialism that drove and characterised imperial Western modernity and modernism. Those European modernities, projected through a triumphant British colonial power, provoked nationalist responses, equally problematic when they incorporated similar essentialisms."[384]

According to R. Siva Kumar "The Santiniketan artists were one of the first who consciously challenged this idea of modernism by opting out of both internationalist modernism and historicist indigenousness and tried to create a context sensitive modernism." He had been studying the work of the Santiniketan masters and thinking about their approach to art since the early 80s. The practice of subsuming Nandalal Bose, Rabindranath Tagore, Ram Kinker Baij and Benode Behari Mukherjee under the Bengal School of Art was, according to Siva Kumar, misleading. *This happened because early writers were guided by genealogies of apprenticeship rather than their styles, worldviews, and perspectives on art practice.*

The literary critic Ranjit Hoskote while reviewing the works of contemporary artist Atul Dodiya writes, "The exposure to Santinketan, through a literary detour, opened Dodiya's eyes to the historical circumstances of what the art historian R Siva Kumar has called a "contextual modernism" developed in eastern India in the 1930s and '40s during the turbulent decades of the global Depression, the Gandhian liberation struggle, the Tagorean cultural renaissance and World War II."

Contextual Modernism in the recent past has found its usage in other related fields of studies, specially in Architecture.

Vernacular Indian Painting

Vernacular art is an art alive (contemporary art), based on the past (the mythes, the traditions and the religion) and made by defined groups. Vernacular art is based on the collective memory of this group.

Examples of Vernacular Indian Painting:

Tribal Painting:

- Bhil painting
- Warli painting
- Gond painting
- Santhal painting
- Saora painting
- Kurumba painting

Rural Painting:

- Pattachitra painting
- Madhubani painting
- Kalamkari painting
- Kolam painting
- Kalam painting
- Mandana Paintings

Modern Indian Painting

During the colonial era, Western influences started to make an impact on Indian art. Some artists developed a style that used Western ideas of composition, perspective and realism to illustrate Indian themes. Others, like Jamini Roy, consciously drew inspiration from folk art.Bharti Dayal has chosen to handle the traditional Mithila Painting in most contemporary way and uses both realism as well abstractionism in her work with a lot of fantasy mixed in to both .Her work has an impeccable sense of balance, harmony and grace.

By the time of Independence in 1947, several schools of art in India provided access to modern techniques and ideas. Galleries were established to showcase these artists. Modern Indian art typically shows the influence of Western styles, but is often inspired by Indian themes and images. Major artists are beginning to gain international recognition, initially among the Indian diaspora, but also among non-Indian audiences.

The Progressive Artists' Group, established shortly after India became independent in 1947, was intended to establish new ways of expressing India in the post-colonial era. The founders were six eminent artists – K. H. Ara, S. K. Bakre, H. A. Gade, M.F. Husain, S.H. Raza and F. N. Souza, though the group was dissolved in 1956, it was profoundly influential in changing the idiom of Indian art. Almost all India's major artists in the 1950s were associated with the group. Some of those who are well-known today are Bal Chabda, Manishi Dey, V. S. Gaitonde, Krishen Khanna, Ram Kumar, Tyeb Mehta, Beohar Rammanohar Sinha and Akbar Padamsee. Other famous painters like Jahar Dasgupta, Prokash Karmakar, John Wilkins, and Bijon Choudhuri enriched the art culture of India. They have become the icon of modern Indian art. Art historians like Prof. Rai Anand Krishna have also referred to those works of modern artistes that reflect Indian ethos.

Also, the increase in the discourse about Indian art, in English as well as vernacular Indian languages, appropriated the way art was perceived in the art schools. Critical approach became rigorous, critics like Geeta Kapur, R . Siva Kumar,[385] contributed to re-thinking contemporary art practice in India.Their voices represented Indian art not only in India but across the world. The critics also had an important role as curators of important exhibitions, re-defining modernism and Indian-art.

Indian Art got a boost with the economic liberalisation of the country since the early 1990s. Artists from various fields now started bringing in varied styles of work. Post-liberalisation Indian art thus works not only within the confines of academic traditions but also outside it. In this phase, artists have introduced even newer concepts which have hitherto not been seen in Indian art. Devajyoti Ray has introduced a new genre of art called Pseudorealism. Pseudorealist

Art is an original art style that has been developed entirely on the Indian soil. Pseudorealism takes into account the Indian concept of abstraction and uses it to transform regular scenes of Indian life into a fantastic images.

In post-liberalisation India, many artists have established themselves in the international art market like Anish Kapoor and Chintan whose mammoth artworks have acquired attention for their sheer size. Many art houses and galleries have also opened in USA and Europe to showcase Indian artworks.Some artists like chiman dangi(painter, printmaker) Bhupat Dudi, Subodh Gupta, Piu Sarkar, Vagaram Choudhary, Amitava Sengupta and many others have done magic worldwide.Chhaya Ghosh is a gifted painter, and is pretty active in Triveni Art Gallery, New Delhi.

Gallery

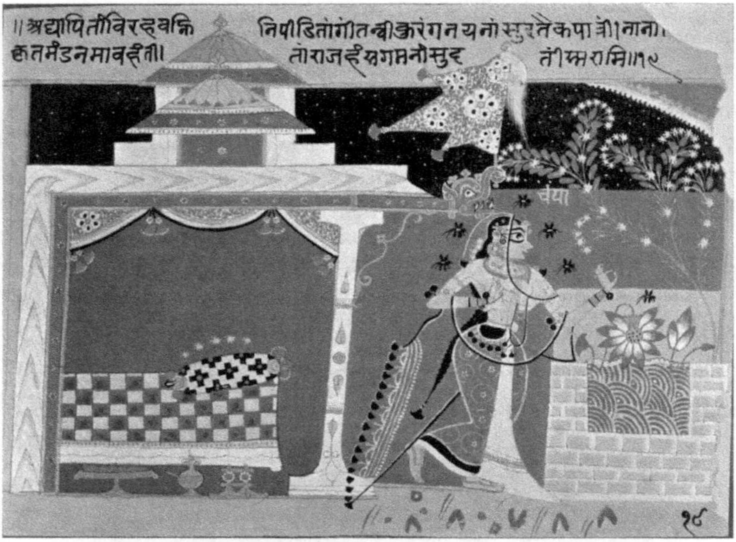

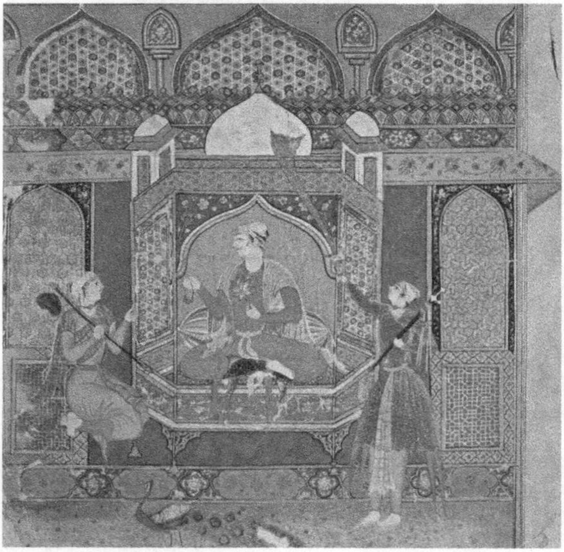

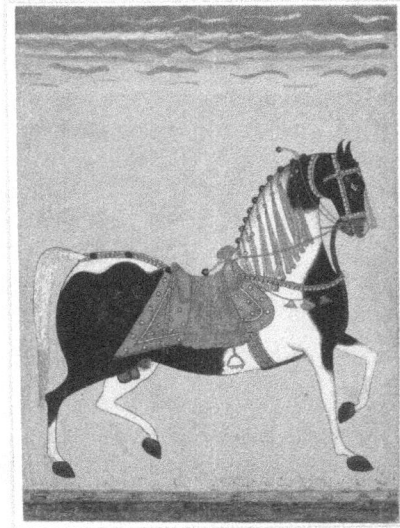

Some notable Indian paintings

- Hemen Majumdar's "Lady with the Lamp"
- Sudip Roy's "Charulata Series"
- Rabindranath Tagore's "Self portrait"
- Abanindranath Tagore's Bharat Mata
- Raja Ravi Varma's Shakuntala
- Ramkinkar Baij's "Jakkha 0 Jakkhi"
- Bikash Bhattacharjee's "Doll-series"
- Geeta Vadhera's Jogia "Dhoop series"
- Jahar Dasgupta's "Confrontation"
- MF Hussain's "Horses-series"
- Jamini Roy's "Jesus"
- John Wilkins's "Gossip",
- Rakesh Vijay "Persian and Mogul styles"
- Jainul Abedin's "Series on Bengal Famine"
- Sunil Das's "Bull Series"
- Devajyoti Ray's "In Despair"
- Tyeb Mehta's "Mahisasur"
- B. G. Sharma's Krishna miniatures
- ShakthiDass's
- Amrita-Sher-Gil
- M. Narayan's "Indian Ethnic" "Horses" Mother Teresa"

Further reading

- Havell, E. B. (1908). *Indian sculpture and painting*[386]. John Murray, London.<templatestyles src="Module:Citation/CS1/styles.css"></templatestyles>
- Coomaraswamy, Ananda K. (1914). *Viśvakarmā ; examples of Indian architecture, sculpture, painting, handicraft*[387]. London.<templatestyles src="Module:Citation/CS1/styles.css"></templatestyles>
- Havell, E. B. (1920). *A Handbook of Indian Art*[388]. John Murray, London.<templatestyles src="Module:Citation/CS1/styles.css"></templatestyles>
- *Indian Painting*, by Percy Brown. Published by Y. M. C. A. publishing house, 1960.
- *Indian Painting*, by Philip S. Rawson. Published by P.Tisné, 1961.
- *Indian Painting: The Scene, Themes, and Legends*, by Mohindar Singh Randhawa, John Kenneth Galbraith. Published by Houghton Mifflin, 1968.
- *Indian Painting*, by Douglas E. Barrett, Basil Gray. Published by Skira, 1978. <templatestyles src="Module:Citation/CS1/styles.css" />ISBN 0-8478-0160-8.
- Kossak, Steven. (1997). *Indian court painting, 16th–19th century.*[389] Metropolitan Museum of Art. <templatestyles src="Module:Citation/CS1/styles.css" />ISBN 0-87099-783-1
- Lerner, Martin (1984). The flame and the lotus: Indian and Southeast Asian art from the Kronos collections[390]. New York: The Metropolitan Museum of Art. ISBN 0-87099-374-7.<templatestyles src="Module:Citation/CS1/styles.css"></templatestyles>
- *A History of Indian Painting: The Modern Period*[391] by Krishna Chaitanya. Published by Abhinav Publications, 1994. <templatestyles src="Module:Citation/CS1/styles.css" />ISBN 81-7017-310-8.
- Ramayana by Valmiki illustrated with Indian miniatures from the 16th to the 19th century[392], Diane de Selliers Publisher, 2011, <templatestyles src="Module:Citation/CS1/styles.css" />ISBN 978-2-903656-76-8
- Welch, Stuart Cary (1985). India: art and culture, 1300-1900[393]. New York: The Metropolitan Museum of Art. ISBN 978-0-944142-13-4.<templatestyles src="Module:Citation/CS1/styles.css"></templatestyles>

External links

> Wikimedia Commons has media related to *Paintings from India*.

- Indian State Traditional Paintings[394]
- Miniature Painting[395], Wall paintings[396], and modern Indian painting[397], Indian Government, Centre for Cultural Resources and Training
- Archaeological Survey of India[398]
- Mithila Paintings or Madhubani Paintings[399]
- [400]

Online exhibits

- Metmuseum.org[401]

Sculpture in India

Sculpture in the Indian subcontinent

The first known **sculpture in the Indian subcontinent** is from the Indus Valley civilization (3300–1700 BC). These include the famous small bronze female dancer. However such figures in bronze and stone are rare and greatly outnumbered by pottery figurines and stone seals, often of animals or deities very finely depicted. After the collapse of the Indus Valley civilization there is little record of sculpture until the Buddhist era, apart from a hoard of copper figures of (somewhat controversially) c. 1500 BCE from Daimabad.[402] Thus the great tradition of Indian monumental sculpture in stone appears to begin relatively late, with the reign of Asoka from 270 to 232 BCE, and the Pillars of Ashoka he erected around India, carrying his edicts and topped by famous sculptures of animals, mostly lions, of which six survive.[403] Large amounts of figurative sculpture, mostly in relief, survive from Early Buddhist pilgrimage stupas, above all Sanchi; these probably developed out of a tradition using wood that also embraced Hinduism.[404]

During the 2nd to 1st century BCE in far northern India, in the Greco-Buddhist art of Gandhara from what is now southern Afghanistan and northern Pakistan, sculptures became more explicit, representing episodes of the Buddha's life and teachings. Although India had a long sculptural tradition and a mastery of rich iconography, the Buddha was never represented in human form before this time, but only through some of his symbols. This may be because Gandharan Buddhist sculpture in modern Afghanistan displays Greek and Persian artistic influence. Artistically, the Gandharan school of sculpture is said to have contributed wavy hair, drapery covering both shoulders, shoes and sandals, acanthus leaf decorations, etc.

The pink sandstone Hindu, Jain and Buddhist sculptures of Mathura from the 1st to 3rd centuries CE reflected both native Indian traditions and the Western influences received through the Greco-Buddhist art of Gandhara, and effectively established the basis for subsequent Indian religious sculpture. The style

Figure 167: *Jain figure of tirthankara Suparshvanatha, 14th century, marble*

Figure 168: *Bronze Vishnu*

Figure 169: *One of the first representations of the Buddha, 1st-2nd century CE, Gandhara*

Figure 170: *The Konark Sun Temple Konark Sun Temple, is a World Heritage Site and It is also featured on various lists of Seven Wonders of India.*

Figure 171: *Shrine with Four Jinas- Rishabhanatha, Parshvanatha, Neminatha, and Mahavira, 6th century*

Figure 172: *The Colossal trimurti at the Elephanta Caves*

Figure 173: *The iconic 57 ft high monolithic Statue of Gommateshwara, Shravanabelagola, 10th Century*

was developed and diffused through most of India under the Gupta Empire (c. 320-550) which remains a "classical" period for Indian sculpture, covering the earlier Ellora Caves,[405] though the Elephanta Caves are probably slightly later.[406] Later large scale sculpture remains almost exclusively religious, and generally rather conservative, often reverting to simple frontal standing poses for deities, though the attendant spirits such as apsaras and yakshi often have sensuously curving poses. Carving is often highly detailed, with an intricate backing behind the main figure in high relief. The celebrated bronzes of the Chola dynasty (c. 850–1250) from south India, many designed to be carried in processions, include the iconic form of Shiva as Nataraja,[407] with the massive granite carvings of Mahabalipuram dating from the previous Pallava dynasty.[408]

Figure 174: *The "dancing girl of Mohenjo Daro", 3rd millennium BCE (replica)*

Figure 175: *Ashoka Pillar, Vaishali, Bihar, c. 250 BCE*

Figure 176: *Torana or stupa gateway at Sanchi, c. 100 CE or perhaps earlier, with densely packed reliefs*

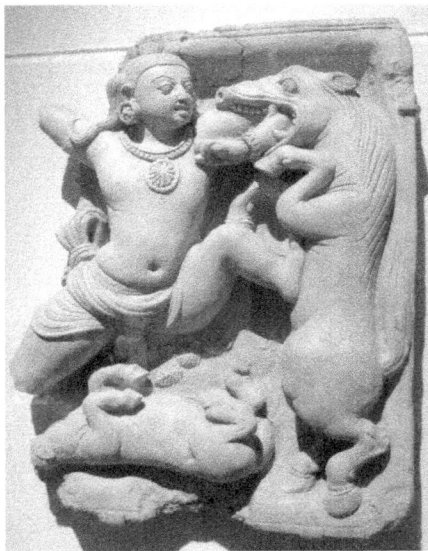

Figure 177: *Hindu Gupta terracotta relief, 5th century CE, of Krishna Killing the Horse Demon Keshi*

Figure 178: *Buddha from Sarnath, 5–6th century CE*

Figure 179: *Seated Ganesha, sandstone sculpture from Rajasthan, 9th century*

Figure 180: *Hindu, Chola period, 1000*

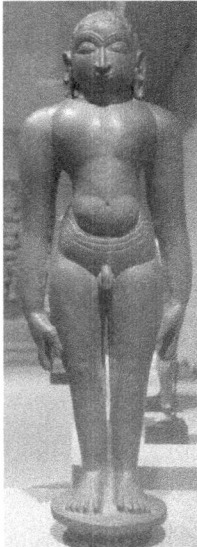

Figure 181: *'Jain Tirthankara', Mysore, India made of bronze with silver content, Honolulu Academy of Arts, 10th-11th century*

Figure 182: *Marble Sculpture of female yak-shi in typical curving pose, c. 1450, Rajasthan*

Figure 183: *Gopuram of the Thillai Nataraja Temple, Chidambaram, Tamil Nadu, densely packed with rows of painted statues*

Greco-Buddhist art

Greco-Buddhist art is the artistic manifestation of Greco-Buddhism, a cultural syncretism between the Classical Greek culture and Buddhism, which developed over a period of close to 1000 years in Central Asia, between the conquests of Alexander the Great in the 4th century BCE, and the Islamic conquests of the 7th century CE. Greco-Buddhist art is characterized by the strong idealistic realism of Hellenistic art and the first representations of the Buddha in human form, which have helped define the artistic (and particularly, sculptural) canon for Buddhist art throughout the Asian continent up to the present. Though dating is uncertain, it appears that strongly Hellenistic styles lingered in the East for several centuries after they had declined around the Mediterranean, as late as the 5th century CE. Some aspects of Greek art were adopted while others did not spread beyond the Greco-Buddhist area; in particular the standing figure, often with a relaxed pose and one leg flexed, and the flying cupids or victories, who became popular across Asia as apsaras. Greek foliage decration was also influential, with Indian versions of the Corinthian capital appearing.[409]

The origins of Greco-Buddhist art are to be found in the Hellenistic Greco-Bactrian kingdom (250 BCE – 130 BCE), located in today's Afghanistan, from which Hellenistic culture radiated into the Indian subcontinent with the establishment of the small Indo-Greek kingdom (180 BCE-10 BCE). Under the Indo-Greeks and then the Kushans, the interaction of Greek and Buddhist culture flourished in the area of Gandhara, in today's northern Pakistan, before spreading further into India, influencing the art of Mathura, and then the Hindu art of the Gupta empire, which was to extend to the rest of South-East Asia. The influence of Greco-Buddhist art also spread northward towards Central Asia, strongly affecting the art of the Tarim Basin and the Dunhuang Caves, and ultimately the sculpted figure in China, Korea, and Japan.[410]

Figure 184: *Gandhara frieze with devotees, holding plantain leaves, in purely Hellenistic style, inside Corinthian columns, 1st–2nd century CE. Buner, Swat, Pakistan. Victoria and Albert Museum*

Figure 185: *970 CE Muktesvara deula, Odisha*

Figure 186: *Fragment of the wind god Boreas, Hadda, Afghanistan.*

Figure 187: *Coin of Demetrius I of Bactria, who reigned circa 200–180 BC and invaded Northern India*

Figure 188: *Buddha head from Hadda, Afghanistan, 3rd–4th centuries*

Figure 189: *Gandhara Poseidon (Ancient Orient Museum)*

Figure 190: *The Buddhist gods Pancika (left)
and Hariti (right), 3rd century, Gandhara*

Figure 191: *Taller Buddha of Bamiyan, c. 547 AD., in 1963 and in 2008 after they were dynamited and destroyed in March 2001 by the Taliban*

Figure 192: *The Konark Sun Temple, is a World Heritage Site and It is also featured on NDTV's list of Seven Wonders of India and Times of India's list of Seven Wonders of India.*

Figure 193: *Statue from a Buddhist monastery 700 AD, Afghanistan*

Gallery

Figure 194: *Didarganj Yakshi Sandstone Sculpture (3rd Century BCE) Mauryan Art-Patna.*

Figure 195: *Chola bronzes*

Figure 196: *Chola bronzes*

Figure 197: *Shiva panel, Kailash Temple (Cave 16), Ellora.*

Figure 198: *Marble figure, Jaisalmer Jain Temple, Rajasthan, 12th Century*

Figure 199: *13th century Ganesha statue*

Figure 200: *Shiva and Uma 14th century*

Figure 201: *Bhudevi*

Figure 202: *Stone Inscription at ASI Museum, Amaravathi*

Figure 203: *Secular scenes*

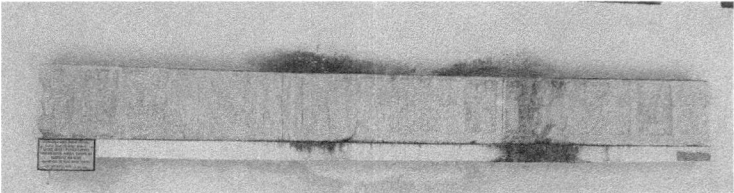

Figure 204: *Lintel Beam Model at ASI Museum, Amaravathi*

Figure 205: *Hindu Goddess*

References

Wikimedia Commons has media related to *Sculptures in India*.

- Boardman, John ed., *The Oxford History of Classical Art*, 1993, OUP, <templatestyles src="Module:Citation/CS1/styles.css" />ISBN 0198143869
- Harle, J.C., *The Art and Architecture of the Indian Subcontinent*, 2nd edn. 1994, Yale University Press Pelican History of Art, <templatestyles src="Module:Citation/CS1/styles.css" />ISBN 0300062176
- Paine, Robert Treat, in: Paine, R. T. & Soper A, *The Art and Architecture of Japan*, 3rd ed 1981, Yale University Press Pelican History of Art, <templatestyles src="Module:Citation/CS1/styles.css" />ISBN 0140561080
- Sickman, Laurence, in: Sickman L & Soper A, *The Art and Architecture of China*, Pelican History of Art, 3rd ed 1971, Penguin (now Yale History of Art), LOC 70-125675

Further reading

- Lerner, Martin (1984). The flame and the lotus: Indian and Southeast Asian art from the Kronos collections[411]. New York: The Metropolitan Museum of Art. ISBN 0870993747. Retrieved 2016-03-06.<templatestyles src="Module:Citation/CS1/styles.css"></templatestyles>
- Welch, Stuart Cary (1985). India: art and culture, 1300-1900][412]. New York: The Metropolitan Museum of Art. ISBN 9780944142134.<templatestyles src="Module:Citation/CS1/styles.css"></templatestyles>

Architecture of India

Architecture of India

The **architecture of India** is rooted in its history, culture and religion. Indian architecture progressed with time and assimilated the many influences that came as a result of India's global discourse with other regions of the world throughout its millennia-old past. The architectural methods practiced in India are a result of examination and implementation of its established building traditions and outside cultural interactions.[413]

Though old, this Eastern tradition has also incorporated modern values as India became a modern nation-state. The economic reforms of 1991 further bolstered the urban architecture of India as the country became more integrated with the world's economy. Traditional *Vastu Shastra* remains influential in India's architecture during the contemporary era.

Indus Valley Civilization (3300 BCE - 1700 BCE)

The Indus Valley Civilization (3300 BCE - 1700 BCE) covered a large area around the Indus River basin and beyond. In its mature phase, from about 2600 to 1900 BCE, it produced several cities marked by great uniformity within and between sites, including Harappa, Lothal, and the UNESCO World Heritage Site Mohenjo-daro. The civic and town planning and engineering aspects of these are remarkable, but the design of the buildings is "of a startling utilitarian character". There are granaries, drains, water-courses and tanks, but neither palaces nor temples have been identified, though cities have a central raised and fortified "citadel".[414] Mohenjo-daro has wells which may be the predecessors of the stepwell. As many as 700 wells have been discovered in just one section of the city, leading scholars to believe that 'cylindrical brick lined wells' were invented by the Indus Valley Civilization.[415]

Figure 206: *The Taj Mahal, the most famous building of Mughal architecture and possibly of Indian architecture as a whole.*

Figure 207: *Dholavira, one of the largest cities of Indus Valley Civilisation, with stepwell steps to reach the water level in artificially constructed reservoirs.*

The architectural decoration is extremely minimal, though there are "narrow pointed niches" inside some buildings. Most of the art found is in miniature forms like seals, and mainly in terracotta, but there are a very few larger sculptures of figures. In most sites fired mud-brick (not sun-baked as in Mesopotamia) is used exclusively as the building material, but a few such as Dholavira are in stone. Most houses have two stories, and very uniform sizes and plans. The large cities declined relatively quickly, for unknown reasons, leaving a less sophisticated village culture behind.[416]

Mahajanapadas (600 BCE—320 BCE)

Urban architecture

<templatestyles src="Multiple_image/styles.css" />

Conjectural reconstruction of the main gate of Kushinagar circa 500 BCE adapted from a relief at Sanchi.

City of Kushinagar in the 5th century BCE according to a 1st century BCE frieze in Sanchi Stupa 1 Southern Gate.

From the time of the Mahajanapadas (600 BCE—320 BCE), walled and moated cities with large gates and multi-storied buildings which consistently used arched windows and doors and made an intense use of wooden architecture, are important features of the architecture during this period. The reliefs of Sanchi, dated to the 1st centuries BCE-CE, show cities such as Kushinagar or Rajagriha as spendid walled cities during the time of the Buddha (5th century BCE), as in the *Royal cortege leaving Rajagriha* or *War over the Buddha's relics*. These views of ancient Indian cities have been relied on for the understanding of ancient Indian urban architecture. Archaeologically, this period corresponds in part to the Northern Black Polished Ware culture.[417] Geopolitically, the Achaemenid Empire started to occupy the northwestern part of the subcontinent from around 518 BCE.

Figure 208: *Jetavana of Sravasti, Sanchi Stupa 1, Northern Gateway.*

Various types of individual housing of the time of the Buddha (c. 563/480 or c. 483/400 BCE), resembling huts with chaitya-decorated doors, are also described in the reliefs of Sanchi. Particularly, the Jetavana at Sravasti, shows the three favourite residences of the Buddha: the Gandhakuti, the Kosambakuti and the Karorikuti, with the throne of the Buddha in the front of each. The Jetavana garden was presented to the Buddha by the rich banker Anathapindika, who purchased it for as many gold pieces as would cover the surface of the ground. Hence, the foreground of the relief is shown covered with ancient Indian coins (karshapanas), just as it is in the similar relief at Bharhut.[418] Although the reliefs of Sanchi are dated to the 1st century BCE/CE, portraying scene taking place during the time of the Buddha, four centuries before, they are considered as an important indication of building traditions in these early times.

Religious architecture

Buddhist caves

During the time of the Buddha (c. 563/480 or c. 483/400 BCE), Buddhist monks were also in the habit of using natural caves, such as the Saptaparni Cave, southwest from Rajgir, Bihar. Many believe it to be the site in which Buddha spent some time before his death,[419] and where the first Buddhist

Figure 209: *Jivakarama vihara monastery. Oblong communal hall (remains), 6th century BCE.*

council was held after the Buddha died (paranirvana). The Buddha himself had also used the Indrasala Cave for meditation, starting a tradition of using caves, natural or man-made, as religious retreats, that would last for over a millennium.[420]

Monasteries

The first monasteries, such as the Jivakarama vihara in Rajgir, Bihar, were built from the time of the Buddha, in the 6th or 5th centuries BCE.[421] The initial Jivakarama monastery was formed of two long parallel and oblong halls, large dormitories where the monks could eat and sleep, in conformity with the original regulations of the samgha, without any private cells. Other halls were then constructed, mostly long, oblong building as well, which remind of the construction of several of the Barabar caves. The Buddha is said to have been treated once in the monastery, after having been injured by Devadatta.

Stupas

Religious buildings in the form of the Buddhist stupa, a dome shaped monument, started to be used in India as commemorative monuments associated with storing sacred relics of the Buddha.[422] The relics of the Buddha were spread between eight stupas, in Rajagriha, Vaishali, Kapilavastu, Allakappa, Ramagrama, Pava, Kushinagar, and Vethapida. The Piprahwa stupa also seems to have been one of the first to be built. Guard rails —consisting of posts, crossbars, and a coping— became a feature of safety surrounding a stupa. The Buddha had left instructions about how to pay hommage to the stupas: "And whoever lays wreaths or puts sweet perfumes and colours there with a devout heart, will reap benefits for a long time".[423] This practice would lead to the decoration of the stupas with stone sculptures of flower garlands in the Classical period.

Figure 210: *Stupas at Piprahwa are some of the earliest surviving stupas.*

Classical period (320 BCE-550 CE)

Monumental stone architecture

The next wave of building, relying on the first examples of true stone architecture, appears with the start of the Classical period (320 BCE-550 CE) and the rise of the Mauryan Empire. The capital city of Pataliputra was an urban marvel described by the Greek ambassador Megasthenes. Remains of monumental stone architecture with a strong Achaemenid and Greek influence can be seen through numerous artifacts recovered from Pataliputra, such as the Pataliputra capital. This cross-fertilization between different art streams converging on the subcontinent produced new forms that, while retaining the essence of the past, succeeded in the integrating selected elements of the new influences.

The Indian emperor Ashoka (rule: 273—232 BCE) established the Pillars of Ashoka throughout his realm, generally next to Buddhist stupas. According to Buddhist tradition, Ashoka recovered the relics of the Buddha from the earlier stupas (except from the Ramagrama stupa), and erected 84.000 stupas to distribute the relics across India. In effect, many stupas are thought to date originally from the time of Ashoka, such as Sanchi or Kesariya, where he also erected pillars with his inscriptions, and possibly Bharhut, Amaravati or Dharmarajika in Gandhara.[424]

Figure 211: *The Pataliputra capital, discovered at the Bulandi Bagh site of Pataliputra, c. 4th-3rd BCE.*

Figure 212: *Ashoka pillar at Vaishali, 250 BCE.*

Ashoka also built the initial Mahabodhi temple in Bodh Gaya around the Bodhi tree, including masterpieces such as the Diamond throne ("Vajrasana"). He is also said to have established a chain of hospitals throughout the Mauryan empire by 230 BCE.[425] One of the edicts of Ashoka reads: "Everywhere King Piyadasi (Ashoka) erected two kinds of hospitals, hospitals for people and hospitals for animals. Where there were no healing herbs for people and animals, he ordered that they be bought and planted."[426] Indian art and culture has absorbed extraneous impacts by varying degrees and is much richer for this exposure.

Fortified cities with stūpas, *viharas*, and temples were constructed during the Maurya empire (c. 321–185 BCE).[427] Architectural creations of the Mauryan period, such as the city of Pataliputra, the Pillars of Ashoka, are outstanding in their achievements, and often compare favourably with the rest of the world at that time. Commenting on Mauryan sculpture, John Marshall once wrote about the "extraordinary precision and accuracy which characterizes all Mauryan works, and which has never, we venture to say, been surpassed even by the finest workmanship on Athenian buildings".[428,429]

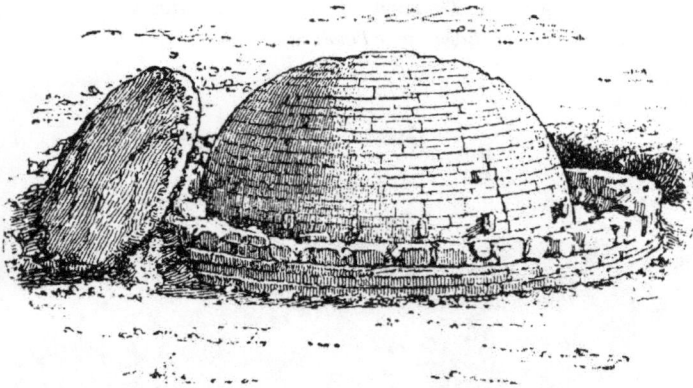

Figure 213: *An early stupa, 6 meters in diameter, with fallen umbrella on side. Chakpat, near Chakdara. Probably Maurya, 3rd century BCE.*

Figure 214: *Ruins of pillared hall at the Kumrahar site at Pataliputra.*

Figure 215: *Mauryan polished stone pillar from Pataliputra.*

Figure 216: *Capital of the Sarnath pillar of Ashoka. 250 BCE.*

Rock-cut caves

<templatestyles src="Multiple_image/styles.css" />

The famous carved door of Lomas Rishi, one of the Barabar Caves, dated
to approximately 250 BCE, displaying the first known Maurya reliefs.

> The quasi-perfect walls of the Barabar Caves were
> dug into the hard rock and polished to a mirror effect
> circa 250 BCE, date of the inscriptions of Ashoka.[430]

Around the same time rock-cut architecture began to develop, starting with the already highly sophisticated and state-sponsored Barabar caves in Bihar, personally dedicated by Ashoka circa 250 BCE. These artificial caves exhibit an amazing level of technical proficiency, the extremely hard granite rock being cut in geometrical fashion and polished to a mirror-like finish.

Probably owing to the 2nd century BCE fall of the Mauryan Empire and the subsequent persecutions of Buddhism under Pushyamitra Sunga, it is thought that many Buddhists relocated to the Deccan under the protection of the Andhra dynasty, thus shifting the cave-building effort to western India: an enormous effort at creating religious caves (usually Buddhist or Jain) continued there until the 2nd century CE, culminating with the Karla caves or the Pandavleni caves. These caves generally followed an apsidal plan with a stupa in the back fot the chaityas, and a rectangular plan with surrounding cells for the viharas. Numerous donors provided the funds for the building of these caves and left donatory inscriptions, including laity, members of the clergy, government officials, and even foreigners such as *Yavanas* (Greeks) representing about 8% of all inscriptions.[431]

The construction of caves would wane after the 2nd century CE, possibly due to the rise of Mahayana Buddhism and the associated intense architectural and artistic production in Gandhara and Amaravati. The building of rock-cut caves would revive briefly in the 5th century CE, with the magnificent achievements of Ajanta and Ellora, before finally subsiding as Hinduism replaced Buddhism in the sub-continent, and stand-alone temples became more prevalent.

Rock-cut architecture also developed with the apparition of stepwells in India, dating from 200–400 CE. Subsequently, the construction of wells at Dhank (550–625 CE) and stepped ponds at Bhinmal (850–950 CE) took place.[432]

Decorated stupas

Stupas were soon to be richly decorated with sculptural reliefs, following the first attempts at Sanchi Stupa No.2 (125 BCE). Full-fledged sculptural decorations and scenes of the life of the Buddha would soon follow at Bharhut (115 BCE), Bodh Gaya (60 BCE), Mathura (125-60 BCE), again at Sanchi for the elevation of the toranas (1st century BCE/CE) and then Amaravati (1st-2nd century CE).[433] The decorative embellishment of stupas also had a considerable development in the northwest in the area of Gandhara, with decorated stupas such as the Butkara Stupa ("monumentalized" with Hellenistic decorative elements from the 2nd century BCE)[434] or the Loriyan Tangai stupas

(2nd century CE). Stupa architecture was adopted in Southeast and East Asia, where it became prominent as a Buddhist monument used for enshrining sacred relics. The Indian gateway arches, the *torana*, reached East Asia with the spread of Buddhism.[435] Some scholars hold that *torii* derives from the torana gates at the Buddhist historic site of Sanchi (3rd century BCE – 11th century CE).[436]

Figure 217: *Sanchi Stupa No.2, the earliest known stupa with important displays of decorative reliefs, circa 125 BCE. UNIQ-ref-0-9c34fa5f9dcb4f28-QINU*

Figure 218: *The Great Stupa at Sanchi.*[413] *Decorated toranas built from the 1st c. BCE to the 1st c. CE.*

Figure 219: *Ashoka's Mahabodhi Temple and Diamond throne in Bodh Gaya, built circa 250 BCE. The inscription between the Chaitya arches reads: "Bhagavato Sakamunino/ bodho" ie 'The building round the Bodhi tree of the Holy Sakamuni (Shakyamuni)". Bharhut frieze (circa 100 BCE).*

Stand-alone temples

Temples —built on elliptical, circular, quadrilateral, or apsidal plans— were initially constructed using brick and timber. Some temples of timber with wattle-and-daub may have preceded them, but none remain to this day.

Circular temples

Some of the earliest free-standing temples may have been of a circular type, as the Bairat Temple in Bairat, Rajasthan, formed of a central stupa surrounded by a circular colonnade and an enclosing wall. It was built during the time of Ashoka, and near it were found two of Ashoka's Minor Rock Edicts.[437] Ashoka also built the Mahabodhi Temple in Bodh Gaya circa 250 BCE, also a circular structure, in order to protect the Bodhi tree under which the Buddha had found enlightenment. Representations of this early temple structure are found on a 100 BCE relief sculpted on the railing of the stupa at Bhārhut, as well as in Sanchi.[438] From that period the Diamond throne remains, an almost intact slab of sandstone decorated with reliefs, which Ashoka had established at the foot of the Bodhi tree.[439,440] These circular-type temples were also found in later rock-hewn caves such as Tulja Caves or Guntupalli.

Figure 220: *Remains of the circular Bairat Temple, circa 250 BCE. A stupa was located in the center.*

Figure 221: *Relief of a circular temple, Bharhut, circa 100 BCE.*

Figure 222: *Relief of a multi-storied temple, 2nd century CE, Ghantasala Stupa.*[441]

Apsidal temples

Another early free-standing temple in India, this time apsidal in shape, appears to be Temple 40 at Sanchi, which is also dated to the 3rd century BCE.[442] It was an apsidal temple built of timber on top of a high rectangular stone platform, 26.52x14x3.35 metres, with two flights of stairs to the east and the west. The temple was burnt down sometime in the 2nd century BCE. This type of apsidal structure was also adopted for most of the cave temple (Chaitya-grihas), as in the 3rd century BCE Barabar Caves and most caves thereafter, with side, and then frontal, entrances. A freestanding apsidal temple remains to this day, although in a modified form, in the Trivikrama Temple in Ter, Maharashtra.

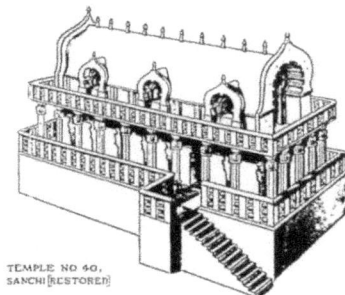

Figure 223: *Illustration of Temple 40 at Sanchi, dated to the 3rd century BCE.*

Figure 224: *Trivikrama Temple at Ter: an early Buddhist apsidal temple, in front of which was later added an Hindu square mandapa.*

Figure 225: *Chejarla apsidal temple, also later converted to Hinduism.*

Truncated pyramidal temples

<templatestyles src="Multiple_image/styles.css" />

The Mahabodhi Temple in 150-200 CE.

The Mahabodhi Temple: a stepped pyramid with round stupa on top.

It is thought that the temple in the shape of a truncated pyramid was derived from the design of the stepped stupas which had developed in Gandhara. The Mahabodhi Temple in Bodh Gaya is one such example, adapting the Gandharan design of a succession of steps with niches containing Buddha images, alternating with Greco-Roman pillars, as seen in the stupas of Jaulian.[443] The structure is crowned by the shape of an hemispherical stupa topped by finials, forming a logical elongation of the stepped Gandharan stupas.

Although the current structure of the Mahabdhodi Temple dates to the Gupta period (5th century CE), the "Plaque of Mahabhodi Temple", discovered in Kumrahar and dated to 150-200 CE based on its dated Kharoshthi inscriptions and combined finds of Huvishka coins, suggests that the pyramidal structure already existed in the 2nd century CE. This is confirmed by archaeological excavations in Bodh Gaya.

This truncated pyramid design also marked the evolution from the aniconic stupa dedicated to the cult of relics, to the iconic temple with multiple images of the Buddha and Bodhisattvas. This design was very influential in the development of later Hindu temples.[444]

Square prostyle temples

The Gupta Empire later also built Buddhist stand-alone temples (following the great cave temples of Indian rock-cut architecture), such as Temple 17 at Sanchi, dating to the early Gupta period (5th century CE). It consists of a flat roofed square sanctum with a portico and four pillars. From an architectural perspective, this is a tetrastyle prostyle temple of Classical appearance.[445] The interior and three sides of the exterior are plain and undecorated but the front and the pillars are elegantly carved, not unlike the 2nd century rock-cut cave temples of the Nasik caves. Nalanda and Valabhi universities, housing thousands of teachers and students, flourished between the 4th–8th centuries.[446]

Figure 226: *A Gupta period tetrastyle prostyle Buddhist temple of Classical appearance at Sanchi (Temple 17) (5th century CE).*

End of the Classical period

This period ends with the destructive invasions of the Alchon Huns in the 6th century CE. During the rule of the Hunnic king Mihirakula, over a thousand Buddhist monasteries throughout Gandhara are said to have been destroyed. The Chinese pilgrim Xuanzang, writing in 630 CE, explained that Mihirakula ordered the destruction of Buddhism and the expulsion of monks.[447] He reported that Buddhism had drastically declined, and that most of the monasteries were deserted and left in ruins.[448] The Buddhist art of Gandhara, in particular Greco-Buddhist art, becomes essentially extinct around that period. The invasions mark the beginning of the decline of Buddhism in India.

Although only spanning a few decades, the invasions had long-term effects on India, and in a sense brought an end to Classical India.[449] Soon after the invasions, the Gupta Empire, already weakened by these invasions and the rise of local rulers, ended as well.[450] Following the invasions, northern India was left in disarray, with numerous smaller Indian powers emerging after the crumbling of the Guptas.[451]

Figure 227: *Kailasa temple, Ellora, the largest rock-cut Hindu temple.*

Early Middle Ages (550 CE—1200 CE)

South Indian temple architecture—visible as a distinct tradition during the 7th century CE.[452]

Māru-Gurjara temple architecture originated somewhere in the sixth century in and around areas of Rajasthan. Māru-Gurjara Architecture shows the deep understanding of structures and refined skills of Rajasthani craftsmen of the bygone era. Māru-Gurjara Architecture has two prominent styles *Maha-Maru* and *Maru-Gurjara*. According to *M. A. Dhaky*, *Maha-Maru* style developed primarily in Marudesa, Sapadalaksha, *Surasena* and parts of *Uparamala* whereas *Maru-Gurjara* originated in Medapata, Gurjaradesa-Arbuda, Gurjaradesa-Anarta and some areas of Gujarat.[453] Scholars such as George Michell, M.A. Dhaky, Michael W. Meister and U.S. Moorti believe that *Māru-Gurjara Temple Architecture* is entirely *Western Indian* architecture and is quite different from the North Indian Temple architecture.[454] There is a connecting link between *Māru-Gurjara Architecture* and Hoysala Temple Architecture. In both of these styles architecture is treated sculpturally.[455] Regional styles include Architecture of Karnataka, Kalinga architecture, Dravidian architecture, Western Chalukya architecture, and Badami Chalukya Architecture.

Figure 228: *An aerial view of the Meenakshi Temple from the top of the southern gopuram, looking north. The temple was rebuilt by the Vijayanagar Empire and an example of Dravidian architecture.*

The South Indian temple consists essentially of a square-chambered sanctuary topped by a superstructure, tower, or spire and an attached pillared porch or hall (maṇḍapa or maṇṭapam), enclosed by a peristyle of cells within a rectangular court. The external walls of the temple are segmented by pilasters and carry niches housing sculpture. The superstructure or tower above the sanctuary is of the kūṭina type and consists of an arrangement of gradually receding stories in a pyramidal shape. Each story is delineated by a parapet of miniature shrines, square at the corners and rectangular with barrel-vault roofs at the centre.

North Indian temples showed increased elevation of the wall and elaborate spire by the 10th century.[456] Richly decorated temples—including the complex at Khajuraho—were constructed in Central India. Indian traders brought Indian architecture to South east Asia through various trade routes.[457] Grandeur of construction, beautiful sculptures, delicate carvings, high domes, gopuras and extensive courtyards were the features of temple architecture in India. Examples include the Lingaraj Temple at Bhubaneshwar in Odisha, Sun Temple at Konark in Odisha, Brihadeeswarar Temple at Thanjavur in Tamil Nadu.

Late Middle Ages (1100 CE—1526 CE)

Vijaynagara Architecture

Vijayanagara Architecture of the period (1336 – 1565 CE) was a notable building style evolved by the Vijayanagar empire that ruled most of South India from their capital at Vijayanagara on the banks of the Tungabhadra River in present-day Karnataka.[458] The architecture of the temples built during the reign of the Vijayanagara empire had elements of political authority.[459] This resulted in the creation of a distinctive imperial style of architecture which featured prominently not only in temples but also in administrative structures across the deccan.[460] The Vijayanagara style is a combination of the Chalukya,

Figure 229: *Qutub Minar at Delhi is the best example of Early Indo-Islamic Architecture*

Hoysala, Pandya and Chola styles which evolved earlier in the centuries when these empires ruled and is characterised by a return to the simplistic and serene art of the past.[461]

Hoysala Architecture

Hoysala architecture is the distinctive building style developed under the rule of the Hoysala Empire in the region historically known as *Karnata*, today's Karnataka, India, between the 11th and the 14th centuries.[462] Large and small temples built during this era remain as examples of the Hoysala architectural style, including the Chennakesava Temple at Belur, the Hoysaleswara Temple at Halebidu, and the Kesava Temple at Somanathapura. Other examples of fine Hoysala craftmanship are the temples at Belavadi, Amrithapura, and Nuggehalli. Study of the Hoysala architectural style has revealed a negligible Indo-Aryan influence while the impact of Southern Indian style is more distinct.[463] A feature of Hoysala temple architecture is its attention to detail and skilled craftsmanship. The temples of Belur and Halebidu are proposed UNESCO world heritage sites.[464] About a 100 Hoysala temples survive today.[465]

Early Indo-Islamic Architecture

The earliest examples of Indo-Islamic Architecture were constructed during this period by the Delhi Sultanates, most famously the Qutb Minar complex, which was designated a UNESCO World Heritage Site in 1993. The complex consists of Qutb Minar, a brick minaret commissioned by Qutub-ud-Din Aibak, as well as other monuments built by successive Delhi Sultans. Alai Minar, a minaret twice the size of Qutb Minar was commissioned by Alauddin Khilji but never completed.

Early Modern period (1500 CE—1947 CE)

Rajput Architecture

The Mughal architecture and painting influenced indigenous Rajput styles of art and architecture. Rajput Architecture represents different types of buildings, which may broadly be classed either as secular or religious. The secular buildings are of various scales. These include temples, forts, stepwells, gardens, and palaces. The forts were specially built for defense and military purposes due to the Islamic invasions.

Buddhist Architecture

Buddhist architecture developed in the Indian subcontinent. Three types of structures are associated with the religious architecture of early Buddhism: monasteries (viharas), places to venerate relics (stupas), and shrines or prayer halls (chaityas, also called *chaitya grihas*), which later came to be called temples in some places. The initial function of a stupa was the veneration and safe-guarding of the relics of Gautama Buddha. The earliest surviving example of a stupa is in Sanchi (Madhya Pradesh). In accordance with changes in religious practice, stupas were gradually incorporated into chaitya-grihas (prayer halls). These are exemplified by the complexes of the Ajanta Caves and the Ellora Caves (Maharashtra). The Mahabodhi Temple at Bodh Gaya in Bihar is another well-known example. The Pagoda is an evolution of the Indian stupa.

Figure 230: *Thikse Monastery is the largest gompa in Ladakh, built in the 1500s.*

Figure 231: *Tawang Monastery in Arunachal Pradesh, was built in the 1600s, is the largest monastery in India and second largest in the world after the Potala Palace in Lhasa, Tibet.*

Figure 233: *Humayun's Tomb, Delhi, the first fully developed Mughal imperial tomb, 1569-70*

Figure 232: *Rumtek Monastery in Sikkim was built under the direction of Changchub Dorje, 12th Karmapa Lama in the mid-1700s.*[466]

Late Indo-Islamic Architecture

The most famous Indo-Islamic style is Mughal architecture. Its most prominent examples are the series of imperial mausolea, which started with the pivotal Tomb of Humayun, but is best known for the Taj Mahal. The Red Fort at Agra (1565–74) and the walled city of Fatehpur Sikri (1569–74) are among the architectural achievements of this time—as is the Taj Mahal, built as a tomb for Queen Mumtaz Mahal by Shah Jahan (1628–58).[456] Employing the double dome, the recessed archway, the depiction of any animal or human—an essential part of the Indian tradition—was forbidden in places of worship under Islam. The Taj Mahal does contain tilework of plant ornaments. The architecture during the Mughal Period, with its rulers being of Turco-Mongol origin, has shown a notable blend of Indian style combined with the Islamic. Taj Mahal in Agra, India is one of the wonders of the world.

The Bahmani and Deccan sultanates in the Southern regions of the Indian subcontinent developed the Indo-Islamic architectural styles of the Deccan. The notable examples are Charminar, Mecca Masjid, Qutb Shahi Tombs, Madrasa Mahmud Gawan and Gol Gumbaz.[467]

Within the Indian subcontinent, the Bengal region developed a distinct regional style under the independent Bengal Sultanate. It incorporated influences from Persia, Byzantium and North India, which were with blended indigenous Bengali elements, such as curved roofs, corner towers and complex terracotta ornamentation. One feature in the sultanate was the relative absence of minarets.[468] Many small and medium-sized medieval mosques, with multiple domes and artistic niche mihrabs, were constructed throughout the region. The grand mosque of Bengal was the 14th century Adina Mosque, the largest mosque in the Indian subcontinent. Built of stone demolished from temples, it featured a monumental ribbed barrel vault over the central nave, the first such giant vault used anywhere in the subcontinent. The mosque was modeled on the imperial Sasanian style of Persia. The Sultanate style flourished between the 14th and 16th centuries. A provincial style influenced by North India evolved in Mughal Bengal during the 17th and 18th centuries. The Mughals also copied the Bengali do-chala roof tradition for mausoleums in North India.[469]

Figure 234: *Buland Darwaza was built by Akbar the Great to commemorate his victory over the Gujarat Sultanate.*

Figure 235: *Red Fort was the main residence of the Mughal emperors for nearly 200 years, until 1856.*

Figure 236: *Gol Gumbaz built by the Bijapur Sultanate in Deccani style, the world's 2nd largest pre-modern.*[470]

Figure 237: *Charminar at Old City in Hyderabad, leg-end has it that it was built by Muhammad Quli Qutb Shah to commemorate the end of a plague that ravaged the city.*

Figure 238: *Adina Mosque, the largest mosque of Bengali Muslim architecture.*

Maratha Architecture

<templatestyles src="Multiple_image/styles.css" />

Shaniwarwada palace fort in Pune, it was the seat of the Peshwa rulers of the Maratha Empire until 1818.

Thanjavur Maratha palace is the official residence of the Bhonsle family.

The Marathas ruled over much of the Indian subcontinent from the mid-17th to the early 19th centuries.[471] Their religious activity took full shape and soon the skylines of Maharashtrian towns were dominated by rising temple spires. Old forms returned with this 'renewal' of Hindu architecture, infused by the Sultanate and later the Mughal traditions. The architecture of Maratha period was planned with courtyards suited to tropical climates. The Maratha Architecture is known for its simplicity, visible logic and austere aesthetic, made rich by beautiful detailing, rhythm, and repetition. The aisles and arcades, punctured by delicate niches, doors, and windows create space in which the articulation of open, semi-open and covered areas is effortless and enchanting. The materials used during those times for construction were –

1. Thin bricks
2. Lime mortar
3. Lime plaster
4. Wooden columns
5. Stone bases
6. Basalt stone flooring
7. Brick pavements

Maharashtra is famous for its caves and rock-cut architectures. It is said that the varieties found in Maharashtra are wider than the caves and rock-cut architectures found in the rock-cut areas of Egypt, Assyria, Persia, and Greece. The Buddhist monks first started these caves in the 2nd century BC, in search of serene and peaceful environment for meditation, and they found these caves on the hillsides.

Sikh Architecture

<templatestyles src=”Multiple_image/styles.css” />

Harmandir Sahib is culturally the most significant place of worship for the Sikhs.

Akal Takht is one of five takhts (seats of power) of the Sikhs.

Sikh Architecture is a style of architecture that is characterized by values of progressiveness, exquisite intricacy, austere beauty and logical flowing lines. Due to its progressive style, it is constantly evolving into many newly developing branches with new contemporary styles. Although Sikh architecture was initially developed within Sikhism its style has been used in many non-religious buildings due to its beauty. 300 years ago, Sikh architecture was distinguished for its many curves and straight lines; Shri Keshgarh Sahib and the Sri Harmandir Sahib (Golden Temple) are prime examples.

European colonial architecture

As with the Mughals, under European colonial rule, architecture became an emblem of power, designed to endorse the occupying power. Numerous European countries invaded India and created architectural styles reflective of their ancestral and adopted homes. The European colonizers created architecture that symbolized their mission of conquest, dedicated to the state or religion.[472]

The British, French, Dutch and the Portuguese were the main European powers that colonized parts of India.[473]

British Colonial Era: 1615 to 1947

The British arrived in 1615 and over the centuries, gradually overthrew the Maratha and Sikh empires and other small independent kingdoms. Britain was present in India for over three hundred years and their legacy still remains through some building and infrastructure that exist in their former colonies.[474] The major cities colonized during this period were Madras, Calcutta, Bombay, Delhi, Agra, Bankipore, Karachi, Nagpur, Bhopal and Hyderabad,[475] which saw the rise of Indo-Saracenic Revival architecture.

St Andrews Kirk, Madras is known for its colonial architecture. The building is circular in form and is sided by two rectangular sections one is the entrance porch. The entrance is lined with twelve colonnades and two British lions and motto of East India Company engraved on them. The interior holds sixteen columns and the dome is painted blue with decorated with gold stars.[476]

Black Town described in 1855 as "the minor streets, occupied by the natives are numerous, irregular and of various dimensions. Many of them are extremely narrow and ill-ventilated ... a hallow square, the rooms opening into a courtyard in the centre."[477]

Garden houses were originally used as weekend houses for recreational use by the upper class British. Nonetheless, the garden house became ideal a full-time dwelling, deserting the fort in the 19th Century.[478]

Calcutta – Madras and Calcutta were similarly bordered by water and division of Indian in the north and British in the south. An Englishwoman noted in 1750 "the banks of the river are as one may say absolutely studded with elegant mansions called here as at Madras, garden houses." Esplanade-row is fronts the fort with lined palaces.[479]

Indian villages in these areas consisted of clay and straw houses which later transformed into the metropolis of brick and stone.[480]

The Victoria Memorial in Calcutta is the most effective symbolism of British Empire, built as a monument in tribute to Queen Victoria's reign. The plan of the building consists of one large central part covered with a larger dome. Colonnades separate the two chambers. Each corner holds a smaller dome and is floored with marble plinth. The memorial stands on 26 hectares of garden surrounded by reflective pools.[481]

Republic of India (1947 CE—present)

In recent times there has been a movement of population from rural areas to urban centres of industry, leading to price rise in property in various cities of India.[482] Urban housing in India balances space constrictions and is aimed to serve the working class.[483] Growing awareness of ecology has influenced architecture in India during modern times.[484]

Climate responsive architecture has long been a feature of India's architecture but has been losing its significance as of late. Indian architecture reflects its various socio-cultural sensibilities which vary from region to region.[485] Certain areas are traditionally held to be belonging to women. Villages in India have features such as courtyards, loggias, terraces and balconies. Calico, chintz, and palampore—of Indian origin—highlight the assimilation of Indian textiles in global interior design.[456] Roshandans, which are skylights-cum-ventilators, are a common feature in Indian homes, especially in North India.

References

- Foekema, Gerard (1996), *A Complete Guide to Hoysaḷa Temples*, Abhinav Publications, <templatestyles src="Module:Citation/CS1/styles.css" />ISBN 81-7017-345-0.
- Gast, Klaus-Peter (2007), *Modern Traditions: Contemporary Architecture in India*, Birkhäuser, <templatestyles src="Module:Citation/CS1/styles.css" />ISBN 978-3-7643-7754-0.
- Harle, J.C., *The Art and Architecture of the Indian Subcontinent*, 2nd edn. 1994, Yale University Press Pelican History of Art, <templatestyles src="Module:Citation/CS1/styles.css" />ISBN 0300062176
- Jaffar, S.M (1936). *The Mughal Empire From Babar To Aurangzeb.* Peshawar City: Muhammad Sadiq Khan. OU_1 60252.<templatestyles src="Module:Citation/CS1/styles.css"></templatestyles>
- Keay, John, *India, a History*, 2000, HarperCollins, <templatestyles src="Module:Citation/CS1/styles.css" />ISBN 0002557177
- Lach, Donald F. (1993), *Asia in the Making of Europe (vol. 2)*, University of Chicago Press, <templatestyles src="Module:Citation/CS1/styles.css" />ISBN 0-226-46730-9.
- Livingston, Morna & Beach, Milo (2002), *Steps to Water: The Ancient Stepwells of India*, Princeton Architectural Press, <templatestyles src="Module:Citation/CS1/styles.css" />ISBN 1-56898-324-7.
- Michell, George, (1977) *The Hindu Temple: An Introduction to its Meaning and Forms*, 1977, University of Chicago Press, <templatestyles src="Module:Citation/CS1/styles.css" />ISBN 978-0-226-53230-1

- Nilsson, Sten (1968). *European Architecture in India 1750 – 1850*. London: Faber and Faber. ISBN 0-571-08225-4.<templatestyles src="Module:Citation/CS1/styles.css"></templatestyles>
- Rowland, Benjamin, *The Art and Architecture of India: Buddhist, Hindu, Jain*, 1967 (3rd edn.), Pelican History of Art, Penguin, <templatestyles src="Module:Citation/CS1/styles.css" />ISBN 0140561021
- Savage, George (2008), *interior design*, Encyclopædia Britannica.
- Tadgell, Christopher (1990). *The history of architecture in India : from the dawn of civilization to the end of the Raj*. London: Architecture Design and Technology Press. ISBN 1-85454-350-4.<templatestyles src="Module:Citation/CS1/styles.css"></templatestyles>
- Thapar, Bindia (2004). *Introduction to Indian Architecture*. Singapore: Periplus Editions. ISBN 0-7946-0011-5.<templatestyles src="Module:Citation/CS1/styles.css"></templatestyles>
- Vastu-Silpa Kosha, Encyclopedia of Hindu Temple architecture and Vastu/S.K.Ramachandara Rao, Delhi, Devine Books, (Lala Murari Lal Chharia Oriental series) <templatestyles src="Module:Citation/CS1/styles.css" />ISBN 978-93-81218-51-8 (Set)
- Chandra, Pramod (2008), *South Asian arts*, Encyclopædia Britannica.
- Evenson, Norma (1989). *The Indian Metropolis*. New Haven and London: Yale University press. ISBN 0-300-04333-3.<templatestyles src="Module:Citation/CS1/styles.css"></templatestyles>
- Mankekar, Kamla (2004). *Temples of Goa*. India: Ministry of Information and Broadcasting, Govt. of Ind. ISBN 978-81-2301161-5.<templatestyles src="Module:Citation/CS1/styles.css"></templatestyles>
- Moffett, Marion; Fazio, Michael W.; Wodehouse Lawrence (2003), *A World History of Architecture*, McGraw-Hill Professional, <templatestyles src="Module:Citation/CS1/styles.css" />ISBN 0-07-141751-6.
- Piercey, W. Douglas & Scarborough, Harold (2008), *hospital*, Encyclopædia Britannica.
- Possehl, Gregory L. (1996), "Mehrgarh", *Oxford Companion to Archaeology* edited by Brian Fagan, Oxford University Press.
- Rodda & Ubertini (2004), *The Basis of Civilization-Water Science?*, International Association of Hydrological Science, <templatestyles src="Module:Citation/CS1/styles.css" />ISBN 1-901502-57-0.
- Sinopoli, Carla M. (2003), *The Political Economy of Craft Production: Crafting Empire in South India, C. 1350–1650*, Cambridge University Press, <templatestyles src="Module:Citation/CS1/styles.css" />ISBN 0-521-82613-6.

- Sinopoli, Carla M. (2003), "Echoes of Empire: Vijayanagara and Historical Memory, Vijayanagara as Historical Memory", *Archaeologies of memory* edited by Ruth M. Van Dyke & Susan E. Alcock, Blackwell Publishing, <templatestyles src="Module:Citation/CS1/styles.css" />ISBN 0-631-23585-X.
- Singh, Vijay P. & Yadava, R. N. (2003), *Water Resources System Operation: Proceedings of the International Conference on Water and Environment*, Allied Publishers, <templatestyles src="Module:Citation/CS1/styles.css" />ISBN 81-7764-548-X.
- Teresi, Dick (2002), *Lost Discoveries: The Ancient Roots of Modern Science—from the Babylonians to the Maya*, Simon & Schuster, <templatestyles src="Module:Citation/CS1/styles.css" />ISBN 0-684-83718-8.

Further reading

- Havell, E.B. (1913). *Indian Architecture, its psychology, structure, and history from the first Muhammadan invasion to the present day*[486]. J. Murray, London.<templatestyles src="Module:Citation/CS1/styles.css"></templatestyles>
- Coomaraswamy, Ananda K. (1914). *Viśvakarmā ; examples of Indian architecture, sculpture, painting, handicraft*[487]. London.<templatestyles src="Module:Citation/CS1/styles.css"></templatestyles>
- Havell, E. B. (1915). *The Ancient and Medieval Architecture of India: a study of Indo-Aryan civilisation*[488]. John Murray, London.<templatestyles src="Module:Citation/CS1/styles.css"></templatestyles>
- Fletcher, Banister; Cruickshank, Dan, *Sir Banister Fletcher's a History of Architecture*[489], Architectural Press, 20th edition, 1996 (first published 1896). <templatestyles src="Module:Citation/CS1/styles.css" />ISBN 0-7506-2267-9. Cf. Part Four, Chapter 26.

External links

- Kamiya, Taeko, *The Architecture of India.*[490]

Further reading

External links

Sports and martial arts

Sport in India

Part of a series on the
Culture of India
History
People
Cuisine
Religion
Sport
• ⚖ **India portal**
• v
• t
• e[491]

India is home to a diverse population playing many different kinds of sports across the country. Cricket is the most popular sport in India. Field hockey is the most successful sport for India at Olympics in which India has won eight

Olympic gold medals. Kabaddi is the most popular indigenous sport in the country. Other popular sports in India are Badminton, Football, Basketball, Chess, Shooting, Wrestling, Boxing, Tennis, Squash, Weightlifting, Gymnastic, Athletics and Table Tennis. Some indigenous sports are also popular in India such as Kho-kho, Kabaddi, Fighter kite, Polo and Gillidanda among others. There are some popular sports which has originated in India such as Chess, Snooker and Kabbadi. India has won Olympic medals in Badminton, Wrestling, Shooting, Weightlifting, Boxing and Tennis. India has also won World Cups in Cricket, Field Hockey and Kabbadi.

India has hosted and co-hosted several international sporting events including the 2010 Commonwealth Games, the 1951 and 1982 Asian Games, the 1987, 1995 and 2016 South Asian Games, the 1987, 1996, 2011 Cricket World Cup and 2016 ICC World Twenty20, the 2003 Afro-Asian Games, the 1989, 2013 and 2017 Asian Athletics Championships, the 1982 and 2010 Men's Field hockey World Cup, 2016–17 Men's FIH Hockey World League, the 1979, 1987, 1991, 2003, 2010, 2013 and 2017 Asian Wrestling Championships, the 2009 BWF World Championships, the 2004, 2007 and 2016 Kabaddi World Cup (Standard style), the 1980,1992 and 2009 Asian Table Tennis Championships, the 1981 ABC Championship, the 2009 FIBA Asia Championship for Women, the 1989, 2005, 2013 and 2017 Asian Cycling Championships. India has recently hosted the 2017 FIBA Women's Asia Cup, the 2017 FIFA U-17 World Cup, the 2017 ISSF World Cup and will host the 2018 Men's Hockey World Cup. India has some premier domestic leagues in different sports which are very popular in the country. Indian Premier League (IPL) is a premier Twenty20 & the most popular cricket league in the world held every year since 2008. The I-League and Indian Super League are premier football league tournaments held since 2007 and 2014 respectively, the Pro Kabaddi league is the most popular indigenous league in the country held since 2014, the Hockey India League is the premier hockey league held since 2013, the Premier Badminton League is the badminton premier league held since 2013, the Pro Wrestling League premier Wrestling league held since 2015 and Ultimate Table Tennis[492] league held since 2017.

Major international sporting events annually held in India include the Chennai Open in tennis, the Indian Masters in golf, the India Open since 2008 and Royal Indian Open since 2001 in badminton. From 2011 to 2013, India hosted the Indian Grand Prix Formula 1 race at the Buddh International Circuit, Greater Noida.

The National Games of India is a national domestic sports event which has been held in the country since 1924 and for developing multi-sports culture in India Khelo India School Games, an event for under-17 school kids, had been started from 2018 as its first edition.

History

Before independence

The geography of sports in India dates back to the Vedic era. Physical culture in ancient India was fuelled by religious rights. The mantra in the Atharvaveda, says, "Duty is in my right hand and the fruits of victory in my left." In terms of an ideal, these words hold the same sentiments as the traditional Olympic Oath: "For the Honour of my Country and the Glory of Sport.[493]" Badminton probably originated in India as a grownup's version of a very old children's game known in England as battledore and shuttlecock, the battledore being a paddle and the shuttlecock a small feathered cork, now usually called a "bird." Games like chess (chaturanga), Snooker snakes and ladders, playing cards, originated in India, and it was from here that these games were transmitted to foreign countries, where they were further modernised.

After independence

India hosted the Asian Games in New Delhi in 1951 and 1982. The Ministry of Youth Affairs and Sports was initially set up as the Department of Sports in 1982 at the time of organisation of the IX Asian Games in New Delhi. Its name was changed to the Department of Youth Affairs & Sports during celebration of the International Youth Year in 1985. India has also hosted or co-hosted several international sporting events, including the 1987 and 1996 Cricket World Cup, the 2003 Afro-Asian Games, the 2010 Hockey World Cup, and the 2010 Commonwealth Games. Major international sporting events annually held in India include the Chennai Open, Mumbai Marathon, Delhi Half Marathon, and the Indian Masters. The country co-hosted the 1987, 1996, 2011 Cricket World Cup and the first Indian Grand Prix in 2011.

Administration and funding

Political responsibility for sport in India is with the Ministry of Youth Affairs and Sports, which is headed by a cabinet minister and managed by National Sport Federations. The only major exception is the BCCI which is the administrative body of Cricket, is not a NSF. Presently there are more than 70 recognised national sports federations (NSF), of which 38 have politicians at the helm.[494]

Sports Authority of India, the field arm of the Ministry, supports and nurtures talent in youth, and provides them with requisite infrastructure, equipment, coaching facilities and competition exposure. Dorabji Tata, with the support of Dr. A.G. Noehren, then director of YMCA, established the Indian

Olympic Association (IOA) in 1927. IOA is responsible for the Indian continent's participation in the Olympic Games, Commonwealth Games, Asian Games (outdoor, indoor and beach), and South Asian Games. Each Olympic and non-Olympic sport has a federation at the national level.

The selection of the national teams is done by the respective national federations and then recommend to IOA for official sponsorship for participation in the games conducted under the auspices of the International Olympic Committee, Olympic Council of Asia, Commonwealth Games Federation, and SAG. A special feature of the Indian Olympic Association is that the National Federations and the State Olympic Associations are affiliated with and recognised by it. The main task of the State Olympic Associations is to promote the Olympic sport and to ensure co-ordination among the State Sports Associations. In 2010–11, the total budget for sports and physical education schemes is ☐31,177 million (US$430 million).[495] Hockey, in which India has an impressive record with eight Olympic gold medals, is said to be the national sport. The Rajiv Gandhi Khel Ratna and the Arjuna Award are India's highest awards for achievement in sports, while the Dronacharya Award is awarded for excellence in coaching.

India has been criticised for neglecting women in sports, as depicted in the film "Chak De! India", where women's sports associations are under-sponsored and out of funds.

International sports events held in India

Following is a list of international sports events held in India:

International Sports Events Hosting Record			
Sport	**Event name**	**Year/-Date**	**Venue**
Multi-sport event	Asian Games	1951	New Delhi
Table tennis	World Table Tennis Championships	1952	Mumbai
Billiards	IBSF World Billiards Championship	1952	Kolkata
Snooker	IBSF World Snooker Championship	1958	Kolkata
Snooker	IBSF World Snooker Championship	1963	Kolkata
Snooker	IBSF World Snooker Championship	1973	Mumbai

Table tennis	World Table Tennis Championships	1975	Kolkata
Wrestling	Asian Wrestling Championships	1979	Jalandhar
Boxing	Men's Asian Amateur Boxing Championships	1980	Bombay
Table tennis	Asian Table Tennis Championships	1980	Kolkata
Archery	Asian Archery Championships	1980	Kolkata
Basketball	FIBA Asia Cup	1981	Kolkata
Snooker	IBSF World Snooker Championship	1981	New Delhi
Field hockey	Field Hockey World Cup	1982	BHA Stadium, Bombay
Multi-sport event	Asian Games	1982	New Delhi
Table tennis	World Table Tennis Championships	1987	New Delhi
Cricket (ODI)	Cricket World Cup	1987	Multiple venues
Wrestling	Asian Wrestling Championships	1987	Mumbai
Snooker	IBSF World Snooker Championship	1987	Bangalore
Multi-sport event	South Asian Games	1987	Kolkata
Archery	Asian Archery Championships	1988	Kolkata
Snooker	ACBS Asian Snooker Championship	1989	India
Cycling	Asian Cycling Championships	1989	Yamuna Velodrome, Delhi
Rowing	Asian Rowing Championships	1989	Sukhna Lake, Chandigarh
Athletics	Asian Athletics Championships	1989	New Delhi
Snooker	IBSF World Snooker Championship	1990	Bangalore
Wrestling	Asian Wrestling Championships	1991	New Delhi
Table tennis	Asian Table Tennis Championships	1992	New Delhi

Judo	Asian Judo Championships	1995	New Delhi
Multi-sport event	South Asian Games	1995	Chennai
Cricket (ODI)	Cricket World Cup	1996	Multiple Venues
Field Hockey	Men's Hockey Champions Trophy	1996	Mayor Radhakrishnan Stadium, Chennai
Tennis	Chennai Open	1996–	SDAT Tennis Stadium, Chennai
Cricket (ODI)	Women's Cricket World Cup	1997	Multiple Venues
Basketball	FIBA Asia Under-18 Championship	1998	Kolkata
Chess	World Chess Championship	2000	New Delhi
Wrestling	Asian Wrestling Championships	2003	New Delhi
Multi-sport event	Afro-Asian Games	2003	Hyderabad
Boxing	Women's Asian Amateur Boxing Championships	2003	Hisar District
Canoeing	Asian Canoeing Championships Canoe sprint	2003	Bhopal
Kabaddi	Kabaddi World Cup (Standard style)	2004	Mumbai, Maharastra
Basketball	FIBA Asia Under-18 Championship	2004	Bangalore
Sailing	Asian Sailing Championship	2004	Mumbai
Marathon	IAAF Road Race Label Events Mumbai Marathon	2004-(recur)	Mumbai
Half marathon	IAAF Road Race Label Events Delhi Half Marathon	2005-(recur)	Delhi
Rowing	Asian Rowing Championships	2005	Hussain Sagar, Hyderabad
Cycling	Asian Cycling Championships	2005	Punjab Agriculture University Velodrome
Field Hockey	Men's Hockey Champions Trophy	2005	Mayor Radhakrishnan Stadium, Chennai
Archery	Asian Archery Championships	2005	New Delhi
Boxing	AIBA Women's World Boxing Championships	2006	New Delhi
Gymnastics	Asian Artistic Gymnastics Championships	2006	Surat

	Rhythmic Gymnastics Asian Championships	2006	
犬: Kabaddi	Kabaddi World Cup (Standard style)	2007	Panvel, Maharastra
Beach Volleyball	Asian Beach Volley-ball Championship	2008	Hyderabad
Boxing	Women's Asian Amateur Boxing Championships	2008	Guwahati
Football	AFC Challenge Cup	2008	Ambedkar Stadium, New Delhi Gachibowli Athletic Stadium, Hyderabad
Multi-sport event	Common-wealth Youth Games	2008	Pune
Badminton	BWF World Junior Championships	2008	Pune
Snooker	IBSF World Snooker Championship	2008	Bangalore
Badminton	BWF World Championships	2009	Hyderabad
Snooker	IBSF World Snooker Championship	2009	Hyderabad
Basketball	FIBA Asia Champi-onship for Women	2009	Chennai
Table tennis	Asian Table Tennis Championships	2009	Lucknow
Snooker	IBSF World Snooker Championship	2010	Maharashtra
Wrestling	Asian Wrestling Championships	2010	New Delhi
Field hockey	Field Hockey World Cup	2010	New Delhi (Dhyan Chand National Stadium)
Multi-sport event	Common-wealth Games	2010	New Delhi
Field hockey	Men's Hockey Champions Trophy	2011	New Delhi
Cricket (ODI)	Cricket World Cup	2011	Multiple Venues
Snooker	ACBS Asian Snooker Championship	2011	Indore
Multi-sport event	South Asian Winter Games	2011	Dehradun and Auli
Snooker	IBSF World Snooker Championship	2011	Bangalore
Motor sports	Formula One2011 Indian Grand Prix	2011	Buddh International Cir-cuit, Greater Noida

Field hockey	2012 Summer Olympics (London) Qualification Tournament 1	2012	New Delhi (Dhyan Chand National Stadium)
Field Hockey	FIH Men's Hockey World League (*2013 Round 2 (Delhi leg)*)	2012–13 season	New Delhi (Dhyan Chand National Stadium)
	FIH Men's Hockey World League (*2013 Round 4 (Final round)*)		
	FIH Women's Hockey World League (*2013 Round 2 (Delhi leg)*)	2012–13 season	
Wrestling	Asian Wrestling Championships	2013	New Delhi
Canoeing	Asian Canoeing Championships Canoe Polo	2013	New Delhi
Cycling	Asian Cycling Championships	2013	New Delhi (Yamuna Velodrome)
Motor sports	Formula One2013 Indian Grand Prix	2013	Buddh International Circuit,Greater Noida
Athletics	Asian Athletics Championships	2013	Pune
Cricket (ODI)	Women's Cricket World Cup	2013	Multiple Venues
Chess	World Chess Championship	2013	Chennai
Multi-sport event	Lusophony Games	2014	Goa
Tennis	Davis Cup World Group Play-offs	2014	KSLTA Tennis Stadium, Bangalore
Snooker	IBSF World Snooker Championship	2014	Bangalore
Badminton	Thomas Cup Uber Cup	2014	Siri Fort Indoor Stadium, New Delhi
Field Hockey	Men's Hockey Champions Trophy	2014	Kalinga Stadium, Bhubaneshwar
	FIH Women's Hockey World League (*2015 Round 2 (Delhi leg)*)	2014–15 season	Dhyan Chand National Stadium, New Delhi
	FIH Men's Hockey World League (*2015 Round 4 (Final round)*)	2014–15 season	Raipur
Golf	Asian Tour Indian Open (golf)	2015	Delhi Golf Club
Snooker	IBSF World Snooker Championship	2016	Bangalore

Cricket (T20)	ICC World Twenty20	2016	Multiple Venues
Cricket (T20)	ICC Women's World Twenty20	2016	Multiple Venues
Kabaddi	Kabaddi World Cup (Standard style)	2016	The Arena, Ahmedabad
Golf	Asian Tour Indian Open (golf)	2016	Delhi Golf Club
Multi-sport event	South Asian Games	2016	Guwahati and Shillong
Athletics	Asian Athletics Championships	2017	Bhubaneswar
Wrestling	Asian Wrestling Championships	2017	Indira Gandhi Sports Complex, New Delhi
Cycling	Asian Cycling Championships	2017	Indira Gandhi Arena, New Delhi
Badminton	BWF Super Series India Open	2017	Siri Fort Indoor Stadium, New Delhi
Squash	Asian Individual Squash Championships	2017	Express Avenue Mall, Chennai
Shooting	ISSF World Cup	2017	New Delhi
Table tennis	ITTF World Tour India Open (table tennis)	2017	Thyagaraj Sports Complex, New Delhi
Football	FIFA U-17 World Cup	2017	Multiple Venues
Basketball	FIBA Asia Women's Cup	2017	Banglore
Basketball	FIBA Asia Under-16 Championship for Women	2017	Bangalore
Boxing	AIBA Women's Youth World Championships	2017	Guwahati
Golf	Asian Tour Indian Open (golf)	2017	DLF Golf and Country Club
Lawn Bowls	Asian Lawn Bowls Championships	2017	New Delhi
	Asian Under 25 Lawn Bowls Championship		
Field hockey	FIH Men's Hockey World League (*2017 Round 4 (Final round)*)	2016–17 season	Kalinga Stadium, Bhubaneshwar
	Field Hockey World Cup	2018	
Golf	Asian Tour Indian Open (golf)	2018	DLF Golf and Country Club
Boxing	AIBA Women's World Boxing Championships	2018	New Delhi

| 🏹 Boxing | AIBA Men's World Boxing Championships | 2021 | New Delhi |
| Cricket (ODI) | Cricket World Cup | 2023 | Multiple Venues |

India at major international sports events

Olympics

A single athlete, Norman Pritchard, represented India in the 1900 Olympics, winning two silver medals. India sent its first national team to the Olympics in 1920, and has participated in every Summer Olympic Games ever since. India has also competed at several Winter Olympic Games since 1964.

India has won a total of 26 Olympic medals. India won its first gold medal in men's field hockey in the 1928 Olympic Games. Abhinav Bindra became the first Indian to win an individual gold medal at the Olympic Games, and India's first gold medal since 1980, when the men's field hockey team won the gold.[496,497]

India has won very few Olympic medals, despite a population exceeding one billion, around half of them under the age of 25. Numerous explanations have been offered for the dearth, including poverty, malnutrition, neglected infrastructure, the lack of sponsorship, the theft of money and equipment, political corruption, institutional disorganisation, social immobility, the predominance of cricket, and other cultural factors.[498,499,500,501]

According to several informal statistics, India is the country with the lowest number of total Olympic medals per capita (out of those countries which have won at least one medal). In the Winter Olympic Games, India has seen four consecutive representations–Nagano (Japan, 1998), Salt Lake City (Utah, USA, 2002), Turin (Italy, 2006), and Vancouver (British Columbia, Canada, 2010). Shiva Keshavan, Asian Champion in luge represented India in all four winter games.

Commonwealth Games

India has competed in fourteen of the eighteen previous Commonwealth Games; starting at the second Games in 1934 hosted the games one time. India hosted the Games in 2010, at Delhi. India is the fourth most successful country with a total of 436 medals including 156 gold medals.

Figure 239: *The Indian Hockey team at the 1936 Berlin Olympics, later going on to defeat Germany 8–1 in the final.*

Asian Games

India hosted the Asian Games in 1951 and 1982 at New Delhi. India is the 4th most successful country winning 602 medals including 139 gold. India has won the gold medal in Kabbadi ever since its inception except in 2018.

The National Games of India

The National Games of India is a sporting event held in India. It comprises various disciplines in which sportsmen from the different states of India participate against each other. The country's first few Olympic Games, now christened as National Games.

Shooting is an important Olympic sport in India. Of India's 26 Olympic medals, 4 have come from Shooting including a Gold by Abhinav Bindra in the 2008 Olympics. Indian shooters who have excelled at the world stage include Abhinav Bindra, Jitu Rai, Rajyavardhan Singh Rathore, Vijay Kumar, Gagan Narang, Apurvi Chandela, Ronjan Sodhi and Anjali Bhagwat.

The Indian shooting contingent for the 2012 London was one of the largest to date. There were a total of 11 shooters including 4 female shooters. India's first medal in the 2012 Olympics was when Gagan Narang won the bronze in the 10m Air Rifle event. This was the same event in which Abhinav Bindra won India's first individual gold medal in the 2008 Summer Olympics Beijing. The second medal came from the unheralded army man Vijay Kumar when he won the silver in the 25m rapid fire pistol event after finishing 4th in the qualification rounds. He had to fend off some tough competition from the third-placed Chinese Ding Feng.

A notable performance was made by Joydeep Karmakar who finished 4th in the 50m rifle prone event. A strong medal prospect Ronjan Sodhi who is an Asian Games gold medallist, however, crashed out in the qualification rounds of the Double trap event.

Olympic sports

Field Hockey

Field Hockey is a popular sport in India. Until the mid-1970s, India men's team dominated international field hockey, winning 7 Olympic gold medals and won the 1975 Men's Hockey World Cup. Since then, barring a gold medal at the 1980 Olympics, India's performance in field hockey has been dismal, with other hockey-playing nations such as Australia, Netherlands and Germany improving their standards and catching up with India. Its decline is also due to the change in rules of the game, introduction of artificial turf, and internal politics in Indian field hockey bodies. The popularity of field hockey has also declined massively parallel to the decline of the Indian hockey team. In recent years, the standard of Indian hockey has gone from bad to worse, with the Men's team not qualifying for the 2008 Olympics and finishing last in the 2012 Olympics. Since 2014, the men's team is trying to regain its lost glory little by little as they become runners up at the 2014 Commonwealth Games, then winning a much needed 2014 Asian Games gold and 2017 Men's Hockey Asia Cup to finally establishing the Asian dominance after long time but before that India lost to Belgium in the quarter final of 2016 Rio Olympics. India men's hockey team is eyeing for gold at the 2018 Men's Hockey World Cup as its going to hold in India, as support of home crowds which is a must need to defeat the aura of the Australians who constantly dominating the Indian team in the recent years in various finals such as the 2014 & 2018 Hockey Champions Trophy. Currently, the Indian men's team is 5th in the rankings of the Fédération Internationale de Hockey sur Gazon (FIH, English:International Hockey Federation), the international governing body of field hockey and indoor field hockey.

The Women's team came of age in 1980 when they first participated at the Summer Olympics and achieved the 4th place. The first golden moment for the team was in 1982 at the Asian Games. Since then not much of happening moments in the team history, though in 2016 after 34 years, its a little hope when Indian women's team qualified for the Summer Olympics and they went on to win the 2017 Women's Hockey Asia Cup claiming the Asian dominance after 2004. India Women's team failed to win any medal in the Women's Hockey World Cup. The present team is ranked 10th by the Fédération Internationale de Hockey.

India has hosted two Men's Hockey World Cups–one in 1982 in Mumbai, and another in 2010 in Delhi, where they finished fifth and eighth respectively. India also hosted the annual Hockey Champions Trophy in 1996, 2005 and 2014. Until 2008, the Indian Hockey Federation (IHF) was the apex body for hockey in the country. However, following revelations of corruption and other scandals in the IHF, the federation was dissolved and de-recognised, and a new apex body for Indian hockey called Hockey India (HI) was formed on 20 May 2009, with support from the IOA and former hockey players. HI, recognised by the International Hockey Federation (FIH), has the sole mandate to govern and conduct all activities for both men's and women's field hockey in India. Although the IHF was reinstated in 2010, it is not recognised by the FIH. The IHF conducts a franchise-based tournament called World Series Hockey (WSH), with its first season conducted in 2012. However, it is not approved by HI or the FIH.

HI also conducts a franchise-based tournament called the Hockey India League (HIL). Its first season was in 2013 and is inspired from the Board of Control for Cricket in India's (BCCI's) highly successful Indian Premier League. The tournament is recognised by the FIH, which has also decided to provide a 30-day window for the forthcoming seasons so that all top players can participate.

Football

Football was introduced to India during the British colonial period. Although India has never been represented in any FIFA World Cup, it did qualify in 1950, though it did not take part, as they were not allowed to play barefoot. India was an Asian powerhouse in football in the 1950s and 1960s. During this golden era, India created history as the first Asian team to reach semi-finals in an Olympic football tournament in 1956 Summer Olympics at Melbourne and Neville D'Souza became the first Asian and Indian to score a hat-trick (record remains unbeaten) in an Olympic match. India also finished as runners-up in the 1964 AFC Asian Cup. But later on, the standard of football started to decline due to lack of professionalism and fitness culture. India currently ranks 97th in the FIFA rankings as of 10 August 2017.

Football is, nevertheless, widely popular both as a spectator sport, and as a participation sport in some parts of the country such as Kerala, West Bengal, Goa and the Northeast. The India national football team represents India in all

Figure 240: *Sayed Rahim Nabi of East Bengal FC and Daniel of Chirag United SC during I league at Salt Lake Stadium.*

FIFA tournaments. The Yuva Bharati Krirangan of Kolkata was the second largest non-auto racing stadium in the world.

In June 1937, at the Army Headquarters, Shimla, the All India Football Federation (AIFF) was formed at a meeting of the representatives of football associations of six regions where the game was very popular in those days. It is the governing body for football in India. Domestic competitions for men's football include the Indian Super League, I-League, I-League 2nd Division in the Indian League System and the annual knock-out style Federation Cup. For women's football the India women's football championship. However, it is European football, such as the English Premier League, Spanish La Liga, and the UEFA Champions League, which are very popular among Indian football fans, especially in metropolitan cities.

The 2017 FIFA U-17 World Cup will be the 17th tournament of the FIFA U-17 World Cup. FIFA revealed on 5 December 2013 (as part of their Executive Committee meets in Salvador, Brazil), that India will be the host. This will be the first time India will host an international football competition at world level.[502] To help increase interest in youth football in advance of the 2017 U-17 World Cup, India has launched the Mission XI Million programme.

Figure 241: *Mahesh Bhupati (left), Leander Paes (right)*

Tennis

Tennis is a sport among Indians in urban areas. Tennis has gained popularity after the exploits of Vijay Amritraj. India's fortunes in Grand Slam singles have been unimpressive, although Leander Paes won a singles bronze medal at the 1996 Olympics. Since the late 1990s India has had impressive results in Grand Slam doubles, Leander Paes and Mahesh Bhupathi have won many men's doubles and mixed doubles Grand Slam titles. Sania Mirza is the most notable Indian woman tennis player, having won a WTA title and breaking into the Top 30 WTA rankings, also winning three Grand Slam doubles events, the first at Wimbledon in 2015. On the men's side, young Somdev Devvarman and Yuki Bhambri are flying India's flag on the ATP Tour. Yuki was the Australian Open junior singles champion in 2009. Rohan Bopanna has won two mixed doubles titles.

Badminton

Badminton is played widely in India and it is one of the most popular sports in India. Badminton is a fast growing sport in India. Badminton's popularity has grown in recent years. Indian shuttlers Saina Nehwal, K. Srikanth and P.V. Sindhu are ranked amongst top-10 in current BWF ranking. Prakash Padukone

Figure 242: *Jwala Gutta, the most successful doubles player from India.*

was the first player from India to achieve world no.1 spot in the game and after him K. Srikanth made it to the top spot as male player for second time in April 2018 and Saina Nehwal is the first female player from India to achieve World no.1 spot in April 2015. The most successful doubles player from India is Jwala Gutta, who is the only Indian to have been ranked in the top-10 of two categories. She peaked at no. 6 with Valiyaveetil Diju in mixed doubles and at no. 10 with Ashwini Ponnappa in women's doubles. Other successful players include Aparna Popat, Pullela Gopichand, Syed Modi, Chetan Anand, Parupalli Kashyap, Prannoy Kumar, Ashwini Ponnappa, Chirag Shetty, Satwiksairaj Rankireddy and N. Sikki Reddy.

Padukone and Gopichand, both won the All England Open in 1980 and 2001 respectively making them the only Indians to ever win the prestigious title. At the 2012 London Olympic Games, Nehwal won the bronze medal in the individual women's competition, the first for the country in badminton and in the next edition at Rio 2016 P.V.Sindhu won silver in Women's singles, 2nd medal in badminton for India. India has won medals at the BWF World Championships as well, with Padukone winning in 1982. The doubles pairing of Gutta and Ponnappa became the first women to win the medal when they won the bronze in 2011.[503] Sindhu won consecutive medals at 2013 and 2014 editions. Nehwal won a silver at 2015 Championships. Saina is the only gold medalist for India in BWF World Junior Championships, won in 2008, where

Figure 243: *Members of India's women's national basketball team at the 2009 Asian Indoor Games in Vietnam*

as Sindhu and Lakshya Sen are the only gold medalists in Badminton Asia
Junior Championships in their respective category for the country, won in 2012
and 2018.

Basketball

Basketball is a popular sport in India, played in almost every school, although
very few people follow it professionally. India has both men's and women's
national basketball teams. Both teams have hired head coaches who have
worked extensively with NBA players and now aim to popularise the game
in India.[504] Satnam Singh Bhamara officially marks the first player from India
to be selected in the NBA by being taken by the Dallas Mavericks as the 52nd
pick of the 2015 NBA draft, as well as the first player to be drafted straight out
of high school as a postgraduate.

The *Young Cagers*, as the national team is nicknamed, made one Olympic appearance in basketball, and appeared 20 times in the Asian Championship.
India is currently ranked 58th in the world in basketball. The Indian national team had its best result at the 1975 Asian Championship, when the
team finished ahead of teams including the Philippines, one of Asia's basketball strongholds. Internationally, one of the most recognised Indian basketball

Figure 244: *Jeev Milkha Singh*

players has been Sozhasingarayer Robinson.[505] Affiliated into the International Basketball Federation (FIBA) since 1936, India has one of Asia's longest basketball traditions.[506]

India's women had their best result at the recent 2011 FIBA Asia Championship for Women when they finished 6th. The team has several internationally known players including Geethu Anna Jose, who was invited to tryouts for the WNBA in 2011.[507]

Table tennis

Table tennis is a popular indoor recreation sport in India, which has caught on in states including West Bengal and Tamil Nadu. The Table Tennis Federation of India is the official governing body of the sport. India, which is ranked 30th in the world, has produced a single player ranked in the top 50, Sharat Kamal.

Golf

Golf is a growing sport in India. It is especially popular among the wealthier classes, but has not yet caught on with others due the expenses involved in playing.

Figure 245: *Vijender preparing for a boxing match on a television show.*

The most successful Indian golfers are Jeev Milkha Singh and Anirban Lahiri. Singh won three titles on the European Tour, four on the Japan Golf Tour, and six on the Asian Tour. His highest world ranking was 28th in March 2009. Singh has won the Asian Tour Order of Merit twice. Meanwhile, Lahiri has two European Tour wins and seven Asian Tour wins. He qualified for the 2015 Presidents Cup.

Other Indians who have won the Asian Tour Order of Merit are Jyoti Randhawa in 2002 (the first Indian to do so), and Arjun Atwal, who went on in 2010 to become the first India-born player to become a member of the US-based PGA Tour and win the 2010 Wyndham Championship.

In golf at the Asian Games, India's men's golf team won gold at the 1982 Asian Games, and silver at the 2006 Asian Games. Lakshman Singh won the individual gold at the 1982 Asian Games.

There are numerous golf courses all over India, and a Professional Golf Tour of India. The main tournament is the Hero Indian Open, co-sanctioned by the Asian Tour and European Tour.

Boxing

Boxing is a highly profiled sport in India, and although it is a regular medal-holder at the Asian Games and Commonwealth Games, though India has not

Figure 246: *Military World Games in Hyderabad, India.*

yet produced a world champion in any weight class. In November 2007, India's Mary Kom won the best boxer title and secured a hat-trick of titles. During the 2008 Beijing Olympics, Vijender Singh won a bronze medal in the middleweight division, and Akhil Kumar and Jitender Kumar qualified for the quarterfinals. Akhil Kumar, Jitender Kumar, A.L. Lakra, and Dinesh Kumar each won a bronze medal at the 2008 World Championship. India's lone women boxer, M.C. Mary Kom, won the bronze medal at the 2012 London Olympic Games.

Wrestling

Considered one of the most ancient and oldest sports in the world, wrestling in India has a glorious past. The sport of wrestling began its journey in India several centuries ago, during the Middle Ages. Wrestling is among the most prestigious and oldest events in the Olympic Games. It was included in the Olympics in 708 BC. In ancient times, wrestling in India was mainly used as a way to stay physically fit. It was also used as a military exercise without any weapons. Wrestling in India is also known as *dangal,* and it is the basic form of a wrestling tournament.

In India, wrestling is mostly known as *Malla-Yuddha*. There are mentions of wrestling in the ancient times, found in the Sanskrit epic of Indian history, *Mahabharata*. One of the premier characters in Mahabharata, Bhima, was considered to be a great wrestler. Other great wrestlers included Jarasandha, Dury-

Figure 247: *Weightlifting training room*

odhana, and Karna. Another Indian epic, Ramayana, also mentions wrestling in India, describing Hanuman as one of the greatest wrestlers of that time. The 13th-century *Malla Purana* references a group of Gujarati Brahmin wrestlers known as Jyesthimallas.

Weightlifting and powerlifting

Karnam Malleswari won a bronze medal at the 2000 Summer Olympics in Sydney, making her the first Indian woman to win an Olympic medal. The headquarters of the Indian Weightlifting Federation is in New Delhi. The federation is affiliated with the Indian Olympic Association (Delhi), and is also a member of the Asian Weightlifting Federation (Tehran) and International Weightlifting Federation (IWF, Budapest). The International Weightlifting Federation banned the Indian Weightlifting Federation from participating in all international competitions for one year when three Indian women weightlifters were accused of doping offences in various international competitions in a single year.

Archery

The game of archery has historical significance, as royals in the ancient days used to practice archery. Modern-day archery in India began in the early 1970s, before its introduction as an Olympic event in 1972, and it was formalised in 1973 when the Archery Association of India (AAI) came into existence. Since its inception, AAI has been promoting an organisation for the sport. India has been producing some world class players who are the medal hopefuls in international events of archery.

Volleyball

Volleyball is a popular recreation sport played all over India, both in rural and urban areas. India is ranked fifth in Asia, and 27th in the world. In the youth and junior levels, India came in second in the 2003 World Youth Championships. The Indian senior men's team is ranked 46th in the world. A major problem for the sport is the lack of sponsors.

Handball

Handball is a popular sport in India, played at the local level, but hasn't yet made an impact at the domestic level. India's handball team began on 27 April 1989, although it hasn't yet made an impact on the world stage, at the international level or the World Cup. The Handball Federation of India manages handball in India.

Taekwondo

Taekwondo in India is administered by the Taekwondo Federation of India which was founded by Jimmy R. Jagtiani.[508] Surendra Bhandari won a bronze medal in taekwondo at the 2002 Asian Games. Taekwondo is widely practised in India, with actors Neetu Chandra, Akshay Kumar and Isha Koppikar holding black belts.

Rugby

Rugby union is a minor, but fast-growing, sport in India. Some Indian sporting clubs are beginning to embrace the game, and it is the second most popular winter sport after football in India, Wikipedia:Citation needed which itself trails in popularity after cricket and field hockey.

Cycling

The history of cycling in India dates back to 1938, and the Cycling Federation of India governs the sport. Though cycling is unknown as a professional sport in India, it is popular as a common recreational sport and a way to keep fit.

Mountain biking

Mountain biking is becoming a popular sport in India. For the last six years, Mtb himachal, a hardcore endurance event, has been organised regularly by Himalayan Adventure Sports & Tourism Promotion Association (HASTPA), a non-governmental organisation (NGO). A number of national and international riders participate, including Indian Army, Indian Air Force, Indo-Tibetan Border Police (ITBP), and a number of young and energetic mountain biking individual riders from cities including Pune, Bangalore, Delhi and Chandigarh. Last yearWikipedia:Manual of Style/Dates and numbers#Chronological items, the government of Sikkim (Department of Tourism) introduced its own mountain biking race, with Southeast Asia's biggest prize money. The second edition saw 48 professional participants from around the globe.

Road Cycling/ Touring

The Tour of Nilgiris is a major non-competitive & non-commercial touring event in South Asia that covers 1,000 kilometres in under 10 days. The Tour of Nilgiris (TfN), India's first Day Touring Cycle Ride, was born in December 2008 with the twin objectives of promoting bicycling as an activity and spreading awareness about the bio-diversity, flora and fauna of the Nilgiris.

It soon grew into something a lot more, with an eclectic riding community in 2008 wanting to take part in. The community soon got together, chalked out plans, figured out a route and realised they would need a framework to support such a large group of people, got sponsors on board to mitigate costs as well as popularise the Tour and the Cause of popularising Cycling as a viable and sustainable means of travel. Ever since its first edition, the TfN has stayed true to the Community of Cyclists in India by being a Tour for the Community, Of the Community and By the Community. It has grown in size, stature and visibility. From 40 riders in the first edition, its grown to 100 cyclists in 2013.

The tour has grown bigger & the routes tougher, allowing cyclists to test their endurance, enjoy the biodiversity of the Nilgiris covering 3 southern states in India (Karnataka, Tamil Nadu & Kerala). For the racing aficionado's, there are racing segments on the tour with colour coded jerseys, recognition and prizes. TfN as its lovingly called is pushing cycling to new frontiers with more and more interested cyclists, applying for the tour. The tour has acquired quite a name, and currently about 25% of registrations are selected for the tour by the organisers.

Equestrian sports

India has a wide following in various equestrian sports, including show jumping, eventing, dressage, endurance riding and tent pegging. Supported by the Equestrian Federation of India, eventing is the most popular of the five, with teams representing the country at most Asian Games, winning a bronze medal in the 2002 and 2006 games. India has been represented at the Olympics twice, by Wing Commander I.J. Lamba, and Imtiaz Anees.

Kayaking

Flat water and sea kayaking

Indian flat water kayakers are an emerging powerhouse on the Asian circuit. Outside of professional flat water kayaking, there is very limited recreational kayaking. The potential to generate interest in flat water kayaking is held by leisure resorts located near the sea or other water bodies. Indian tourists tend to consider kayaking a one-time activity, rather than a sport to be pursued.

Whitewater kayaking

Enthusiasts of whitewater kayaking are concentrated in the north towards the Himalayas, with some in the south in Bangalore in Karnataka. Most of these enthusiasts are or were whitewater raft guides who took to the sport of whitewater kayaking. Some of the prominent whitewater kayakers include Abhinav Kala, Shalabh Gahlaut, and John Pollard. Many of them have notched first descents (similar to climbing ascents) on rivers in India and Nepal.

"Bangalore Kayakers" or "Southern River Runners" are India's first amateur group of white water kayakers. Based out of Bangalore, they explore rivers around Western Ghats. The lure for most of these participants is adventure. Whitewater kayaking in India allows for exploration of places where, literally, no human has been before.

Gear availability is a problem that plagues kayakers. While the global designs for whitewater boats and paddles change annually, Indian kayakers have to pay high fees if they want to import any kind of gear, or they have to buy used gear in Nepal. More often than not, one will see Indian kayaking guides riding down the river in a Perception Amp, Piroutte or Dancer designs, while the kayakers from abroad ride the river in their new design, planing hull, centred volume kayaks from Riot, Pyranha, or Wave Sport.

Kayaking India groups on Facebook are good resources for kayakers in India.

Athletics: Track, Field and Road

India is unfortunately not affluent in the field of athletics and track events. There are very few athletes who won any medal in any global or major events. But the scenario is changing in the 20th century, when people started taking interest in athletics and facility are providing to improve the meager situation of athletics. Anju Bobby George made history when she won the bronze medal in Women's long jump at the 2003 World Championships in Athletics in Paris. With this achievement, she became the first Indian athlete ever to win a medal in a World Championships in Athletics jumping 6.70 m. Till 2010 Milkha Singh was the only athlete to win an individual gold medal at a Commonwealth Games but at 2010 Commonwealth Games, Krishna Punia created history by winning the Women's discus throw gold medal for India after 52 years and as first woman to win a gold in athletics at Commonwealth Games. In the same edition of Commonwealth games Manjeet Kaur, Sini Jose, Ashwini Akkunji & Mandeep Kaur won the Women's 4 × 400 m (Relay) gold medal. At 2014 Commonwealth Games Vikas Gowda won the Men's Discus Throw gold medal.

Hima Das is only Indian track athlete to win a medal at any IAAF global event. She won the gold medal in Women's 400 metres at 2018 IAAF World U20 Championships at Tampere, Finland, on 12 July 2018, clocking a time of 51.46 seconds.She is second gold medalist in athletics at IAAF World U20 Championships after Neeraj Chopra who won Men's javelin throw gold at 2016 IAAF World U20 Championships by setting world junior record with a throw of 86.48 m. Later Neeraj went on to win the Men's javelin throw gold at 2018 Commonwealth Games. Performances at Olympics Games are not satisfactory, till now no Indian athlete won any medal at the Olympics. At 2016 Summer Olympics Lalita Babar becomes the first Indian athlete since 1984 to reach Olympics finale in the event of Women's 3000 metres steeplechase, before her, P.T. Usha reach the finale of Women's 400 metres hurdles at 1984 Summer Olympics.

P.T. Usha won multiple gold medals in different editions of Asian Games and Asian Athletics Championships. Lavy Pinto was the first Indian to win a gold medal in the Asian Games which he won in the first Asian Games held at New Delhi in 1951 in 100 and 200-meter categories. Christine Brown, Stephie D'Souza, Violet Peters, Mary D'Souza gave India its first women athletics gold medal when they won 4 × 100 m relay in 1954 Asian Games but current Asian record is held by Priyanka Pawar,Tintu Luka, Mandeep Kaur, Machettira Raju Poovamma when they won Women's 4 × 400 metres relay at 2014 Asian Games clocking 3:28:68. Kamaljeet Sandhu was the first Indian female athlete to win individual gold medal at any Asian games by winning 400m track event at 1970 Asian Games. Sunita Rani holds the current Asian record in 1500 m track event winning at Busan 2002 Asian Games clocking 4:06:03.

Madhurjya Borah, an Indian triathlete holds silver medal at South Asian Triathlon Championship

Anu Vaidyanathan, an Indian triathlete, is the first Asian to compete in Ultraman.

In May 2016, Arunaabh Shah from Delhi became the 1st Indian male and the youngest Indian to finish Ultraman, at Ultraman Australia.

Gymnastics

Gymnastics came of age in India, when at the 2010 Commonwealth Games, Ashish Kumar won the first-ever medal in gymnastics for India in the form of bronze. However, soon after the win, the president of the Gymnastics Federation of India, controversially asked Kumar's chief coach from the Soviet Union, Vladimir Chertkov, "Is this all that you can deliver, a bronze?" The comment was widely reported in the press. Later, the coach revealed that, "In August 2009, we had no equipment. Ashish trained on hard floor till February 2010, and then we got equipment around 20 years old." The federation announced that no Indian team would travel to Rotterdam for the World Championships in October, which would mean that Indian gymnasts would not have the opportunity to qualify as a team for the 2012 Summer Olympics. Ashish also won a silver medal in the Men's vault at 2010 Commonwealth Games.

It was Glasgow 2014 Commonwealth Games, from where India's glorious path in gymnastics started taking shape slowly, when Dipa Karmakar from Tripura, a small state of India, went on to win bronze medal in the Women's vault finale. But it was not her medal that stuns the world, but its her 2nd vault, the most difficult vault with a D-score of 7, the Produnova vault, named after famous Yelena Produnova of Russia, also known as the **vault of death** due to its difficulty and likelihood of injury, which she executed with a score of 15.1 (D-7, Ex- 8.1) which help her to get the precious bronze. With this attempt she became 5th gymnast to ever execute the Produnova just after legendary gymnast Oksana Chusovitina who executed multiples times.In October 2015, Karmakar became the first Indian gymnast to qualify for a final stage at the World Artistic Gymnastics Championships. Later in 2016 when she qualified for Rio Olympics, she became first Indian gymnast to do so and also hours after her qualification at 2016 Gymnastics Olympic Test Event she clinched gold medal in Women's vault event stunning Oksana Chusovitina with her prudunova again who came second to her. On 6 July 2016, FIG honored Dipa by naming her **World Class Gymnast**. At Rio Olympics she achieved 4th place in vaults. After a long break due to injury when she ran for vaults and landed with a gold at

Figure 248: *Viswanathan Anand*

World Challenge Cup series. Her medal is second to first ever medal won by any Indian, was won by Aruna Reddy at FIG Artistic Gymnastics World Cup Melbourne, where she secured the bronze medal in the individual vaults.

Non-olympic sports

Billiards and snooker

India has been a force in world billiards competitions. Champions including Wilson Jones, Michael Ferreira, Geet Sethi and now the domination of Pankaj Advani have underlined the powerhouse status of the country. The Snooker Federation of India, the apex body, plays a proactive role in popularising the game. Many efforts have been made by the Billiards and Snooker Federation of India in the recent past to enhance the popularity of the game in the country. Several training camps for developing budding talent and providing them with regional and state sponsorship have been organised by the Billiards and Snooker Federation in various parts of the country.

Chess

Chess has risen in popularity in India over the last few decades, primarily due to its star player Viswanathan Anand. He is a multiple World Champion. The

Figure 249: *In a career of twenty four-year span, Sachin Tendulkar has created many batting records, and is often regarded as one of the most successful cricketer of all time.*

game may have originated from India as a successor to Chaturanga or Shatranj. The All India Chess Federation is the governing body for chess in India.

Cricket

Cricket has a long history in India, having been introduced in the country during the British rule. It is the most popular sport by a wide margin in India . Cricket is played on local, national, and international levels, and enjoys consistent support from people in most parts of India. Its development has been closely tied in with the history of the country, mirroring many of the political and cultural developments around issues such as caste, gender, religion, and nationality. The Indian national cricket team played its first official match (a Test) in 1932 against England, and the team's performance since then has generally been mixed, sometimes enjoying stupendous success and sometimes suffering outright failure. The highest profile rival of the Indian cricket team is the Pakistani cricket team, though, in recent times, it has gained other rivals, including Australia, South Africa and England.

Although cricket is the most popular sport in India, it is not the nation's official national sport as India does not have a national sport. The governing body for cricket in India, the Board of Control for Cricket in India (BCCI), was formed

Figure 250: *Kabaddi is one of the most popular sports in India.*

in December 1928 and is based in Mumbai. Today, BCCI is the richest sporting body in the world.

India has hosted or co-hosted a large number of multi-nation major international cricket tournaments, including the 1987 Cricket World Cup (co-hosted with Pakistan), the 1996 Cricket World Cup (co-hosted with Pakistan and Sri Lanka), the 2006 ICC Champions Trophy and the 2011 Cricket World Cup (co-hosted with Sri Lanka and Bangladesh). The India national cricket team has won major tournaments, including the 1983 Cricket World Cup in England, the 2007 ICC World Twenty20 in South Africa, the 2011 Cricket World Cup (which they won by beating Sri Lanka in the final at home), and the 2013 ICC Champions Trophy, and has shared the 2002 ICC Champions Trophy with Sri Lanka. It had also briefly held the position of the No. 1 team in Tests. The domestic competitions include the Ranji Trophy, the Duleep Trophy, the Deodhar Trophy, the Irani Trophy, and the Challenger Series, all of which are not widely followed, despite cricket's popularity in the country. This parallels the global situation in cricket, where the international game is more widely followed than the domestic game in all major cricketing countries. In addition, the BCCI conducts the Indian Premier League, a domestic franchise-based Twenty20 competition, during March–April every year and is extremely popular.

Kabaddi

Kabaddi is a popular national sport in India, played mainly among people in villages. It is regarded as a team-contact sport and as a recreational form of combat training.

Two teams occupy opposite halves of a small field and take turns sending a raider into the other half to win points by tagging and wrestling members of the opposing team. The raider then attempts to return to his own half while holding his breath and chanting "kabaddi, kabaddi, kabaddi" during the whole raid.

India has won gold in all the Asian Games in kabaddi excepting 2018 Asian games where they got bronze. The four forms of kabaddi recognised by Kabaddi federation in India are Amar, Sanjeevni, Gaminee and Punjabi rules Kabaddi. India won the Kabaddi World Championship in 2007, beating Iran 29–19.

Motorsports

Motorsport is a popular spectator sport in India, although there are relatively few competitors compared to other sports, due to the high costs of competing. Coimbatore is often referred to as the "Motor sports Capital of India" and the "Backyard of Indian Motorsports". S.Karivardhan, spearheaded motor racing, making Coimbatore the country's motor racing hub when he designed and built entry level race cars. Before Buddh International Circuit was constructed, the country's only two permanent race ways were the Kari Motor Speedway, Coimbatore and Madras Motor Racing Track, Chennai. MRF built the first Formula 3 car in 1997. MRF in collaboration with Maruti established the Formula Maruti racing, a single-seater, open wheel class motorsport racing event for race cars made in India. MRF Challenge is a Formula 2000 open-wheel motorsport formula based series organised by Madras Motor Sports Club in association with MRF. Narain Karthikeyan and Karun Chandhok are the only drivers from to represent India in Formula 1.

On 1 February 2005, Narain Karthikeyan became India's first Formula One racing driver. On March 2007, he also became the first-ever Indian-born driver to compete in a NASCAR Series. He debuted in the NASCAR Camping World Truck Series in the Kroger 250. Force India F1 is a Formula One motor racing team. The team was formed in October 2007, when a consortium led by Indian businessmen Vijay Mallya and Michiel Mol bought the Spyker F1 team for €88 million. After competing in 29 races without a point, Force India won their first Formula One World Championship points and podium place when Giancarlo Fisichella finished second in the 2009 Belgian Grand Prix. New Delhi hosted the Indian Grand Prix in 2011 at Buddh International

Figure 251: *Force India drivers at the 2008 Canadian Grand Prix.*

Circuit in Greater Noida, 50 km from New Delhi. Karun Chandhok was the test driver for Team Lotus & Narain Karthikeyan raced for HRT during the first half of the 2011 Formula One season. Karun Chandhok participated in Friday'sWikipedia:Manual of Style/Dates and numbers#Chronological items practice session and Karthikeyan (stepping in for Daniel Ricciardo) raced at the 2011 Indian Grand Prix; it was the first time two Indian drivers associated with the same Formula One Grand Prix directly.

Team MRF's Gaurav Gill the first Indian rally driver to win FIA Asia-Pacific Rally Championship in 2013.[509]

Korfball

Korfball, a mixed-gender ball sport, with similarities to netball and basketball, is played by over 50 countries in the world. It is not as popular in India as other sports, but is still played by a significant amount of people. India came in third place twice (2002 & 2006) in the Asia-Oceania Korfball Championships.

Karate

Karate in India is administered by the Karate Association of India[510] whose president is Karate R Thiagarajan and General Secretary Bharat Sharma of KAI. India has produced many accomplished *karatekas* like Aniket Gupta, Deepika Dhiman, Sunil Rathee , Supriya Jatav and Gaurva Sindhiya. The 2015 Commonwealth Karate Games were held in Delhi, India.

Figure 252: *Jump korfball in the Netherlands between ZKV Zaandam and ALO.*

Floorball

Floorball, an indoor team sport, a type of floor hockey, is gaining popularity in India. The Floorball Federation of India was started in 2001 and, since then, it has expanded rapidly. There have been four national floorball championships held, with Uttar Pradesh becoming the champions. Women's floorball has also expanded, and Mumbai is the first national floorball champion of India. India is a provisional member of the International Floorball Federation. India has participated in many international friendlies and steps are being taken to make India an ordinary member of floorball.

Netball

Netball, derived from early versions of basketball, is a popular sport in India, especially among Indian women. India's national team is ranked 25th in the world and has played only a few matches. The team has failed to qualify for any of the World Netball Championships. They played 18 matches in total. In the 2010 Commonwealth Games in Delhi, India, netball was included as a medal sport. However, the Indian team failed to win a medal.

Throwball

Throwball, a non-contact competitive ball sport played across a net between two teams of seven players on a rectangular court, is gaining popularity in India. Indian authorities of the game were instrumental in organising an Asian level and, later, a world level association for the sport. Throwball is played in gym class, colleges, and clubs throughout Asian countries such as India, Sri Lanka, Korea, Thailand, Malaysia, Japan, China, Pakistan, Nepal, Bhutan, and Bangladesh. The sport is also slowly gaining in popularity in other countries including France, Australia, Brazil, Canada, and the United Kingdom. India's junior throwball team visited Sri Lanka in 1982. Vijay Dahiya from Haryana was captain of the team. The Indian team won the test series.

Lacrosse

Lacrosse is a relatively new sport in India, introduced in 2006. The governing body for lacrosse in India is the Indian National Lacrosse Federation. It is now being played by schools in Shillong, Meghalaya, while being mostly unknown in the rest of the country.

American football

Introduced in 2011 by various American football figures, including Mike Ditka and Ron Jaworski, the Elite Football League of India was India's first professional American football league. Their first league play was to commence in 2012, and feature teams from eight different Indian cities, including Mumbai, Kolkata, Delhi, and Jaipur.

Polo

India is considered the cradle of modern polo. Babur, the founder of the Mughal Empire in the 15th century, firmly established its popularity. The period between the decline of the Mughal dynasty and the upsurgence of the British Imperial rule, polo almost vanished from mainland India. Fortunately, the game survived in a few remote mountainous enclaves of the subcontinent, notably Gilgit, Chitral, Ladakh, and Manipur.

In India, the popularity of polo has waned and risen many times. However, it has never lost its regal status. In the last few decades, the emergence of privately owned teams has ensured a renaissance in Indian polo. Today, polo is not just restricted to the royalty and the Indian Army.

Figure 253: *Polo*

Baseball and softball

Baseball has recently begun to show up in India. Softball is played in school and at the university level. Two Indian pitchers were selected by the "Million Dollar Arm" competition to play in the United States. A talent hunt-style competition conducted by Major League Baseball to find baseball talent in India found the teenagers Rinku Singh and Dinesh Patel, who were taken to the US and received professional coaching. These two players were selected to play for Pittsburgh Pirates minor league organisations. Rinku Singh played for the Canberra Cavalry of the Australian Baseball League for the competition's inaugural 2010–11 season.

Rock climbing

Rock climbing has been around in India for a long time. Presumably, the mountaineers headed for Himalayan ascents had to train somewhere, and would have imparted some of the initial technical climbing culture. Documented evidence of rock climbing is associated with bouldering and climbing around Bangalore's famous Ramanagara crags and Turahalli boulders, around Western Ghats closer to Mumbai and Pune. The Deccan Plateau and south of the Vindhya Range are considered the prime locations for rock climbing in India. There is an established climbing tradition associated with Mumbai, Pune,

Figure 254: *Sepak takraw ball*

and Bangalore. For example, Hampi is considered the bouldering capital of India. Climbers congregate here during New Year's Eve and climb through the weeks preceding and after. Badami is popular for its free and sport routes (numbering over 200).

Sepak takraw

Sepak takraw, though not very well known in India, was a demonstration sport at the Delhi Asian Games in 1982. The Sepak Takraw Federation, with its headquarters in Nagpur, Maharashtra, was founded on 10 September 1982. It is recognised by the Indian Olympic Association and Ministry of Youth Affairs and Sports since 2000.[511] So far, the federation has conducted 14 senior, seven junior, and six sub-junior national championships in different cities, and is conducting Federation Cup Tournaments and zonal National Championships.

The game is very popular in the northeastern state of Manipur, and some of the best players came from there. In the 22nd King's Cup International Sepak Takraw Tournament held in Bangkok, the India men's team lost in the semi-finals and claimed bronze in the team event. In the doubles event, the women's team lost in the semi-finals, but earned bronze medals.[512]

On 21st August 2018, at the 2018 Asian Games, the national men's team created history as the team won a bronze after losing 2-0 to Thailand. It was Indian's fisrt medal in Sepak takraw in Asian games.

Winter sports

Winter sports are common in India in the Himalayan areas. Skiing tournaments take place every winter in Gulmarg, and Manali. Winter sports are generally more common in the northern states of Jammu and Kashmir, Himachal Pradesh, Uttarakhand, Sikkim, and Arunachal Pradesh. Skiing, snow rugby, snow cycling, and snow football are some of the common winter sports played in India. Skiing is more popular, although India has taken part in luge in Winter Olympics since 1998. Shiva Keshavan is the only Indian to have won medals in international meets in winter sports (Asian Gold 2011, Asian Silver 2009, Asian Bronze 2008, Asian Silver (doubles) 2005, Asian Bronze (singles) 2005), and to have participated in four Olympic Games. He is the Asian speed record holder at 134.4 km/h, making him the fastest man in Asia on ice. Luge is practised in a big way by the mountain residents in an improvised form called "reri".

Bandy

India has a national bandy team. The Bandy Federation of India governs bandy in India. Its headquarters are in Mandi in Himachal Pradesh. Bandy, a team winter sport played on ice, in which skaters use sticks to direct a ball into the opposing team's goal, is generally played in northern India, where there is snow and ice. India is one of seven countries in Asia and out of a total of 28 to be a member of Federation of International Bandy. BFI planned to send a team to the 2011 Asian Winter Games in Astana-Almaty, but ultimately did not.

Ice hockey

Ice hockey is played in the colder parts of India, including Kashmir, Ladakh, and parts of Himachal Pradesh.

Figure 255: *Seval sandai, traditional cock fight*

Traditional and regional sports

Seval Sandai

Seval Sandai or Seval Porr (cockfighting) is a popular rural sport. Three or four-inch blades are attached to the cocks' feet and the winner is decided after three or four rounds of no hold barred fighting. The sport involves major gambling in recent times.

Jallikattu

Jallikattu is a popular bull taming sport practiced particularly during Pongal festival. Jallikattu was a popular sport since the Tamil classical period. Rekla race is an associated sport which is a form of bullock cart racing. In May 2014, the Supreme Court of India banned both the sports citing animal welfare issues.[513]

Gilli-danda

Gilli-danda is a sport played by using one small stick (*gilli*) and a large stick (*danda*) like cricket, with the ball replaced by *gilli*. It is still played in villages of Karnataka, Tamil Nadu, Rajasthan, Uttar Pradesh, Madhya Pradesh, Bihar, Maharashtra and Gujarat in India only as a recreational sport among boys.

Figure 256: *Jallikattu, taming the bull*

Figure 257: *Rekla, bullock cart race*

Figure 258: *Young boys playing Gilli-danda, a traditional Indian sport.*

Kancha

Kancha is played by using marbles. Marbles are glass balls which are very popular among children. It is popular in small Indian cities and villages, among small boys only as a gully sport. It is rarely played by girls. The participant has to hit the marble kept in a circle. If he hits the target properly, he wins. The winner gets the kancha of the other participant boys.

Kite-flying

Kite-flying is pursued by many people in India, in cities as well as villages. The festival of Makar Sankranti features kite-flying competitions. It is festival which is a passion among Indians.

Indian martial arts

India has many traditional regional forms of martial arts like lathi khela, sqay, kalari, kushti, thang-ta and silambam.

Kho-kho

Kho kho is a tag sport played by teams of twelve players who try to avoid being touched by members of the opposing team, only 9 players of the team enter the field. It is one of the two most popular traditional tag games played in schools, the other being kabbadi.

===Others=== ball badminton as combination of badminton and volleyball Uriyadi involves smashing a small earthen pot with a long stick usually with a cloth wrapped around the eyes to prevent the participants from seeing the pot. Other minor sports include Ilavatta kal where lift huge spherical rocks, Gilli-danda played with two pieces of sticks, Nondi played by folding one leg and hopping squares. Some of the indoor games include Pallanguzhi involving beads, Bambaram involving spinning of top, Dhayakattai which is a modified dice game, Aadu puli attam, Nungu vandi and Seechangal. Other regional sports and games, including air sports, atya patya, langdi, surr, sitolia bridge, carrom, cycle polo, fencing, judo, Gatka, kho-kho, mallakhamb, roller skating, rowing, shooting ball, soft tennis, squash, swimming, ten-pin bowling, tennikoit, tug of war, yachting, and yoga, have dedicated followers and their own national sports federations. There are other seasonal sports like "Dahi Handi" which have a great public following as well.

Sports Broadcasting in India

Local sporting events broadcasting is in a stagnant stage in India due to the mandatory sharing of sporting events of live feed and rights made by ordnance in favour of Prasar Bharathi. Thus, all sports broadcasters playout from outside the country, which only allows the capability to produce international events and fades the production, distribution, invention of the new local field of sporting events.

Major sports television networks include Star Sports, Star Sports Network, Sony Ten, Sony Six, Sony ESPN, ESPN Asia, DSport and DD Sports.

Sports Leagues in India

National

Green background for the major IPL-Style sports leagues. Blue background for the major sports leagues.

The no of season are as on August 2016.

League	Current Sponsored	Game	Partic- ipation	Sea- sons	Teams
All India & South Asia Rugby Tournament		⚡ Rugby Union	Club Teams	6	10
Champions Tennis League (CTL)	Aircel	🎾 Tennis	Club Teams	2	6
Deodhar Trophy		🏏 Cricket (List A)	Zonal Teams	44	5
Duleep Trophy		🏏 Cricket (First Class)	Zonal Teams	56	5
Elite Football League of India		🏈 American Football	Club Teams	2	24
Golf Premier League		⛳ Golf	Club Teams	1	8
Hockey India League (HIL)	Hero	🏑 Hockey	Club Teams	4	6
Indian Premier League (IPL)	Vivo	🏏 Cricket (Twenty20)	Club Teams	10	8
Indian Super League (ISL)	Hero	⚽ Football	Club Teams	3	10
Indian Volley League		🏐 Volleyball	Club Teams	1	6
I-League	Hero	⚽ Football	Club Teams	10	10
I-League 2nd Division		⚽ Football	Club Teams	10	18
Premier Badminton League (PBL)		🏸 Badminton	Club Teams	2	6
Premier Futsal		⚽ Futsal	Club Teams	1	6
Pro Kabaddi League (PKL)	Star Sports	🤼 Kabaddi	Club Teams	5	12
Pro Wrestling League (PWL)		🤼 Wrestling	Club Teams	1	8
Ranji Trophy	Paytm	🏏 Cricket (First Class)	State Teams	82	27
UBA Pro Basketball League		🏀 Basketball	Club Teams	4	8
Vijay Hazare Trophy		🏏 Cricket (List A)	State Teams	15	27
Women's Kabaddi Challenge (PKL)	Star Sports	🤼 Kabaddi	Club Teams	1	3
World Series Hockey (WSH)		🏑 Field Hockey	Club Teams	1	8

Indian Women's League	Hero	🏃 Football	Club Teams	1	6 (Main Round)

International

League	Current Sponsored	Game	Partic-ipation	Sea-sons	Teams	Indian Teams
AFC Cup		🏃 Football	Club Teams	13	32	2
International Premier Tennis League (IPTL)	Coca-Cola	🎾 Tennis	Club Teams	2	4	1

Youth Sports Leagues

- I-League U19 (association football)

Others

- Ring Ka King (Professional Wrestling)
- Super Fight League (Mixed Martial Arts)

Proposed League

League	Current Sponsored	Game	Partic-ipation	Sea-sons	Teams
Indian Athletics League		🏃 Athletics	Club Teams		
Indian Series of Boxing[514]		🥊 Boxing	Club Teams		TBA
i1 Super Series		🏎 Motor-sports	Club Teams		9 (Pro-posed)

Leagues that are defunct

League	Game	Participation	Seasons	Teams
Indian Cricket League (ICL)	⅄ Cricket (Twenty20)	Club Teams	2	9
ICL World Series (ICL World Series)	⅄ Cricket (Twenty20)	Club Teams	2	4
National Football League	⇗ Association Football	Club Teams	11	10
Premier Hockey League (PHL)	⚹ Field Hockey	Club Teams	4	7

External links

- The mystery of the missing medals[515]
- Ministry of Youth Affairs and Sports[516]
- Budget for Sports in India[517]

Template:Sport Federation of India

Indian martial arts

Part of a series on
Indian martial arts

Styles

Gatka
Huyen langlon
Kalaripayattu
Mardani khel
Silambam
Sqay
Boxing

Musti-yuddha

Wrestling

Malla-yuddha
Pehlwani
Vajra-musti

Legendary Figures

- Agastya
- Balarama
- Bhima
- Bodhidharma
- Duryodhana
- Ganesha
- Hanuman
- Harihara
- Jambavan
- Jarasandha
- Kali
- Krishna
- Kartikeya
- Parashurama
- Shiva
- Unniyarcha
- Vajrapani

Notable Practitioners

- Guru Hargobind
- Shivaji
- Kittur Chennamma
- Lakshmibai

Related terms
• Akhara
• Hatha yoga
• Kshatriya
• Nihang
• Paika akhada
• Varma kalai

• v
• t
• e[518]

Indian martial arts refers to the fighting systems of the Indian subcontinent. A variety of terms are used for the English phrases "Indian martial arts", usually deriving from Sanskrit or Dravidian sources. While they may seem to imply specific disciplines (e.g. archery, armed combat), by Classical times they were used generically for all fighting systems.

Translations of *Indian martial arts*

Term (in Sanskrit)	Translation
yuddhakalā (युद्धकला)	warfare art
āyudhavidyā (आयुधविद्या)	knowledge of arms
vīravidyā (वीरविद्या)	science of being a warrior
śastravidyā (शस्त्रविद्या)	science of weaponry
dhanurveda (धनुर्वेद)	science of archery
svarakshākalā (स्वरक्षाकला) (in Sanskrit)	art of self-defence

Among the most common terms today, *śastra-vidyā*, is a compound of the words *śastra* (weapon) and *vidyā* (knowledge).[519] *Dhanurveda* derives from the words for bow (*dhanushya*) and knowledge (*veda*), the "science of archery" in Puranic literature, later applied to martial arts in general.[520] The Vishnu Purana text describes dhanuveda as one of the traditional eighteen branches of "applied knowledge" or upaveda, along with *shastrashastra* or military science. A later term, *yuddha kalā*, comes from the words *yuddha* meaning fight or combat and *kalā* meaning art or skill. The related term *śastra kalā* (lit. weapon art) usually refers specifically to armed disciplines. Another term, *yuddha-vidyā* or "combat knowledge", refers to the skills used on the battlefield, encompassing not only actual fighting but also battle formations and strategy. Martial arts are usually learnt and practiced in the traditional akharas.

History

Antiquity (pre-Gupta)

Dhanurveda, a section found in the Vedas (1700 BCE - 1100 BCE) contains references to martial arts. Indian epics contain the earliest accounts of combat, both armed and bare-handed. Most deities of the Hindu-Buddhist pantheon are armed with their own personal weapon, and are revered not only as master martial artists but often as originators of those systems themselves. The *Mahabharata* tells of fighters armed only with daggers besting lions, and describes a prolonged battle between Arjuna and Karna using bows, swords, trees, rocks and fists. Another unarmed battle in the Mahabharata describes two combatants boxing with clenched fists and fighting with kicks, finger strikes, knee strikes and headbutts.[521]

The oldest recorded organized unarmed fighting art in South Asia is mallayuddha or combat-wrestling, codified into four forms and pre-dating the Vedic Period. Stories describing Krishna report that he sometimes engaged in wrestling matches where he used knee strikes to the chest, punches to the head, hair pulling, and strangleholds. Based on such accounts, Svinth (2002) traces press ups and squats used by South Asian wrestlers to the pre-classical era.

In Sanskrit literature the term *dwandwayuddha* referred to a duel, such that it was a battle between only two warriors and not armies. Epics often describe the duels between deities and god-like heroes as lasting a month or more. The malla-yuddha (wrestling match) between Bhima and Jarasandha lasts 27 days. Similarly, the *dwandayuddha* between Parasurama and Bhishma lasts for 30 days, while that between Krishna and Jambavan lasts for 28 days. Likewise, the *dwandwayudda* between Bali and Dundubhi, a demon in the form of a water buffalo, lasts for 45 days. The Manusmriti tells that if a warrior's topknot comes loose during such a fight or duel, the opponent must give him time to bind his hair before continuing.

The *Charanavyuha* authored by Shaunaka mentions four *upaveda* (applied Vedas). Included among them are archery (*dhanurveda*) and military sciences (*shastrashastra*), the mastery of which was the duty (*dharma*) of the warrior class. Kings usually belonged to the kshatria (warrior) class and thus served as heads of the army. They typically practiced archery, wrestling, boxing, and swordsmanship as part of their education. Examples include such rulers as Siddhartha Gautama and Rudradaman. The Chinese monk Xuanzang writes that the emperor Harsha was light on his feet despite his advancing age and managed to dodge and seize an assailant during an assassination attempt.

Many of the popular sports mentioned in the Vedas and the epics have their origins in military training, such as boxing (*musti-yuddha*), wrestling (*maladwandwa*), chariot-racing (*rathachalan*), horse-riding (*aswa-rohana*) and archery (*dhanurvidya*). Competitions were held not just as a contest of the players' prowess but also as a means of finding a bridegroom. Arjuna, Rama and Siddhartha Gautama all won their consorts in such tournaments.

In the 3rd century, elements from the Yoga Sutras of Patanjali, as well as finger movements in the *nata* dances, were incorporated into the fighting arts. A number of South Asian fighting styles remain closely connected to yoga, dance and performing arts. Some of the choreographed sparring in kalaripayat can be applied to dance and kathakali dancers who knew kalaripayat were believed to be markedly better than other performers. Until recent decades, the chhau dance was performed only by martial artists. Some traditional Indian classical dance schools still incorporate martial arts as part of their exercise regimen.[522]

Written evidence of martial arts in Southern India dates back to the Sangam literature of about the 2nd century BC to the 2nd century AD. The Akananuru and Purananuru describe the use of spears, swords, shields, bows and silambam in the Sangam era. The word kalari appears in the *Puram* (verses 225, 237, 245, 356) and *Akam* (verses 34, 231, 293) to describe both a battlefield and combat arena. The word *kalari tatt* denoted a martial feat, while *kalari kozhai* meant a coward in war. Each warrior in the Sangam era received regular military training[523] in target practice and horse riding. They specialized in one or more of the important weapons of the period including the spear (*vel*), sword (*val*), shield (*kedaham*), and bow and arrow (*vil ambu*). The combat techniques of the Sangam period were the earliest precursors to kalaripayat. References to "Silappadikkaram" in Sangam literature date back to the 2nd century. This referred to the silambam staff which was in great demand with foreign visitors.

The ten fighting styles of northern sastra-vidya were said to have been created in different areas based on animals and gods, and designed for the particular geography of their origin.Wikipedia:Citation needed Tradition ascribes their convergence to the 6th-century Buddhist university of Takshashila,Wikipedia:Citation needed ancient India's intellectual capital. Located in present-day Panjab, Pakistan, the Ramayana ascribes the city's founding to Bharata who named it after his son Taksha. From the 7th to the 5th centuries BC it was held in high regard as a great centre of trade and learning, attracting students from throughout present-day Pakistan and northern India. Among the subjects taught were the "military sciences", and archery was one of its prime arts.

Some measures were put into place to discourage martial activity during the Buddhist period. The Khandhaka in particular forbids wrestling, boxing, archery, and swordsmanship. However, references to fighting arts are found in early Buddhist texts, such as the Lotus Sutra (c. 1st century AD) which refers to a boxing art while speaking to Manjusri.[524] It also categorised combat techniques as joint locks, fist strikes, grapples and throws. The Lotus Sutra makes further mention of a martial art with dance-like movements called *Nara*. Another Buddhist sutra called *Hongyo-kyo* (佛本行集經) describes a "strength contest" between Gautama Buddha's half-brother Prince Nanda and his cousin Devadatta. Siddhartha Gautama himself was a champion wrestler and swordsman before becoming the Buddha.

Classical period (3rd to 10th centuries)

Like other branches of Sanskrit literature, treatises on martial arts become more systematic in the course of the 1st millennium AD. Vajra-musti, an armed grappling style, is mentioned in sources of the early centuries AD. Around this time, tantric philosophers developed important metaphysical concepts such as kundalini, chakra, and mantra.

The *Sushruta Samhita* (c. 4th century) identifies 107 vital points on the human body[525] of which 64 were classified as being lethal if properly struck with a fist or stick. Sushruta's work formed the basis of the medical discipline ayurveda which was taught alongside various martial arts. With numerous other scattered references to vital points in Vedic and epic sources, it is certain that South Asia's early fighters knew and practised attacking or defending vital points.

Around 630, King Narasimhavarman of the Pallava dynasty commissioned dozens of granite sculptures showing unarmed fighters disarming armed opponents. This is similar to the style described in the *Agni Purana*.

Martial arts were not exclusive to the kshatriya caste, though the warrior class used them more extensively. The 8th-century text *Kuvalaymala* by Udyotanasuri recorded fighting techniques being taught at educational institutions, where non-kshatriya students from throughout the subcontinent "were learning and practicing archery, fighting with sword and shield, with daggers, sticks, lances, and with fists, and in duels (*niyuddham*)". Hindu priests of the traditional gurukula still teach unarmed fighting techniques to their students as a way of increasing stamina and training the physical bodyWikipedia:Citation needed.

The Gurjara-Pratihara came into power during the 7th century and founded a kyshatria dynasty in northern India which exceeded the preceding Gupta Empire. During this period, Emperor Nagabhata I (750–780 AD) and Mihir Bhoja I (836–890) commissioned various texts on martial arts, and were themselves practitioners of these systems. *Shiva Dhanuveda* was composed in this era. The *khadga*, a two-handed broad-tipped heavy longsword, was given special preference. It was even used for *khadga-puja*, ritualised worship of the sword. The Gurjara-Pratiharas continuously fought off Arab invasions, particularly during the Caliphate campaigns in India. The Arab chronicler Sulaiman wrote of the Gurjara ruler as the greatest foe to Islamic expansion, while at the same time praising his cavalry. The Gurjara people still keep up their tradition of gatka and kushti, and until today there are world-class wrestlers from the community competing at national and international levels.

Middle Ages (11th to 15th centuries)

Kalaripayat had developed into its present form by the 11th century, during an extended period of warfare between the Chera and Chola dynasties. The earliest treatise discussing the techniques of malla-yuddha is the *Malla Purana* (c. 13th century), unlike the earlier *Manasollasa* which gives the names of movements but no descriptions.

Over a period of several centuries, invading Muslim armies managed to occupy much of present-day Pakistan and northern India. In response to the spread of Muslim rule,[526] the kingdoms of south India united in the 14th century to found the Vijayanagara Empire. Physical culture was given much attention by both royalty and commoners in the empire, with wrestling being particularly popular with both men and women. Gymnasiums have been discovered inside royal quarters of Vijayanagara, and records speak of regular physical training for commanders and their armies during peace time. Royal palaces and market places had special arenas where royalty and common people alike amused themselves by watching matches such as cock fights, ram fights and wrestling. One account describes an akhara in Chandragiri where noblemen practiced jumping exercises, boxing, fencing and wrestling almost everyday before dinner to maintain their health, and observed that "men as old as seventy years look only thirty".

The Italian traveller Pietro Della Valle wrote of cane-fighting in southern India. According to Pietro, it was the custom for soldiers to specialise in their own particular weapon of expertise and never use any other even during war, "thereby becoming very expert and well practised in that which he takes to".

As their ancient predecessors, swordplay and wrestling were commonly practiced by the royalty of Vijayanagara. Krishna Deva Raya is said to have arranged a duel between a champion swordsman and the prince of Odisha who was known for being an expert with both the sword and dagger. The prince accepted the challenge until he learned he would be fighting one not of royal blood and so killed himself rather than having to "soil his hands". Fernao Nunes and the Persian envoy Adbur Razzak relate that Deva Raya II survived an assassination attempt "as he was a man who knew how to use both sword and dagger better than anyone in his kingdom, avoided by twists and turns of his

Figure 259: *Mughal warriors practicing horse-*
back archery, a skill they were highly renowned for

body the thrusts aimed at him, freed himself from him, and slew him with a
short sword that he had."

Mughal era (1526–1857)

After a series of victories, the Central Asian conqueror Babur established
Mughal rule in north India during the 16th century. The Mughals were patrons of India's native arts, not only recruiting akhara-trained Rajput fighters
for their armies but even practicing these systems themselves.[527]   The *Au-*
sanasa Dhanurveda Sankalanam dates to the late 16th century, compiled under the patronage of Akbar. The *Ain-i-Akbari* tells that the Mughal court had
various kinds of fighting men from around the empire who would demonstrate
their skills every day in exchange for rewards. Among them were said to be
both native and Mughal wrestlers, slingers from Gujarat, Hindustani athletes,
boxers, stone-throwers and many others.

> *'There are several kinds of gladiators, each performing astonishing feats.*
> *In fighting they show much speed and agility and blend courage and skill in*
> *squatting down and rising up again. Some of them use shields in fighting,*
> *others use cudgels. Others again use no means of defence, and fight with*
> *one hand only; these are called ek-hath. Those who come from the eastern*

districts of Hindostan use a small shield called "chirwah". Those from the southern provinces have shields of such magnitude as to cover a man and a horse. This kind of shield is called tilwah. Another class use a shield somewhat less than the height of a man. Some again use a long sword, and seizing it with both hands they perform extraordinary feats of skill. There is another famous class called Bankúlis. They have no shield but make use of a peculiar kind of sword which, though curved towards the point, is straight near the handle. They wield it with great dexterity. The skill that they exhibit passes all description. Others are skilful in fighting with daggers and knives of various forms; of these there are upwards of a hundred thousand. Each class has a different name; they also differ in their performances. At court there are a thousand gladiators always in readiness."

Avid hunters, a popular sport among the Mughals was *shikar* or tiger-hunting. While often done with arrows and later even rifles, it was considered most impressive to kill a tiger with a hand-to-hand weapon such as a sword or dagger. A warrior who managed to best a tiger would be awarded the title of *Pachmar*.

In the 16th century, Madhusudana Saraswati of Bengal organised a section of the Naga tradition of armed sannyasi in order to protect Hindus from the intolerant Mughal rulers. Although generally said to abide by the principle of non-violence (*ahimsā*), these Dashanami monks had long been forming akhara for the practice of both yoga and martial arts. Such warrior-ascetics have been recorded from 1500 to as late as the 18th century, although tradition attributes their creation to the 8th-century philosopher Sankaracharya. They began as a stratum of Rajput warriors who would gather after harvest and arm peasants into militarised units, effectively acting as a self-defense squad. Prevalent in Rajasthan, Maharashtra and Bengal, they would give up their occupations and leave their families to live as mercenaries. Naga sadhu today rarely practice any form of fighting other than wrestling, but still carry trishula, swords, canes and spears. To this day their retreats are called *chhauni* or armed camps, and they have been known to hold mock jousts among themselves. As recently as the 1950s, it was not unusual for Naga sadhu to strike to kill someone over issues of honour.

There is also a 17th-century *Dhanurveda-samhita* attributed to Vasistha.

Maratha dynasty (1674–1859)

Coming from a hilly region characterized by valleys and caves, the Marathas became expert horsemen who favoured light armour and highly mobile cavalry units during war. Known especially as masters of swords and spears, their heavily martial culture and propensity for the lance is mentioned as early as

Figure 260: *Statue of Shivaji, the warrior-king who brought
the Maratha people and fighting style to prominence*

the 7th century by Xuanzang.[528] After serving the Dakshin sultanates of the
early 17th century, the scattered Marathas united to found their own kingdom
under the warrior Shivaji Raje. Having learned the native art of mardani khela
from a young age, Chhatrapati Shivaji Maharaj was a master swordsman and
proficient in the use of various weapons. He took advantage of his people's
expertise in guerilla tactics (*Shiva sutra*) to re-establish *Hindavi Swarajya* (native [Hindu being a term traditionally applied to the native inhabitants of India
throughout antiquity] self-rule) at a time of Muslim supremacy and increasing
intolerance. Utilizing speed, focused surprise attacks (typically at night and
in rocky terrain), and the geography of Maharashtra, Karnataka, & South India; the Maratha rulers were successfully able to defend their territory from
the more numerous and heavily armed Mughals.[529] The still-existing Maratha
Light Infantry is one of the "oldest and most renowned" regiments of the Indian
Army, tracing its origins to 1768.

Paika Rebellion

Paika is the Odia word for fighter or warrior. Their training schools, known
as paika akhada, can be traced back to ancient Kalinga and their art was at
one time patronised by King Kharavela. In March 1817, under the leadership

of Bakshi Jagabandhu Bidyadhar Mohapatra, nearly 400 Khanda of Ghumusar in Ganjam marched towards Khordha in protest against British colonial rule. Many government buildings were burnt down and all the officials fled. The British commander of one detachment was killed during a battle at Gangapada. The paika managed to capture two bases at Puri and Pipli before spreading the rebellion further to Gop, Tiran, Kanika and Kujang. The revolt lasted a year and a half before being quelled by September 1818. Today the paika akhada are known mainly for their street performances during festivals.

Modern period (1857—present)

South Asian martial arts underwent a period of decline after the full establishment of British colonial rule in the 19th century. More European modes of organizing kings, armies and governmental institutions, and the increasing use of firearms, gradually eroded the need for traditional combat training associated with caste-specific duties. The British colonial government banned kalaripayat in 1804 in response to a series of revolts. Silambam was also banned and became more common in the Malay Peninsula than its native Tamil Nadu. Nevertheless, traditional fighting systems persisted, sometimes even under the patronage of enthusiastic British spectators who tended to remark on the violence of native boxing and the acrobatic movements characteristic of South Asian fighting styles.Wikipedia:Citation needed

The British took advantage of communities with a heavily militaristic culture, characterising them as "martial races" and employing them in the armed forces. Sikhs - already known among Indians for their martial practices - were particularly valued by the colonists as soldiers and guards, and were posted throughout not only India but Southeast Asia and other parts of the British EmpireWikipedia:Citation needed. Members of the army were allowed to box as a way of settling disputes, provided that they were still able to carry out their duties as soldiers after a match. The particular form of boxing used by the Punjabi soldiers was *loh-musti*,Wikipedia:Citation needed as the kara worn by Sikhs could be wielded like brass knuckles.

The resurgence of public interest in kalaripayat began in the 1920s in Tellicherry as part of a wave of rediscovery of the traditional arts throughout south India which characterised the growing reaction against British colonial rule. During the following three decades, other regional styles were subsequently revived such as silambam in Tamil Nadu, thang-ta in Manipur and paika akhada in Orissa.

Texts

Agni Purana

One of the earliest extant manual of Indian martial arts is in the Agni Purana (dated to between the 8th and the 11th century), The dhanurveda section in the Agni Purana spans chapters 248–251, categorizing weapons into thrown and unthrown classes and further divided into several sub-classes. It catalogs training into five major divisions for different types of warriors, namely charioteers, elephant-riders, horsemen, infantry, and wrestlers.

The nine asanas (stances) in the fight are listed below:

1. *samapada* ("holding the feet even"): standing in closed ranks with the feet put together (248.9)
2. *vaiśākha*: standing erect with the feet apart (248.10)
3. *maṇḍala* ("disk"): standing with the knees apart, arranged in the shape of a flock of geese (248.11)
4. *ālīḍha* ("licked, polished"): bending the right knee with the left foot pulled back (248.12)
5. *pratyālīḍha*: bending the left knee with the right foot pulled back (248.13)
6. *jāta* ("origin"): placing the right foot straight with the left foot perpendicular, the ankles being five fingers apart (248.14)
7. *daṇḍāyata* ("extended staff"): keeping the right knee bent with the left leg straight, or vice versa; called *vikaṭa* ("dreadful") if the two legs are two palm-lengths apart (248.16)
8. *sampuṭa* ("hemisphere") (248.17)
9. *swastika* ("well-being"): keeping the feet 16 fingers apart and lifting the feet a little (248.19)

Then there follows a more detailed discussion of archery technique.

The section concludes with listing the names of actions or "deeds" possible with a number of weapons, including 32 positions to be taken with sword and shield (*khaḍgacarmavidhau*),[530] 11 names of techniques of using a rope in fighting, along with 5 names of "acts in the rope operation" along with lists of "deeds" pertaining to the chakram (war-quoit), the spear, the *tomara* (iron club), the gada (mace), the axe, the hammer, the *bhindipāla* or *laguda*, the vajra, the dagger, the slingshot, and finally deeds with a bludgeon or cudgel. A short passage near the end of the text returns to the larger concerns of warfare and explains the various uses of war elephants and men. The text concludes with a description of how to appropriately send the well-trained fighter off to war.

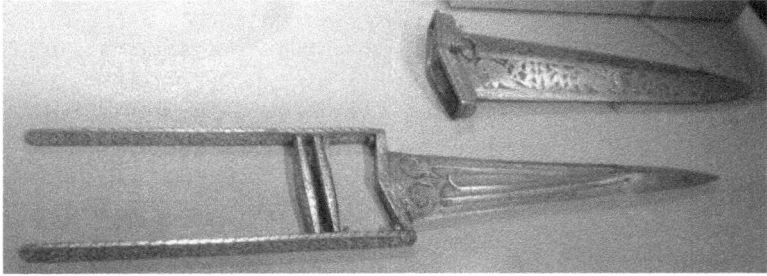

Figure 261: *The katara, the most characteristic of South Asian daggers*

Arthashastra

The Arthashastra, c. 4th century BCE, typically attributed to Chanakya chief advisor of Chandragupt Maurya is one of the earliest treatises on state craft, including diverse topics such as economics, politics, diplomacy and military strategy.

Others

There is an extant *Dhanurveda-Samhita* dating to the mid-14th century, by Brhat Sarngadhara Paddhati (ed. 1888).
Other scattered references to fighting arts in medieval texts include the:
Kamandakiya Nitisara (c. 8th century ed. Manmatha Nath Dutt, 1896),
The *Nitivakyamrta* by Somadeva Suri (10th century),
The *Yuktikalpataru* of Bhoja (11th century) and
The *Manasollasa* of Somesvara III (12th century)

Weapons & Arts

A wide array of weapons are used in South Asia, some of which are not found anywhere else. According to P.C. Chakravati in *The Art of War in Ancient India*, armies used standard weapons such as wooden or metal tipped spears, swords, thatched bamboo, wooden or metal shields, axes, short and long bows in warfare as early as the 4th century BC. Military accounts of the Gupta Empire (c. 240–480) and the later Agni Purana identify over 130 different weapons.

The *Agni Purana* divides weapons into thrown and unthrown classes. The thrown (*mukta*) class includes twelve weapons altogether which come under four categories, viz.

- *yantra-mukta*: projectile weapons such as the sling or the bow

- *pāṇi-mukta*: weapons thrown by hand such as the javelin
- *mukta-sandarita*: weapons that are thrown and drawn back, such as the rope-spear
- *mantra-mukta*: mythical weapons that are thrown by magic incantations (mantra), numbering 6 types

These were opposed to the much larger unthrown class of three categories.

- *hasta-śastra* or *amukta*: melee weapons that do not leave the hand, numbering twenty types
- *muktāmukta*: weapons that can be thrown or used in-close, numbering 98 varieties
- *bāhu-yuddha* or *bhuja-yuddha*: weapons of the body, i.e. unarmed fighting

The duel with bow and arrows is considered the most noble, fighting with the spear ranks next, while fighting with the sword is considered unrefined, and wrestling is classed as the meanest or worst form of fighting. Only a Brahmins could be an acharya (teacher) of sastravidya, Kshatriya and vaishya should learn from the Acharya, while a shudra could not take a teacher, left to "fight of his own in danger".

Over time, weaponry evolved and India became famous for its flexible wootz steel. The most commonly taught weapons in the Indian martial arts today are types of swords, daggers, spears, staves, cudgels and maces.

Weapons are linked to several superstitions and cultural beliefs in South Asia. Drawing a weapon without reason is forbidden and considered by Hindus to be disrespectful to the goddess Chandika. Thus the saying that a sword cannot be sheathed until it has drawn blood. It was a mother's duty to tie a warrior's sword around his waist before war or a duel. In addition, she would cut her finger with the sword and make a tilak on his head from a drop of her blood. Weapons themselves were also anointed with tilak, most often from the blood of a freshly-decapitated goat (*chatanga*). Other taboos include looking at one's reflection in the blade, telling the price or source of acquisition, throwing it on the ground or using it for domestic purposes.

Swordsmanship (Khadgavidya)

Nakula and Sahadeva are said to be skilled swordsmen in Mahabharata. Sword-fighting is one of the common Indian fighting arts. Varieties include the curved single-edge sword, the straight double-edge sword, the two-handed longsword, the gauntlet-sword, and the urumi or flexible sword. Techniques differ from one state to another but all make extensive use of circular movements, often circling the weapon around the user's head. The flexible nature and light weight of Indian swords allows for speed but provides little defensive

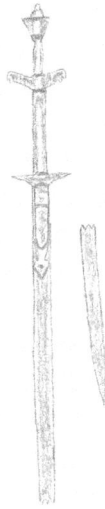

Figure 262: *A southern two-handed sword*

ability, so that the swordsman must instead rely on body maneuvers to dodge attacks. Entire systems exist focusing on drawing the sword out of the opponent's body. Stances and forms traditionally made up the early training before students progress to free sparring with sticks to simulate swords in an exercise called gatka, although this term is more often used in English when referring to the Panjabi-Sikh fighting style. A common way to practice precision-cutting is to slice cloves or lemons, eventually doing so while blindfolded. Pairing two swords of equal length, though considered impractical in some parts of the world, is common and was considered highly advantageous in South Asia.

Staffplay (Lathikhela)

Stick-fighting (lathi khela) may be taught as part of a wider system like Gatka, silambam or on its ownWikipedia:Citation needed. In the *Kama Sutra* the sage Vātsyāyana enjoins all women to practice fighting with single-stick, quarterstaff, sword and bow and arrow in addition to the art of love-making. The stick (*lathi* in Prakrit) is typically made of bamboo with steel caps at the ends to prevent it from splinteringWikipedia:Citation needed. Wooden sticks made from Indian ebony may also be usedWikipedia:Citation needed. It ranges from the length of a cudgel to a staff equal to the wielders heightWikipedia:Citation needed. The stick used during matches is covered in leather to cushion the impactWikipedia:Citation needed. Points are awarded based on which part of the body is hit. Techniques differ from system to system, but northern styles tend to primarily use only one end of the staff for attacking while the other end is held with both handsWikipedia:Citation needed.

Sikh martial art Gatka was developed in the North by sixth Sikh Guru, Guru Hargobind Sahib and it was further developed and preached by tenth Sikh Guru, Guru Gobind Singh. Gatka is associated with the Sikhs history and an integral part of an array of Sikh Shastar Vidiya developed during 15th century for self-defense. Southern styles like also make use of this technique but will more often use both ends of the staff to strike. The latter is the more common method of attacking in the eastern states and Bangladesh, combined with squatting and frequent changes in height.Wikipedia:Citation needed

Spearplay

Yudhishthira is said to be a master in spearplay warfare in *Mahabharata*, while Shalya was also noted to be an excellent warrior in the field of spearplay. Also according to Indian Hindu myths, Kartikeya, the son of Lord Shiva, is said to be skilled in spear-fighting, by holding his divine spear called Vel. The South Asian spear is typically made of bamboo with a steel blade. It can be used in hand-to-hand combat or thrown when the fighters are farther apart. Despite primarily being a thrusting weapon, the wide spearhead also allows for many slashing techniques. By the 17th century, Rajput mercenaries in the Mughal army were using a type of spear which integrated a pointed spear butt and a club near the head, making it similar to a mace. On the other hand, the longer cavalry spear was made of wood, with red cloth attached near the blade to prevent the opponent's blood from dripping to the shaft. The Marathas were revered for their skill of wielding a ten-foot spear called *bothati* (ਬੋਥਾਟੀ) from horseback. Bothati fighting is practiced with a ball-tipped lance, the end of which is covered in dye so that hits may easily be confirmed. In solo training, the spear is aimed at a pile of stones. From this was eventually developed the uniquely Indian *vita* which has a 5 feet (1.5 m) length of cord attached to the butt end of the weapon and tied around the spearman's wrist. Using this cord the spear can be pulled back after it has been thrown.

Archery (Dhanurvidya)

Archery is noted to be one of the noblest form of defense within Indian cultural heritage. Siddharta Gautama was a champion with the bow, while Rama, Arjuna, Karna, Bhishma, Drona and Ekalavya of the epics were all said to be peerless archers.

Indian bows were described as the height of their users by Arrian, and Deccan bows in 1518 as "long like those of England".[531] Composite bows are shown in Mughal artwork.

Traditional archery is today practiced mainly in the far northern states of Ladakh and Arunachal. One sport which has persisted into the present day is *thoda* from Himachal Pradesh, in which a team of archers attempt to shoot blunt arrows at the legs of the opposing team.

Mace-fighting (Gadayuddha)

Mace (gada) is the weapon of God Hanuman in Ramayana. Lord Vishnu also carries a gada named Kaumodaki in one of his four hands. In the Mahabharata epic, the fighters Bhima, Duryodhana, Jarasandha and Balarama were said to be masters of the gada. In the mace combat, Bhima wins the final battle against Duryodhana by hitting his inner thigh. Such an attack below the waist was said to be against the etiquette of mace duels, implying a degree of commonality to this type of fighting. It was and still is used as training equipment by wrestlers. The traditional gada (mace) was essentially a wooden or steel sphere mounted on a handle and with a single spike at the top. An alternative mace-head was the lotus-shaped *padam*. According to the *Agni Purana*, the gada can be handled in twenty different ways. Due to its weight, the gada is said to be best suited to fighters with a large build or great strength. The Mughal club or mace, known as a *gurj* or *gargaj*, had a head consisting of 8-10 petal-shaped blades. Fitted with basket-hilt, a spherical pommel, and a spiked top, this type of club was designed for beating down armour-clad opponents. Alternatively, some gurj had a spiked top and a hand-guard.

Wrestling (Mallayuddha)

Grappling arts (*malla-vidya*), practiced either as sport or fighting style, are found throughout the entirety of South Asia. True combat-wrestling is called malla-yuddha, while the term malakhra refers to wrestling for sport. Malla-yuddha was codified into four forms which progressed from purely sportive contests of strength to actual full-contact fights known as *yuddha*. Due to the extreme violence, this final form is generally no longer practised. The second form, wherein the wrestlers attempt to lift each other off the ground for three seconds, persists in Karnataka. Under Mughal influence, malla-yuddha incorporated new training methods and became known as kusti, which soon came to dominate most of South AsiaWikipedia:Citation needed. Traditional malla-yuddha is virtually extinct in the north where it has been supplanted by kusti, but another form called malakhra still exists in parts of India and Sindh, PakistanWikipedia:Citation needed. Vajra-musti was another old grappling art in which the competitors wrestled while wearing a horned knuckleduster. In a later style called *naki ka kusti* (claw wrestling), the duellists fought with bagh nakha. Numerous styles of folk wrestling are also found in India's countryside, such as mukna from Manipur and Inbuan wrestling from Mizoram.

Boxing (Mushtiyuddha)

Boxing (musti-yuddha) is traditionally considered the roughest form of South
Asian unarmed combat. In ancient times it was popular throughout what are
now Pakistan and northern India, but is rarely practiced today. Boxers harden
their fists by striking stone and other hard objects. Matches may be either
one-on-one or group fights. All kinds of strikes and grabs are allowed, and
any part of the body may be targeted except the groin. Another form of boxing was *loh-musti* (meaning "iron fist"), saidWikipedia:Manual of Style/Words
to watch#Unsupported attributions to have been practiced by the God Kr-
ishnaWikipedia:Citation needed. In this variation, boxers fought while wielding a kara or steel bracelet like a knuckledusterWikipedia:Citation needed.
Grabs, kicks, biting and attacks to the groin were all legal, the only prohi-
bition being spitting on the opponent which was considered crude and dishon-
ourableWikipedia:Citation needed. The kara used for regular matches was un-
adornedWikipedia:Citation needed, but the form employed during war had one
or more spikes around its edgeWikipedia:Citation needed. The kara may be
paired with one on each handWikipedia:Citation needed, but it was generally
only worn on one hand so the other hand could be left freeWikipedia:Citation
needed. In some cases the free hand could be paired with another weapon,
most commonly the bagh nakhaWikipedia:Citation needed.

Kicking

Kick-fighting(*aki kiti*) is the preserve of tribes from Nagaland. While the entire Naga population of northeast India and northwest Myanmar was traditionally known for their skill with broadswords (*dao*) and other weapons, disputes
among tribesmen and between tribes were settled with a solely kick-based form
of unarmed fighting. The goal is to either drive the opponent to their knees or
outside of the ring. Only the feet are used to strike, and even blocking must
be done with the legs.[532]

Pugilism

Many forms of unarmed combat (*bāhu-yuddha* or *bhuja-yuddha*) incorporate
too wide an array of techniques to be accurately categorized. In modern times
when the carrying of weapons is no longer legal, teachers of the martial arts
often emphasise the unarmed techniques as these are seen to be more practical for self-defense purposes. A warrior who fights unarmed is referred to as
a *bhajanh*, literally meaning someone who fights with their arms. The bare-
handed components of Indian fighting arts are typically based on the movements of animals or Hindu deities. Binot, a Central Indian art which focuses
on defending against both armed and unarmed opponents, may be the earliest

system of its kind. In the Mughal era, such fighters were known as *ek-hath* (lit. "one-hand"), so named because they would demonstrate their art using only one arm.

Bal Vidya

64 different types of skills & arts existed in ancient India which lead to well developed individuals boosting their mind, body and intellect making them capable of performing their responsibilities efficiently and effectively on personal, social and national level. Today, unhealthy and irregular lifestyles, frustrations and rising competitions in every sphere of life are affecting the health of people, especially the youth. In such a scenario, one of the ancient Indian arts referred to as "Bal Vidya" can help not only to improve the physical health but also upscale the mental and intellectual well-being of a person. A strong mind and intellect is equally important along with a strong body. Shree Aniruddha Upasana Foundation (Mumbai, India) attempts to review these ancient Indian martial arts form and provides "Bal Vidya" training to both men and women free of charge. Art forms like Mudgal Vidya, Vajra Mushthi, Surya Bhedan, Ashwa and various types of Yashwanti Malla Vidya using various weapons like Laathi (iron-bound bamboo stick), Kaathi (Pole), Fari-Gadga, Dorkhand (rope)and Dandpatta (gauntlet-sword). A book detailing all these art forms with the title "Bhartiya Prachin Bal Vidya" (The Ancient Indian Bal Art) is also available for achieving proficiency through practice post attending training sessions.[533,534,535]WP:NOTRS[536]

Systems

As in other respects of Indian culture, South Asian martial arts can be roughly divided into northern and southern styles. The northern systems (including Pakistan and Bangladesh) may generically be referred to as *shastra-vidiya*, although this term is often used synonymously with gatka. The main difference is that the north was more exposed to Persianate influence during the Mughal period, while the south is more conservative in preserving ancient and medieval traditions. The exception to this rule are the northeastern states which, due to their geographic location, were closed off from most pre-European foreign invaders. As a result, northeast Indian culture and fighting methods are also closely related to that of Southeast Asia. In addition to the major division between north and south, martial systems in South Asia tend to be associated with certain states, cities, villages or ethnic groups.

Regional Styles

Andhra Pradesh

Masters in Andhra Pradesh trace their lineage to the Vijayanagara empire, popular in Konaseema region. The native system of *Chedi Talimkhana* or *yudhkaushalya che talim* is often abbreviated to **Talimkhana** or simply **Talim**. The art makes use of several weapons which are used in preset forms. These include knife fighting (*baku samu*), sword fighting (*katti samu*), and staff fighting (*kara samu*) in addition to other weapons such as the gada (mace) and pata (guantlet sword).

Bengal (West Bengal and Bangladesh)

Bengali war-dances bear testament to the weapons once used in the Bengal region. Today most of these weapons are used only in choreographed fights, including *dao khela* (knife fighting) and *fala khela* (sword fighting)Wikipedia:Citation needed. Traditional stick-fighting (lathi khela) is still used in free sparring todayWikipedia:Citation needed. The sticks may be short like a cudgel or a long staff. The former are sometimes paired with a shield.Wikipedia:Citation needed

Bihar

"Pari-khanda" is a fighting form created by Rajputs and is still practised in many parts of Bihar. "Pari" means shield and "khanda" means sword according "Chhau" region, therefore this art uses sword and shield for fighting. This fighting form has given birth to a local dance form named "Chhau" dance and its martial elements have been fully absorbed by this dance. It is even practised in some parts of Jharkhand and Odisha. Chhau is the name of the traditional dance- drama of the eastern regions of India and is of three types. The three forms of "Chhau" are named after the district or village where they are performed, i.e. the Purulia Chau of Bengal, the Seraikella Chau of Bihar and the Mayurbhanj Chau of Orissa.

Karnataka

The Kannada fighting arts are taught exclusively at traditional training halls or *garadi mane*. Disciplines include unarmed combat (*kai varase*), staff-fighting (*kolu varase*) and sword-fighting (*katti varase*) among various other weapons. These are most often seen today only during choreographed demonstrations at festivals.

Figure 263: *Kalaripayat sword-fighting*

Kashmir

Kashmiri swordsmanship is said to have an ancient history, but it was only much later that it acquired its modern name of sqay. Sqay survived a decline following the partition of India by adopting competitive methodologies of karate and taekwondo. Types of competition include sparring, breaking, and forms or *khawankay*. Pracitioners spar using fake swords called *tora* which are paired with a shield. Sparring is point-based, the points being awarded for successful hits with the tora or with the foot.

Kerala

The Keralite art of fighting came into its present form through the kalari, the local variation of the gurukula educational institution. Historically, the warrior groups of Kerala practiced Kalaripayut. Today there are three branches of kalaripayat: northern, central and southern. Training progresses from footwork and stances to unarmed techniques, blunt weapons, and finally to edged weapons. The most common weapons today are the staff, stick, sword, shield, spear, dagger and flexible sword.

Maharashtra

The Marathas developed their fighting style based on the state's hilly geography. Mardani khel today teaches armed techniques for use in single combat as well as defense against several opponents. Other weapons include the sword, shield, spear, dagger, kukri, double deer horns, and bow and arrow.

Manipur

The Manipuri art of *huyen lalong* was once practiced by the state's indigenous hill tribes who would engage in duels governed by strict rules of conduct. The armed component called thang-ta is named after the system's main weapons, the *thang* (sword) and *ta* (spear). Practitioners spar through *cheibi gatka* in which a foam sword is used together with a shield. Unarmed huyen lalong is called *sarit-sarak* and is used in conjunction with thang-ta when the fighter loses their weapon.

Odisha

The Orissan martial art traces back to the *paika* class of warriors who were particularly knownWikipedia:Manual of Style/Words to watch#Unsupported attributions for their use of the *khanda* or double-edge straight sword-Wikipedia:Citation needed. During times of peace, the paika would hone their skills through martial dances, forms-training and various acrobatic-sWikipedia:Citation needed. Their descendants have preserved these exercises in training halls called paika akhadaWikipedia:Citation needed, and demonstrate them mainly through street performances. Their method of sword training called *pari-khanda* is still used as the first part of the chhau dance.Wikipedia:Citation needed Other weapons include the staff and guantlet-sword.

Panjab region and Rajasthan

Martial arts in northwest India and adjacent Pakistan were traditionally referred to by several terms but the most common today is *shastara-vidiya* or "science of self defense"Wikipedia:Citation needed. Swordsmen practiced their techniques either in routines using real swords, or freestyle sparring with wooden sticks called gatka, a form of stick-fighting. Gatka is associated with the Sikhs history and an integral part of an array of Sikh Shastar Vidiya. During the colonial period, the term *gatka* was extended to mean northwestern martial arts in generalWikipedia:Citation needed. Some aspects of the art, such as the unarmed techniques or fighting in armour, are today practiced almost exclusively by the Nihang order of SikhsWikipedia:Citation needed. Gatka incorporates several forms, each with their own set of weapons, strategies and footwork. In the late 18th century, this martial art further developed as a recreational game and Panjab University Lahore codified its rules for playing it as a game.

Figure 264: *Wrestling match in Bharatpur, 2013.*

Tamil Nadu

The native Tamil martial art has come to be referred to as silambam after its main weapon, the bamboo staff. Training begins with footwork patterns before progressing to stances and subsequently fighting techniques. Aside from its namesake, silambam includes a variety of weapons such as the sword, twin sticks, double deer horns, whip, sword, shield and sword, dagger, flexible sword and sickle. Unarmed silambam (*kai silambam*) is based on animal movements such as the snake, eagle, tiger and elephant. Other Martial Arts of Tamil Nadu are Varma Kalai, Kalari payattu, Adi Thadi, Malyutham AND Gusthi (Boxing form of Tamil Nadu, not to be confused with North Indian Kushti which is a Wrestling art.)

External links

- Guru Hemang Shastar Vidiya[537]
- Hegarty, Stephanie. " The only living master of a dying martial art[538] ." *BBC*. 29 October 2011.
- Sanatan Sikh Shastar Vidiya[539]

Media

Television in India

Part of a series on the
Culture of India
History
People
Cuisine
Religion
Sport
•   India portal
• v
• t
• e[540]

Indian television
Main articles:
• India
Nationwide
• English • Hindi
Regional
• Assamese • Bengali • Bhojpuri • English • Gujarati • Hindi • Kannada • Konkani • Malayalam • Marathi • Odia • Punjabi • Tamil • Telugu • Urdu
Niche
• News • 4K • 3D • HD
• v • t • e[541]

Television in India is a huge industry which has thousands of programs in many languages. The small screen has produced numerous celebrities. More than half of all Indian households own a television. As of 2016, the country has a collection of over 857 channels of which 184 are pay channels.[542]

History

In January 1950, *The Indian Express* reported that a television was put up for demonstration at an exhibition in the Teynampet locality of Madras (now Chennai) by B. Sivakumaran, a student of electrical engineering. A letter was scanned and its image displayed on a cathode ray tube screen. The report said that "[i]t may be this is not the whole of television but it is certainly the most significant link in the system" and added that the demonstration of the sort could be the "first in India".

In Kolkata, television was first used in the house of the wealthy Neogi family. Terrestrial television in India started with the experimental telecast starting in Delhi on 15 September 1959 with a small transmitter and a makeshift studio. Daily transmission began in 1965 as a part of All India Radio (AIR). Television service was later extended to Bombay and Amritsar in 1972. Up until 1975, only seven Indian cities had television services. Satellite Instructional Television Experiment (SITE) was an important step taken by India to use television for development. The programmes were mainly produced by Doordarshan (DD) which was then a part of the AIR. The telecast happened twice a day, in the mornings and evenings. Other than information related to agriculture, health and family planning were the other important topics dealt with in these programmes. Entertainment was also included in the form of dance, music, drama, folk and rural art forms. Television services were separated from radio in 1976. National telecast was introduced in 1982. In the same year, color television was introduced in the Indian market.

Indian small screen programming started off in the early 1980s. During this time, there was only one national channel, the government-owned Doordarshan. The *Ramayana* and *Mahabharata*, both based on the Indian epics of the same names, were the first major television series produced. They notched up world record in viewership numbers. By the late 1980s, more people began to own television sets. Though there was a single channel, television programming had reached saturation. Hence the government opened up another channel which had part national programming and part regional. This channel was known as DD 2, later renamed DD Metro. Both channels were broadcast terrestrially. In 1997, Prasar Bharati, a statutory autonomous body was established. Doordarshan along with the AIR were converted into government corporations under Prasar Bharati. The Prasar Bharati Corporation was established to serve as the public service broadcaster of the country which would achieve its objectives through AIR and Doordashan. This was a step towards greater autonomy for Doordarshan and AIR. However, Prasar Bharati has not succeeded in shielding Doordarshan from government control.

The transponders of the American satellites PAS 1 and PAS-4 helped in the transmission and telecast of DD. An international channel called DD International was started in 1995 and it telecasts programs for 19 hours a day to foreign countries-via PAS-4 to Europe, Asia and Africa, and via PAS-1 to North America.

The 1980s was the era of DD with shows like *Hum Log* (1984), *Wagle Ki Duniya* (1988), *Buniyaad* (1986–87) and comedy shows like *Yeh Jo Hai Zindagi* (1984), other than the widely popular mythological dramas like *Ramayan* (1987–88) and *Mahabharat* (1989–90) glued millions to Doordarshan and later on *Chandrakanta*. Hindi film songs based programs like *Chitrahaar*, *Rangoli*, *Superhit Muqabla* and crime thrillers like *Karamchand*, *Byomkesh Bakshi*. Shows targeted at children included *Divyanshu ki Kahaniyan*, *Vikram Betal*, *Malgudi Days*, *Tenali Rama*. It is also noted that Bengali filmmaker Prabir Roy had the distinction of introducing colour television coverage in India in February–March 1982 during the Nehru Cup, a football tournament which was held at Eden Gardens, Kolkata, with five on-line camera operation, before Doordarshan started the same during the Delhi Asian Games in November that year.

The central government launched a series of economic and social reforms in 1991 under Prime Minister Narasimha Rao. Under the new policies the government allowed private and foreign broadcasters to engage in limited operations in India. This process has been pursued consistently by all subsequent federal administrations. Foreign channels like CNN, STAR TV and private domestic channels such as Zee TV, ETV and Sun TV started satellite broadcasts. Starting with 41 sets in 1962 and one channel, by 1995, television in India had covered more than 70 million homes giving a viewing population of more than 400 million individuals through more than 100 channels.

Broadcast media

There are at least five basic types of television in India: broadcast or "over-the-air" television, unencrypted satellite or "free-to-air", Direct-to-Home (DTH), cable television, and IPTV.

Over-the-air and free-to-air TV is free with no monthly payments while Cable, DTH, and IPTV require a monthly payment that varies depending on how many channels a subscriber chooses to pay for. Channels are usually sold in groups or a la carte. All television service providers are required by law to provide a la carte selection of channels.

Broadcast television

In India, the broadcast of free-to-air television is governed through state-owned Prasar Bharati Corporation, with the Doordarshan group of channels being the only broadcaster. As such, cable television is the primary source of TV programming in India. Private channels were started in about 1995.

Cable television

As per the TAM Annual Universe Update - 2015, India now has over 167 million households (out of 234 million) with television sets, of which over 161 million have access to Cable TV or Satellite TV, including 84 million households which are DTH subscribers. Digital TV households have grown by 32% since 2013 due to migration from terrestrial and analog broadcasts. TV owning households have been growing at between 8-10%. Digital TV penetration is at 64% as of September 2014. The growth in digital broadcast has been due to the introduction of a multi-phase digitisation policy by the Government of India. An ordinance was introduced by the Govt. of India regarding the mandatory digitization of the Cable Services. According to this amendment made in the section 9 of the Cable Television Networks (Regulation) Amendment Ordinance, 1995, the I&B ministry is in the process of making Digital Addressable System mandatory. As per the policy, viewers would be able to access digital services only through a set top box (STB).

It is also estimated that India now has over 823 TV channels covering all the main languages spoken in the nation.

Star TV Network introduced five major television channels into the Indian broadcasting space that had so far been monopolised by the Indian government-owned Doordarshan: MTV, STAR Plus, Star Movies, BBC, Prime Sports and STAR Chinese Channel. Soon after, India saw the launch of Zee TV, the first privately owned Indian channel to broadcast over cable followed by Asia Television Network (ATN). A few years later CNN, Discovery Channel and National Geographic Channel made their foray into India. Later, Star TV Network expanded its bouquet with the introduction of STAR World India, STAR Sports, ESPN, Channel V and STAR Gold.

With the launch of the Tamil Sun TV in 1992, South India saw the birth of its first private television channel. With a network comprising more than 20 channels in various South Indian languages, Sun TV network recently launched a DTH service and its channels are now available in several countries outside India. Following Sun TV, several television channels sprung up in the south. Among these are the Tamil channel Raj Television and the Malayalam channel Asianet, both launched in 1993. These three networks and their channels today take up most of the broadcasting space in South India. In 1994, industrialist N.

P. V. Ramasamy Udayar launched a Tamil channel called *GEC* (Golden Eagle Communication), which was later acquired by Vijay Mallya and renamed as Vijay TV. In Telugu, Telugu daily newspaper Eenadu started its own channel called ETV in 1995 later diversified into other Indian languages. The same year, another Telugu channel called Gemini TV was launched which was later acquired by the Sun Group in 1998.

Throughout the 1990s, along with a multitude of Hindi-language channels, several regional and English language channels flourished all over India. By 2001, international channels HBO and History Channel started providing service. In 1999–2003, other international channels such as Nickelodeon, Cartoon Network, VH1, Disney and Toon Disney entered the market. Starting in 2003, there has been an explosion of news channels in various languages; the most notable among them are NDTV, CNN IBN and Aaj Tak. The most recent channels/networks in the Indian broadcasting industry include UTV Movies, UTV Bindass, Zoom, Colours, 9X and 9XM. There are several more new channels in the pipeline, including Leader TV.

Currently the major four cable general entertainment channels (GECs) that dominate the TRP rivalry are StarPlus, Sony Entertainment Television, Colors TV and Zee TV.[543]

Conditional access system

CAS or conditional access system, is a digital mode of transmitting TV channels through a set-top box (STB). The transmission signals are encrypted and viewers need to buy a set-top box to receive and decrypt the signal. The STB is required to watch only pay channels.

The idea of CAS was mooted in 2001, due to a furore over charge hikes by channels and subsequently by cable operators. Poor reception of certain channels; arbitrary pricing and increase in prices; bundling of channels; poor service delivery by Cable Television Operators (CTOs); monopolies in each area; lack of regulatory framework and redress avenues were some of the issues that were to be addressed by implementation of CAS

It was decided by the government that CAS would be first introduced in the four metros. It has been in place in Chennai since September 2003, where until very recently it had managed to attract very few subscribers. It has been rolled out recently in the other three metros of Delhi, Mumbai and Kolkata.

As of April 2008[544] only 25 per cent of the people have subscribed the new technology. The rest watch only free-to-air channels. As mentioned above, the inhibiting factor from the viewer's perspective is the cost of the STB.

Analog switchover

The Ministry of Information and Broadcasting issued a notification on 11 November 2011, setting 31 March 2015 as the deadline for complete shift from analogue to digital systems. In December 2011, Parliament passed *The Cable Television Networks (Regulation) Amendment Act* to digitise the cable television sector by 2014.[545,546] Chennai, Delhi, Kolkata, and Mumbai had to switch by 31 October 2012. The second phase of 38 cities, including Bangalore, Chandigarh, Nagpur, Patna, and Pune, was to switch by 31 March 2013. The remaining urban areas were to digitise by 30 November 2014 and the rest of the country by 31 March 2015.

Phase (planned date)	City/Region	Date of switchover†
Phase I (31 October 2012)	Delhi	31 October 2012
	Mumbai	31 October 2012
	Kolkata	*15 January 2013*
	Chennai	*Not completed*
Phase II (31 March 2013)	38 cities in 15 states	31 March 2013
Phase III (30 September 2014)	All remaining urban areas	31 March 2016
Phase IV (31 December 2014)	Rest of India	31 December 2016

†Indicates the date when analogue signals were switched off and not necessarily the date when 100% digitisation was achieved.

Phase I

From midnight on 31 October 2012, analogue signals were switched off in Delhi and Mumbai. Pirated signals were available in parts of Delhi even after the date. In Kolkata, on 30 October 2012, the state government refused to switch off analogue signals citing low penetration of set-top boxes (STBs) required for receiving digital signals. The I&B Ministry did not push for switching off of analogue signals in Kolkata. After approximately the Centre estimated that 75% of Kolkata households had installed STBs, the ministry issued a directive to stop airing analogue channels in some parts of the city beginning 16 December and completely switch off analogue signals after 27 December. On 17 December 2012, the West Bengal government openly defied the directive and stated that it would not implement it. The state government then announced that it would extend the deadline to 15 January 2013. The I&B ministry had initially threatened to cancel the license of multi system operators

(MSOs) in Kolkata if they did not switch off all analogue channels. However, the ministries softened their stand following a letter from MSOs, explaining how it they were sandwiched between divergent orders from the Central and State Governments.

In Chennai, the deadline was extended twice to 5 November by the Madras High Court. The extension was in response to a petition filed by the Chennai Metro Cable TV Operators Association (CMCOA), who argued at the beginning of November that only 164,000 homes in Chennai had the proper equipment, and three million households would be left without service. When a week later only a quarter of households had their set-top boxes, the Madras High Court further extended the deadline to 9 November. The Ministry of Information and Broadcasting stated that it would allow an additional extension to 31 December. As of March 2013, out of 3 million subscribers, 2.4 million continued to be without set-top boxes.[547]

A similar petition, filed by a local cable operator (LCO), to extend the deadline in Mumbai was rejected by the Bombay High Court on 31 October 2012.[548]

Phase II

In the second phase, 38 cities in 15 states had to digitise by 31 March 2013. Of the 38, Maharashtra has 9 cities, Uttar Pradesh has 7 and Gujarat has 5.[549]

About 25% of the 16 million households covered did not have their equipment installed before the deadline. Secretary Uday Kumar Varma extended a 15-day grace period. The I&B ministry estimated that as of 3 April 2013, 25% of households did not have set-top boxes.[550] Enforcement of the switchover varied from city to city.[551] Vishakhapatnam had the lowest rate of conversion to the new system at 12.18 per cent. Other cities that had low figures included Srinagar (20 per cent), Coimbatore (28.89 per cent), Jabalpur (34.87 per cent) and Kalyan Dombivli (38.59 per cent).[552]

Satellite television

As of 2016, over 1600 TV satellite television channels are broadcast in India. This includes channels from the state-owned Doordarshan, 21st Century Fox owned STAR TV, Sony owned Sony Entertainment Television, Zee TV, Sun Network and Asianet. Direct To Home service is provided by Airtel Digital Tv, BIG TV owned by Reliance, DD Direct Plus, DishTV, Sun Direct DTH, Tata Sky and Videocon D2H. Dish TV was the first one to come up in Indian Market, others came only years later.

These services are provided by locally built satellites from ISRO such as INSAT 4CR, INSAT 4A, INSAT-2E, INSAT-3C and INSAT-3E as well as private

Figure 265: *Tata Sky Dish India*

satellites such as the Dutch-based SES, Global-owned NSS 6, Thaicom-2 and Telstar 10.

DTH is defined as the reception of satellite programs with a personal dish in an individual home. As of December 2012, India had roughly 54 million DTH subcribers.

DTH does not compete with CAS.Wikipedia:Citation needed Cable TV and DTH are two methods of delivery of television content. CAS is integral to both the systems in delivering pay channels.

Cable TV is through cable networks and DTH is wireless, reaching direct to the consumer through a small dish and a set-top box. Although the government has ensured that free-to-air channels on cable are delivered to the consumer without a set-top box, DTH signals cannot be received without the set-top box.

India currently has 7 major DTH service providers and a total of over 54 million subscriber households in as of December 2012. DishTV (a ZEE TV subsidiary), Tata Sky, Videocon D2H, Sun Network owned ' Sun Direct DTH', Reliance Digital TV, Bharti Airtel's DTH Service 'Airtel Digital TV' and the public sector DD Direct Plus. As of 2012, India has the most competitive Direct-broadcast satellite market with 7 operators vying for more than 135 million TV homes. India overtook the USA as the world's largest Direct-broadcast satellite market in 2012.

The rapid growth of DTH in India has propelled an exodus from cabled homes, the need to measure viewership in this space is more than ever; aMap, the overnight ratings agency, has mounted a peoplemeter panel to measure viewership and interactive engagement in DTH homes in India.[553]

Internet Protocol Television (IPTV)

There are currently five IPTV Platforms available for Subscription in India in the main cities as Broadband Internet penetration is confined to urban areas of the country, They are

- liControl IPTV[554] A joint venture between MTNL and BSNL also in association with Aksh Optifiber[555] a company that also provides FTTH and VoIP services available in some of the main cities in India such as Mumbai which has about 200 Television Channels on offer with Time Shift TV in a number of Basic and Premium Packages including Movies on Demand offered at various Basic, Premium and Pay Per View Rates and other services such as an Interactive Karaoke channel, The IPTV Operator uses the UTStarcom RollingStream IPTV Solution as its end-to-end Delivery Platform.
- Airtel IPT available in some of the main cities in India such as New Delhi and Bangalore which has about 175 Television Channels on offer with Time Shift TV in a number of TV Packages and a small number of Television Channels offered on Premium Subscription Rates including Movies on Demand offered at Premium and Pay Per View Rates SVOD and other services such as Digital Radio and Games, The IPTV Operator uses the UTStarcom RollingStream IPTV Solution as its end-to-end Delivery Platform.
- Smart TV Group also Operates an IPTV Platform based on the SeaChange International IPTV and Cisco IPTV Standards in many parts of India with the following services:
  - 185 TV channels on various basic and premium packages
  - 40 TV channel Catch up TV service
  - 250 Hour Personal Video Recorder
  - A 5000+ Hour Movie Library
  - Digital Radio and Karaoke Service

The service is available to MTNL and BSNL Broadband Internet customers.

- Reliance IPTV is an IPTV service Operated by Reliance Communication the Telco uses the Microsoft Mediaroom IPTV Middleware Software as its end-to-end delivery Platform, with around three TV packages on offer. the service is currently only available in Mumbai.

Programming

The typical Indian soap opera is by-far the most common genre on Indian television. Fiction shows (which also includes thriller dramas and sitcoms) are extremely popular among Indian audiences, as they reflect real family issues portrayed in a melodramatic fashion.

There are thousands of television programs in India, all ranging in length, air time, genre and language. The Hindi and Tamil television industry is by far the biggest. However, some have much greater influence on the audiences, and therefore make the annual list of the best Hindi shows. The present status follows:

List of top five Hindi GEC (Urban+Rural) Television shows in India (Week 8, 2018)

Source: Barc India

Rank	Series	Genre	Net-work	Air date	Air time	Impressions (000s)
1	Kumkum Bhagya	Indian soap opera	Zee Anmol	Since 15 April 2014	Mon-Fri 9:00PM IST	12847
2	Kundali Bhagya	Indian soap opera	Zee TV	Since 12 July 2017	Mon-Fri 9:30PM IST	12480
3	Kumkum Bhagya	Indian soap opera	Zee TV	Since 15 April 2014	Mon-Fri 9:00PM IST	10893
4	Kya Hal, Mr. Panchal	Indian soap opera	Star Bharat	Since 28 August 2017	Mon-Fri 8:00PM IST	9860
5	Ye Hai Mo-habbatein	Indian soap opera	Star Plus	Since 3 December 2013	Mon-Sat 7:30PM IST	9585

List of top five Tamil GEC (Urban+Rural) Television shows in India (Week 1, 2018)

Source: Barc India

Rank	Series	Genre	Net-work	Air date	Air time	Impressions (000s)
1	*Deivama-gal*	Tamil soap opera	Sun TV	25 March 2013 – 17 February 2018	Mon-Sat 8:30PM IST	14030
2	*Nandini*	Tamil soap opera	Sun TV	Since 23 January 2017	Mon-Sat 9:00PM IST	12483
3	*Kula Deivam*	Tamil soap opera	Sun TV	11 May 2015 – 13 April 2018	Mon-Sat 7:00PM IST	10357
4	*Azhagu*	Tamil soap opera	Sun TV	Since 20 November 2017	Mon-Sat 8:30PM IST	10196
5	*Vani Rani*	Tamil soap opera	Sun TV	Since 3 December 2013	Mon-Sat 9:30PM IST	9674

Sports

Major sports networks include Star Sports, Star Sports Network, Sony Ten, Sony Six, Sony ESPN, ESPN Asia, DSport and DD Sports.

Audience metrics

Television metrics in India have gone through several phases in which it fragmented, consolidated and then fragmented again.

DART

During the days of the single channel Doordarshan monopoly, DART (Doordarshan Audience Research Team) was the only metric available. This used the notebook method of recordkeeping across 33 cities across India.[556] DART continues to provide this information independent of the Private agencies. DART is one of the rating system that measures audience metrics in Rural India.[557]

TAM & INTAM

In 1994, claiming a heterogeneous and fragmenting television market ORG-MARG introduced INTAM (Indian National Television Audience Measurement). Ex-officials of DD (Doordarshan) claimed that INTAM was introduced by vested commercial interests who only sought to break the monopoly of DD and that INTAM was significantly weaker in both sample size, rigour and the range of cities and regions covered.[558]

In 1997, a joint industry body appointed TAM (backed by AC Nielsen[559]) as the official recordkeeper of audience metrics. Due to the differences in methodology and samples of TAM and INTAM, both provided differing results for the same programs.

In 2001, a confidential list of households in Mumbai that were participating in the monitoring survey was released, calling into question the reliability of the data.[560,561] This subsequently led to the merger of the two measurement systems into TAM.[562] For several years after this, in spite of misgivings about the process, sample and other parameters, TAM was the de facto standard and monopoly in the audience metrics game.[563]

aMap

In 2004, a rival ratings service funded by American NRI investors, called Audience Measurement Analytics Limited (aMap) was launched.[564,565,566] Although initially, it faced a cautious uptake from clients, the TAM monopoly was broken.

What differentiates aMap is that its ratings are available within one day as compared to TAM's timeline of one week.

Broadcast Audience Research Council

BARC (Broadcast Audience Research Council) India is an industry body set up to design, commission, supervise and own an accurate, reliable and timely television audience measurement system for India. It currently measures TV Viewing habits of 183 million TV households in the country, using 30,000 sample panel homes. This will go up to 50,000 in the next couple of years, as mandated by the Ministry of Information & Broadcasting.

As per BARC India's Broadcast India (BI) 2018 Survey released in July 2018, based on a sample of 3 lakh homes in the country, TV homes in the country have seen a 7.5% jump, outpacing the growth of homes in India which grew at 4.5%. India currently boasts of 298 million homes, of which 197 million have a TV set, having an opportunity of almost 100mn more TV homes in the country.

Guided by the recommendations of the TRAI (Telecom Regulatory Authority of India) and MIB notifications of January 2014, BARC India brings together the three key stakeholders in television audience measurement - broadcasters, advertisers, and advertising and media agencies, via their apex bodies.

BARC India is committed towards establishing a robust, transparent and accountable governance framework for providing data points that are required to plan media spends more effectively.[567]

Cinema of India

Indian cinema	
No. of screens	9,000 single screens (2016) 2,100 multi
· Per capita	6 per million (2016)
Produced feature films (2017)	
Total	1,986
Number of admissions (2016)	
Total	2,200,000,000
Gross box office	
Total	⎕156 billion (US$2.2 billion) (2017)
National films	India: US$2.1 billion (2015)

South Asian cinema
• **Cinema of Bangladesh** • **Cinema of India** • **Cinema of Nepal** • **Cinema of Pakistan** • **Cinema of Sri Lanka**

Indian cinema

- Assamese
- Bengali (Tollywood)
- Bhojpuri
- Badaga
- Bihari
- Chhattisgarhi
- Deccani (Deccanwood)
- Dogri
- Gujarati (Gollywood/Dhollywood)
- Haryanvi
- Hindi (Bollywood)
- Jharkhandi (Jollywood)
- Kashmiri
- Kannada (Sandalwood)
- Konkani
- Kosli
- Kutchi
- Malayalam (Mollywood)
- Marathi

- Meitei
- Odia
- Punjabi
- Rajasthani
- Sanskrit
- Santali
- Tamil (Kollywood)
- Telugu (Tollywood)
- Tulu (Coastalwood)

Part of a series on the
Culture of India
History
People
Cuisine
Religion
Sport
• 　 India portal
• v
• t
• e[568]

The **Cinema of India** consists of films produced in the nation of India. Cinema is immensely popular in India, with as many as 1,600 films produced in various languages every year. Indian cinema produces more films watched by more people than any other country; in 2011, over 3.5 billion tickets were sold across the globe, 900,000 more than Hollywood.[569]

As of 2013 India ranked first in terms of annual film output, followed by Nigeria, Hollywood and China. In 2012, India produced 1,602 feature films. The

Indian film industry reached overall revenues of $1.86 billion ([]93 billion) in 2011. In 2015, India had a total box office gross of US$2.1 billion, third largest in the world.

Indian cinema is a global enterprise.[570] Its films have a following throughout Southern Asia, and across Asia, Europe, the Greater Middle East, North America, Eastern Africa, China and elsewhere, reaching in over 90 countries.[571] Biopics including *Dangal* became transnational blockbusters grossing over $300 million worldwide.

Global enterprises such as 20th Century Fox, Sony Pictures, Walt Disney Pictures and Warner Bros invested in the industry along with Indian enterprises such as AVM Productions, Prasad's Group, Sun Pictures, PVP Cinemas, Zee, UTV, Suresh Productions, Eros Films, Ayngaran International, Pyramid Saimira, Aascar Films and Adlabs. By 2003 as many as 30 film production companies had been listed in the National Stock Exchange of India.[572]

The overall revenue of Indian cinema reached US$1.3 billion in 2000.[573] The industry is segmented by language. The Hindi language film industry is known as Bollywood, the largest sector, representing 43% of box office revenue. Combined Tamil (Kollywood) and Telugu (Tollywood) film industries revenues represent 36%. The South Indian film industry encompasses five film cultures: Tamil, Telugu, Malayalam, Kannada and Tulu.

Millions of Indians overseas watch Indian films, accounting for some 12% of revenues.[574] Music rights alone account for 4–5% of net revenues.

History

The history of cinema in India extends back to the beginning of the film era. The Indian film Industry is the 2nd oldest in the world. Following the screening of the Lumière and Robert Paul moving pictures in London (1896), animated photography became a worldwide sensation and by mid-1896 both Lumière and Robert Paul films had been shown in Bombay.[575]

Silent films (1910s–1920s)

In 1897 a film presentation by one Professor Stevenson featured a stage show at Calcutta's Star Theatre. With Stevenson's encouragement and camera Hiralal Sen, an Indian photographer, made a film of scenes from that show, namely *The Flower of Persia* (1898). *The Wrestlers* (1899) by H. S. Bhatavdekar, showing a wrestling match at the Hanging Gardens in Bombay, was the first film to be shot by an Indian and the first Indian documentary film.Wikipedia:Citation needed

The first Indian film released in India was *Shree Pundalik,* a silent film in Marathi by Dadasaheb Torne on 18 May 1912 at Coronation Cinematograph, Bombay. Some have argued that *Pundalik* was not the first Indian film, because it was a photographic recording of a play, and because the cameraman was a British man named Johnson and the film was processed in London.

History of Indian cinema

Figure 266: *Producer-director-screenwriter Dadasaheb Phalke, the "father of Indian cinema" UNIQ-ref-0-9c34fa5f9dcb4f28-QINU UNIQ-ref-1-9c34fa5f9dcb4f28-QINU*

Figure 267: *AVM Studios in Chennai, India's oldest surviving film studio*

Figure 268: *Advertisement in The Times of India of 25 May 1912 announcing the screening of the first feature film of India, Shree Pundalik by Dadasaheb Torne*

Figure 269: *A scene from Raja Harishchandra (1913), the first full-length Indian motion picture*

The first full-length motion picture in India was produced by Dadasaheb Phalke, Phalke is seen as the pioneer of the Indian film industry and a scholar of India's languages and culture. He employed elements from Sanskrit epics to produce his *Raja Harishchandra* (1913), a silent film in Marathi. The female characters in the film were played by male actors.[576] Only one print of the film was made, for showing at the Coronation Cinematograph on 3 May 1913. It was a commercial success. The first silent film in Tamil, *Keechaka Vadham* was made by R. Nataraja Mudaliar in 1916.

The first chain of Indian cinemas, Madan Theatre was owned by Parsi entrepreneur Jamshedji Framji Madan, who oversaw production of 10 films annually and distributed them throughout India beginning in 1902. He founded Elphinstone Bioscope Company in Calcutta. Elphinstone merged into Madan Theatres Limited in 1919, which had brought many of Bengal's most popular literary works to the stage. He also produced *Satyawadi Raja Harishchandra* in 1917, a remake of Phalke's *Raja Harishchandra* (1913).

Raghupathi Venkaiah Naidu was an Indian artist and a film pioneer.[577] From 1909, he was involved in many aspects of Indian cinema, travelling across Asia. He was the first to build and own cinemas in Madras. He was credited as the father of Telugu cinema. In South India, the first Tamil talkie *Kalidas was* released on 31 October 1931. Nataraja Mudaliar established South India's first film studio in Madras.

Film steadily gained popularity across India. Tickets were affordable to the masses (as low as an *anna* (one-sixteenth of a rupee) in Bombay) with additional comforts available at a higher price.

Young producers began to incorporate elements of Indian social life and culture into cinema. Others brought ideas from across the world. Global audiences and markets soon became aware of India's film industry.[578]

In 1927, the British Government, to promote the market in India for British films over American ones, formed the Indian Cinematograph Enquiry Committee. The ICC consisted of three Brits and three Indians, led by T. Rangachari, a Madras lawyer. This committee failed to support the desired recommendations of supporting British Film, instead recommending support for the fledgling Indian film industry. Their suggestions were shelved.

Talkies (1930s–mid-1940s)

Ardeshir Irani released *Alam Ara,* the first Indian talkie, on 14 March 1931. Irani later produced the first south Indian talkie film *Kalidas* directed by H. M. Reddy released on 31 October 1931.[579] *Jumai Shasthi* was the first Bengali talkie. Chittor V. Nagaiah, was one of the first multilingual film actor/singer/composer/producer/directors in India. He was known as India's Paul Muni.

In 1932, the name "Tollywood" was coined for the Bengali film industry because Tollygunge rhymed with "Hollywood". Tollygunge was then the centre of the Indian film industry. Bombay later overtook Tollygunge as the industry's center, spawning "Bollywood" and many other Hollywood-inspired names.

In 1933, East India Film Company produced its first Telugu film, *Savitri*. Based on a stage play by Mylavaram Bala Bharathi Samajam, the film was directed by C. Pullaiah with stage actors Vemuri Gaggaiah and Dasari Ramathilakam. The film received an honorary diploma at the 2nd Venice International Film Festival.

On 10 March 1935, another pioneer film maker Jyoti Prasad Agarwala made his first film *Joymoti* in Assamese. Jyoti Prasad went to Berlin to learn more about films. Indramalati is another film he himself produced and directed after Joymoti. The first film studio in South India, Durga Cinetone was built in 1936 by Nidamarthi Surayya in Rajahmundry, Andhra Pradesh. The 1930s saw the rise of music in Indian cinema with musicals such as *Indra Sabha* and *Devi Devyani* marking the beginning of song-and-dance in Indian films. Studios emerged by 1935 in major cities such as Madras, Calcutta and Bombay as filmmaking became an established craft, exemplified by the success of *Devdas*.[580] directed by an Assamese film maker Pramathesh Baruah. In 1937, *Kisan Kanhiya* directed by Moti B was released, the first colour film made in India. The 1940 film, *Vishwa Mohini*, is the first Indian film to depict the Indian movie world. The film was directed by Y. V. Rao and scripted by Balijepalli Lakshmikanta Kavi.

Swamikannu Vincent, who had built the first cinema of South India in Coimbatore, introduced the concept of "Tent Cinema" in which a tent was erected on a stretch of open land to screen films. The first of its kind was in Madras, called Edison's Grand Cinemamegaphone. This was due to the fact that electric carbons were used for motion picture projectors. Bombay Talkies opened in 1934 and Prabhat Studios in Pune began production of Marathi films meant. R. S. D. Choudhury produced *Wrath* (1930), which was banned by the British Raj for its depiction of Indian actors as leaders during the Indian independence movement. *Sant Tukaram*, a 1936 film based on the life of Tukaram (1608–50), a Varkari Sant and spiritual poet became the first Indian film to be screened at an international film festival, at the 1937 edition of the Venice Film Festival. The film was judged one of the three best films of the year. In 1938, Gudavalli Ramabrahmam, co-produced and directed the social problem film, *Raithu Bidda*, which was also banned by the British administration, for depicting the peasant uprising among the Zamindars during the British raj.

The Indian *Masala film*—a term used for mixed-genre films that combined song, dance, romance etc.—arose following World War II. During the 1940s cinema in South India accounted for nearly half of India's cinema halls and cinema came to be viewed as an instrument of cultural revival. The partition of India following independence divided the nation's assets and a number of studios moved to Pakistan. Partition became an enduring film subject thereafter.

Figure 270: *Satyajit Ray is recognized as one of the greatest filmmakers of the 20th century.*

After Indian independence the film industry was investigated by the S. K. Patil Commission.[581] Patil recommended setting up a Film Finance Corporation (FFC) under the Ministry of Finance. This advice was adopted in 1960 and FFC provide financial support to filmmakers.[582] The Indian government had established a Films Division by 1948, which eventually became one of the world's largest documentary film producers with an annual production of over 200 short documentaries, each released in 18 languages with 9,000 prints for permanent film theatres across the country.[583]

The Indian People's Theatre Association (IPTA), an art movement with a communist inclination, began to take shape through the 1940s and the 1950s. Realist IPTA plays, such as *Nabanna* (1944, Bijon Bhattacharya) prepared the ground for realism in Indian cinema, exemplified by Khwaja Ahmad Abbas's *Dharti Ke Lal* (*Children of the Earth*) in 1946. The IPTA movement continued to emphasize realism and went on to produce *Mother India* and *Pyaasa*, among India's most recognizable cinematic productions.[584]

Golden Age (late 1940s–1960s)

The period from the late 1940s to the early 1960s is regarded by film historians as the Golden Age of Indian cinema.

This period saw the emergence of the Parallel Cinema movement, mainly led by Bengalis, which then accounted for a quarter of India's film output. The movement emphasized social realism. Early examples include *Dharti Ke Lal* (1946, Khwaja Ahmad Abbas), *Neecha Nagar* (1946, Chetan Anand),[585] *Nagarik* (1952, Ritwik Ghatak) and *Do Bigha Zamin* (1953, Bimal Roy), laying the foundations for Indian neorealism and the Indian New Wave.

The Apu Trilogy (1955–1959, Satyajit Ray) won major prizes at all the major international film festivals and firmly established the Parallel Cinema movement. *Pather Panchali* (1955), the first part of the trilogy, marked Ray's entry in Indian cinema.[586] The trilogy's influence on world cinema can be felt in the "youthful coming-of-age dramas that flooded art houses since the mid-fifties", which "owe a tremendous debt to the Apu trilogy".

Cinematographer Subrata Mitra, who debuted in the trilogy, had his own important influence on cinematography globally. One of his most important techniques was bounce lighting, to recreate the effect of daylight on sets. He pioneered the technique while filming *Aparajito* (1956), the second part of the trilogy. Ray pioneered other effects such as the photo-negative flashbacks and X-ray digressions in *Pratidwandi* (1972).

During the 1960s, Indira Gandhi's intervention during her reign as the Information and Broadcasting Minister of India supported production of off-beat cinematic by FFC.

Commercial Hindi cinema began thriving, including acclaimed films *Pyaasa* (1957) and *Kaagaz Ke Phool* (1959, Guru Dutt) *Awaara* (1951) and *Shree 420* (1955, Raj Kapoor). These films expressed social themes mainly dealing with working-class urban life in India; *Awaara* presented the city as both a nightmare and a dream, while *Pyaasa* critiqued the unreality of city life.

Epic film *Mother India* (1957, Mehboob Khan), a remake of his earlier *Aurat* (1940), was the first Indian film to be nominated for the Academy Award for Best Foreign Language Film. *Mother India* defined the conventions of Hindi cinema for decades. It spawned a new genre of dacoit films. *Gunga Jumna* (1961, Dilip Kumar) was a dacoit crime drama about two brothers on opposite sides of the law, a theme that became common in Indian films in the 1970s. *Madhumati* (1958, Bimal Roy) popularised the theme of reincarnation in Western popular culture.

Dilip Kumar (Muhammad Yusuf Khan) debuted in the 1940s and rose to fame in the 1950s and was one of the biggest Indian movie stars. He was a pioneer of method acting, predating Hollywood method actors such as Marlon Brando. Much like Brando's influence on New Hollywood actors, Kumar inspired Indian actors, including Amitabh Bachchan, Naseeruddin Shah, Shah Rukh Khan and Nawazuddin Siddiqui.[587]

Neecha Nagar won the Palme d'Or at Cannes, putting Indian films in competition for the Palme d'Or for nearly every year in the 1950s and early 1960s, with many winning major prizes. Ray won the Golden Lion at the Venice Film Festival for *Aparajito* (1956) and the Golden Bear and two Silver Bears for Best Director at the Berlin International Film Festival. The films of screenwriter Khwaja Ahmad Abbas were nominated for the Palme d'Or three times. (*Neecha Nagar* won, with nominations for *Awaara* and *Pardesi* (1957)).

Ray's contemporaries Ghatak and Dutt were overlooked in their own lifetimes, but generated international recognition in the 1980s and 1990s. Ray is regarded as one of the greatest auteurs of 20th century cinema, with Dutt and Ghatak. In 1992, the *Sight & Sound* Critics' Poll ranked Ray at No. 7 in its list of "Top 10 Directors" of all time, while Dutt ranked No. 73 in the 2002 *Sight & Sound* poll.

Multiple films from this era are included among the greatest films of all time in various critics' and directors' polls. Multiple Ray films appeared in the *Sight & Sound* Critics' Poll, including *The Apu Trilogy* (ranked No. 4 in 1992 if votes are combined), *Jalsaghar* (ranked No. 27 in 1992), *Charulata* (ranked No. 41 in 1992) and *Aranyer Din Ratri* (ranked No. 81 in 1982). The 2002 *Sight & Sound* critics' and directors' poll also included the Dutt films *Pyaasa* and *Kaagaz Ke Phool* (both tied at #160), Ghatak's films *Meghe Dhaka Tara* (ranked #231) and *Komal Gandhar* (ranked #346), and Raj Kapoor's *Awaara*, Vijay Bhatt's *Baiju Bawra*, Mehboob Khan's *Mother India* and K. Asif's *Mughal-e-Azam* all tied at #346. In 1998, the critics' poll conducted by the Asian film magazine *Cinemaya* included *The Apu Trilogy* (ranked No. 1 if votes are combined), Ray's *Charulata* and *Jalsaghar* (both tied at #11), and Ghatak's *Subarnarekha* (also tied at #11).

South Indian cinema saw the production works based on the epic Mahabharata, such as *Mayabazar* (listed by IBN Live's 2013 Poll as the greatest Indian film of all time). Sivaji Ganesan became India's first actor to receive an international award when he won the "Best Actor" award at the Afro-Asian film festival in 1960 and was awarded the title of *Chevalier* in the Legion of Honour by the French Government in 1995. Tamil cinema is influenced by Dravidian politics,[588] with prominent film personalities C N Annadurai, M G Ramachandran, M Karunanidhi and Jayalalithaa becoming Chief Ministers of Tamil Nadu.

Contemporary Indian cinema (1970s–present)

Realistic Parallel Cinema continued throughout the 1970s,[589] practiced in many Indian film cultures. The FFC's art film orientation came under criticism during a Committee on Public Undertakings investigation in 1976, which accused the body of not doing enough to encourage commercial cinema.[590]

Hindi commercial cinema continued with films such as *Aradhana* (1969), *Sachaa Jhutha* (1970), *Haathi Mere Saathi* (1971), *Anand* (1971), *Kati Patang* (1971) *Amar Prem* (1972), *Dushman* (1972) and *Daag* (1973).

<templatestyles src=”Multiple_image/styles.css” />

The screenwriting duo Salim-Javed, consisting of Salim Khan (l) and Javed Akhtar (r), revolutionized Indian cinema in the 1970s, and are considered Bollywood's greatest screenwriters.

Salim-Javed

By the early 1970s, Hindi cinema was experiencing thematic stagnation, dominated by musical romance films. The arrival of screenwriter duo Salim-Javed, consisting of Salim Khan and Javed Akhtar, revitalized the industry. They established the genre of gritty, violent, Bombay underworld crime films, with films such as *Zanjeer* (1973) and *Deewaar* (1975). They reinterpreted the rural themes of *Mother India* and *Gunga Jumna* in an urban context reflecting 1970s India, channeling the growing discontent and disillusionment among the masses, unprecedented growth of slums and urban poverty, corruption and crime, as well as anti-establishment themes. This resulted in their creation of the "angry young man", personified by Amitabh Bachchan, who reinterpreted Kumar's performance in *Gunga Jumna*, and gave a voice to the urban poor.

By the mid-1970s, crime-action films like *Zanjeer* and *Sholay* (1975) solidified Bachchan's position as a lead actor. The devotional classic *Jai Santoshi Ma* (1975) was made on a shoe-string budget and became a box office success and a cult classic. Another important film was *Deewaar* (1975, Yash Chopra). This crime film pitted "a policeman against his brother, a gang leader based on the real-life smuggler Haji Mastan", portrayed by Bachchan. Danny Boyle described it as "absolutely key to Indian cinema".

"Bollywood" was named in the 70s, when the conventions of commercial Bollywood films were established. Key to this was Nasir Hussain and Salim-Javed's creation of the masala film genre, which combines elements of action, comedy, romance, drama, melodrama and musical. Another Hussain/Salim-Javed concoction, *Yaadon Ki Baarat* (1973), was identified as the first masala film and the "first" quintessentially "Bollywood" film.[591] Salim-Javed wrote more successful masala films in the 1970s and 1980s. Masala films made Bachchan the biggest Bollywood movie star of the period. Another landmark was *Amar Akbar Anthony* (1977, Manmohan Desai). Desai further expanded the genre in the 1970s and 1980s.

Salim-Javed was highly influential in South Indian cinema. In addition to writing two Kannada films, many of their Bollywood films had remakes produced in other regions, including Tamil, Telugu and Malayalam cinema. While the Bollywood directors and producers held the rights to their films in Northern India, Salim-Javed retained the rights in South India, where they sold remake rights, usually for around ₹1 lakh (equivalent to ₹27 lakh or US$38,000 in 2017) each, for films such as *Zanjeer*, *Yaadon Ki Baarat* and *Don*. Several of these remakes became breakthroughs for Rajinikanth, who portrayed Bachchan's role for several Tamil remakes.

South Indian industries

Kannada film *Samskara* (1970, Pattabhirama Reddy), pioneered the parallel cinema movement in south Indian cinema. The film won Bronze Leopard at the Locarno International Film Festival.

Telugu film *Sankarabharanam* (1980) dealt with the revival of Indian classical music and won the Prize of the Public at the 1981 Besancon Film Festival.

Tamil language films appeared at multiple film festivals. *Kannathil Muthamittal* (Ratnam), *Veyyil* (Vasanthabalan) and *Paruthiveeran. Kanchivaram* (2009, Ameer Sultan) premiered at the Toronto International Film Festival. Tamil films were submitted by India for the Academy Award for Best Foreign Language on eight occasions. *Nayakan* (1987, Kamal Hassan) was included in Time magazine's "All-TIME" 100 best movies list.[592] In 1991, *Marupakkam* directed by K.S. Sethu Madhavan, became the first Tamil film to win the National Film Award for Best Feature Film, the feat was repeated by *Kanchivaram* in 2007.

Malayalam cinema experienced its own Golden Age in the 1980s and early 1990s. Acclaimed Malayalam filmmakers industry, included Adoor Gopalakrishnan, G. Aravindan, T. V. Chandran and Shaji N. Karun. Gopalakrishnan,

Figure 271: *Sridevi in 2012. The most successful Indian actress during the 1980s–1990s, she is considered one of India's greatest and most influential movie stars and is cited as the "First Female Superstar of Bollywood cinema".*

is often considered to be Ray's spiritual heir. He directed some of his most acclaimed films during this period, including *Elippathayam* (1981) which won the Sutherland Trophy at the London Film Festival, as well as *Mathilukal* (1989) which won major prizes at the Venice Film Festival. Karun's debut film *Piravi* (1989) won the Camera d'Or at the 1989 Cannes Film Festival, while his second film *Swaham* (1994) was in competition for the Palme d'Or at the 1994 event. Commercial Malayalam cinema began gaining popularity with the action films of Jayan, a popular stunt actor who died while filming a helicopter stunt.

Sridevi is widely considered as the first female *superstar* of Bollywood cinema due to her pan-Indian appeal and a rare actor who had an equally successful career in the major Indian film industries: Hindi, Tamil and Telugu . she's also the only movie star in history of Bollywood to star in the top 10 highest grossers of the year throughout her active period (1983-1997).

New Bollywood

Commercial Hindi cinema grew in the 1980s, with films such as *Ek Duuje Ke Liye* (1981), *Himmatwala* (1983), *Tohfa* (1984), *Naam* (1986), *Mr India* (1987), and *Tezaab* (1988). But by the late 1980s, Hindi cinema experienced a period of stagnation, with a decline in box office turnout, due to increasing violence, decline in musical melodic quality, and rise in video piracy, leading to middle-class family audiences abandoning theaters. The turning point came with *Qayamat Se Qayamat Tak* (1988), directed by Mansoor Khan, written and produced by his father Nasir Hussain, and starring his cousin Aamir Khan with Juhi Chawla. Its blend of youthfulness, wholesome entertainment, emotional quotients and strong melodies lured family audiences back to the big screen. It set a new template for Bollywood musical romance films that defined Hindi cinema in the 1990s. Commercial Hindi cinema grew in the 1990s, with the release of *Chaalbaaz* (1989), *Chandni* (1989), *Maine Pyar Kiya* (1989), *Saajan* (1991), *Khalnayak* (1993), *Darr* (1993), *Hum Aapke Hain Koun..!* (1994), *Dilwale Dulhania Le Jayenge* (1995), *Dil To Pagal Hai* (1997), *Pyar Kiya Toh Darna Kya* (1998) and *Kuch Kuch Hota Hai* (1998). Cult classic *Bandit Queen* (1994, Shekhar Kapur) received international recognition and controversy.[593,594]

In the late 1990s, Parallel Cinema began a resurgence in Hindi cinema, largely due to the critical and commercial success of crime films *Satya* (1998 and Vaastav). These film's launched a genre known as *Mumbai noir*, urban films reflecting social problems there.

Since the 1990s, the three biggest Bollywood movie stars have been the "Three Khans": Aamir Khan, Shah Rukh Khan, and Salman Khan. Combined, they starred in the top ten highest-grossing Bollywood films. The three Khans have had successful careers since the late 1980s, and have dominated the Indian box office since the 1990s.[595] Shah Rukh Khan was the most successful for most of the 1990s and 2000s, while Aamir Khan has been the most successful since the late 2000s; according to *Forbes*, Aamir Khan is "arguably the world's biggest movie star" as of 2017, due to his immense popularity in India and China. Other Hindi stars include Anil Kapoor, Madhuri Dixit and Kajol. *Haider* (2014, Vishal Bhardwaj), the third instalment of the Indian Shakespearean Trilogy after *Maqbool* (2003) and *Omkara* (2006), won the *People's Choice Award* at the 9th Rome Film Festival in the Mondo Genere category making it the first Indian film to achieve this honor.

Aamir Khan Productions has been credited for redefining and modernizing the masala film (which originated from his uncle Nasir Hussain's *Yaadon Ki Baarat*, which he first appeared in), with Aamir Khan's own distinct brand of socially conscious cinema in the early 21st century. His films blur the distinction between commercial masala films and realistic parallel cinema, combining

the entertainment and production values of the former with the believable narratives and strong messages of the latter, earning both commercial success and
critical acclaim, in India and overseas.

Global discourse

During colonial rule Indians bought film equipment from Europe. The British
funded wartime propaganda films during World War II, some of which showed
the Indian army pitted against the Axis powers, specifically the Empire of
Japan, which had managed to infiltrate India.[596] One such story was *Burma
Rani*, which depicted civilian resistance to Japanese occupation by British and
Indian forces in Myanmar. Pre-independence businessmen such as J. F. Madan
and Abdulally Esoofally traded in global cinema.

Early Indian films made early inroads into the Soviet Union, Middle East,
Southeast Asia[597] and China. Mainstream Indian movie stars gained international fame across Asia and Eastern Europe. For example, Indian films were
more popular in the Soviet Union than Hollywood films[598] and occasionally
domestic Soviet films. From 1954 to 1991, 206 Indian films were sent to the
Soviet Union, drawing higher average audience figures than domestic Soviet
productions, Films such as *Awaara* and *Disco Dancer* drew more than 60 million viewers. Films such as *Awaara*, *3 Idiots* and *Dangal*,[599] were one of the
20 highest-grossing films in China.[600]

Indian films frequently appeared in international fora and film festivals. This
allowed Parallel Bengali filmmakers to achieve worldwide fame.

Tamil films gained viewers in South East Asia and other parts of the world.
Chandralekha and *Muthu* were dubbed into Japanese and grossed a record
$1.6 million in 1998. In 2010, *Enthiran* grossed a record $4 million in North
America.

Many Asian and South Asian countries increasingly found Indian cinema as
more suited to their sensibilities than Western cinema. Jigna Desai holds that
by the 21st century, Indian cinema had become 'deterritorialized', spreading to
parts of the world where Indian expatriatres were present in significant numbers, and had become an alternative to other international cinema.[601]

Indian cinema more recently began influencing Western musical films, and
played a particularly instrumental role in the revival of the genre in the Western world. Ray's work had a worldwide impact, with filmmakers such as Martin Scorsese, James Ivory, Abbas Kiarostami, François Truffaut, Carlos Saura,
Isao Takahata and Gregory Nava citing his influence, and others such as Akira
Kurosawa praising his work. The "youthful coming-of-age dramas that have
flooded art houses since the mid-fifties owe a tremendous debt to the Apu

Figure 272: *Victoria Public Hall, is a historical building in Chennai, named after Victoria, Empress of India. It served as a theatre in the late 19th century and the early 20th century.*

trilogy". Since the 1980s, overlooked Indian filmmakers such as Ghatak and Dutt posthumously gained international acclaim. Baz Luhrmann stated that his successful musical film *Moulin Rouge!* (2001) was directly inspired by Bollywood musicals. That film's success renewed interest in the then-moribund Western musical genre, subsequently fuelling a renaissance. Danny Boyle's Oscar-winning film *Slumdog Millionaire* (2008) was directly inspired by Indian films, and is considered to be an "homage to Hindi commercial cinema".

Indian cinema has been recognised repeatedly at the Academy Awards. Indian films *Mother India* (1957), *Salaam Bombay!* (1988) and *Lagaan* (2001), were nominated for the Academy Award for Best Foreign Language Film. Indian Oscar winners include Bhanu Athaiya (costume designer), Ray (filmmaker), A. R. Rahman (music composer), Resul Pookutty (sound editor) and Gulzar (lyricist), Cottalango Leon and Rahul Thakkar Sci-Tech Award.

Influences

Moti Gokulsing and Wimal Dissanayake identify six major influences that have shaped Indian popular cinema:

Figure 273: *Prasads IMAX Theatre located at Hyderabad, is the world's largest 3D-IMAX screen, and also the most attended screen in the world.*

Figure 274: *Ramoji Film City located in Hyderabad, holds Guinness World Record as the World's largest film studio.*

Figure 275: *PVR Cinemas is one of the largest cinema chains in India*

- The ancient epics of *Mahabharata* and *Ramayana* influenced the narratives of Indian cinema. Examples of this influence include the techniques of a side story, back-story and story within a story. Indian popular films often have plots that branch into sub-plots; such narrative dispersals can clearly be seen in the 1993 films *Khalnayak* and *Gardish*.
- Ancient Sanskrit drama, with its emphasis on spectacle, combined music, dance and gesture combined "to create a vibrant artistic unit with dance and mime being central to the dramatic experience". Sanskrit dramas were known as *natya*, derived from the root word *nrit* (dance), featuring spectacular dance-dramas. The *Rasa* method of performance, dating to ancient times, is one of the fundamental features that differentiate Indian from Western cinema. In the *Rasa* method, empathetic "emotions are conveyed by the performer and thus felt by the audience", in contrast to the Western Stanislavski method where the actor must become "a living, breathing embodiment of a character" rather than "simply conveying emotion". The *rasa* method is apparent in the performances of Hindi actors such as Bachchan and Shah Rukh Khan and in Hindi films such as *Rang De Basanti* (2006), and Ray's works.
- Traditional folk theatre became popular around the 10th century with the decline of Sanskrit theatre. These regional traditions include the Yatra of West Bengal, the Ramlila of Uttar Pradesh, Yakshagana of Karnataka, 'Chindu Natakam' of Andhra Pradesh and the Terukkuttu of Tamil Nadu.
- Parsi theatre "blended realism and fantasy, music and dance, narrative and spectacle, earthy dialogue and ingenuity of stage presentation, integrating them into a dramatic melodrama. The Parsi plays contained crude humour, melodious songs and music, sensationalism and dazzling stagecraft." These influences are clearly evident in *masala* films such as *Coolie* (1983), and to an extent in more recent critically acclaimed films

such as *Rang De Basanti*.
- Hollywood made popular musicals from the 1920s through the 1960s. Indian musical makers departed from their Hollywood counterparts in several ways. "For example, the Hollywood musicals had as their plot the world of entertainment itself. Indian filmmakers, while enhancing the elements of fantasy so pervasive in Indian popular films, used song and music as a natural mode of articulation in a given situation in their films. There is a strong Indian tradition of narrating mythology, history, fairy stories and so on through song and dance." In addition, "whereas Hollywood filmmakers strove to conceal the constructed nature of their work so that the realistic narrative was wholly dominant, Indian filmmakers made no attempt to conceal the fact that what was shown on the screen was a creation, an illusion, a fiction. However, they demonstrated how this creation intersected with people's day-to-day lives in complex and interesting ways."
- Western musical television, particularly MTV, had an increasing influence in the 1990s, as can be seen in the pace, camera angles, dance sequences and music of recent Indian films. An early example of this approach was *Bombay* (1995, Mani Ratnam).

Sharmistha Gooptu and Bhaumik identify Indo-Persian/Islamicate culture as another major influence. In the early 20th century, Urdu was the lingua franca of popular performances across northern India, established in performance art traditions such as nautch dancing, Urdu poetry and Parsi theater. Urdu and related Hindi dialects were the most widely understood across northern India, thus Hindi-Urdu became the standardized language of early Indian talkies. *One Thousand and One Nights* (*Arabian Nights*) had a strong influence on Parsi theater, which adapted "Persianate adventure-romances" into films, and on early Bombay cinema where *"Arabian Nights* cinema" became a popular genre. Stadtman identifies foreign influences on commercial Bollywood masala films: New Hollywood, Hong Kong martial arts cinema and Italian exploitation films.

Like mainstream Indian popular cinema, Indian Parallel Cinema was influenced by a combination of Indian theatre and Indian literature (such as Bengali literature and Urdu poetry), but differs when it comes to foreign influences, where it is influenced more by European cinema (particularly Italian neorealism and French poetic realism) than by Hollywood. Ray cited Vittorio De Sica's *Bicycle Thieves* (1948) and Jean Renoir's *The River* (1951), on which he assisted, as influences on his debut film *Pather Panchali* (1955).

Multilinguals

Some Indian films are known as "multilinguals", filmed in similar but non-identical versions in different languages. This was done in the 1930s. According to Rajadhyaksha and Willemen in the *Encyclopaedia of Indian Cinema* (1994), in its most precise form, a multilingual is <templatestyles src="Template:Quote/styles.css"/>

> *a bilingual or a trilingual [that] was the kind of film made in the 1930s in the studio era, when different but identical takes were made of every shot in different languages, often with different leading stars but identical technical crew and music.*[15]

Rajadhyaksha and Willemen note that in seeking to construct their *Encyclopedia*, they often found it "extremely difficult to distinguish multilinguals in this original sense from dubbed versions, remakes, reissues or, in some cases, the same film listed with different titles, presented as separate versions in different languages ... it will take years of scholarly work to establish definitive data in this respect".[15]

Regional industries

Films are made in many cities and regions in India including Andhra Pradesh and Telangana, Assam, Bengal, Bihar, Gujarat, Haryana, Jammu, Kashmir, Jharkhand, Karnataka, Konkan (Goa), Northern Telangana, Northern Karnataka and Ranchi (Jharkhand), Kerala, Maharashtra, Manipur, Odisha, Punjab, Rajasthan, Tamil Nadu and Uttrakhand.

Breakdown by languages

2017 Indian feature films certified by the Central Board of Film Certification by languages.
Note: This table indicates the number of films certified by the CBFC's regional offices in nine cities. The actual number of films produced may be less.

Language	No. of films
Hindi	364 (digital) and 0 (celluloid), total of 364
Tamil	304 (digital) and 0 (celluloid), total of 304
Telugu	294 (digital) and 0 (celluloid), total of 294
Kannada	220 (digital) and 0 (celluloid), total of 220
Bengali	163 (digital) and 0 (celluloid), total of 163
Malayalam	153 (digital) and 0 (celluloid), total of 153
Marathi	117 (digital) and 0 (celluloid), total of 117
Bhojpuri	102 (digital) and 0 (celluloid), total of 102

Gujarati	73 (digital) and 0 (celluloid), total of 73
Odia	42 (digital) and 0 (celluloid), total of 42
Punjabi	38 (digital) and 0 (celluloid), total of 38
Assamese	16 (digital) and 0 (celluloid), total of 16
Konkani	13 (digital) and 0 (celluloid), total of 13
English	11 (digital) and 0 (celluloid), total of 11
Rajasthani (Rollywood)	10 (digital) and 0 (celluloid), total of 10
Chhattisgarhi	9 (digital) and 0 (celluloid), total of 9
Tulu	9 (digital) and 0 (celluloid), total of 9
Khasi	7 (digital) and 0 (celluloid), total of 7
Garhwali	4 (digital) and 0 (celluloid), total of 4
Maithili	4 (digital) and 0 (celluloid), total of 4
Awadhi	3 (digital) and 0 (celluloid), total of 3
Lambadi	2 (digital) and 0 (celluloid), total of 2
Haryanvi	2 (digital) and 0 (celluloid), total of 2
Mishing	2 (digital) and 0 (celluloid), total of 2
Nepali	2 (digital) and 0 (celluloid), total of 2
Pnar	2 (digital) and 0 (celluloid), total of 2
Others	1 each
Total	1986 (digital) and 0 (celluloid), total of 1986

Assam

The Assamese language film industry traces its origin to the works of revolutionary visionary Rupkonwar Jyotiprasad Agarwala, who was a distinguished poet, playwright, composer and freedom fighter. He was instrumental in the production of the first Assamese film *Joymati* in 1935, under the banner of Critrakala Movietone. Due to the lack of trained technicians, Jyotiprasad, while making his maiden film, had to shoulder the added responsibilities as the screenwriter, producer, director, choreographer, editor, set and costume designer, lyricist and music director. The film, completed with a budget of 60,000 rupees, was released on 10 March 1935. The picture failed miserably. Like many early films, the negatives and prints of *Joymati* are missing. Some effort has been made privately by Altaf Mazid to restore and subtitle what is left of the prints. Despite the significant financial loss from *Joymati*, a second picture, *Indramalati*, was released in 1939. The 21st century has produced Bollywood-style Assamese movies.[602]

Figure 276: *First Assamese motion picture, Joymati, filmed in 1935*

Figure 277: *A scene from Dena Paona, 1931, the first Bengali talkie*

Bengali cinema

The Bengali language cinematic tradition of Tollygunge located in West Bengal hosted masters such as Ray, Ghatak and Sen.[603] Recent Bengali films that have captured national attention include *Choker Bali*.(Rituparno Ghosh)[604] Bengal has produced science fiction and issue films.[605]

Bengali cinema dates to the 1890s, when the first "bioscopes" were shown in theatres in Calcutta. Within five years, Hiralal Sen set up the Royal Bioscope Company, producing scenes from the stage productions of a number of popular shows at the Star Theatre, Calcutta, Minerva Theatre and Classic Theatre. Following a long gap after Sen, Dhirendra Nath Ganguly (Known as D.G.) established Indo British Film Co, the first Bengali owned production company, in 1918. The first Bengali Feature film *Billwamangal* was produced in 1919 under the banner of Madan Theatre. *Bilat Ferat* (1921) was the IBFC's first production. Madan Theatres production of *Jamai Shashthi* was the first Bengali talkie.[606]

In 1932, the name "Tollywood" was coined for the Bengali film industry because Tollygunge rhymes with "Hollywood" and because it was then the centre of the Indian film industry. The 'Parallel Cinema' movement began in Bengal. Bengali stalwarts such as Ray, Mrinal Sen, Ghatak and others earned international acclaim. Actors including Uttam Kumar and Soumitra Chatterjee led the Bengali film industry.

Other Bengali art film directors include Mir Shaani, Buddhadeb Dasgupta, Gautam Ghose, Sandip Ray and Aparna Sen.

Brajbhasha cinema

Braj Bhasha language films present Brij culture mainly to rural people, predominant in the nebulous Braj region centred around Mathura, Agra, Aligarh and Hathras in Western Uttar Pradesh and Bharatpur and Dholpur in Rajasthan. It is the predominant language in the central stretch of the Ganges-Yamuna Doab in Uttar Pradesh. The first Brij Bhasha movie India was *Brij Bhoomi* (1982, Shiv Kumar), which was a success throughout the country. Later Brij Bhasha cinema saw the production of films like *Jamuna Kinare*, *Brij Kau Birju*, *Bhakta Surdas* and *Jesus*. The culture of Brij is presented in *Krishna Tere Desh Main* (Hindi), *Kanha Ki Braj Bhumi*, Brij ki radha dwarika ke shyam and *Bawre Nain*.

Bhojpuri

Bhojpuri language films predominantly cater to residents of western Bihar and eastern Uttar Pradesh and also have a large audience in Delhi and Mumbai due to migration of Bhojpuri speakers to these cities. Besides India, markets for these films developed in other Bhojpuri speaking countries of the West Indies, Oceania and South America.

Bhojpuri film history begins with *Ganga Maiyya Tohe Piyari Chadhaibo* (*Mother Ganges, I will offer you a yellow sari*, 1962, Kundan Kumar). Throughout the following decades, few films were produced. Films such as *Bidesiya* (*Foreigner*, 1963, S. N. Tripathi) and *Ganga* (*Ganges*, 1965, Kumar) were profitable and popular, but in general Bhojpuri films were not common in the 1960s and 1970s.

The industry experienced a revival in 2001 with the hit *Saiyyan Hamar* (*My Sweetheart*, Mohan Prasad), which shot Ravi Kissan to superstardom. This was followed by several other successes, including *Panditji Batai Na Biyah Kab Hoi* (*Priest, tell me when I will marry*, 2005, Prasad), and *Sasura Bada Paisa Wala* (*My father-in-law, the rich guy*, 2005.) Both did much better business in Uttar Pradesh and Bihar than mainstream Bollywood hits, and both earned more than ten times their production costs.[607] Although smaller than other Indian film industries, these successes increased Bhojpuri cinema's visibility, leading to an awards show and a trade magazine, *Bhojpuri City*.

Chhattisgarh (Chhollywood)

Chhollywood was born in 1965 with the first Chhattisgarhi film *Kahi Debe Sandesh* (*In Black and White,* Manu Nayak). NaiduWikipedia:Manual of Style/Words to watch#Unsupported attributions wrote the lyrics for the film, and two songs were sung by Mohammad Rafi. That film and *Ghar Dwar* (1971, Niranjan Tiwari) bombed. No Chhollywood movie was produced for nearly 30 years thereafter.

English

Deepa Mehta, Anant Balani, Homi Adajania, Vijay Singh, Vierendrra Lalit and Sooni Taraporevala have garnered recognition in Indian English cinema.

Gujarat

Before the arrival of talkies, several silent films were closely related to Gujarati culture. Many film directors, producers and actors associated with silent films were Gujarati and Parsi. Twenty leading film company and studios were owned by Gujaratis between 1913 and 1931. They were mostly located in Mumbai. At least forty-four major Gujarati directors worked during this period.

Gujarati cinema dates to 9 April 1932, when the first Gujarati film, *Narsinh Mehta*, was released. *Leeludi Dharti* (1968) was the first colour Gujarati film. After flourishing through the 1960s to 1980s, the industry declined although it later revived. More than one thousand films were released.

Gujarati cinema ranges from mythology to history and from social to political. Gujarati films originally targeted a rural audience, but after its revival catered to an urban audience.

Hindi (Bollywood)

The Hindi language film industry of Bombay—also known as Bollywood—is the largest and most powerful branch. Hindi cinema explored issues of caste and culture in films such as *Achhut Kanya* (1936) and *Sujata* (1959).[608] International visibility came to the industry with Raj Kapoor's *Awara* and later in Shakti Samantha's *Aradhana*.[609] Hindi cinema grew during the 1990s with the release of as many as 215 films annually.

Many actors signed contracts for simultaneous work in 3–4 films. Institutions such as the Industrial Development Bank of India financed Hindi films. Magazines such as *Filmfare*, *Stardust* and *Cine Blitz* became popular.[610]

Figure 278: *Amitabh Bacchan has been a popular Bollywood actor for over 45 years.*

In Hindi cinema audiences participate by clapping, singing and reciting familiar dialogue.

Art film directors include Kaul, Kumar Shahani, Ketan Mehta, Govind Nihalani, Shyam Benegal, Mira Nair, Nagesh Kukunoor, Sudhir Mishra and Nandita Das.

Kannada (Sandalwood)

The Kannada film industry, also referred to as *Sandalwood*, is based in Bengaluru and caters mostly to Karnataka. Gubbi Veeranna (1891 – 1972) was an Indian theatre director and artist and an awardee of the Padma Shri award conferred by the President of India. He was one of the pioneers and most prolific contributors to Kannada theatre. Kannada actor Rajkumar began working with Veeranna and later became an important actor.

Veeranna founded *Karnataka Gubbi Productions*. He produced *Sadarame* (1935, Raja Chandrasekar), in which he acted in the lead role. He then produced *Subhadra and Jeevana Nataka* (1942). He took the lead role in *Hemareddy Mallamma* (1945). Karnataka Gubbi Productions was later called Karnataka Films Ltd., and is credited with starting the career of Rajkumar when it offered him the lead role in his debut film *Bedara Kannappa*. He produced silent movies including *His Love Affair,* (Raphel Algoet). Veeranna was the lead, accompanied by his wife, Jayamma.

Veeranna produced *Bedara Kannappa* (1954, H. L. N. Simha) which received the first Certificate of Merit. However, the first "President's Silver Medal for Best Feature Film in Kannada" was awarded at the 5th National Film Awards ceremony to *Premada Puthri (1957,* R. Nagendra Rao).

Vishnuvardhan and Rajkumar were eminent actors along with Ambarish, Anant Nag, Shankar Nag, Prabhakar, Udaya Kumar, Kalyan Kumar, Gangadhar, Ravichandran, Girish Karnad, Prakash Raj, Charan Raj, B Jayamma, Shivaraj kumar, Leelavathi, Kalpana, Bharathi, Jayanthi, Pandari Bai, Aarathi, Jaimala, Tara, Umashri and Ramya.

Kannada directors include H. L. N. Simha, R. Nagendra Rao, B. R. Panthulu, M. S. Sathyu, Puttanna Kanagal, G. V. Iyer, Karnad, T. S. Nagabharana Siddalingaiah, B. V. Karanth, A K Pattabhi, T. V. Singh Thakur, Y. R. Swamy, M. R. Vittal, Sundar Rao Nadkarni, P. S. Moorthy, S. K. A. Chari, Hunsur Krishnamurthy, Prema Karanth, Rajendra Singh Babu, N. Lakshminarayan, Shankar Nag, Girish Kasaravalli, Umesh Kulkarni and Suresh Heblikar. Other noted film personalities in Kannada are, Bhargava, G.K. Venkatesh, Vijaya Bhaskar, Rajan-Nagendra, Geethapriya, Hamsalekha, R. N. Jayagopal, M. Ranga Rao and Yogaraj Bhat.

Kannada cinema contributed to Indian parallel cinema. Influential Kannada films in this genre include *Samskara, Chomana Dudi* (B. V. Karanth), *Tabarana Kathe, Vamshavruksha, Kaadu Kudure, Hamsageethe, Bhootayyana Maga Ayyu, Accident, Maanasa Sarovara, Bara, Chitegoo Chinte, Galige, Ijjodu, Kaneshwara Rama,Ghatashraddha, Tabarana Kathe, Mane, Kraurya, Thaayi Saheba, Bandhana, Muthina Haara, Banker Margayya, Dweepa, Munnudi, Bettada Jeeva, Mysore Mallige and Chinnari Muththa.*

The Government Film and Television Institute, Bangalore (formerly a part of S.J. Polytechnic) is believed to be the first government institute in India to start technical film courses.

Konkani

Konkani language films are mainly produced in Goa. It is one of India's smallest film regions, producing four films in 2009. Konkani language is spoken mainly in the states of Goa, Maharashtra and Karnataka and to a smaller extent in Kerala. The first full length Konkani film was *Mogacho Anvddo* (1950, Jerry Braganza), under the banner of Etica Pictures. The film's release date, 24 April, is celebrated as Konkani Film Day. Karnataka is the hub of many Konkani speaking people. An immense body of Konkani literature and art is a

Figure 279: *Movie poster of Vigathakumaran*

resource for filmmakers. *Kazar (Marriage,* 2009, Richard Castelino) and *Uj-vaadu (Shedding New Light on Old Age Issues,* Kasaragod Chinna) are major releases. The pioneering Mangalorean Konkani film is *Mog Ani Maipas.*

Malayalam

The Malayalam film industry, India's fourth largest, is based in Kochi. Malayalam films are known for bridging the gap between parallel cinema and mainstream cinema by portraying thought-provoking social issues with technical flair and low budgets. Filmmakers include Gopalakrishnan, Karun, Aravindan, K. G. George, Padmarajan, Sathyan Anthikad, Chandran and Bharathan.

The first full-length Malayalam feature was *Vigathakumaran (*1928, J. C. Daniel). This movie is credited as the first Indian social drama feature film. Daniel is considered the father of the Malayalam film industry. *Balan (*1938, S. Nottani) was the first Malayalam "talkie".

Malayalam films were mainly produced by Tamil producers until 1947, when the first major film studio, Udaya Studio, opened in Kerala. *Neelakkuyil* (1954) captured national interest by winning the President's silver medal. Scripted by the well-known Malayalam novelist, Uroob (P. Bhaskaran and Ramu Kariat) is often considered the first authentic Malayali film. *Newspaper Boy (1955),*

Figure 280: *A promotional notice of Balan*

made by a group of students, was the first neo-realistic film offering. *Chemmeen* (1965, Ramu Kariat) based on a story by Thakazhi Sivasankara Pillai, became the first South Indian film to win the National Film Award for Best Feature Film.

The first neorealistic film *Newspaper Boy* (1955-P. Ramdas), The first CinemaScope film *Thacholi Ambu* (1978-Navodaya Appachan), The first 70 mm film film *Padayottam* (1982-Jijo Punnoose), The first 3D film *My Dear Kuttichathan* (1984-Jijo Punnoose), The first Digital film *Moonnamathoral* (2006-V. K. Prakash),[611] The first Smartphone film *Jalachhayam* (2010-Sathish Kalathil), The first 8K resolution film *Villain* (2017-B. Unnikrishnan) of India were made in Malayalam.

The period from the late 1980s to early 1990s is regarded as the Golden Age of Malayalam cinema with the emergence of actors Mohanlal, Mammootty, Suresh Gopi, Jayaram, Bharath Gopi, Murali, Thilakan and Nedumudi Venu. The major actors who emerged after the Golden Age include Dileep, Jayasurya, Fahadh Faasil, Nivin Pauly, Prithviraj Sukumaran, Dulquer Salmaan, Kunchacko Boban and Asif Ali (actor) and Manju Warrier.

Notable filmmakers such as I. V. Sasi, Bharathan, Padmarajan, K. G. George, Sathyan Anthikad, Priyadarshan, A. K. Lohithadas, Siddique-Lal, T. K. Rajeev Kumar and Sreenivasan. Art film directors include Puttanna Kanagal,

Dore Bhagavan, Siddalingaiah in Kannada; Gopalakrishnan, Karun and T.V. Chandran.

K. R. Narayanan National Institute of Visual Science and Arts (KRNNIVSA) is an autonomous institute established by the Government of Kerala at Thekkumthala in Kottayam District in Kerala state as a training-cum-research centre in film/audio-visual technology.

Meitei

Meitei cinema is a small industry in the state of Manipur. This region's debut was a full-length black and white film *Matamgee Manipur* (1972). Meitei cinema started in the 1980s. *Langlen Thadoi* (1984) was Meitei cinema's first full-length colour film.

Meitei cinema gained momentum following a ban on the screening of Hindi films in entertainment houses in Manipur. Screening of Hindi movies came to a halt despite reiterated appeals made by successive Chief Ministers.

80-100 movies are made each year. Cinemas opened in Imphal after World War II. The first full-length Meitei movie was made in 1972, followed by a boom in 2002.

Imagi Ningthem (Aribam Syam Sharma) won the Grand Prix in the 1992 Nantes International Film Festival. A nationwide French telecast of *Imagi Ningthem* expanded the audience. After watching *Ishanou* (Aribam Syam Sharma), westerners began research on Lai Haraoba and Manipur's rich folklore. *Maipak, Son of Manipur* (1971) was the first Meitei documentary film.

Among the notable Meitei films are *Phijigee Mani*, *Leipaklei* and *Pallepfam*.

Marathi

Marathi films are produced in the Marathi language in Maharashtra. It is one of the oldest efforts in Indian cinema. Dadasaheb Phalke made the first indigenous silent film *Raja Harishchandra* (1913) with a Marathi crew, which is considered by IFFI and NIFD to be part of Marathi cinema.

The first Marathi talkie, *Ayodhyecha Raja* (1932, Prabhat Films). *Shwaas* (2004) and *Harishchandrachi Factory* (2009), became India's official Oscar entries. Today the industry is based in Mumbai, but it began in Kolhapur and then Pune.

Some of the more notable films are *Sangte Aika*, *Ek Gaon Bara Bhangadi*, *Pinjara*, *Sinhasan*, *Pathlaag*, *Jait Re Jait*, *Saamana*, *Santh Wahate Krishnamai*, *Sant Tukaram* and *Shyamchi Aai*.

Marathi films feature the work of actors including Durga Khote, V. Shantaram, Lalita Pawar, Nanda, Shriram Lagoo, Ramesh Deo, Seema Deo, Nana Patekar, Smita Patil, Sadashiv Amrapurkar, Sonali Kulkarni, Sonali Bendre, Urmila Matondkar, Reema Lagoo, Padmini Kolhapure, Ashok Saraf, Laxmikant Berde and Sachin Khedekar.

Gorkha

Gorkha cinema consists of Nepali language films produced by Nepali-speaking Indians.

Odia (Ollywood)

The Odia language film industry operates in Bhubaneswar and Cuttack. The first Odia talkie Sita Bibaha (1936) came from Mohan Sunder Deb Goswami. Shreeram Panda, Prashanta Nanda, Uttam Mohanty and Bijay Mohanty started the Oriya film industry by finding an audience and a fresh presentation. The first colour film, *Gapa Hele Be Sata* (*Although a Story, It Is True*), was made by Nagen Ray and photographed by Pune Film Institute-trained cinematographer Surendra Sahu. The best year for Odia cinema was 1984 when *Maya Miriga* (Nirad Mohapatra) and *Dhare Alua* were showcased in Indian Panorama and *Maya Miriga* was invited to Critics Week at Cannes. The film received the Best Third World Film award at Mannheim Film Festival, Jury Award at Hawaii and was shown at the London Film Festival.

Punjab (Pollywood)

K.D. Mehra made the first Punjabi film, *Sheela* (also known as *Pind di Kudi* (*Rustic Girl*)). Baby Noor Jehan was introduced as an actress and singer in this film. *Sheela* was made in Calcutta and released in Lahore; it was a hit across the province. Its success led many more producers to make Punjabi films. As of 2009, Punjabi cinema had produced between 900 and 1,000 movies. The average number of releases per year in the 1970s was nine; in the 1980s, eight; and in the 1990s, six. In the 2000s Punjabi cinema revived with more releases every year featuring bigger budgets. Manny Parmar made the first 3D Punjabi film, *Pehchaan* 3D (2013).

Figure 281: *Kalidas (1931), Tamil cinema's first talkie*

Sindh

The Sindhi film industry produces movies at intervals. The first was *Abana* (1958), which was a success throughout the country. Sindhi cinema then produced some Bollywood-style films such as *Hal Ta Bhaji Haloon*, *Parewari*, *Dil Dije Dil Waran Khe*, *Ho Jamalo*, *Pyar Kare Dis: Feel the Power of Love* and *The Awakening*. Numerous Sindhi have contributed in Bollywood, including G P Sippy, Ramesh Sippy, Nikhil Advani, Tarun Mansukhani, Ritesh Sidhwani and Asrani.

Sherdukpen

Director Songe Dorjee Thongdok introduced the first Sherdukpen-language film *Crossing Bridges* (2014). Sherdukpen is native to the north-eastern state of Arunachal Pradesh.

Tamil (Kollywood)

Chennai once served as a base for all South Indian films It is the second largest industry in India after Bollywood and is South India's largest production centre.

The first south Indian talkie film *Kalidas* (H. M. Reddy) was shot in Tamil and Telugu. Sivaji Ganesan became India's first actor to receive an international award when he won Best Actor at the Afro-Asian film festival in 1960 and the title of *Chevalier* in the Legion of Honour by the French Government in 1995.

Tamil cinema is influenced by Dravidian politics, led by film personalities such as C N Annadurai, M G Ramachandran, M Karunanidhi and Jayalalithaa who became Chief Ministers of Tamil Nadu. K. B. Sundarambal was the first film personality to enter a state legislature in India. She was also the first to command a salary of one lakh rupees.

Tamil films are distributed to various parts of Asia, Southern Africa, Northern America, Europe and Oceania.[612] The industry inspired Tamil film-making in Sri Lanka, Malaysia, Singapore and Canada.

Rajnikanth is referred to as "Superstar" and holds matinee idol status in South India. The ₹26 crore (US$3.6 million) he earned for *Sivaji* (2007), made him the highest-paid actor in Asia after Jackie Chan.Kamal Haasan debuted in *Kalathur Kannamma*, for which he won the President's Gold Medal for Best Child Actor. Haasan is tied with Mammootty and Bachchan for the most Best Actor National Film Awards, with three. With seven submissions, Kamal Haasan has starred in the highest number of Academy Award submissions. Critically acclaimed composers such as Ilaiyaraaja and A. R. Rahman work in Tamil cinema. Art film directors include Santosh Sivan.

Telugu (Tollywood)

India's greatest number of theatres are located in Andhra Pradesh / Telangana and feature films in Telugu. As of 2018, it is the third largest film industry in India after Bollywood and Kollywood in terms of box office collections and footfalls, and in terms of number of theatrical releases. . Ramoji Film City, which holds the Guinness World Record for the world's largest film production facility, is located in Hyderabad. The Prasad IMAX in Hyderabad is the world's largest 3D IMAX screen and is the world's most viewed screen. The highest-grossing Telugu movie is *Baahubali 2: The Conclusion*. Raghupathi Venkaiah Naidu is considered the "father of Telugu cinema". The annual Raghupati Venkaiah Award was incorporated into the Nandi Awards to recognize contributions to the industry.

Chittor V. Nagaiah was the first multilingual Indian film actor, thespian, composer, director, producer, writer and playback singer. Nagaiah made significant contributions to Telugu cinema, and starred in some two hundred productions. Regarded as one of the finest Indian method actors, he was Telugu's first matinee idol. His forte was intense characters, often immersing himself in the character's traits and mannerisms. He was the first from South India to be

Figure 282: *Raghupati Venkayya, "father of Telugu cinema"*

honoured with the Padma Shri. He became known as India's Paul Muni. S. V. Ranga Rao was one of the first Indian actors to receive the international award at the Indonesian Film Festival, held in Jakarta, for *Narthanasala* in 1963.[613] N. T. Rama Rao was one of the most successful Telugu actors of his time.

B. Narsing Rao, K. N. T. Sastry and Pattabhirama Reddy garnered international recognition for their pioneering work in Parallel Cinema. Adurthi Subba Rao won ten National Film Awards, Telugu cinema's highest individual awards, for his directorial work. N .T. Rama Rao was an Indian actor, producer, director, editor and politician who earned three National Film Awards. He served as Chief Minister of Andhra Pradesh for seven years over three terms.

Bhanumathi Ramakrishna was a multilingual Indian film actress, drector, music director, singer, producer, author and songwriter. Widely known as the first female super star of Telugu cinema, she is also known for her work in Tamil cinema.

Ghantasala Venkateswara Rao was an Indian film, composer, playback singer known for his works predominantly in Telugu cinema, and other languages. In 1970, he received the Padma Shri award.

S. P. Balasubramanyam holds the Guinness World Record of having sung the most number of songs for any male playback singer; the majority were in Telugu.

S. V. Ranga Rao, N. T. Rama Rao, Kanta Rao, Bhanumathi Ramakrishna, Savitri, Gummadi and Sobhan Babu received the Rashtrapati Award for best performance in a leading role. Sharada, Archana, Vijayashanti, Rohini, Akkineni Nageswara Rao, and P. L. Narayana received the National Film Award for the best performance in acting. Chiranjeevi was listed among "the men who changed the face of the Indian Cinema" by IBN-live India.

Art film directors include K. N. T. Sastry, B. Narsing Rao, Akkineni Kutumba Rao and Deva Katta.

Tulu

30 to 40 films are made annually in Tulu. K. N. Tailor and Machchendra nath Pandeshwar are Tulu icons. Usually Tulu films are released in theatres across the Kanara region of Karnataka.

Enna Thangadi, was the first, released in 1971. The critically acclaimed *Suddha* won the award for Best Indian Film at the Osian film festival held at New Delhi in 2006. *Oriyardori Asal*, released in 2011, is the most successful. *Koti Chennaya* (1973, Vishu Kumar) was the first history-based. The first colour film was *Kariyani Kattandi Kandani* (1978, Aroor Bhimarao).

Genres and styles

Masala films

Masala is a style of Indian cinema that mix genres in one work, especially in Bollywood, West Bengal and South India. For example, one film can portray action, comedy, drama, romance and melodrama. These films tend to be musicals, with songs filmed in picturesque locations. Plots for such movies may seem illogical and improbable to unfamiliar viewers. The genre is named after masala, a mixture of spices in Indian cuisine.

Parallel cinema

Parallel Cinema, also known as Art Cinema or the Indian New Wave, is known for its realism and naturalism, addressing the sociopolitical climate. This movement is distinct from mainstream Bollywood cinema and began around the same time as the French and Japanese New Waves. The movement began in Bengal (led by Ray, Sen and Ghatak) and then gained prominence in the regions. The movement was launched by Roy's *Do Bigha Zamin* (1953), which was both a commercial and critical success, winning the International Prize at the 1954 Cannes Film Festival. Ray's films include *The Apu Trilogy*. Its three films won major prizes at the Cannes, Berlin and Venice Film Festivals, and are frequently listed among the greatest films of all time.[614]

Other neo-realist filmmakers were Shyam Benegal, Karun, Gopalakrishnan and Kasaravalli.[615]

Production organizations

More than 1000 production organizations operate in the Indian film industry, but few are successful. AVM Productions is the oldest surviving studio in India. Other major production houses include Yash Raj Films, Red Chillies Entertainment, Dharma Productions, Eros International, Ajay Devgn FFilms, Balaji Motion Pictures, UTV Motion Pictures, Raj Kamal Films International,Wunderbar studios, Indian Movies Limited and Geetha Arts.

Music

Music is a substantial revenue generator, with music rights alone accounting for 4–5% of net revenues. The major film music companies are Saregama and Sony Music. Film music accounts for 48% of net music sales. A typical film may feature 5–6 choreographed songs.[616]

The demands of a multicultural, increasingly globalized Indian audience led to a mixing of local and international musical traditions. Local dance and music remain a recurring theme in India and followed the Indian diaspora. Playback singers such as Mohammad Rafi, Kishore Kumar, Lata Mangeshkar, S. P. Balasubrahmanyam and Yesudas drew crowds to film music stage shows. In the 21st century interaction increased between Indian artists and others.[617]

Film locations

In filmmaking, a location is any place where acting and dialogue are recorded. Sites where filming without dialog takes place is termed a second unit photography site. Filmmakers often choose to shoot on location because they believe that greater realism can be achieved in a "real" place. Location shooting is often motivated by budget considerations.

The most popular locations are the main cities for each regional industry. Other locations include Manali and Shimla in Himachal Pradesh, Srinagar and Ladakh in Jammu and Kashmir, Lucknow, Agra and Varanasi in Uttar Pradesh, Ooty in Tamil Nadu, Amritsar in Punjab, Darjeeling in West Bengal, Udaipur, Jodhpur, Jaisalmer and Jaipur in Rajasthan, Delhi, Kerala and Goa.

Awards

Dadasaheb Phalke is known as the "Father of Indian cinema". The Dadasaheb Phalke Award, for lifetime contribution to cinema, was instituted in his honour by the Government of India in 1969, and is the country's most prestigious and coveted film award.

Prominent government-sponsored film awards

Award	Year of Inception	Awarded by
National Film Awards	1954	Directorate of Film Festivals, Government of India
Bengal Film Journalists' Association Awards	1937	Government of West Bengal
Maharashtra State Film Awards	1963	Government of Maharashtra
Nandi Awards	1964	Governments of Andhra Pradesh and Telangana
Punjab Rattan Awards	1940	Government of Punjab
Tamil Nadu State Film Awards	1967	Government of Tamil Nadu
Karnataka State Film Awards	1967	Government of Karnataka
Orissa State Film Awards	1968	Government of Odisha
Kerala State Film Awards	1969	Government of Kerala

Prominent non-governmental awards

Award	Year of Inception	Awarded by
Filmfare Awards Filmfare Awards South	1954	Bennett, Coleman and Co. Ltd.
Screen Awards	1994	Screen Weekly
Zee Cine Awards	1998	Zee Entertainment Enterprises
Asianet Film Awards	1998	Asianet
IIFA Awards	2000	Wizcraft International Entertainment Pvt Ltd
Stardust Awards	2003	Stardust
Zee Gaurav Puraskar	2003	Zee Entertainment Enterprises
Apsara Awards	2004	Apsara Producers Guilt awards
Vijay Awards	2007	STAR Vijay
Marathi International Film and Theatre Awards	2010	Marathi Film Industry
South Indian International Movie Awards	2012	South Indian Film Industry
Punjabi International Film Academy Awards	2012	Parvasi Media Inc.
Prag Cine Awards	2013	Prag AM Television
Filmfare Awards East	2014	Bennett, Coleman and Co. Ltd.

Institutes

Government-run and private institutes provide formal education in various aspects of filmmaking. Some of the prominent ones include:

- State Institute of Film and Television
- AJK Mass Communication Research Centre, Jamia Millia Islamia, New Delhi
- Annapurna International School of Film and Media, Hyderabad
- Asian Academy of Film and Television
- Biju Pattnaik Film and Television Institute of Odisha
- BOFTA - Blue Ocean Film and Television Academy, Kodambakkam, Chennai, Tamil Nadu
- Centre for advanced media studies, Patiala
- Department of Culture and Media studies, Central University of Rajasthan
- Film and Television Institute of India (FTII), Pune
- Film-Theater Studies, SOH, Tamil Nadu Open University, Saidapet, Chennai

- Government Film and Television Institute, Bangalore
- K. R. Narayanan National Institute of Visual Science and Arts (KRN-NIVSA), Kottayam, Kerala
- L. V. Prasad Film and TV Academy, Chennai
- MGR Film and Television institute, Chennai
- Matrikas Film School
- National Institute of Design, Ahmedabad
- Palme Deor Media College, Tambaram west, Chennai and Arulananda Nagar, Thanjavur
- Regional Government Film and Television Institute (RGFTI), Guwahati
- Satyajit Ray Film and Television Institute, Calcutta
- School of Media and Cultural Studies, Tata Institute of Social Sciences, Mumbai
- Srishti School of Art, Design and Technology, Bangalore, Karnataka
- Whistling Woods International
- National school of Drama Delhi

Further reading

- Suresh Chabria; Paolo Cherchi Usai (1994). *Light of Asia: Indian Silent Cinema, 1912–1934*[618]. Wiley Eastern. ISBN 978-81-224-0680-1.<templatestyles src="Module:Citation/CS1/styles.css"></templatestyles>
- Stanley A. Wolpert (2006). *Encyclopedia of India*. ISBN 978-0-684-31350-4.<templatestyles src="Module:Citation/CS1/styles.css"></templatestyles>
- Desai, Jigna (2004). *Beyond Bollywood: The Cultural Politics of South Asian Diasporic Film*. Psychology Press. ISBN 978-0-415-96684-9.<templatestyles src="Module:Citation/CS1/styles.css"></templatestyles>
- K. Moti Gokulsing; Wimal Dissanayake (2004). *Indian Popular Cinema: A Narrative of Cultural Change*. Trentham Books Limited. ISBN 978-1-85856-329-9.<templatestyles src="Module:Citation/CS1/styles.css"></templatestyles>
- Gulzar, Govin Nihalanni, & Saibel Chatterjee. *Encyclopaedia of Hindi Cinema* New Delhi: Encyclopædia Britannica, 2003. <templatestyles src="Module:Citation/CS1/styles.css" />ISBN 81-7991-066-0.
- Khanna, Amit (2003), "The Business of Hindi Films", *Encyclopaedia of Hindi Cinema: historical record, the business and its future, narrative forms, analysis of the medium, milestones, biographies*, Encyclopædia Britannica (India) Private Limited, <templatestyles src="Module:Citation/CS1/styles.css" />ISBN 978-81-7991-066-5.

- Gopal, Sangita; Moorti, Sujata (2008). *Global Bollywood: Travels of Hindi Song and Dance*. University of Minnesota Press. ISBN 978-0-8166-4578-7.<templatestyles src="Module:Citation/CS1/styles.css"></templatestyles>
- Narweker, Sanjit, ed. *Directory of Indian Film-Makers and Films*. Flicks Books, 1994. <templatestyles src="Module:Citation/CS1/styles.css" />>ISBN 0-948911-40-9
- Stanley A. Wolpert (2006). *Encyclopedia of India*. ISBN 978-0-684-31351-1.<templatestyles src="Module:Citation/CS1/styles.css"></templatestyles>
- Nowell-Smith, Geoffrey (1996). *The Oxford History of World Cinema*. Oxford University Press, US. ISBN 978-0-19-811257-0.<templatestyles src="Module:Citation/CS1/styles.css"></templatestyles>
- Passek, Jean-Loup, ed. (1983). *Le cinéma indien*. Paris: Centre national d'art et de culture Georges Pompidou. ISBN 9782864250371. OCLC 10696565[619].<templatestyles src="Module:Citation/CS1/styles.css"></templatestyles>
- Rajadhyaksha, Ashish; Willemen, Paul (1999). *Encyclopedia of Indian Cinema*. Routledge. ISBN 978-1-57958-146-6.<templatestyles src="Module:Citation/CS1/styles.css"></templatestyles>
- Stanley A. Wolpert (2006). *Encyclopedia of India*. ISBN 978-0-684-31351-1.<templatestyles src="Module:Citation/CS1/styles.css"></templatestyles>
- Velayutham, Selvaraj (2008). *Tamil Cinema: The Cultural Politics of India's Other Film Industry*. Psychology Press. ISBN 978-0-415-39680-6.<templatestyles src="Module:Citation/CS1/styles.css"></templatestyles>
- Watson, James L. (2009), *Globalization*, Encyclopædia Britannica.
- Gopal, Sangita; Moorti, Sujata (2008). *Global Bollywood: Travels of Hindi Song and Dance*. University of Minnesota Press. ISBN 978-0-8166-4578-7.<templatestyles src="Module:Citation/CS1/styles.css"></templatestyles>
- *Report of the Indian Cinematograph Committee 1927–1928*[620]. Superintendent, The Government Press, Madras. 1928.<templatestyles src="Module:Citation/CS1/styles.css"></templatestyles>
- Dwyer, Rachel; Patel, Divia (2002). *Cinema India: The Visual Culture of Hindi Film*. ISBN 978-0-8135-3175-5.<templatestyles src="Module:Citation/CS1/styles.css"></templatestyles>
- Culture and Representation: The Emerging Field of Media Semiotics/J A H Khatri/ Ruby Press & Co.[621]/<templatestyles src="Module:Citation/CS1/styles.css" />>ISBN 978-93-82395-12-6/ 2013.

External links

Wikimedia Commons has media related to *Cinema of India*.

Appendix

References

[1] Robert M. W. Dixon, Y. Alexandra, *Adjective Classes: A Cross-linguistic Typology*, page 74, Oxford University Press, 2004,

[2] RJ LaPolla, The Sino-Tibetan Languages, La Trobe University

[3] Matti Miestamo & Bernhard Wälchli, *New Challenges in Typology*, page 90, Walter de Gruyter, 2007,

[4] David Levinson & Karen Christensen, *Encyclopedia of Modern Asia: a berkshire reference work*, page 494, Charles Scribner's Sons, 2002,

[5] Martin Haspelmath, The World Atlas of Language Structures https://books. google.com/books?id=sCRcARRN9nsC&pg=PA569&dq=indosphere&lr=&ei= cObSR7zSINC4igH0ldirBQ&sig=NZzfitQOiVvLf3LOSI04oXn3Rzs, page 569, Oxford University Press, 2005,

[6] Umberto Ansaldo, Stephen Matthews & Lisa Lim, *Deconstructing Creole*, page 113, John Benjamins Publishing Company, 2007,

[7] Alexandra Y. Aikhenvald & Robert M. W. Dixon, *Grammars in Contact*, page 4, Oxford University Press, 2006,

[8] Carol Genetti, *A Grammar of Dolakha Newar*, page 3, Walter de Gruyter, 2007,

[9] Colin Renfrew, April M. S. McMahon & Robert Lawrence Trask, *Time Depth in Historical Linguistics*, page 334, McDonald Institute for Archaeological Research, 2000,

[10] https://web.archive.org/web/20071102144300/http://pacling.anu.edu.au/catalogue/555.html

[11] https://web.archive.org/web/20071201144245/http://www.ogmios.org/91.htm

[12] https://web.archive.org/web/20060715124751/http://www.iias.nl/host/himalaya/conferences/ hls/1st_abstracts/wow.html

[13] https://web.archive.org/web/20071120043520/http://www.questhimalaya.com/journal/turin-tibeto-burman-02.htm

[14] http://www.uwm.edu/~noonan/806/Enfield.Areal-SEA.pdf

[15] //en.wikipedia.org/w/index.php?title=Template:Greater_India&action=edit

[16] Pierre-Yves Manguin, "From Funan to Sriwijaya: Cultural continuities and discontinuities in the Early Historical maritime states of Southeast Asia", in *25 tahun kerjasama Pusat Penelitian Arkeologi dan Ecole française d'Extrême-Orient*, Jakarta, Pusat Penelitian Arkeologi / EFEO, 2002, p. 59-82.

[17] Bayly, S. (2004). "Imagining 'Greater India': French and Indian Visions of Colonialism in the Indic Mode". *Modern Asian Studies*, 38(3), 703-744. doi:10.1017/S0026749X04001246

[18] Quote: "Azurara's hyperbole, indeed, which celebrates the Navigator Prince as joining Orient and Occident by continual voyaging, as transporting to the extremities of the East the creations of Western industry, does not scruple to picture the people of the *Greater and the Lesser India*"

[19] Quote: "Among all the confusion of the various Indies in Mediaeval nomenclature, "Greater India" can usually be recognized as restricted to the "India proper" of the modern [c. 1910] world."

[20] Quote: "Subsequently the whole area came to be identified with one of the "Three Indies," though whether *India Major* or *Minor*, *Greater* or *Lesser*, *Superior* or *Inferior*, seems often to have been a personal preference of the author concerned. When Europeans began to penetrate into Southeast Asia in earnest, they continued this tradition, attaching to various of the constituent territories such labels as Further India or Hinterindien, the East Indies, the Indian Archipelago, Insulinde, and, in acknowledgment of the presence of a competing culture, Indochina."

[21] "Review: New Maps," (1912) *Bulletin of the American Geographical Society* 44(3): 235–240.

[22] Argand, E., 1924. La tectonique de l'Asie. Proc. 13th Int. Geol. Cong. 7 (1924), 171–372.

[23] Quote: "Starting in the 1920s under the leadership of Kalidas Nag - and continuing even after independence - a number of Indian scholars wrote extensively and rapturously about the ancient Hindu cultural expansion into and colonisation of South and Southeast Asia. They called this

vast region "Greater India" – for a region which had been influenced by Indian religion, art, architecture, literature and administrative customs. Indeed, Congress leaders made occasional references to Greater India while the organisation's abiding interest in the problems of overseas Indians lent indirect support to the Indian hope of restoring the cultural and spiritual unity of South and Southeast Asia."

[24] Quote: "At another level, it was believed that the dynamics of many Asian cultures, particularly those of Southeast Asia, arose from Hindu culture, and the theory of Greater India derived sustenance from Pan-Hinduism. A curious pride was taken in the supposed imperialist past of India, as expressed in sentiments such as these: "The art of Java and Kambuja was no doubt derived from India and fostered by the Indian rulers of these colonies." (Majumdar, R. C. et al. (1950), *An Advanced History of India*, London: Macmillan, p. 221) "

[25] National Library of Australia. Asia's French Connection : George Coedes and the Coedes Collection http://www.nla.gov.au/asian/form/coedes2.html

[26] Theories of Indianisation http://www.oeaw.ac.at/sozant/files/working_papers/suedostasien/soa001.pdf Exemplified by Selected Case Studies from Indonesia (Insular Southeast Asia), by Dr. Helmut Lukas

[27] Higham, C., 2001, The Civilization of Angkor, London: Weidenfeld & Nicolson,

[28] Some Aspects of Asian History and Culture by Upendra Thakur p.2

[29] Ram Gopal and K. V. Paliwal, *Hindu renaissance*, page 83, Hindu Writers Forum, 2005 Quote: "Colonial and Cultural Expansion (of Ancient India)", written by R. C. Majumdar, concluded with: "We may conclude with a broad survey of the Indian colonies in the Far East. For nearly fifteen hundred years, and down to a period when the Hindus had lost their independence in their own home, Hindu kings were ruling over Indo-China and the numerous islands of the Indian Archipelago, from Sumatra to New Guinea. Indian religion, Indian culture, Indian laws and Indian government moulded the lives of the primitive races all over this wide region, and they imbibed a more elevated moral spirit and a higher intellectual taste through the religion, art, and literature of India. In short, the people were lifted to a higher plane of civilisation."

[30] Review by 'SKV' of *The Hindu Colony of Cambodia* by Phanindranath Bose [Adyar, Madras: Theosophical Publishing House 1927] in The Vedic Magazine and Gurukula Samachar 26: 1927, pp. 620–1.

[31] Lyne Bansat-Boudon, Roland Lardinois, and Isabelle Ratié, *Sylvain Lévi (1863-1935)*, page 196, Brepols, 2007, Quote: "The ancient Hindus of yore were not simply a spiritual people, always busy with mystical problems and never troubling themselves with the questions of 'this world'... India also has its Napoleons and Charlemagnes, its Bismarcks and Machiavellis. But the real charm of Indian history does not consist in these aspirants after universal power, but in its peaceful and benevolent Imperialism — a unique thing in the history of mankind. The colonisers of India did not go with sword and fire in their hands; they used... the weapons of their superior culture and religion... The Buddhist age has attracted special attention, and the French savants have taken much pains to investigate the splendid monuments of the Indian cultural empire in the Far East."

[32] Quote: "Starting in the 1920s under the leadership of Kalidas Nag - and continuing even after independence - a number of Indian scholars wrote extensively and rapturously about the ancient Hindu cultural expansion into and colonisation of South and Southeast Asia. They called this vast region "Greater India" – a dubious appellation for a region which to a limited degree, but with little permanence, had been influenced by Indian religion, art, architecture, literature and administrative customs. As a consequence of this renewed and extensive interest in Greater India, many Indians came to believe that the entire South and Southeast Asian region formed the cultural progeny of India; now that the sub-continent was reawakening, they felt, India would once again assert its non-political ascendancy over the area.... While the idea of reviving the ancient Greater India was never officially endorsed by the Indian National Congress, it enjoyed considerable popularity in nationalist Indian circles. Indeed, Congress leaders made occasional references to Greater India while the organisation's abiding interest in the problems of overseas Indians lent indirect support to the Indian hope of restoring the alleged cultural and spiritual unity of South and Southeast Asia."

[33] Quote: "At another level, it was believed that the dynamics of many Asian cultures, particularly those of Southeast Asia, arose from Hindu culture, and the theory of Greater India derived

sustenance from Pan-Hinduism. A curious pride was taken in the supposed imperialist past of India, as expressed in sentiments such as these: "The art of Java and Kambuja was no doubt derived from India and fostered by the Indian rulers of these colonies." (Majumdar, R. C. et al. (1950), *An Advanced History of India*, London: Macmillan, p. 221) This form of historical interpretation, which can perhaps best be described as being inspired by Hindu nationalism, remains an influential school of thinking in present historical writings.

[34] Quote:"The Greater India visions which Calcutta thinkers derived from French and other sources are still known to educated anglophone Indians, especially but not exclusively Bengalis from the generation brought up in the traditions of post-Independence Nehruvian secular nationalism. One key source of this knowledge is a warm tribute paid to Sylvain Lévi and his ideas of an expansive, civilising India by Jawaharlal Nehru himself, in his celebrated book, *The Discovery of India*, which was written during one of Nehru's periods of imprisonment by the British authorities, first published in 1946, and reprinted many times since.... The ideas of both Lévi and the Greater India scholars were known to Nehru through his close intellectual links with Tagore. Thus Lévi's notion of ancient Indian voyagers leaving their invisible 'imprints' throughout east and southeast Asia was for Nehru a recapitulation of Tagore's vision of nationhood, that is an idealisation of India as a benign and uncoercive world civiliser and font of global enlightenment. This was clearly a perspective which defined the Greater India phenomenon as a process of religious and spiritual tutelage, but it was not a Hindu supremacist idea of India's mission to the lands of the trans-gangetic *Sarvabhumi* or *Bharat Varsha*."

[35] Quote: "To him (Nehru), the so-called practical approach meant, in practice, shameless expediency, and so he would say, "the sooner we are not practical, the better". He rebuked a Member of Indian Parliament who sought to revive the concept of *Greater India* by saying that 'the honorable Member lived in the days of Bismarck; Bismarck is dead, and his politics more dead!' He would consistently plead for an idealistic approach and such power as the language wields is the creation of idealism—politics' arch enemy—which, however, liberates the leader of a national movement from narrow nationalism, thus igniting in the process a dead fact of history, in the sneer, "For him the Bastille has not fallen!" Though Nehru was not to the language born, his utterances show a remarkable capacity for introspection and sense of moral responsibility in commenting on political processes."

[36] Quote: "The tide of revisionism that is currently sweeping through Southeast Asian historiography has in effect taken us back almost to the point where we have to consider reevaluating almost every text bearing on the protohistoric period and many from later times. Although this may seem a daunting proposition, it is nonetheless supremely worth attempting, for the process by which the peoples of western Southeast Asia came to think of themselves as part of *Bharatavarsa* (even though they had no conception of "India" as we know it) represents one of the most impressive instances of large-scale acculturation in the history of the world. Sylvain Levi was perhaps overenthusiastic when he claimed that India produced her definitive masterpieces — he was thinking of Angkor and the Borobudur — through the efforts of foreigners or on foreign soil. Those masterpieces were not strictly Indian achievements: rather were they the outcome of a Eutychian fusion of natures so melded together as to constitute a single cultural process in which Southeast Asia was the matrix and South Asia the mediatrix."

[37] Quote: "An equally significant movement is one that brought about among the Indian intelligentsia of Calcutta a few years ago the formation of what is known as the "Greater India Society," whose membership is open "to all serious students of the Indian cultural expansion and to all sympathizers of such studies and activities." Though still in its infancy, this organisation has already a large membership, due perhaps as much as anything else to the enthusiasm of its Secretary and Convener, Dr. Kalidas Nag, whose scholarly affiliations with the Orientalists in the University of Paris and studies in Indochina, Insulindia and beyond, have equipped him in an unusual way for the work he has chosen, namely stimulating interest in and spreading knowledge of Greater Indian culture of the past, present and future. The Society's President is Professor Jadunath Sarkar, Vice-Chancellor of Calcutta University, and its Council is made up largely of professors on the faculty of the University and members of the staff of the Calcutta Museum, as well as of Indian authors and journalists. Its activities have included illustrated lecture series at the various universities throughout India by Dr. Nag, the assembling of a research library, and the publication of monographs of which four very excellent examples have

447

already been printed: 1)*Greater India*, by Kalidas Nag, M.A., D.Litt(Paris), 2) *India and China*, by Prabodh Chandra Bagchi, M.A., D.Litt., 3) *Indian Culture in Java and Sumatra*, by Bijan Raj Chatterjee, D.Litt. (Punjab), Ph.D. (London), and 4) *India and Central Asia*, by Niranjan Prasad Chakravarti, M.A., Ph.D.(Cantab.)."

[38] Martin Haspelmath, The World Atlas of Language Structures https://books.google.com/books? id=sCRcARRN9nsC&pg=PA569 , page 569, Oxford University Press, 2005,

[39] Balinese Religion http://philtar.ucsm.ac.uk/encyclopedia/indon/balin.html

[40] Buddhist Channel | Buddhism News, Headlines | Thailand | Phra Prom returns to Erawan Shrine http://buddhistchannel.tv/index.php?id=52,2733,0,0,1,0

[41] See this page from the Indonesian Wikipedia for a list

[42] https://books.google.co.in/books?id=-01JisWpJbEC&q=Indian&source=gbs_word_cloud_ r&cad=5#v=snippet&q=Indian&f=false

[43] //doi.org/10.1016%2Fj.earscirev.2005.07.005

[44] //doi.org/10.1017%2FS0026749X04001246

[45] //doi.org/10.2307%2F1776846

[46] //www.jstor.org/stable/1776846

[47] //doi.org/10.1098%2Frstl.1767.0018

[48] //doi.org/10.2307%2F2750560

[49] //www.jstor.org/stable/2750560

[50] //doi.org/10.2307%2F2757594

[51] //www.jstor.org/stable/2757594

[52] //doi.org/10.1111%2Fj.1467-971X.1986.tb00728.x

[53] //doi.org/10.2307%2F2504471

[54] //www.jstor.org/stable/2504471

[55] //doi.org/10.2307%2F2055365

[56] //www.jstor.org/stable/2055365

[57] https://books.google.com/books?id=jLZAAAAAMAAJ

[58] https://books.google.com/?id=wiUTOanLClcC&printsec=frontcover#v=onepage&q&f=false

[59] https://web.archive.org/web/20071120043520/http://www.questhimalaya.com/journal/turin-tibeto-burman-02.htm

[60] http://www.oeaw.ac.at/sozant/files/working_papers/suedostasien/soa001.pdf

[61] //en.wikipedia.org/w/index.php?title=Template:Asian_philosophy_sidebar&action=edit

[62] //en.wikipedia.org/w/index.php?title=Template:Philosophy_sidebar&action=edit

[63] John Bowker, *Oxford Dictionary of World Religions*, p. 259

[64] Cowell and Gough, p. xii.

[65] Nicholson, pp. 158-162.

[66] Ben-Ami Scharfstein (1998), *A comparative history of world philosophy: from the Upanishads to Kant*, Albany: State University of New York Press, pp. 9-11

[67] Flood, op. cit., p. 231–232.

[68] Michaels, p. 264.

[69] Nicholson 2010.

[70] Mike Burley (2012), Classical Samkhya and Yoga - An Indian Metaphysics of Experience, Routledge, , pages 43-46

[71] Tom Flynn and Richard Dawkins (2007), The New Encyclopedia of Unbelief, Prometheus, , pages 420-421

[72] Edwin Bryant (2011, Rutgers University), *The Yoga Sutras of Patanjali* http://www.iep.utm. edu/yoga/ IEP

[73] Nyaya Realism http://plato.stanford.edu/entries/perception-india/, in Perceptual Experience and Concepts in Classical Indian Philosophy, Stanford Encyclopedia of Philosophy (2015)

[74] Nyaya: Indian Philosophy http://www.britannica.com/EBchecked/topic/423058/Nyaya Encyclopædia Britannica (2014)

[75] Dale Riepe (1996), Naturalistic Tradition in Indian Thought, , pages 227-246

[76] Analytical philosophy in early modern India http://plato.stanford.edu/entries/early-modern-india/#VaiAto J Ganeri, Stanford Encyclopedia of Philosophy

[77] Oliver Leaman (2006), Shruti, in *Encyclopaedia of Asian Philosophy*, Routledge, , page 503

[78] Mimamsa http://www.britannica.com/EBchecked/topic/383181/Mimamsa Encyclopædia Britannica (2014)

[79] JN Mohanty (2001), Explorations in Philosophy, Vol 1 (Editor: Bina Gupta), Oxford University Press, page 107-108

[80] Oliver Leaman (2000), Eastern Philosophy: Key Readings, Routledge, , page 251;
R Prasad (2009), A Historical-developmental Study of Classical Indian Philosophy of Morals, Concept Publishing, , pages 345-347

[81] Roy Perrett (2000), Indian Philosophy, Routledge, , page 88

[82] Sushil Mittal & Gene Thursby (2004), The Hindu World, Routledge, , pages 729-730

[83] Flood 1996, pp. 82, 224–49.

[84]

[85] Sarvepalli Radhakrishnan and Charles A. Moore. *A Sourcebook in Indian Philosophy '249.*

[86] Reginald Ray (1999), Buddhist Saints in India, Oxford University Press, , pages 237-240, 247-249

[87] Padmanabh S Jaini (2001), Collected papers on Buddhist Studies, Motilal Banarsidass, , pages 57-77

[88] AL Basham (1951), History and Doctrines of the Ajivikas - a Vanished Indian Religion, Motilal Banarsidass, , pages 94-103

[89] https//books.google.co.in

[90] Dundas 2002, pp. 30–31.

[91] https//books.google.co.in

[92] , Quote: "[Buddhism's ontological hypotheses] that nothing in reality has its own-being and that all phenomena reduce to the relativities of pratitya samutpada. The Buddhist ontological hypothesese deny that there is any ontologically ultimate object such a God, Brahman, the Dao, or any transcendent creative source or principle."

[93] Anatta Buddhism http://www.britannica.com/topic/anatta, Encyclopædia Britannica (2013)

[94] [a]
[b] Gombrich (2006), page 47, **Quote:** "(...) Buddha's teaching that beings have no soul, no abiding essence. This 'no-soul doctrine' (anatta-vada) he expounded in his second sermon."

[95] [a] Anatta http://www.britannica.com/topic/anatta, Encyclopædia Britannica (2013), Quote: "Anatta in Buddhism, the doctrine that there is in humans no permanent, underlying soul. The concept of anatta, or anatman, is a departure from the Hindu belief in atman ("the self").";
[b] Steven Collins (1994), Religion and Practical Reason (Editors: Frank Reynolds, David Tracy), State Univ of New York Press, , page 64; "Central to Buddhist soteriology is the doctrine of not-self (Pali: anattā, Sanskrit: anātman, the opposed doctrine of ātman is central to Brahmanical thought). Put very briefly, this is the [Buddhist] doctrine that human beings have no soul, no self, no unchanging essence.";
[c] John C. Plott et al (2000), Global History of Philosophy: The Axial Age, Volume 1, Motilal Banarsidass, , page 63, Quote: "The Buddhist schools reject any Ātman concept. As we have already observed, this is the basic and ineradicable distinction between Hinduism and Buddhism";
[d] Katie Javanaud (2013), Is The Buddhist 'No-Self' Doctrine Compatible With Pursuing Nirvana? https://philosophynow.org/issues/97/Is_The_Buddhist_No-Self_Doctrine_Compatible_With_Pursuing_Nirvana, Philosophy Now;
[e] David Loy (1982), Enlightenment in Buddhism and Advaita Vedanta: Are Nirvana and Moksha the Same?, International Philosophical Quarterly, Volume 23, Issue 1, pages 65-74

[96] Jeffrey D Long (2009), Jainism: An Introduction, Macmillan, , page 199

[97] Basham 1951, pp. 145-146.

[98] Basham 1951, Chapter 1.

[99] Johannes Quack (2014), The Oxford Handbook of Atheism (Editors: Stephen Bullivant, Michael Ruse), Oxford University Press, , page 654

[100] Analayo (2004), Satipaṭṭhāna: The Direct Path to Realization, , pages 207-208

[101] Basham 1951, pp. 240-261, 270-273.

[102] Cowell and Gough, p. 4

[103] Bhattacharya, Ramkrishna. Materialism in India: A Synoptic View http://www.carvaka4india.com/2011/08/materialism-in-india-synoptic-view.html. Retrieved 27 July 2012.

[104]

[105] Gananath Obeyesekere (2005), Karma and Rebirth: A Cross Cultural Study, Motilal Banarsidass, , page 106

[106] Damien Keown (2013), Buddhism: A Very Short Introduction, 2nd Edition, Oxford University Press, , pages 32-46

[107] Haribhadrasūri (Translator: M Jain, 1989), Saddarsanasamuccaya, Asiatic Society,

[108] Halbfass, Wilhelm (2000), Karma und Wiedergeburt im indischen Denken, Diederichs, München,

[109] Patrick Olivelle (2005), *The Blackwell Companion to Hinduism* (Editor: Flood, Gavin), Wiley-Blackwell, , pages 277-278

[110] Karel Werner (1995), Love Divine: Studies in Bhakti and Devotional Mysticism, Routledge, , pages 45-46

[111] John Cort, Jains in the World : Religious Values and Ideology in India, Oxford University Press, ISBN, pages 64-68, 86-90, 100-112

[112] Christian Novetzke (2007), Bhakti and Its Public, International Journal of Hindu Studies, Vol. 11, No. 3, page 255-272

[113] [a] Knut Jacobsen (2008), Theory and Practice of Yoga : 'Essays in Honour of Gerald James Larson, Motilal Banarsidass, , pages 15-16, 76-78;
[b] Lloyd Pflueger, Person Purity and Power in Yogasutra, in Theory and Practice of Yoga (Editor: Knut Jacobsen), Motilal Banarsidass, , pages 38-39

[114] [a] Karl Potter (2008), Encyclopedia of Indian Philosophies Vol. III, Motilal Banarsidass, , pages 16-18, 220;
[b] Basant Pradhan (2014), Yoga and Mindfulness Based Cognitive Therapy, Springer Academic, , page 13 see A.4

[115] U Tahtinen (1976), Ahimsa: Non-Violence in Indian Tradition, London, , pages 75-78, 94-106

[116] U Tahtinen (1976), Ahimsa: Non-Violence in Indian Tradition, London, , pages 57-62, 109-111

[117] U Tahtinen (1976), Ahimsa: Non-Violence in Indian Tradition, London, , pages 34-43, 89-97, 109-110

[118] Christopher Chapple (1993), Nonviolence to Animals, Earth, and Self in Asian Traditions, State University of New York Press, , pages 16-17

[119]

[120] Karin Meyers (2013), Free Will, Agency, and Selfhood in Indian Philosophy (Editors: Matthew R. Dasti, Edwin F. Bryant), Oxford University Press, , pages 41-61

[121] Howard Coward (2008), The Perfectibility of Human Nature in Eastern and Western Thought, State University of New York Press, , pages 103-114;
Harold Coward (2003), Encyclopedia of Science and Religion, Macmillan Reference, see Karma,

[122] AL Basham (1951), History and Doctrines of the Ajivikas - a Vanished Indian Religion, Motilal Banarsidass, , pages 237

[123] Damien Keown (2004), A Dictionary of Buddhism, Oxford University Press, , Entry for *Prapañca*, Quote: "Term meaning 'proliferation', in the sense of the multiplication of erroneous concepts, ideas, and ideologies which obscure the true nature of reality".

[124] Lynn Foulston and Stuart Abbott (2009), Hindu Goddesses: Beliefs and Practices, Sussex Academic Press, , pages 14-16

[125] Wendy Doniger O'Flaherty (1986), Dreams, Illusion, and Other Realities, University of Chicago Press, , page 119

[126]

[127] Ramkrishna Bhattacharya (2011), Studies on the Carvaka/Lokayata, Anthem, , page 216

[128] Anatta http://www.britannica.com/topic/anatta Encyclopædia Britannica, Quote:"In Buddhism, the doctrine that there is in humans no permanent, underlying substance that can be called the soul. (...) The concept of anatta, or anatman, is a departure from the Hindu belief in atman (self)."

[129] Oliver Leaman (2000), Eastern Philosophy: Key Readings, Routledge, , page 251

[130] Mike Burley (2012), Classical Samkhya and Yoga - An Indian Metaphysics of Experience, Routledge, , page 39

[131] Paul Hacker (1978), Eigentumlichkeiten dr Lehre und Terminologie Sankara: Avidya, Namarupa, Maya, Isvara, in Kleine Schriften (Editor: L. Schmithausen), Franz Steiner Verlag, Weisbaden, pages 101-109 (in German), also pages 69-99

[132] D Sharma (1966), Epistemological negative dialectics of Indian logic — Abhāva versus Anupalabdhi, Indo-Iranian Journal, 9(4): 291-300

[133] MM Kamal (1998), The Epistemology of the Carvaka Philosophy, Journal of Indian and Buddhist Studies, 46(2), pages 13-16

[134]

[135] Eliott Deutsche (2000), in Philosophy of Religion : Indian Philosophy Vol 4 (Editor: Roy Perrett), Routledge, , pages 245-248

[136] Christopher Bartley (2011), An Introduction to Indian Philosophy, Bloomsbury Academic, , pages 46, 120

[137] Elisa Freschi (2012): The Vedas are not deontic authorities and may be disobeyed, but still recognized as an epistemic authority by a Hindu.<ref>Elisa Freschi (2012), *Duty, Language and Exegesis in Prabhakara Mimamsa*, BRILL, , page 62

[138] Catherine Cornille (2009), Criteria of Discernment in Interreligious Dialogue, Wipf & Stock, , pages 185-186

[139] AL Basham (1951), History and Doctrines of the Ajivikas - a Vanished Indian Religion, Motilal Banarsidass, , pages 227

[140] Jerald Gort (1992), On Sharing Religious Experience: Possibilities of Interfaith Mutuality, Rodopi, , pages 209-210

[141] John Cort (2010), Framing the Jina: Narratives of Icons and Idols in Jain History, Oxford University Press, , pages 80, 188

[142] Andrew Fort (1998), Jivanmukti in Transformation, State University of New York Press,

[143] Masao Abe and Steven Heine (1995), Buddhism and Interfaith Dialogue, University of Hawaii Press, , pages 105-106

[144] Chad Meister (2009), Introducing Philosophy of Religion, Routledge, , page 60; Quote: "In this chapter, we looked at religious metaphysics and saw two different ways of understanding Ultimate Reality. On the one hand, it can be understood as an absolute state of being. Within Hindu absolutism, for example, it is Brahman, the undifferentiated Absolute. Within Buddhist metaphysics, fundamental reality is Sunyata, or the Void."

[145] Christopher Key Chapple (2004), Jainism and Ecology: Nonviolence in the Web of Life, Motilal Banarsidass, , page 20

[146] PT Raju (2006), Idealistic Thought of India, Routledge, , page 426 and Conclusion chapter part XII

[147] Roy W Perrett (Editor, 2000), Indian Philosophy: Metaphysics, Volume 3, Taylor & Francis, , page xvii;
AC Das (1952), Brahman and Māyā in Advaita Metaphysics, Philosophy East and West, Vol. 2, No. 2, pages 144-154

[148] "Transcendentalism".*The Oxford Companion to American Literature*. James D. Hart ed.Oxford University Press, 1995. *Oxford Reference Online*. Web. 24 Oct.2011

[149] https://books.google.com/books?id=X8iAAgAAQBAJ

[150] https://books.google.com.np/books?id=BiGQzc5lRGYC

[151] https://books.google.ca/books?id=nfOPCgAAQBAJ&dq

[152] https://books.google.com/books?id=xkrCRbOq-HUC

[153] https://archive.org/details/Sarvepalli.Radhakrishnan.Indian.Philosophy.Volume.1-2

[154] https://www.wisdomlib.org/hinduism/book/a-history-of-indian-philosophy-volume-1/index.html

[155] https://www.wisdomlib.org/hinduism/book/a-history-of-indian-philosophy-volume-2/index.html

[156] https://www.wisdomlib.org/hinduism/book/a-history-of-indian-philosophy-volume-3/index.html

[157] https://www.wisdomlib.org/hinduism/book/a-history-of-indian-philosophy-volume-4/index.html

[158] https://www.wisdomlib.org/hinduism/book/a-history-of-indian-philosophy-volume-5/index.html

[159] http://www.ucl.ac.uk/philosophy/LPSG/Indian.pdf

[160] http://www.iep.utm.edu/category/traditions/indian/

[161] http://ipi.org.in

[162] https://archive.org/details/AHistoryOfIndianPhilosophyBySurendranathDasgupta-5Volumes

[163] https://archive.org/details/Indian.Idealism.by.Surendranath.Dasgupta

[164] https://archive.org/details/Mysore.Hiriyanna-The.Essentials.of.Indian.Philosophy

[165] https://archive.org/details/Mysore.Hiriyanna-Outlines.of.Indian.Philosophy

[166] https://archive.org/details/Radhakrishnan-History.of.Philosophy-Eastern.and.Western-Volume.1-2

[167] http://www.jiva.org/indian-schools-of-philosophy-and-theology/

[168] //en.wikipedia.org/w/index.php?title=Template:Wildlife_of_India&action=edit

[169] Encyclopedia of World Geography By Peter Haggett https://books.google.com/books?id=IROIY4ONOSEC&pg=PA2648

[170] South India By Sarina Singh, Stuart Butler, Virginia Jealous, Amy Karafin, Simon Richmond, Rafael Wlodarski https://books.google.com/books?id=ywx4f4WczMEC&pg=PA86&dq=wildlife+of+india+diverse&lr=&as_brr=3&client=firefox-a

[171] Biodiversity and its conservation in India By Sharad Singh Negi https://books.google.com/books?id=PjfVFGM4p6wC&pg=PA172&dq=wildlife+of+india+species+number&lr=&as_brr=3&client=firefox-a

[172] Explorations in Applied Geography By Dutt Misra & Chatterjee (eds.), L. R. Singh, Ashok K. Dutt, H. N. Misra, Meera Chatterjee https://books.google.com/books?id=YcaFp3g36l8C&pg=PA104&dq=wildlife+of+india+diverse&lr=&as_brr=3&client=firefox-a

[173] Indira Gandhi Conservation Monitoring Centre (IGCMC), New Delhi and the United Nations Environmental Programme (UNEP), World Conservation Monitoring Centre http://www.unep-wcmc.org/, Cambridge, UK. 2001. *Biodiversity profile for India* http://ces.iisc.ernet.in/hpg/cesmg/indiabio.html.

[174] K. Praveen Karach. (2006). Out-of-India Gondwanan origin of some tropical Asian biota http://www.iisc.ernet.in/currsci/mar252006/789.pdf

[175] Groombridge, B. (ed). 1993. *The 1994 IUCN Red List of Threatened Animals.* IUCN, England, Switzerland and Cambridge, UK. lvi + 286 pp.

[176] Jhala, Y. V., Qureshi, Q., Sinha, P. R. (Eds.) (2011). *Status of tigers, co-predators and prey in India, 2010.* https://web.archive.org/web/20120120232451/http://www.projecttiger.nic.in/whtsnew/Tiger_Status_oct_2010.pdf National Tiger Conservation Authority, Govt. of India, New Delhi, and Wildlife Institute of India, Dehradun. TR 2011/003 pp-302

[177] Botanical Survey of India. 1983. *Flora and Vegetation of India — An Outline.* Botanical Survey of India, Howrah. 24 pp.

[178] Valmik Thapar, *Land of the Tiger: A Natural History of the Indian Subcontinent*, 1997.

[179]

[180] Fungi or Fungus Wikipedia Fungus

[181] Classification of Organisms Wikipedia Kingdom (biology)

[182] Fungal biodiversity: Distribution, conservation and prospecting of fungi from India http://www.iisc.ernet.in/currsci/jul102005/58.pdf

[183] Fungi of India 1989-2001 http://www.vedamsbooks.com/no33639/fungi-india-19892001-jamaluddin-mg-goswami-bm-ojha;

[184] Krausman, PR & AT Johnson (1990) Conservation and wildlife education in India. Wild. Soc. Bull. 18:342-347

[185] Project Tiger http://projecttiger.nic.in/ Accessed February 2007

[186] NDTV http://www.ndtv.com/article/india/tiger-census-295-tigers-added-population-estimated-at-1706-94584

[187] corbett-national-park.com http://www.corbett-national-park.com/blog/tourists-thronging-tiger-reserves-india.html

[188] Shashwat, D.C. (27 June 2007) "The Last Roar?" http://shashwatdc.blogspot.com/2007/07/last-roar.html, *Dataquest Magazine*, India.

[189] Threatened birds of Asia http://www.rdb.or.id/detailbird.php?id=693 Accessed October 2006

[190] *The Nation*, 6 March 2007 http://www.nationmultimedia.com/2007/03/07/headlines/headlines_30028700.php

[191] Dolphin becomes India's national aquatic animal http://www.hindustantimes.com/News/india/Dolphin-becomes-India-s-national-aquatic-animal/Article1-461628.aspx

[192] UNESCO, Man and the Biosphere (MAB) Programme list http://www.unesco.org/mab/BRs/AsiaBRlist.shtml*I

[193] http://oldwww.wii.gov.in/envis/species_database.html

[194] http://oldwww.wii.gov.in/envis/database.html
[195] http://oldwww.wii.gov.in/envis/threatened_plants/special_habitat_threatened_plants_of_india.pdf
[196] http://www.ecoheritage.cpreec.org/index.php
[197] http//google.com
[198] https://www.worldcat.org/search?fq=x0:jrnl&q=n2:0564-3295
[199] http://144.16.93.203/energy/water/paper/Conservation_of_wetlands_of_India.pdf
[200] http://www.iisc.ernet.in/currsci/jul102005/58.pdf
[201] http://www.vedamsbooks.com/no33639/fungi-india-19892001-jamaluddin-mg-goswami-bm-ojha
[202] http://www.envfor.nic.in/
[203] http://www.envfor.nic.in/legis/legis.html
[204] http://www.envfor.nic.in/legis/legis.html#S
[205] http://www.envfor.nic.in/legis/legis.html#R
[206] https://www.intltravelnews.com/2006/04/eight-lions-15-tigers-and-a-whole-lot-of-elephants-——an-indian-wildlife-safari/
[207] //en.wikipedia.org/w/index.php?title=Template:Indian_cuisine&action=edit
[208] //en.wikipedia.org/w/index.php?title=Template:Culture_of_India&action=edit
[209] Padmanabh S Jaini (2001), Collected papers on Buddhist Studies, Motilal Banarsidass, , pages 57–77
[210] Padmanabh S Jaini (2000), Collected papers on Jaina Studies, Motilal Banarsidass, , pages 3–14
[211] *Autobiography Of A Yogi*, Paramahansa Yogananda, Self Realization Fellowship, 1973, p. 22
[212] Maharishi Mahesh Yogi on the Bhagavad Gita Translation and Commentary, Arkana, 1990 p. 236
[213] Chandigarh Cuisine http://www.chandigarh.co.uk/culture/cuisines.html.
[214] Game cuisine: A Rajput legacy by madhulika dash
[215] The Sunday Tribune – Spectrum – Lead Article http://www.tribuneindia.com/2003/20030713/spectrum/main2.htm. *The Tribune*. (13 July 2003). Retrieved 2012-08-06.
[216] https://curlie.org/Home/Cooking/World_Cuisines/Asian/Indian/
[217] https://www.indianfoodrecipesonline.com/
[218] //en.wikipedia.org/w/index.php?title=Template:Culture_of_India&action=edit
[219] Admin. "Traditional Dresses and Fashion Culture across different Indian States" http://www.lisaadelhi.com/traditional-dresses-and-fashion-culture-across-different-indian-states/, [*LisaaDelhi*], Retrieved 10 May 2018.
[220] These were vegetable dyes, commonly used in textiles. Non vegetable dyes were also used such as *gairika* (red ochre), *sindura* (red lead), *kajal* (lampblack), sulphate of iron, sulphate of antimony and carmine. UNIQ-ref-0-9c34fa5f9dcb4f28-QINU
[221] The Rig Veda, Mandala 10, hymn 75, mentions the valley of *Sindhu* as *suvasa urnavati* i.e home to plenty of sheepWikipedia:Citation needed
[222] The Periplus states the various regions of production of cloth, including the Gangetic plain. Ancient Romans called Indian textiles by names such as *gangetika*, nebula and *venti* meaning woven wind. Marco Polo's Description of the world gives an idea of textile trade of the time, with a mention that Gujarat has the best textiles in the world.Admin. "Traditional Dresses and Fashion Culture across different Indian States" http://www.lisaadelhi.com/traditional-dresses-and-fashion-culture-across-different-indian-states/, [*LisaaDelhi*], Retrieved 10 May 2018.
[223] Alkazi, Roshan (1983) "Ancient Indian costume", Art Heritage; Ghurye (1951) "Indian costume", Popular book depot (Bombay); Boulanger, Chantal; (1997)
[224] http://www.culturalindia.net/indian-clothing/sari.html
[225] Boulanger, C (1997) Saris: An Illustrated Guide to the Indian Art of Draping, Shakti Press International, New York.
[226] Ghurye (1951) "Indian costume", Popular book depot (Bombay)
[227] Kapur, Manohar Lal (1992) Social and economic history of Jammu and Kashmir State, 1885-1925 A.D. https://books.google.com/books?ei=ADmDVfeOMML4ygPY4YP4Dw&id=3ecbAAAAIAAJ&dq=jammu+suthan&focus=searchwithinvolume&q=suthan
[228] http://dawn.com/2012/02/12/legend-anarkali-myth-mystery-and-history/

229 Zaira Mis, Marcel Mis (2001) Asian Costumes and Textiles: From the Bosphorus to Fujiama https://books.google.com/books?id=V-wcAQAAIAAJ&q=angarkha+ +sanskrit&dq=angarkha++sanskrit&hl=en&sa=X&ved=0CCIQ6AEwAWoVChMIiIfj-e3dxgIVqhbbCh1dWgDU

230 Kumar, Ritu (2006) Costumes and textiles of royal India https://books.google.com/ books?id=qYK1AAAAIAAJ&q=angarkha&dq=angarkha&hl=en&sa=X&ved= 0CC0Q6AEwAWoVChMI9PzF2_jdxgIV6QfbCh0zwArh

231 Ghurye, Govind Sadashiv (1966) Indian Costume https//books.google.com

232 Tierney, Tom (2013) Fashions from India https//books.google.com

233 Sarosh Medhora (02.09.2000) The Tribune. Focus on men's formals http://www.tribuneindia. com/2000/20000902/windows/main7.htm

234 https://archive.org/stream/textilemanufactu00watsrich#page/n5/mode/2up

235 https://archive.org/stream/CAI1057660001Images/CAI_105766_0001_Images#page/n3/ mode/2up

236 https://archive.org/stream/blockprintsfromi01lewi#page/n3/mode/2up

237 https://books.google.com/books?id=R531j7QrmGUC

238 https://books.google.com/books?id=Wx11yQK3J3QC

239 //en.wikipedia.org/w/index.php?title=Template:Culture_of_India&action=edit

240 //en.wikipedia.org/w/index.php?title=Template:Indian_literature&action=edit

241 //en.wikipedia.org/w/index.php?title=Template:History_of_literature_by_era&action=edit

242 "Kannada literature", *Encyclopædia Britannica*, 2008. Quote: "The earliest literary work is the Kavirajamarga (c. AD 450), a treatise on poetics based on a Sanskrit model."

243 Official website of Bharatiya Jnanpith http://jnanpith.net/

244 //en.wikipedia.org/w/index.php?title=Template:History_of_literature_by_region_or_ country&action=edit

245 Fallon, Oliver. 2009. Bhatti's Poem: The Death of Rávana (Bhaṭṭikāvya). New York: Clay Sanskrit Libraryhttp://www.claysanskritlibrary.org/. ||

246 Narang, Satya Pal. 2003. An Analysis of the Prākṛta of Bhāśā-sama of the Bhaṭṭi-kāvya (Canto XII). In: Prof. Mahapatra G.N., Vanijyotih: Felicitation Volume, Utkal University, *Bhu-vaneshwar.

247 Lalthangliana, B., *Mizo tihin ṭawng a nei lo tih kha* http://www.vanglaini.org/index.php? option=com_content&view=article&id=12917:mizo-tihin-tawng-a-nei-lo-tih-kha&catid= 105:articles&Itemid=466/

248 Sigfried J. de Laet. *History of Humanity: From the seventh to the sixteenth century* https/ /books.google.nl UNESCO, 1994. p 734

249 http://www.iiste.org/Journals/index.php/NMMC/article/view/1769, iiste-international knowl-edge sharing platform.

250 http://www.indohistory.com/literature.html

251 http://indianreview.in

252 http://lawpark.jimdo.com/other-lists-1/south-asian-canonical-texts/

253 http://www.worldrecordsindia.com/2014/06/longest-poem-on-indian-constitution/

254 http://literatureinindia.com

255 //en.wikipedia.org/w/index.php?title=Template:Culture_of_India&action=edit

256 Williams 2004, pp. 83-84, the other major classical Indian dances are: Bharatanatyam, Kathak, Odissi, Kathakali, Kuchipudi, Sattriya, Chhau, Manipuri, Yaksagana and Bhagavata Mela.

257

258 , **Quote:** "It would be appropriate here to comment on Hindu classical dance. This developed in a religious context and was given high profile as part of temple worship. There are a number of regional and other styles as well as source texts, but the point we wish to stress is the partici-pative nature of such dance. In form and content, the heart of dance as worship in Hinduism has always been 'expression' (abhinaya), i.e. the enacting of various themes".

259 , **Quote:** Hindu classical dance-forms, like Hindu music, are associated with worship. Refer-ences to dance and music are found in the vedic literature, (...)".

260 , **Quote:** All of the dances considered to be part of the Indian classical canon (Bharata Natyam, Chhau, Kathak, Kathakali, Kuchipudi, Manipuri, Mohiniattam, Odissi, Sattriya and Yakshagana)

trace their roots to religious practices (...) the Indian diaspora has led to the translocation of Hindu dances to Europe, North America and to the world."

[261] Maurice Winternitz 2008, pp. 181–182.

[262] ML Varadpande (1990), History of Indian Theatre, Volume 1, Abhinav, , page 48

[263]

[264] Farley P. Richmond, Darius L. Swann & Phillip B. Zarrilli 1993, p. 30.

[265] Tarla Mehta 1995, pp. xxiv, xxxi–xxxii, 17.

[266] Natalia Lidova 2014.

[267] Tarla Mehta 1995, pp. xxiv, 19–20.

[268] Wallace Dace 1963, p. 249.

[269] Emmie Te Nijenhuis 1974, pp. 1–25.

[270] Bharata-natyam https://www.britannica.com/art/bharata-natyam *Encyclopædia Britannica*. 2007

[271] Williams 2004, pp. 83-84, the other major classical Indian dances are: Kathak, Kuchipudi, Odissi, Kathakali, Manipuri, Cchau, Satriya, Yaksagana and Bhagavata Mela.

[272] T Balasaraswati (1976), Bharata Natyam, *NCPA Quarterly Journal*, Volume 4, Issue 4, pages 1-8

[273] Massey 1999, p. 15.

[274] Williams 2004, p. 83.

[275] Ragini Devi 1990, pp. 60-68.

[276] Sunil Kothari & Avinash Pasricha 2001, pp. 43-46, 80 footnote 8.

[277] Massey 2004, pp. 79-81.

[278] Ragini Devi 1990, pp. 67-68.

[279] Ragini Devi 1990, p. 73.

[280] Sunil Kothari & Avinash Pasricha 2001.

[281] Farley P. Richmond, Darius L. Swann & Phillip B. Zarrilli 1993, p. 173.

[282] Sunil Kothari & Avinash Pasricha 2001, pp. 43-45, 97-104, 117-121.

[283] Sunil Kothari & Avinash Pasricha 2001, pp. 147-149.

[284] Sunil Kothari & Avinash Pasricha 2001, pp. 20-21, 190-204.

[285] Odissi https://www.britannica.com/art/odissi *Encyclopædia Britannica* (2013)

[286] Centre for Cultural Resources and Training (CCRT) http://ccrtindia.gov.in/classicaldances.php; Guidelines for Sangeet Natak Akademi Ratna and Akademi Puraskar

[287] , **Quote:** "There are other temples too in Orissa where the *maharis* used to dance. Besides the temple of Lord Jagannatha, *maharis* were employed in temples dedicated to Shiva and Shakti."

[288] Farley P. Richmond, Darius L. Swann & Phillip B. Zarrilli 1993, p. 22.

[289] Ankiya Nat http://www.accu.or.jp/ich/en/arts/A_IND1.html, UNESCO: Asia-Pacific Database on Intangible Cultural Heritage (ICH), Japan

[290] Massey 2004, p. 177.

[291] Massey 2004, pp. 177-187.

[292] Ragini Devi 1990, pp. 175-180.

[293] Massey 2004, pp. 177-180.

[294] Saryu Doshi 1989, pp. 19-20, 93-99.

[295] Farley P. Richmond, Darius L. Swann & Phillip B. Zarrilli 1993, pp. 174-175.

[296] Ragini Devi 1990, p. 176.

[297] Mohini Attam https://www.britannica.com/art/mohini-attam, Encyclopædia Britannica (2016)

[298] "Thirayattam" (folklore Text- mallayalam, moorkkanad Peethambaran), State Institute of Language, kerala

[299] (Campbell, 2007)

[300] https://books.google.com/books?id=KRz5ykKRVAEC

[301] https://books.google.com/books?id=xRbkAAAAMAAJ

[302] https://books.google.com/books?id=Xa8FamiJJKgC

[303] //doi.org/10.1093%2Fobo%2F9780195399318-0071

[304] https://books.google.com/books?id=3TKarwqJJP0C

[305] https://books.google.com/books?id=yFXkPk3zMeYC

[306] https://books.google.com/books?id=l7naMj1UxIkC

[307] https://books.google.com/books?id=NrgfAAAAIAAJ

[308] http://jashm.press.illinois.edu/12.3/12-3IntheShadow_Williams78-99.pdf

[309] //doi.org/10.1080%2F08949460490274013

[310] https://books.google.com/books?id=OroCOEqkVg4C

[311] //doi.org/10.2307%2F3204783

[312] //www.jstor.org/stable/3204783

[313] http://ncpamumbai.com/arts-dance.html

[314] http://www.india-arts.pitt.edu/

[315] http://www.goethe.de/ins/in/en/lp/kul/mag/foc/kus/tut.html

[316] http://www.stonybrook.edu/commcms/india/events/artseries.html

[317] http://www.hunter.cuny.edu/educationabroad/programs/short-term-programs/all-winter-2014-15-programs/India-performing-arts

[318] http://www.darpana.com

[319] http://studyabroad.sit.edu/programs/semester/fall-2016/inr/

[320] https://www.jstor.org/stable/2155853

[321] //en.wikipedia.org/w/index.php?title=Template:Culture_of_India&action=edit

[322] Richmond, Swann, and Zarrilli (1993, 12).

[323] Brandon (1997, 72) and Richmond (1998, 516).

[324] Brandon (1997, 72), Richmond (1998, 516), and Richmond, Swann, and Zarrilli (1993, 12).

[325] Richmond (1998, 516) and Richmond, Swann, and Zarrilli (1993, 13).

[326] Brandon (1996, 70) and Richmond (1998, 516).

[327] Richmond, Swann, and Zarrilli (1993, 21).

[328] Brandon (1981, xvii) and (1998, 516-517).

[329] Richmond (1998, 516).

[330] Richmond (1998, 517).

[331] Rachel Van M. Baumer and James R. Brandon (ed.), *Sanskrit Drama in Performance* https://books.google.com/books?id=Ix-RShGgZUAC&pg=PA11&dq=actor+drama+pali#v=onepage&q=actor%20drama%20pali&f=false (University of Hawaii Press, 1981), pp.11

[332] According to later Buddhist texts, King Bimbisara (a contemporary of Gautama Buddha) had a drama performed for another king. This would be as early as the 5th century BCE, but the event is only described in much later texts, from the 3rd-4th centuries CE.<ref> *Sanskrit Drama in Performance* https://books.google.com/books?id=Ix-RShGgZUAC&pg=PA11&dq=actor+drama+pali#v=onepage&q=actor%20drama%20pali&f=false, p.11

[333] Brandon (1981, xvii) and Richmond (1998, 517).

[334] Richmond (1998, 518).

[335] Richmond (1998, 518). The literal meaning of *abhinaya* is "to carry forwards".

[336] Brandon (1981, xvii).

[337] Banham (1998, 1051).

[338] Article in Eenadu

[339] Sharma, Shrikrishna, ed. 1996. Rangkarmi. Cultural Societies of Rajasthan. (1996, 139)

[340] https://www.youtube.com/playlist?list=PLnfpS117nLitk6bgGQZHc_6-S9yayqSyj

[341] Pravara art studio https://www.thehindu.com/todays-paper/tp-features/tp-metroplus/the-stage-and-the-journey/article24756932.ece

[342] https://archive.org/stream/selectspecimenso01wils#page/n5/mode/2up

[343] https://archive.org/stream/dasarupatreatise00dhanrich#page/n5/mode/2up

[344] https://archive.org/stream/cu31924012568535#page/n5/mode/2up

[345] http://www.jagrancityplus.com/storydetail.aspx?cityid=22...155

[346] //en.wikipedia.org/w/index.php?title=Template:Music_of_India&action=edit

[347] //en.wikipedia.org/w/index.php?title=Template:Culture_of_India&action=edit

[348] origin of Indian music and arts http://shodhganga.inflibnet.ac.in/bitstream/10603/13634/8/08_chapter%202.pdf. Shodhganga.

[349] see e.g. ; *Sanskrit literature* (2003) in Philip's Encyclopedia. Accessed 2007-08-09

[350] see e.g. ; Witzel, Michael, "Vedas and ", in: ; ; *Sanskrit literature* (2003) in Philip's Encyclopedia. Accessed 2007-08-09

[351] Sanujit Ghose (2011). " Religious Developments in Ancient India http://www.ancient.eu.com/article/230/" in *Ancient History Encyclopedia*.

[352] Maurice Winternitz 2008, pp. 181–182.

353

354 Sorrell & Narayan 1980, pp. 3-4.

355 Patrick Olivelle 1999, pp. xxiii.

356 Jan Gonda (1970 through 1987), A History of Indian Literature, Volumes 1 to 7, Otto Harrassowitz Verlag,

357 Teun Goudriaan and Sanjukta Gupta (1981), Hindu Tantric and Śākta Literature, A History of Indian Literature, Volume 2, Otto Harrassowitz Verlag, , pages 7–14

358 Ananda W. P. Guruge, 1991, The Society of the Ramayana https//books.google.com.sg, Page 180-200.

359 Beale, T.W., An Oriental Biographical Dictionary, p.145

360 Suresh Kant Sharma and Usha Sharma, 2005, Discovery of North-East India https//books.google.com.sg, Page 288.

361 pp. 193-94.

362 Ghosh, p. xiii

363 *Tagore: At Home in the World* pp. 253-254

364 reggaetonline.net http://www.reggaetonline.net/luny-tunes-04262006_inside-reggaeton

365 https://archive.org/stream/musicmusicalinst00dayc#page/n7/mode/2up

366 https://archive.org/stream/cu31924018413900#page/n5/mode/2up.

367 https://archive.org/stream/musicofhindostan00foxs#page/n7/mode/2up

368 https://archive.org/stream/musicofindia00popl#page/n3/mode/2up

369 https://books.google.com/books?id=kFkVJDlg-4IC&printsec=frontcover&source=gbs_ge_summary_r&cad=0#v=onepage&q&f=false

370 https://www.worldcat.org/oclc/299648131

371 https://archive.org/stream/NatyaShastra/natya_shastra_translation_volume_2_-_bharat_muni#page/n7/mode/2up

372 http://www.bbc.co.uk/programmes/p005xm48

373 http://www.bbc.co.uk/programmes/p005xm4c

374 http://www.bbc.co.uk/programmes/p005xjq8

375 http://www.bbc.co.uk/programmes/p005xjqc

376 http://www.bbc.co.uk/programmes/p005xjqk

377 http://www.bbc.co.uk/programmes/p005xl8n

378 http://www.bbc.co.uk/programmes/p005xl8s

379 http://www.bbc.co.uk/programmes/p005xm4k

380 http://www.moutal.eu/indian-music.html

381 //en.wikipedia.org/w/index.php?title=Template:Culture_of_India&action=edit

382 Coomaraswamy, Ananda K. (1999). *Introduction to Indian Art*,: Munshiram Manoharlal, p. 68-70

383 Giusti, M. and Chakraborty, U. (ed.). *Immagini Storie Parole. Dialoghi di formazione coi dipinti cantati delle donne Chitrakar del West Bengal.* Mantova: Universitas Studiorum, 2014,

384 http://www.huichawaii.org/assets/gall,-david---overcoming-polarized-modernities.pdf

385 http://ngmaindia.gov.in/pdf/The-Last-Harvest-e-INVITE.pdf

386 https://archive.org/stream/cu31924016181798#page/n9/mode/2up

387 https://archive.org/stream/cu31924022942993#page/n3/mode/2up

388 https://archive.org/stream/handbookofindian002882mbp#page/n5/mode/2up

389 http://libmma.contentdm.oclc.org/cdm/compoundobject/collection/p15324coll10/id/12335/rec/74

390 http://libmma.contentdm.oclc.org/cdm/compoundobject/collection/p15324coll10/id/105494

391 https//books.google.com

392 http://www.ramayanabook.com/

393 http://libmma.contentdm.oclc.org/cdm/compoundobject/collection/p15324coll10/id/80045/rec/1

394 https://ceed-mdes.blogspot.com/2017/11/indian-state-paintings-and-famous.html

395 https://web.archive.org/web/20130318231813/http://ccrtindia.gov.in/miniaturepainting.htm

396 http://ccrtindia.gov.in/wallpaintings.php

397 http://ccrtindia.gov.in/modernindianpainting.php

398 http://asi.nic.in/asi_monu_whs_ajanta.asp

[399] http://www.mithilapaintings.com

[400] http://curiokat.com/madhubani-paintings-all-you-need-to-know-about-the-quintessential-elegance/

[401] http://www.metmuseum.org/toah/hd/mugh_2/hd_mugh_2.htm

[402] Harle, 17–20

[403] Harle, 22–24

[404] Harle, 26–38

[405] Harle, 87; his Part 2 covers the period

[406] Harle, 124

[407] Harle, 301-310, 325-327

[408] Harle, 276–284

[409] Boardman, 370–378; Harle, 71–84

[410] Boardman, 370–378; Sickman, 85–90; Paine, 29–30

[411] http://libmma.contentdm.oclc.org/cdm/compoundobject/collection/p15324coll10/id/105494

[412] http://libmma.contentdm.oclc.org/cdm/compoundobject/collection/p15324coll10/id/80045/rec/1

[413] See Raj Jadhav, pp. 7–13 in *Modern Traditions: Contemporary Architecture in India.*

[414] Rowland, 31-34, 32 quoted; Harle, 15-18

[415]

[416] Rowland, 31-34, 33 quoted; Harle, 15-18

[417] J.M. Kenoyer (2006), "Cultures and Societies of the Indus Tradition. In Historical Roots" in *the Making of 'the Aryan'*, R. Thapar (ed.), pp. 21–49. New Delhi, National Book Trust.

[418] John Marshall, A Guide to Sanchi, 1918 p.58ff https://archive.org/stream/in.ernet.dli.2015.459148 (Public Domain text)

[419] Digha Nikaya 16 http://www.metta.lk/tipitaka/2Sutta-Pitaka/1Digha-Nikaya/Digha2/16-mahaparinibbana-e2.html, Maha-Parinibbana Sutta, Last Days of the Buddha, Buddhist Publication Society

[420] Buddhist Architecture, Lee Huu Phuoc, Grafikol 2009, p.97-99

[421] "The rubble-built building complex of Jivakamravana at Rajgir probably represents one of the earliest monasteries of India dating from the Buddha's time." in

[422] Encyclopædia Britannica (2008), *Pagoda.*

[423] Buddhist Architecture, Lee Huu Phuoc, Grafikol 2009, p.143

[424]

[425] Piercey & Scarborough (2008)

[426] See Stanley Finger (2001), *Origins of Neuroscience: A History of Explorations Into Brain Function*, Oxford University Press, p. 12, .

[427]

[428] The Early History of India by Vincent A. Smith https://books.google.com/books?id=8XXGhAL1WKcC&pg=PA165

[429] Annual report 1906-07 p.89 https://archive.org/stream/in.gov.ignca.55105/55105#page/n147/mode/2up

[430] Ashoka in Ancient India by Nayanjot Lahiri https://books.google.com/books?id=bJ_XCgAAQBAJ&pg=PA231

[431] Buddhist architecture, Lee Huu Phuoc, Grafikol 2009, p.98-99 https://books.google.com/books?id=9jb364g4BvoC&pg=PA99&lpg=PA99

[432]

[433] Buddhist Architecture, Lee Huu Phuoc, Grafikol 2009, p.149-150

[434] "De l'Indus a l'Oxus: archaeologie de l'Asie Centrale", Pierfrancesco Callieri, p212: "The diffusion, from the second century BCE, of Hellenistic influences in the architecture of Swat is also attested by the archaeological searches at the sanctuary of Butkara I, which saw its stupa "monumentalized" at that exact time by basal elements and decorative alcoves derived from Hellenistic architecture".

[435] Encyclopædia Britannica (2008), *torii*

[436] Japanese Architecture and Art Net Users System (2001), *torii*. http://www.aisf.or.jp/~jaanus/

[437]

[438] "Sowing the Seeds of the Lotus: A Journey to the Great Pilgrimage Sites of Buddhism, Part I" by John C. Huntington. *Orientations*, November 1985 pg 61

[439] Buddhist Architecture, Huu Phuoc Le, Grafikol, 2010 p.240 https://books.google.com/books?id=9jb364g4BvoC&pg=PA240

[440] A Global History of Architecture, Francis D. K. Ching, Mark M. Jarzombek, Vikramaditya Prakash, John Wiley & Sons, 2017 p.570ff https://books.google.com/books?id=SPqKDgAAQBAJ&pg=PT570

[441] Rowland, 31-34, 32 quoted; Harle, 15-18

[442] Buddhist Architecture, Lee Huu Phuoc, Grafikol 2009, p.147

[443]

[444] Le Huu Phuoc, Buddhist Architecture, p.234

[445]

[446] Encyclopædia Britannica (2008), *education, history of*.

[447] Early Buddhist Transmission and Trade Networks by Jason Neelis p.168 https://books.google.com/books?id=GB-JV2eOr2UC&pg=PA168

[448] The Spread of Buddhism by Ann Heirman,Stephan Peter Bumbacher p.60 sq https://books.google.com/books?id=NuOvCQAAQBAJ&pg=PA60

[449] The First Spring: The Golden Age of India by Abraham Eraly p.48 sq https://books.google.com/books?id=te1sqTzTxD8C&pg=PA48

[450] Ancient Indian History and Civilization by Sailendra Nath Sen p.221 https://books.google.com/books?id=Wk4_ICH_g1EC&pg=PA221

[451] A Comprehensive History Of Ancient India p.174 https://books.google.com/books?id=gE7udqBkACwC&pg=PA174

[452] Encyclopædia Britannica (2008), *South Indian temple architecture*.

[453] The sculpture of early medieval Rajasthan By Cynthia Packert Atherton

[454] Beginnings of Medieval Idiom c. A.D. 900–1000 by George Michell

[455] The legacy of G.S. Ghurye: a centennial festschrift By Govind Sadashiv Ghurye, A. R. Momin, p-205

[456] Encyclopædia Britannica (2008), *North Indian temple architecture*.

[457] Moffett *et al.*, 75

[458] See Percy Brown in Sūryanātha Kāmat's *A concise history of Karnataka: from pre-historic times to the present*, p. 132.

[459] See Carla Sinopoli, *Echoes of Empire: Vijayanagara and Historical Memory, Vijayanagara as Historical Memory*, p. 26.

[460] See Carla Sinopoli, *The Political Economy of Craft Production: Crafting Empire in South India, C. 1350–1650*, p. 209.

[461] See Percy Brown in Sūryanātha Kāmat's *A concise history of Karnataka: from pre-historic times to the present*, p. 182.

[462] MSN Encarta (2008), *Hoysala_Dynasty* http://au.encarta.msn.com/encyclopedia_761588346/Hoysala_Dynasty.html. Archived https://www.webcitation.org/5kwKcQ2xF 2009-10-31.

[463] See Percy Brown in Sūryanātha Kāmat's *A concise history of Karnataka: from pre-historic times to the present*, p. 134.

[464] The Hindu (2004), *Belur for World Heritage Status*. http://www.hindu.com/2004/07/25/stories/2004072501490300.htm

[465] Foekema, 16

[466] Rowland, 31-34, 33 quoted; Harle, 15-18

[467] Michell, George & Mark Zebrowski. Architecture and Art of the Deccan Sultanates (The New Cambridge History of India Vol. I:7), Cambridge University Press, Cambridge, 1999, , p.14 & pp.77–80.

[468] Hasan, Perween (2007). Sultans and Mosques:The Early Muslim Architecture of Bangladesh. United Kingdom: I.B. Tauris. p. 23–27.

[469] Petersen, Andrew (2002). Dictionary of Islamic Architecture. Routledge. p. 33–35.

[470] J.M. Kenoyer (2006), "Cultures and Societies of the Indus Tradition. In Historical Roots" in *the Making of 'the Aryan'*, R. Thapar (ed.), pp. 21–49. New Delhi, National Book Trust.

[471] An Advanced History of Modern India By Sailendra Nath Sen, p.16 https//books.google.com

[472] Thapar 2004, p. 122.

[473] Nilsson 1968, p. 9.

[474] Jaffar 1936, p. 230.

[475] Tadgell 1990, p. 14.

[476] Thapar 2004, p. 125.

[477] Evenson 1989, p. 2.

[478] Evenson 1989, p. 6.

[479] Evenson 1989, p. 20.

[480] Nilsson 1968, pp. 66–67.

[481] Thapar 2004, p. 129.

[482] See Raj Jadhav, p. 11 in *Modern Traditions: Contemporary Architecture in India.*

[483] Gast, 77

[484] Gast, 119

[485]

[486] https://archive.org/stream/indianarchitectu00haveuoft#page/n9/mode/2up

[487] https://archive.org/stream/cu31924022942993#page/n3/mode/2up

[488] https://archive.org/stream/cu31924011010109#page/n9/mode/2up

[489] https://books.google.com/books?id=Gt1jTpXAThwC&printsec=frontcover

[490] http://www.kamit.jp/engl.htm

[491] //en.wikipedia.org/w/index.php?title=Template:Culture_of_India&action=edit

[492] https://www.ultimatetabletennis.in/

[493] Sharma Sushant, https://www.sportskeeda.com/cricket/sports-fanaticism-in-india-history-and-where-are-we-today

[494] http://www.cppr.in/article/government-is-a-spoilsport/

[495] http://yas.nic.in/writereaddata/linkimages/6831719428.pdf

[496] Abhinav Bindra wins 10m air rifle gold http://www.rediff.com/sports/2008/aug/11bindra.htm

[497] Medalists – India http://results.beijing2008.cn/WRM/ENG/INF/GL/92A/IND_T.shtml, The official website of the Beijing 2008 Olympic Games

[498] New York Times: With India's First Gold, Suddenly a Billion People Notice the Olympics https://www.nytimes.com/2008/08/12/sports/olympics/12indiagold.html?ref=olympics

[499] mystery of the missing medals http://www.sportstaronnet.com/tss2738/stories/20040918005300800.htmThe

[500] Track and failed: the making of a sleeping Olympic giant https://www.theguardian.com/world/2008/jul/25/india.olympicgames2008

[501] Olympic machismo: The tale the medals tell http://www.rediff.com/sports/2008/aug/04rajeev.htm

[502] 2017 FIFA U-17 World Cup

[503] http://www.ibnlive.com/news/india/jwala-gutta-ashwini-ponnappa-ousted-from-world-championships-710154.html

[504] The Times of India – Sports – I'm here to create a superstar, says India's NBA coach Kenny Natt, timesofindia.com, written 14 June 2011, accessed 21 October 2011. http://articles.timesofindia.indiatimes.com/2011-06-14/interviews/29656175_1_basketball-federation-nba-player-coaching-basketball

[505] Mumbai Mirror – To hell and back for cager Robinson http://www.mumbaimirror.com/article/8/20090304200903040204246234ecc8f32/To-hell-and-back-for-cager-Robinson.html, Mumbaimirror.com, written 4 March 2009, accessed 15 October 2011.

[506] FIBA.com – National Federations & Leagues http://www.fiba.com/pages/eng/fc/FIBA/fibaStru/nfLeag/nfProf.asp?nationalFederationNumber=301

[507] ESPN.com – Geethu Anna Jose gets 3 tryouts http://sports.espn.go.com/wnba/news/story?id=6414207

[508] http://timesofindia.indiatimes.com/india/Fatherland-of-Taekwondo-ready-to-invest-in-Indian-talent/articleshow/122161

[509] faizpunna 2013.

[510] http://www.karateindia.org/

[511] Sportal – Sports Portal – GOVERNMENT OF INDIA http://sportal.nic.in/innerindex.asp?moduleid=26&maincatid=101&comid=2

[512] Sepak Takraw players and officials felicited:: KanglaOnline ∼ Your Gateway http://www. kanglaonline.com/index.php?template=headline&newsid=38912&typeid=3&Idoc_Session= 675c609a27ff40ff109ba1daaff8ed58

[513] J.Venkatesan," Supreme Court bans jallikattu in Tamil Nadu http://www.thehindu.com/news/ national/tamil-nadu/supreme-court-bans-jallikattu-in-tamil-nadu/article5986025.ece," *The Hindu*, 8 May 2014.

[514] Boxing India plans Indian Series of Boxing, new ranking system http://timesofindia. indiatimes.com/sports/boxing/Boxing-India-plans-Indian-Series-of-Boxing-new-ranking-system/articleshow/46042426.cms

[515] http://www.sportstaronnet.com/tss2738/stories/20040918005300800.htm

[516] http://yas.nic.in/

[517] http://indiabudget.nic.in/ub2010-11/eb/dg105.pdf

[518] //en.wikipedia.org/w/index.php?title=Template:Indian_martial_arts_sidebar&action=edit

[519] attested in Classical Sanskrit only, specifically in the Anargharāghava.

[520] attested from Epic Sanskrit; see

[521] Section XIII: *Samayapalana Parva* http://www.sacred-texts.com/hin/m04/m04013.htm, Book 4: *Virata Parva, Mahabharata*.

[522] Luijendijk 2008

[523] Subramanian, N. (1966). *Sangam polity*. Bombay: Asian Publishing House.

[524] Bruce A. Haines (1995). *Karate's History and Traditions* (p. 23-25). Tuttle Publishing.

[525] G. D. Singhal, L. V. Guru (1973). *Anatomical and Obstetrical Considerations in Ancient Indian Surgery Based on Sarira-Sthana of Susruta Samhita*.

[526] Historians such as P. B. Desai (*History of Vijayanagar Empire*, 1936), Henry Heras (*The Aravidu Dynasty of Vijayanagara*, 1927), B.A. Saletore (*Social and Political Life in the Vijayanagara Empire*, 1930), G.S. Gai (Archaeological Survey of India), William Coelho (*The Hoysala Vamsa*, 1955) and Kamath (Kamath 2001, pp157–160)

[527] For instance, the Akbarnama tells that Emperor Akbar practiced gatka every day

[528]

[529] A History of Warfare: Field-Marshal Viscount Montgomery of Alamein, William Morrow & Co; 1st edition (January 1983),

[530] ' ' (251.1) ' ' (251.2) ' ' (251.3) ' (251.4ab)

[531] no primary attribution, quoted in Dirk H.A. Kolff. Naukar, Rajput, & Sepoy. The ethnohistory of the military labour market in Hindustan, 1450-1860. University of Cambridge Oriental Publications no. 43. Cambridge University Press 1990.

[532] "Nagaland Kickboxing". *Last Man Standing*. BBC and Discovery USA. 17 July 2007

[533] http://ancientindianmartialarts.blogspot.in/2011/08/bal-vidya-and-yashwanti-mall-vidya.html

[534] https://aniruddhafoundation.com/compassion-bala-vidya-men-women/

[535] Kal%C4%81

[536] https://www.slideshare.net/ashoknene/sixty-four-arts-of-ancient-india-45933958

[537] https://web.archive.org/web/20160819174918/http://www.guruhemang.com/

[538] https://www.bbc.co.uk/news/magazine-15480741

[539] http://www.shastarvidhya.org/

[540] //en.wikipedia.org/w/index.php?title=Template:Culture_of_India&action=edit

[541] //en.wikipedia.org/w/index.php?title=Template:Indian_television_topics&action=edit

[542] 23.77 mn DTH subscribers by June 2010: Trai http://www.business-standard.com/india/news/ 2377-mn-dth-subscribers-by-june-2010-trai/111180/on Business Standard

[543] Star, Zee, Colors and Sony fight it out on weekends - Business Standard https://www.business-standard.com/article/management/star-zee-colors-and-sony-fight-it-out-on-weekends-113061301119_1.html

[544] //en.wikipedia.org/w/index.php?title=Television_in_India&action=edit

[545] Cable TV Digitization: Everything you need to know - LCD TVs | Plasma TV & Televisions | ThinkDigit Features http://www.thinkdigit.com/TVs/Cable-TV-Digitization-Everything-you-need-to_9535.html. Thinkdigit.com.

[546] 15-day grace period to get TV set-top box http://www.hindustantimes.com/India-news/ NewDelhi/15-day-grace-period-to-get-TV-set-top-box/Article1-1036983.aspx . Hindustan Times (4 April 2013).

[547] http://timesofindia.indiatimes.com/city/chennai/24-lakh-houses-in-Chennai-still-without-set-top-boxes/articleshow/19285596.cms.THE TIMES OF INDIA

[548] Bombay High Court rejects plea on shifting digitisation deadline http://www.business-standard.com/india/news/bombay-high-court-rejects-pleashifting-digitisation-deadline/193834/on. Business Standard (31 October 2012).

[549] Digitisation: Countdown begins for Phase II http://www.business-standard.com/india/news/digitisation-countdown-begins-for-phase-ii/194791/on. Business Standard (6 November 2012).

[550] No extension of deadline in 2nd phase of digitization: Tewari http://zeenews.india.com/business/news/technology/no-extension-of-deadline-in-2nd-phase-of-digitization-tewari_73488.html. Zeenews.india.com.

[551] Cable digitisation: Govt allows grace period of 15 days http://zeenews.india.com/business/news/technology/digitisation-phase-ii-govt-to-allow-grace-period-of-15-days_73374.html. Zeenews.india.com.

[552] TV Digitisation: Consumers can utilise transition period of 10 to 15 http://ibnlive.in.com/news/tv-digitisation-consumers-can-utilise-transition-period-of-10-to-15/382864-3.html. Ibnlive.in.com (3 April 2013).

[553] aMap secures Tata Sky DTH audience measurement biz And Recently Videocon has launched D2H http://www.indiantelevision.com/mam/headlines/y2k9/dec/decmam77.php Indiantelevision.com

[554] https://web.archive.org/web/20081207052246/http://icontrol.in/

[555] http://akshoptifibre.com/

[556] Identity and Consumerism on Television in India http://list.msu.edu/cgi-bin/wa?A2=ind9909e&L=aejmc&T=0&P=1721 AEJMC Archives

[557] http//www.indiantelevision.com. Indiantelevision.com.

[558] Why is TRP a contentious issue? http://www.screenindia.com/old/fullstory.php?content_id=11144 Screen India

[559] Company Profile http://www.tamindia.com/tamindia/Company_Profile.htm tamindia.com

[560] How real is Tam/Intam rating? http://timesofindia.indiatimes.com/business/india-business/how-real-is-tam/intam-rating/articleshow/1657160735.cms The Times of India

[561] TRP rating: The slip is showing http://ia.rediff.com/money/2001/sep/05trp.htm Business Standard via Rediff.com

[562] Security Check: TAM, INTAM Try To Ensure Data Sanctity http://cricket.expressindia.com/old//fulliestory.php?content_id=38689 Express cricket

[563] Quibbles apart, TAM is only currency industry can use http://indiantelevision.com/perspectives/y2k3/adagerating3.htm indiantelevision.com

[564] New TV rating system to challenge TAM monopoly http://timesofindia.indiatimes.com/business/india-business/new-tv-rating-system-to-challenge-tam-monopoly/articleshow/803398.cms The Times of India

[565] [[Audience Measurement and Analytics Ltd. (aMap)laMap http://www.thehindubusinessline.com/2004/08/04/stories/2004080401660900.htm] brings TV ratings online] Hindu Business Line

[566] Ratings cos fight for market share http://www.business-standard.com/common/news_article.php?leftnm=blife&bKeyFlag=BO&autono=322078 Business Standard

[567] rival to stare TAM in eyeball http://www.financialexpress.com/news/New-rival-to-stare-TAM-in-eyeball/308769/New Financial Express

[568] //en.wikipedia.org/w/index.php?title=Template:Culture_of_India&action=edit

[569] Matusitz, J., & Payano, P. (2011). The Bollywood in Indian and American Perceptions: A Comparative Analysis. *India Quarterly: A Journal of International Affairs*, 67(1), 65–77.

[570] Khanna, 155

[571] Khanna, 158

[572] Khanna, 156

[573] Potts, 75

[574] Potts, 74

[575] Burra & Rao, 252

[576] Burra & Rao, 253

[577] The Hindu : Friday Review Hyderabad : *Nijam cheppamantara, abaddham cheppamantara ...* http://www.hindu.com/thehindu/fr/2007/02/09/stories/2007020901390100.htm

[578] Burra & Rao, 252–253

[579] [Narayanan, Arandhai (2008) (in Tamil) Arambakala Tamil Cinema (1931–1941). Chennai: Vijaya Publications. pp. 10–11. ISBN].

[580] Burra & Rao, 254

[581] Rajadhyaksa, 679

[582]

[583] Rajadhyaksa, 681–683

[584] Rajadhyaksa, 681

[585] Maker of innovative, meaningful movies http://www.hindu.com/fr/2007/06/15/stories/2007061551020100.htm. *The Hindu*, 15 June 2007

[586] Rajadhyaksa, 683

[587] Before Brando, There Was Dilip Kumar https://www.thequint.com/entertainment/2015/12/11/before-brando-there-was-dilip-kumar, The Quint, 11 December 2015

[588] Gokulsing & Dissanayake, 132–133

[589] Rajadhyaksa, 685

[590] Rajadhyaksa, 688

[591] Kaushik Bhaumik, An Insightful Reading of Our Many Indian Identities https://thewire.in/24564/an-insightful-reading-of-our-many-indian-identities/, The Wire, 12/03/2016

[592] Nayakan http://www.time.com/time/2005/100movies/0,23220,nayakan,00.html, All-Time 100 Best Films, *Time*, 2005

[593] Arundhati Roy, Author-Activist http://www.india-today.com/itoday/19991213/roy.html *indiatoday.com*. Retrieved 16 June 2013

[594] "The Great Indian Rape-Trick" http://www.sawnet.org/books/writing/roy_bq1.html , SAWNET - The South Asian Women's NETwork. Retrieved 25 November 2011

[595] After Aamir, SRK, Salman, why Bollywood's next male superstar may need a decade to rise http://www.firstpost.com/entertainment/after-aamir-srk-salman-why-bollywoods-next-male-superstar-may-need-a-decade-to-rise-3049864.html, Firstpost, 16 October 2016

[596] Velayutham, 174

[597] Desai, 38

[598] *Moscow Prime Time: How the Soviet Union Built the Media Empire that Lost the Cultural Cold War*, page 44 https://is.muni.cz/el/1421/podzim2015/FAV291/um/Roth-Ey-Moscow_Prime_Time.pdf#page=5, Cornell University Press, 2011

[599] How To Become A Foreign Movie Star In China: Aamir Khan's 5-Point Formula For Success https://www.forbes.com/sites/robcain/2017/06/11/how-to-become-a-foreign-movie-star-in-china-aamir-khans-5-point-formula-for-success/, *Forbes*, 11 June 2017

[600] 'Dangal' Makes More History In China, Joins List Of All-Time 20 Biggest Box Office Hits https://www.forbes.com/sites/robcain/2017/06/09/dangal-makes-history-in-china-by-joining-list-of-all-time-20-biggest-box-office-hits/, *Forbes*, 9 June 2017

[601] Desai, 37

[602] Lakshmi B. Ghosh, *A rare peep into world of Assamese cinema* The Hindu: New Delhi News: A rare peep into world of Assamese cinema http://www.hindu.com/2006/01/05/stories/2006010504870200.htm, The Hindu, 2006

[603] Gokulsing & Dissanayake, 138

[604] Gokulsing & Dissanayake, 139

[605] Gokulsing & Dissanayake, 138–140

[606] : first Bengali talkie

[607] "Move over Bollywood, Here's Bhojpuri," BBC News Online: http://news.bbc.co.uk/go/pr/fr/-/1/hi/world/south_asia/4512812.stm

[608] Gokulsing & Dissanayake, 10–11

[609] Gokulsing & Dissanayake, 10

[610] Gokulsing & Dissanayake, 11

[611] History of Malayalam Cinema http://www.cinemaofmalayalam.net/malayalam_his_5.html. Cinemaofmalayalam.net. Retrieved on 29 July 2013.

[612] Gokulsing & Dissanayake, 133

[613] Mahabhinishkramana, Viswa Nata Chakravarti, M. Sanjay Kishore, Sangam Akademy, Hyderabad, 2005, pp: 69–70.

[614] The Best 1,000 Movies Ever Made https://www.nytimes.com/ref/movies/1000best.html By THE FILM CRITICS OF THE NEW YORK TIMES, *The New York Times*, 2002.

[615] Gokulsing & Dissanayake, 132

[616] Thompson, 74

[617] Zumkhawala-Cook, 312

[618] https://books.google.com/books?id=CORkAAAAMAAJ

[619] //www.worldcat.org/oclc/10696565

[620] https://archive.org/stream/reportoftheindia030105mbp#page/n5/mode/2up

[621] https://web.archive.org/web/20131019131146/http://www.rubypressco.com/

Article Sources and Contributors

The sources listed for each article provide more detailed licensing information including the copyright status, the copyright owner, and the license conditions.

Indosphere *Source:* https://en.wikipedia.org/w/index.php?oldid=860031588 *License:* Creative Commons Attribution-Share Alike 3.0 *Contributors:* Abc root, Abecedare, Adavidb, Aditya Kabir, AdjunctMonument, AjitPD, AkhilKumarPal, Ambuj.Saxena, Amikake3, Amysze123, Apocalyptic Destroyer, Bakasuprman, BrownHairedGirl, Citation bot 1, DaGizza, Dangerous-Boy, David Marjanović, Dbachmann, Deepak~enwiki, Deeptrivia, Embryomystic, Emperor Genius, Grammarpolice, Green Giant, Grubb, Iamthecheese44, Iridescent, Ism schism, Jarble, JarrahTree, Jerome Charles Potts, Kanguole, Keeper76, KnowledgeHegemony, Kransky, Kristod, Kwamikagami, Le Anh-Huy, Lezela, Linguist8, Master of the Orichalcos, Mrbellamguel, Munci, Night w, Paxse, PhnomPencil, Quest for Truth, Rikyu, Rjwilmsi, Scythian1, Sevilledade, Shyamsunder, SlaveToTheWage, Spencer, Srkris, SteinbDJ, Subbupedia95, Sundar, Suntech, Talalpa, The Transhumanist, TheLeopard, Thegreyanomaly, Toussaint, Vadakkan, Woohookitty, YemeniteCamel, Yug, 28 anonymous edits 3

Greater India *Source:* https://en.wikipedia.org/w/index.php?oldid=864711369 *License:* Creative Commons Attribution-Share Alike 3.0 *Contributors:* A ri gi bod, Aacugna, Adamgerber80, AddWittyNameHere, Aditya Kabir, AgnosticPreachersKid, Alternativity, Anaphysik, Ankhsoprah2, AusLonder, Ayunia C., BD2412, Bagas Chrisara, Beland, Bender235, Bgwhite, Bishal Shrestha, Blazearon21, Bonadea, Callofworld, Ceosad, Cleaner880, CommonsDelinker, Cookiemohnsta, Darwgon0801, Dbachmann, Defm0de, Dewritech, Disthan, Doug Weller, El C, Embryomystic, Enervonsyrup, Fixer88, Fowler&fowler, Fraenir, Gorthian, Gunkarta, Haminoon, HimynameisKeluUrumi, History of Persia, Hms1103, I sense a disturbance in the force, Imtushar, Ism schism, JJMC89, Jarble, Jasper0070, JesseW900, JimRenge, John "Hannibal" Smith, John of Reading, JohnThorne, Joshua Jonathan, Juxlos, JzG, Kautilya3, Keith D, Kingprimeb2, Kmiki87, Lakun.patra, Lezela, Lihaas, LouisAragon, Lyndonbaines, Magioladitis, Manish2542, Matthew Fennell, Milktaco, Monkey122d, MoshiKun, Muffin Wizard, Narky Blert, Neel.arunabh, NewEnglandYankee, Nick Number, Nicoleedalat, Ohnoitsjamie, Onel5969, Oranjelo100, Oshwah, Pelagic, PericlesofAthens, Pfhreak, Philipandrew2, PulauKakatua19, Pv.kalash, R'n'B, RandomCritic, Rantemario, RegentsPark, Reyk, Rich Farmbrough, Smsarmad, Solomon7968, Srednuas Lenoroc, Takafumi1, Tigercompanion25, TwoTwoHello, Uplift Humanity, UserNumber, Utcursch, Verbum Veritas, VerifiedCactus, VulpesVulpes42, Weighty, Wendybelcher, Wikirictor, Work number1987, Worldbruce, 暖城 2016-02-05, 150 anonymous edits 6

Indian philosophy *Source:* https://en.wikipedia.org/w/index.php?oldid=865253315 *License:* Creative Commons Attribution-Share Alike 3.0 *Contributors:* 0nlyth3truth, Abecedare, Allforrous, Amitrochates, AnirvacanIya, Ann 146, Aoidh, Aranea Mortem, Arvind Derhgawen, Aubreybardo, Avaya1, BD2412, Barek, Begoon, Bender235, Bevyriot, Blazearon21, Capankajsmilyo, Capitals00, Chemeleon008, Chukki364, ClueBot NG, CsDix, D4iNa4, DaGizza, David.moreno72, Dazedbythebell, Devatmashishya, Devb, Donner60, Dream of Nyx, Dvaitavada, Editor2020, Effulgence108, El C, Festeeliot, FolkTraditionalist, Fraytel, Friedrich Zarathustra, Fyrael, Gaidinliu, Gazelle55, Gregbard, Guanaco, Hariyali, Herodotus123, Hovard carter, Hu12, Human3015, Hvvisweswaran, I dream of horses, Indian Chronicles, Indopug, JBM1971, JaGa, John of Reading, Joshua Jonathan, Kannadigathewarrior, Kashmiri, Kautilya3, Kedarjk, Kishor Nasery, Liz, Luxure, MBlaze Lightning, Magioladitis, Manoguru, Mark Ironie, Maurice Carbonaro, Money money tickle parsnip, Monitagopal, Moxy, Ms Sarah Welch, NawlinWiki, Nick Number, Ogress, Ohconfucius, Omnipaedista, Operacontralto, Overvalued, Paramahansa-Yo, Parasparograhi1, PhnomPencil, Polyamorph, Presearch, Ramakrishnasurathu, Rcsprinter123, Rich Farmbrough, Rohansingh.31, Ronz, Ronzzzzz, Sabyasachi Mishra, Samanthathepirate, Skbhat, Solomon7968, Solus ipse Inc., Soni Ruchi, SpacemanSpiff, Ssilvers, Suraduttashandilya, Swarnimraj, The Quixotic Potato, Tiarapawn, TomS TDotO, UY Scuti, Ugog Nizdast, Upplapati1, Veganvegan, Venkatesh kadam, Vinay4454, Wavelength, Widr, Woohookitty, Xoloitzcuintle, Yoonadue, 116 anonymous edits 33

Wildlife of India *Source:* https://en.wikipedia.org/w/index.php?oldid=863563954 *License:* Creative Commons Attribution-Share Alike 3.0 *Contributors:* Adityamadhav83, Ahuney123, Amiedits, Amitkskj, Anuandraj, Apparition11, Arjuncm3, Armbrust, Arya Kumar Jena, Aspening, AtreyoMukherjee, Audacity, Bender235, Bentogoa, Bgwhite, Caballero1967, ClueBot NG, CommonsDelinker, Crystallizedcarbon, Cyrus noto3at bulaga, DASonnenfeld, Dcirovic, Devbrahma, Dinofahad, Dirkbb, Donlammers, Editinf, Emmawatson287, Epicgenius, Fafnir1, Faizhaider, FierceJake754, Flyer22 Reborn, FoCuSandLeArN, Freddiejoebob, Fruit and more, GLG GLG, Gadget850, Gilliam, Guanaco, GünniX, Günter2415, HMSLavender, JThu, Jauerback, Jigsaw4753, Jim.henderson, Jim1138, KH-1, KLBot2, Kind Tennis Fan, Kkm010, Kosack, KylieTastic, LakesideMiners, Leo1pard, LittleWink, M.srihari, Manikaushik2, Mar4d, Mark the train, Materialscientist, Maxx786, Mbk551, Md Faisal Ansari, Mean as custard, Melody Concerto, Miljan Simonović, Mr. Guye, My Lord, Niranjan43, Noyster, Oshwah, Pablomartinez, PanchoS, Pbsouthwood, Puru7, Rao JK, Red-eyed demon, Riky patel58, Sambit 1982, Samrth Singh, SchreiberBike, Serols, Shankar Raman, Shellwood, Shyamal, Simplexity22, Snehil10, Solarra, Sonicyouth86, Stephenindia, Stesmo, TYelliot, Takeaway, Theroadislong, Toreightyone, TranquilHope, Ugog Nizdast, Vijay8808, Vinodtiwari2608, VirenVaz, Vozul, WILL.I.AM123654, WOSlinker, Wavelength, Weneedarti, Wiae, Widr, Wiggy!, Winterysteppe, Yathin sk, Ykclite, Yokeshbharathi, फ़िलप्रो, 276 anonymous edits 47

Indian cuisine *Source:* https://en.wikipedia.org/w/index.php?oldid=865472629 *License:* Creative Commons Attribution-Share Alike 3.0 *Contributors:* 0xF8E8, 12qqwa, 19SM85, Acroterion, Alexf, Alwaysjaimatadi, Amanyu, Americanfreedom, Arjayay, Asalgotra, BD2412, Baghabayen, BallenaBlanca, Ballistic-bitflip, Barthateslisa, Beland, Buerish, C.Fred, CAPTAIN RAJU, CLCStudent, Caliburn, CalliopeMuse, Chiswick Chap, Chris the speller, ClueBot NG, Comedora, CommonsDelinker, Craighalles, Dan Koehl, Debasisdev, Deli nk, Dhairya da2, Domasai, Drewmutt, Easylifeforeveryone, Embla Kjartansdóttir, Evaders99, Excirial, Flooded with them hundreds, GaonkarA, Geartooth, Gene Wilson, Godara.rahul, GorillaWarfare, Harsh15nagarkoti, Highpeaks35, Hohum, Hokie96, Hooma Roy Choudhury, INeedSupport, Imaturkeybigandround, Iridescent, IronGargoyle, Jahanzaibk76, Jonathansammy, Jps sahu, Jschnur, Julietdeltalima, JzG, KARTY JazZ, KConWiki, KH-1, Keith D, Kintetsubuffalo, KorealoverfromIndu, Korg432, Krchicago, Kuru, Kvwiki1234, L293D, Laasya3924, Liantluanga, LilHelpa, MBlaze Lightning, Madarasi012, Magioladitis, Mahi2210, Mandymech, Marianna251, Mark Sylvester, Marlo Jonesa, Materialscientist, Melcous, Mksword, Mr Stephen, Mrizvydeen, My Lord, Nacck, Nihlus, Northamerica1000, Onel5969, Optakeover, Oshwah, Patient Zero, Pikamander2, Plantdrew, Pooja Khaneja, Primefac, Princejinu, Ramaksoud2000, Richi, Rodw, Rohini, Rounak Ray, Saima perveen, Serols, Shantimoy, Shatabdi Mukherjee, Shellwood, Sherlock Holmes1902, Shibusingh15, Shikharbls, Shweta0007, SiddharthWest, Smithcharlie, SnapMeUp, Snori, Sohil2520, Som07, Sonakanwar, Sshreinivasan, Sumit.india247, Surender1989, Takeaway, Theindiansun, Utcursch, VagabondStories, Vaibhav007 pro, Vgfun, Victor Sanz, Widr, Wiki-uk, WikiPuppies, Wikipelli, Willondon, Yellow Diamond, Yellow Pearl, Yintan, 214 anonymous edits 81

Clothing in India *Source:* https://en.wikipedia.org/w/index.php?oldid=864995654 *License:* Creative Commons Attribution-Share Alike 3.0 *Contributors:* AlenaCollins, AmanJASS, Amartyabag, Aniruddhbhaidhadhaldhadhal, Anushasam, Apparition11, Arr4, Ash wki, BD2412, Bamyers99, Barthateslisa, Basemetal, Bender235, Bgwhite, Bizay s, CASSIOPEIA, CFynn, Canto55, Capitals00, ClueBot NG, CommonsDelinker, Cpt.a.haddock, Dammitkevin, DemocraticLuntz, DesignerEra, Dinesh.bharatplaza111, Dl2000, Drmies, El cid, el campeador, Flyer22 Reborn, Frosty, Ftwseounli9, Gayjew83, Get that easy, Gilliam, Godara.rahul, HMSSolent, Happysailor, Heliotom, Highpeaks35, Imperfect perfection, Inddus, Iridescent, JaconaFrere, John of Reading, Juhuyuta, Justlettersandnumbers, KH-1, Kkj11210, LaMona, LuK3, MER-C, MRD2014, Mabalu, Malikhpur, Mastermurto10, Materialscientist, Mean as custard, Melonkelon, Metaloaf, MrOllie, MusikAnimal, Nat965, Navyamehrotra, Ohnoitsjamie, Osama57, PlyrStar93, Pranjal Joshi, Queenmiss, R'n'B, Raghvendra99674010, Rajebdras, RandomGryffindor, Raymond3023, RheaTomer, Serols, Sfan00 IMG, Simplexity22, Singanna, Smd75jr, Sourcenet, SpacemanSpiff, Sri6639, Stephenb, Strawberryfields77, Super48paul, Supremewisdom, TheFrog001, Thedrunkindianguy, Theinstantmatrix, TranquilHope, Uparna321, Utbindas, Utcursch, Vieque, Vikas9gupta, Wiae, Widr, Wiki-uk, Wikipediasecond, Yamaguchi先生 , Yann, 225 anonymous edits 129

Indian literature *Source:* https://en.wikipedia.org/w/index.php?oldid=860110076 *License:* Creative Commons Attribution-Share Alike 3.0 *Contributors:* 7Sidz, Abecedare, Adits90, Animallover400, Anitek bhattacharya, AnjanBorah, Ankush 89, Anna Roy, Anshuman.jrt, Anthrophilos, Aoidh, Apparition11, Arunspeel, Ashwin147, Atul Bhattacharyya, Authorabhi, Babumoshai50, Bagworm, Bharu12, Bhawani Gautam, Bijitb, Bishnu Saikia, Biswa bisruta, Biswabiscuit, Bri, CLCStudent, Carel.jonkhout, Carl.bunderson, Chris the speller, ClueBot NG, CommonsDelinker, Coolcolney, Cpt.a.haddock, CsDix, DMacks, Dcirovic, Dffgd, Dl2000, Dream of Nyx, DreamGuy, Drmies, Dsp13, Editor5454, EkAsian, Ekabhishek, Ekkavi, Elaqueate, Fraggle81, Fæ, Gamusa1234, Gazal world, George Sharma, Gherkinmad, Gilliam, GoldenDragon2293Return, Goranmust, GorgeCustersSabre, GregorB, Hendrick 99, Hmains, Hmainsbot1, Hororoka, Ira Leviton, Ish ishwar, ItsZippy, Jagged 85, JimVC3, Jncraton, JohanahoJ, John of Reading, John.kakoty, Johnbarry1978, Jprg1966, Jschnur, Jugaari cross, Jyotithesawant, Kalhause, Kishorechan, Kwamikagami, Kww, Lakun.patra, Lawpark00, LilHelpa, Logical1004, LouisAragon, Malcolmxl5, Mang55, Manuni21, Materialscientist, MatthewVanitas, Max Scharnberg, Me, Myself, and I are Here, Michael Greiner, Navonil1, Neelix, NeilN, NewEnglandYankee, Nikkimaria, Ogress, Ohconfucius, Ohnoitsjamie, Okkisafire, Philip Trueman, Pinethicket, Poetry Watch, Pranav.manangath, Prinshukr, Puffin, Qworty, Qzd, Revent, Richard Reinhardt, Roisterer, Rosarino, Sahityakar, Sailpra, Salvio giuliano, Samaraga, Sarahj2107, SchreiberBike, Serols, Sfan00 IMG, ShelfSkewed, Shreevatsa, Sibasishacharyya, Smmmaniruzzaman, Sria91, Sun Creator, Syeda09, Tachs, Tassedethe, Teejay Tamil arasu, Telfordbuck, Tentinator, Termininja, Titodutta, Toms Berk, Utcursch, Uxbona, Vaibhavjunior, Vinaybhai, VirtualPoetix, Vivo78, Vivvt, Wikiuser13, WilliamThweatt, Woohookitty, WrobjexWiki, Xifiggigi, YellowMonkey, Yogesh Khandke, 205 anonymous edits 153

Dance in India *Source:* https://en.wikipedia.org/w/index.php?oldid=865460320 *License:* Creative Commons Attribution-Share Alike 3.0 *Contributors:* A.amitkumar, Adityamadhav83, Akshta101, Anbu121, Andrewpmk, Anisharm, Anshuman.jrt, Apalaria, B-Null, BD2412, Ballerinailina, Bellus Delphina, Bender235, BethNaught, Bgwhite, Blacknclick, Bob1960evens, Buenorays, CAPTAIN RAJU, ClueBot NG, Dan D. Ric, Dark-World25, Dcirovic, Deepchaitanya, Dev0745, Dipjyotidipankarsattriya, DivineAlpha, Dr.K., EclipseDude, FourViolas, Gandharv aiims, Gareth Griffith-Jones, Gazoth, Gilliam, Girth Summit, Godara.rahul, Highpeaks35, I dream of horses, Ifnord, Isarra (HG), IsraphelMac, JackintheBox, JaconaFrere, Jigneshnat, Jim1138, John.kakoty, Jonathansammy, Jonesey95, Julia W, Karan1974, Karthikndr, Khus2001, Kiran cb, Kkmkumar, Kundanlal33, KylieTastic, Lakun.patra, Little green rosetta, Lugia2453, Magioladitis, Marianna251, Materialscientist, MelbourneStar, Mike Rosoft, Mogism, Ms Sarah Welch,

Msasag, Music1201, Mydreamsparrow, Narky Blert, Neilho, Nick Number, Nitinjog, Noyster, Nritarutya, Paanavalli, Panavalli, Param Mudgal, Paul foord, Pavan santhosh.s, PohranicniStraze, Prashanth1231, Pratyya Ghosh, Prayagpathak, Rachana Sundaresan, Rich Farmbrough, Rusianejohn, Sai santhosh00, Samee, SarithaP, Shellwood, SilverGhost99, Sivavelu, Skinsmoke, Slazenger, SpacemanSpiff, Starpchack, Summerdiary, Svpnikhil, Sxa93, T Yashaswi, TanmayaPanda, Tolly4bolly, Unique.creator, Vedpriyaa, Vishwaradhya k, Viswaprabha, Widr, Wizardman, Yogita ganpat chavan, 215 anonymous edits 181

Theatre of India *Source:* https://en.wikipedia.org/w/index.php?oldid=864576674 *License:* Creative Commons Attribution-Share Alike 3.0 *Contributors:* A22brad22, AKS.9955, Abecedare, Adroit.faizi, Amnawale, Ann Nata, Anna Frodesiak, Apparition11, Arjayay, Arunvrparavur, Ashishtiwari1208, Aspening, AusLondonder, Avantiputra7, Baba Bootler, Bender235, BethNaught, Bgwhite, Bhupesh Joshi gatha, Billi guddu, Brenont, Caballero1967, Chilukamarri nataraj, Chilukamarri nataraja gopala murthy, Chris857, ClueBot NG, Cotton2, DGV Rithvik, Darwin Naz, David.moreno72, Debasishdutta77, Devansh3112, Diannaa, Dl2000, Dr Omendra kumar, Eagleash, Ekabhishek, Emchia1995, Epicgenius, Excirial, Floating Boat, Gilliam, Glasseyesred, HMSLavender, Hanu Ramasanjeeva, Heptametru, Highpeaks35, Hyderabadi101, I dream of horses, Ipigott, Jeansandlungs, John of Reading, Khazar2, Kovooran, KylieTastic, Learnerktm, LilHelpa, Lotje, MLBB1993, Mark Arsten, Meldort, Miteshaaaaa, Mortee, Muralibasa, Natg 19, Niceguyedc, Nizil Shah, Operator873, Perry Middlemiss, PhilKnight, Prabhakar Dabhade, Praween kumar Pandey, Punjabson, Raguks, Rahul Sahu, Rajanalakala, Rikimi, Riyazusman, RomanSpa, Ronz, Rsrikanth05, SHIVESHKR, Scenography center, Serols, SomberiJanma, Surajsingh1, Tassedethe, The Herald, TheAMmollusc, Theintuitus, Theworldhasscience, Thinkopotamus, Tolly4bolly, Troy2807, Tuhin k, Urban.chameleon, Vanarase, Vibhu shivhare, Vinay.iyer1, Waisi11, WereSpielChequers, Widr, Y SHANKER MURTI, Yaditiva, Yogee23, Zocke1r, দিব্য দত্ত, 237 anonymous edits 203

Music of India *Source:* https://en.wikipedia.org/w/index.php?oldid=865208301 *License:* Creative Commons Attribution-Share Alike 3.0 *Contributors:* 72, Aayushjaiswal94, Abhishek0831996, Alexf, Anonym59, Arjayay, AusLondonder, BD2412, Bender235, Bgwhite, Bizcochoso, Blue Edits, BukhariSaeed, Cadillac000, Chetanya yadav, Chris the speller, Classicwiki, ClueBot NG, CommonsDelinker, Coolgama, CyberWarfare, DVdm, DatGuy, David.moreno72, Davros69999, Dcirovic, Deepcruze, Deli nk, DemocraticLuntz, Dilrajnandha, DocWatson42, Ezaid Fabber, Favonian, Filmman3000, Flooded with them hundreds, Flyer22 Reborn, Frosty, Geartooth, Gilliam, GoingBatty, Gsenthil28, Helpsome, Highpeaks35, Huon, IKHazarika, Icensnow42, Ifnord, Indianiamanindianiamanindian, JJMC89, JackintheBox, Jessicapierce, Jim1138, Jonathansammy, JueLinLi, K6ka, Kautuk1, Kbb2, Kieronoldham, Kurousagi, L3X1, LindsayH, Luketheb, LyricsMaya, Maestro2016, Materialscientist, Maximajorian Viridio, McGeddon, Meekv, Mrnit, Msasag, Narky Blert, Niceguyedc, Noteremote, Omnipaedista, Onel5969, Oshwah, PK635, Palmor Redol, Piguy101, Praxidicae, Priyanka Bhambhani, ProphetCSP, Qzd, RA0808, RagaBhakta, Rajeshkelkar, Rk566RUFine, Rmd.iitk, Ronakshah1990, Sacuquire, SchreiberBike, Serols, Shehadsc, Shellwood, Shreymaan, Simplexity22, Skskdh, Songspklive, SrikanthGorthy, Strawberry, Subu hazarika, Sudiptohbk, TVGarfield, Tabletop123, The Transhumanist, Trim02, Ulric1313, Umair Aj, UserNumber, Usmankhalid280, Vanischenu, VarunFEB2003, VasuVR, Verbum Veritas, Widr, Woodlot, Zawl, 229 anonymous edits 223

Indian painting *Source:* https://en.wikipedia.org/w/index.php?oldid=855885887 *License:* Creative Commons Attribution-Share Alike 3.0 *Contributors:* Andershus, Apparition11, B–aAa AaA aAa–b, Bonadea, ClownTracker, Diannaa, Dl2000, Frietjes, Funcoolindia, Hmains, JJMC89, John of Reading, Johnbod, Jonesey95, Mark the train, Mathglot, Rameezraja001, Rodw, Tachs, Thomas.W, Travelbird, Tribe of Tiger, WereSpielChequers, Xover, বাক্যবাগীশ, 27 anonymous edits 243

Sculpture in the Indian subcontinent *Source:* https://en.wikipedia.org/w/index.php?oldid=859681176 *License:* Creative Commons Attribution-Share Alike 3.0 *Contributors:* Arjun01, AxelBoldt, BD2412, ClueBot NG, CommonsDelinker, Cotton2, Csldigicol, Cwobeel, Deepak.of.raj, Deeptrivia, Delljvc, Dharmadhyaksha, Ekabhishek, El C, Freshacconci, Funfood, Ganeshk, Gangesdolphin, Gogo Dodo, Hawkestone, Highpeaks35, ISTB351, Insanity Incarnate, Jdcollins13, John.kakoty, Johnbod, KARTY JazZ, KCVelaga, Kkm010, Kmzayeem, Kndimov, LilHelpa, Lithoderm, Mar4d, Modernist, Mogism, Moortiindia2013, Neddyseagoon, Niceguyedc, Ogress, Onef9day, Pratyk321, Rahulsydney, Roland zh, Salilb, Sbblr geervaanee, SlaveToTheWage, Spartaz, TanmayaPanda, ThaddeusB, The Thing That Should Not Be, Thevikrant, Umais Bin Sajjad, WilliamDigiCol, Yamaguchi先生 , 41 anonymous edits 269

Architecture of India *Source:* https://en.wikipedia.org/w/index.php?oldid=864838268 *License:* Creative Commons Attribution-Share Alike 3.0 *Contributors:* A.Savin, Abecedare, Ahhhh513, Aisteco, Alonso de Mendoza, AmericanAir88, Apparition11, Aristophanes68, Arjayay, Arjuncm3, Arshdeepbahga, Ashish.singh8912, Atulindian, Aymatth2, BD2412, Bender235, Bgag, Bgwhite, Bhattcr, Canadianji, Certes, Chris the speller, Chrisque5, ClueBot NG, CommonsDelinker, Cpt.a.haddock, D4iNa4, Dark-World25, DavidLeighEllis, Dcirovic, Debjitpaul10, Diannaa, Dl2000, DuncanHill, EnglishJoee, Falcon Kirtaran, Fraggle81, Gilliam, Hadescurve, Highpeaks35, Hmains, Hmainsbot1, IM3847, Iridescent, IronGargoyle, Jasonanaggie, JayB91, Jim1138, Jodosma, Johnbod, Kjp993, KylieTastic, Lockesdonkey, Look2See1, LouisAragon, Marianna251, Materialscientist, Mild Bill Hiccup, Mogism, Namaamij, Nihiltres, Ninney, Oculi, Onel5969, Orenburg1, Preerithu, R'n'B, Ritujkr, Robevans123, Roland zh, Serols, Shank2432, Sionk, Sjö, Sreejanshilpa, Srolanh, Subhrajyoti07, TheDJ, Titodutta, Utcursch, Vibhss, Vsmith, Wouterhagens, Zppix, पाटलिपुत्र, కైవల్యం, 141 anonymous edits 291

Sport in India *Source:* https://en.wikipedia.org/w/index.php?oldid=865486252 *License:* Creative Commons Attribution-Share Alike 3.0 *Contributors:* AGreatPhoenixSunsFan, Ak2431989, Ariradha, Arjayay, Arman7073526342, Asmita Ghosh, AusLondonder, BD2412, Bender235, Billinghurst, Broccoli and Coffee, BrownHairedGirl, CLCStudent, CUA 27, Cannolis, Changu'sDad, ClueBot NG, Cnwilliams, CyanoTex, DHinz23, David Biddulph, David.moreno72, Deepak2709, Derorgmas, Dey subrata, Dinesh mikkel, DiplomatTesterMan, Dmuc, Dwanyewest, Eno Lirpa, Filipid011, Funplussmart, Fxjctklm, Ghoshprashant.51, Gilliam, GoingBatty, Groundhopping, GünniX, Hazarasp, Hemant Dabral, Highpeaks35, Ianblair23, Ira Leviton, Iridescent, J04n, JJMC89, Jan Johane Pieter, JayM22, Jessequeira21, John of Reading, Just a guy from the KP, KH-1, Kalpathyram, Keith D, Kya hua, Lakun.patra, Lawrencekhoo, MBlaze Lightning, Madhavbajajskater01, Malikhpur, Marchjuly, Matassileikis, Materialscientist, Mc2175, NewEnglandYankee, Numerounovedant, OkayKenji, Oshwah, PRehse, Pardeep Pandit, Paris1127, Paul Kommu, Praneeth kannegolla, Praxidicae, Purplinko, Ram Bhadouriya2498, Rayman60, Ripdaman.singh01, Rodw, Rsrikanth05, Runawayangel, SJ Defender, Sfimin, ShakespeareFan00, ShivaSah, Shovon76, Some Gadget Geek, Srinivaspon, Stefan2, Stephreef, Steve Quinn, TAnthony, The Discoverer, ThePlatypusofDoom, Tintin1107, Tony1, Tricana8571uno, Upanshu upanshu, Upen150, Utcursch, VISAVASU, Vidhyarv, Vivek Ray, WOSlinker, WereSpielChequers, Wiki.editAnshu, Wikipedia nitin, Will.I.Win, Wtmitchell, Xpyqzr, Yamaguchi先生 , 213 anonymous edits 325

Indian martial arts *Source:* https://en.wikipedia.org/w/index.php?oldid=851496990 *License:* Creative Commons Attribution-Share Alike 3.0 *Contributors:* .Absolution., Abhijithvp411, Adavidb, Akspedia, Alertedlevel2, Arebellion, Arjayay, Arunachalam Mani, BD2412, Banak, Bender235, Bharath chand., Bipin2905, Birdtread, Bladesmulti, Bodha2, Capitals00, Catlemur, Chaubals, Chris the speller, ClueBot NG, Cpt.a.haddock, Curb Chain, Dcirovic, Deathlasersonline, Derek R Bullamore, Dl2000, Download, DynamoDegsy, Ekabhishek, Fixer88, Helpsome, Hmains, Hotmuru, John "Hannibal" Smith, John Hill, Khazar2, King durai k, Kpbolumbu, Kwamikagami, LialSE, Liberal Humanist, MKar, Magioladitis, Mansi Nanavati, Mark Arsten, Mean as custard, Melonkelon, Merlin Immanuel, Mogism, Mohd. Toukir Hamid, Morinae, Mottengott, MusikAnimal, Mykhal, Ogress, Ohconfucius, Onel5969, Oshwah, PRehse, Pigsonthewing, Prodes99, Pv.abhinav, Quarter Nelson, RA0808, Rajaram Sarangapani, Redhotsathya, Richard Keatinge, Rishu Shukla, Rjs.swarnkar, Rsrikanth05, Ryo 625, Saifu77, Samitakalla, Sascode78, SchreiberBike, Serendipodous, Shaibykoshy, Shrish, Sikh-history, Skinsmoke, Solomon7968, Spidey665, Sujato, Svabhiman, TanmayaPanda, The Mol Man, Titodutta, Utcursch, Wagadkar, Wbm1058, WhisperToMe, Widr, Woohookitty, ZarlanTheGreen, Zephyrmaten, 168 anonymous edits 368

Television in India *Source:* https://en.wikipedia.org/w/index.php?oldid=863921431 *License:* Creative Commons Attribution-Share Alike 3.0 *Contributors:* 100 lion, 28bytes, A.amitkumar, Abcdqwerty3698, Abhimanyuvikram, Abhkum, Ajcfreak, Alexf, Ali jafri, AmanKiAsha, Amrabangali, Amrishsingh92, Arunsingh16, Aryan.for.you, BD2412, Bentogoa, Bgwhite, BigJolly9, Blaclef, Brindavijay03, Broadcast Audience Research Council India, Chris the speller, ClueBot NG, DVdm, Danusker, Desiindianserial, Dewritech, Dharmadhyaksha, Diannaa, Dl2000, DocWatson42, Editor5454, Evano1van, Faizan, Frze, Fuddle, GSS, Gpkp, GünniX, Hack, JJMC89, JamesBWatson, Jatinbhatt blap, JayB91, Jim1138, John of Reading, John.kakoty, Jutir, Jyoti Atma, Kanhakris, Kkm010, LeoFrank, LittleWink, Luckykool, M2545, MER-C, Maheshkumaryadav, Managerarc, Mark Arsten, MarnetteD, Materialscientist, MatiW97, Me, Myself, and I are Here, Mehar Ghazanfar Hussain, Meiskam, Miracle Pen, Mogism, MrFawwaz, Mushroom9, Naisarg gamit, Neechalkaran, Neelkamala, Niceguyedc, Nikhil.tiru, Northamerica1000, ObseloV, Ohconfucius, Oluwa2Chainz, Pai Walisongo, Paris1127, Pavankumarchenna, Pearll's sun, Peppy Paneer, R'n'B, Rahul Manivanan, Rams.jan, Rangrasiya., RichardWeiss, Rnikhil1811, Roopeshrao, Sachin.neelkanth, Sambhav Arora, Sanjayrealman, Satellizer, Ser Amantio di Nicolao, Sfan00 IMG, Sodabottle, Solarra, SympatheticIsolation, Tabletop, Tassedethe, Tentinator, The Banner, The Mighty Glen, The Quixotic Potato, Thewikiguru1, Thilakshan, Tigercompanion25, Titodutta, Traitortanmay, Vali ace, ViperSnake151, Vrij, Wandering unicorn, Wiki Wikardo, Wiki-uk, Wizardman, Woohookitty, Xzinger, Zapcommunications, 214 anonymous edits 391

Cinema of India *Source:* https://en.wikipedia.org/w/index.php?oldid=865195537 *License:* Creative Commons Attribution-Share Alike 3.0 *Contributors:* 65HCA7, Aban abhiram, Aggi007, Aj white jr., Anirudh Emani, Anirudhinduchudan56, AnkurWiki, Arjayay, Arp265, Arunnagammal, BD2412, Badriya313, Bollywoodking75, Bonadea, Brandmeister, Bumbravathi, CAPTAIN RAJU, Cait.123, Certes, Chatram, Chris the speller, ClueBot NG, Coolharrypotter, Cop 663, Cuty g, DRAGON BOOSTER, DadaNeem, Dhiraj Sakunde, Dinkar.d, Dl2000, DocWatson42, ESIST, Editor5454, Emir of Wikipedia, Enterprisey, Frietjes, Gatemansgc, Gilo1969, Gpkp, GünniX, Haakonsson, Hammersoft, Headbomb, Howcheng, IdreamofJeanie, Jay Jay Marcus Keize13, JayB91, Jodosma, John of Reading, Jonesey95, Jyotilohkana, Kailash29792, Kaitha Poo Manam, Kallol6195, Kotivalo, Kriti rajput, Kuru, Let There Be Sunshine, Lfstevens, Loginnigol, LynxTufts, MBlaze Lightning, Madrasraj, Maestro2016, Mahmudmasri, Manchivadu, Marchjuly, Mark the train, Markbassett, Materialscientist, MatiW97, Mauricebrownuk, Mild Bill Hiccup, Modest Genius, Mohitkapoor93, Monish Pathy, Mouglii, MoviePhan, MrOllie, My Lord, Nabilahmad27, NineTimes, PKT, Pandit Ramanuj Iyar, Paripoornanand, Pkbwcgs, Plandu, PlyrStar93, Powerlight44, Prad Nelluru, Prajwal Mudiyappa, Prasanth reddy22, Prinsgezinde, Prinsipe Ybarro, Punyaboy, Pveluri, RHcosm, Raawat, Radiphus, Rahulkamal88, Ram33333, Ravensfire, Regaliceratops, Rich Farmbrough, Risu43, Robertgombos, Rodw, Sai santhosh00, Salam1117, Sandstein, Sc..7, Sexymoosa123, Shadab Siddiqui, Shadowowl, Shellwood, Siddiqsazzad001, SpacemanSpiff, Sudhir Attavar, Suydigitra, TAnthony, Tarulan, Tassedethe, Teamspuul, The Immortal Excalibur, Thejdeep, Titodutta, Vensatry, Vibhss, Vijay Allam, Vijay kethavath999, WereSpielChequers, Wldn ss, Yamaguchi先生 , अ आ, 212 anonymous edits 404

Image Sources, Licenses and Contributors

The sources listed for each image provide more detailed licensing information including the copyright status, the copyright owner, and the license conditions.

Image *Source:* https://en.wikipedia.org/w/index.php?title=File:Indian_cultural_zone.svg *License:* Creative Commons Attribution-ShareAlike 3.0 Unported *Contributors:* User:Deeptrivia 6
Figure 1 *Source:* https://en.wikipedia.org/w/index.php?title=File:Prambanan_Complex_1.jpg *License:* Creative Commons Attribution-Sharealike 3.0 *Contributors:* Gunawan Kartapranata 8
Figure 2 *Source:* https://en.wikipedia.org/w/index.php?title=File:Ayutthaya-old.jpg *License:* Creative Commons Attribution-Sharealike 2.0 *Contributors:* Later versions were uploaded by Diliff at en.wikipedia. 10
Figure 3 *Source:* https://en.wikipedia.org/w/index.php?title=File:Angkor_Vat_(6783535194).jpg *License:* Creative Commons Attribution 2.0 *Contributors:* Jean-Pierre Dalbéra from Paris, France 14
Figure 4 *Source:* https://en.wikipedia.org/w/index.php?title=File:Durga_Loro_Jonggrang_copy.jpg *License:* Creative Commons Attribution-Sharealike 3.0 *Contributors:* Gunawan Kartapranata 17
Figure 5 *Source:* https://en.wikipedia.org/w/index.php?title=File:Hinduism_Expansion_in_Asia.svg *Contributors:* User:Gunkarta 21
Figure 6 *Source:* https://en.wikipedia.org/w/index.php?title=File:006_Bujang_Valley_Candi.jpg *License:* Creative Commons Attribution-Sharealike 3.0 *Contributors:* User:Anandajoti 22
Figure 7 *Source:* https://en.wikipedia.org/w/index.php?title=File:Atashgah_Fire_Temple.jpg *License:* Public domain *Contributors:* Not home 23
Figure 8 *Source:* https://en.wikipedia.org/w/index.php?title=File:Character-sphere.png *License:* Creative Commons Attribution-ShareAlike 3.0 Unported *Contributors:* Innn 25
Image *Source:* https://en.wikipedia.org/w/index.php?title=File:Asianphilsidebar.jpg *License:* GNU Free Documentation License *Contributors:* Javierfv1212 33
Image *Source:* https://en.wikipedia.org/w/index.php?title=File:Philbar_3.png *Contributors:* User:Javierfv1212 34
Image *Source:* https://en.wikipedia.org/w/index.php?title=File:Socrates.png *License:* Public Domain *Contributors:* Later versions were uploaded by Optimager at en.wikipedia. 35
Image *Source:* https://en.wikipedia.org/w/index.php?title=File:Yajnavalkya_and_Janaka.jpg *License:* Creative Commons Attribution-Sharealike 3.0 *Contributors:* எஸ். பி. கிருஷ்ணமூர்த்தி 36
Image *Source:* https://en.wikipedia.org/w/index.php?title=File:Jain_statues,_Gwalior.jpg *License:* Creative Commons Attribution-Share Alike *Contributors:* Yann (talk) 36
Image *Source:* https://en.wikipedia.org/w/index.php?title=File:Rock-cut_Lord_-_Buddha-_-_Statue_at_Bojjanakonda_near_Anakapalle_of_Visakhapatnam_dist_in_AP.jpg *License:* Creative Commons Attribution 3.0 *Contributors:* Adityamadhav83 36
Image *Source:* https://en.wikipedia.org/w/index.php?title=File:GuruGobindSinghJiGurdwaraBhaiThanSingh.jpg *License:* Public Domain *Contributors:* Jujhar.pannu, OgreBot 2, Roland zh 36
Figure 9 *Source:* https://en.wikipedia.org/w/index.php?title=File:Raja_Ravi_Varma_-_Sankaracharya.jpg *License:* Public Domain *Contributors:* BeatrixBelibaste, Naveen Sankar, Nvvchar, Praveenp, Redtigerxyz, Roland zh, 2 anonymous edits 37
Figure 10 *Source:* https://en.wikipedia.org/w/index.php?title=File:Photo_of_lord_adinath_bhagwan_at_kundalpur.JPG *License:* Creative Commons Attribution-Sharealike 3.0 *Contributors:* User:Adarshj4 39
Figure 11 *Source:* https://en.wikipedia.org/w/index.php?title=File:Gandhara_Buddha_(tnm).jpeg *License:* Public domain *Contributors:* User:World Imaging 40
Figure 12 *Source:* https://en.wikipedia.org/w/index.php?title=File:Sudama_and_Lomas_Rishi_Caves_at_Barabar,_Bihar,_1870.jpg *License:* Public Domain *Contributors:* Thomas Fraser Peppé 41
Image *Source:* https://en.wikipedia.org/w/index.php?title=File:Commons-logo.svg *License:* logo *Contributors:* Anomie, Callanecc, CambridgeBayWeather, Jo-Jo Eumerus, RHaworth 46
Image *Source:* https://en.wikipedia.org/w/index.php?title=File:Nagzira_Tiger_By_Vijay_Phulwadhawa.jpg *License:* Creative Commons Attribution 3.0 *Contributors:* Vijaymp 47
Figure 13 *Source:* https://en.wikipedia.org/w/index.php?title=File:IndianElephant.jpg *License:* Creative Commons Attribution-Sharealike 2.0 *Contributors:* Jayanand Govindaraj 49
Figure 14 *Source:* https://en.wikipedia.org/w/index.php?title=File:Valley_of_flowers_uttaranchal_full_view.JPG *License:* Creative Commons Attribution-Sharealike 2.5 *Contributors:* () 50
Figure 15 *Source:* https://en.wikipedia.org/w/index.php?title=File:Valley_of_flowers_National_Park,_Uttrakhand_India..jpg *License:* Creative Commons Attribution-Sharealike 3.0 *Contributors:* User:Seemakushaal 51
Figure 16 *Source:* https://en.wikipedia.org/w/index.php?title=File:Ophrysia_superciliosa_hm.jpg *License:* Public Domain *Contributors:* , published in Hume and Marshall 53
Figure 17 *Source:* https://en.wikipedia.org/w/index.php?title=File:Green_Peafowl_Pavo_muticus_Manipur_by_Raju_Kasambe..jpg *Contributors:* User:Dr. Raju Kasambe 54
Figure 18 *Source:* https://en.wikipedia.org/w/index.php?title=File:Boat,_trees_and_water_in_Sundarbans.jpg *License:* Creative Commons Attribution 2.0 *Contributors:* Ranveig, Roland zh 54
Figure 19 *Source:* https://en.wikipedia.org/w/index.php?title=File:RameshwaramScenicView.jpg *License:* Creative Commons Attribution 2.0 *Contributors:* FlickreviewR, Keyan20, Roland zh 55
Figure 20 *Source:* https://en.wikipedia.org/w/index.php?title=File:Rhinoceros_unicornis,_Kaziranga_(2006).jpg *License:* Creative Commons Attribution-Sharealike 3.0 *Contributors:* User:Yathin sk 56
Figure 21 *Source:* https://en.wikipedia.org/w/index.php?title=File:IndianWildAss1.jpg *License:* Creative Commons Attribution-Sharealike 3.0 *Contributors:* User:Asimpatel 56
Figure 22 *Source:* https://en.wikipedia.org/w/index.php?title=File:Male_Gaur_(asiatic_wild_ox)_at_Nagarahole_wildlife_sanctuary.jpg *License:* GNU Free Documentation License *Contributors:* User:Dineshkannambadi 57
Figure 23 *Source:* https://en.wikipedia.org/w/index.php?title=File:Bos_grunniens_at_Letdar_on_Annapurna_Circuit.jpg *License:* Creative Commons Attribution-Sharealike 2.0 *Contributors:* travelwayoflife 57
Figure 24 *Source:* https://en.wikipedia.org/w/index.php?title=File:Sambhar_Deer_by_N_A_Nazeer.jpg *License:* Creative Commons Attribution-Sharealike 2.5 *Contributors:* User:Sreejithk2000 57
Figure 25 *Source:* https://en.wikipedia.org/w/index.php?title=File:Deer2.jpg *License:* Creative Commons Attribution-Sharealike 3.0 *Contributors:* User:Shanmugamp7 58
Figure 26 *Source:* https://en.wikipedia.org/w/index.php?title=File:Boselaphus_tragocamelus1.jpg *License:* GNU Free Documentation License *Contributors:* User:Andrew c 58
Figure 27 *Source:* https://en.wikipedia.org/w/index.php?title=File:Chinkara_(Indian_Gazelle)_in_Ranthambore_National_Park.jpg *Contributors:* User:Bharioke 59
Figure 28 *Source:* https://en.wikipedia.org/w/index.php?title=File:Ranthambore_Tiger.jpg *License:* Creative Commons Attribution 2.0 *Contributors:* Koshyk 59
Figure 29 *Source:* https://en.wikipedia.org/w/index.php?title=File:Asiatic_Lion_and_Lioness.jpg *Contributors:* User:Ranitrkd7 60
Figure 30 *Source:* https://en.wikipedia.org/w/index.php?title=File:Alert_Leopard.jpg *License:* Creative Commons Attribution-Sharealike 3.0,2.5,2.0,1.0 *Contributors:* Kalyan Varma 60
Figure 31 *Source:* https://en.wikipedia.org/w/index.php?title=File:Lightmatter_snowleopard.jpg *License:* Creative Commons Attribution 2.0 *Contributors:* Abujoy, Fabien1309, Hardscarf, MPF, Quadell, Winterkind, 2 anonymous edits 61
Figure 32 *Source:* https://en.wikipedia.org/w/index.php?title=File:Striped_hyena_(Hyaena_hyaena)_at_IGZoo_Park.JPG *License:* Creative Commons Attribution-Sharealike 3.0 *Contributors:* User:Adityamadhav83 61
Figure 33 *Source:* https://en.wikipedia.org/w/index.php?title=File:Canis_lupus_pallipes_Mysore_Zoo_1.jpg *License:* Creative Commons Attribution 2.0 *Contributors:* Pavan Kunder 62
Figure 34 *Source:* https://en.wikipedia.org/w/index.php?title=File:Golden_Jackal_-_Corbett_National_Park.jpg *License:* Creative Commons Attribution-Sharealike 2.0 *Contributors:* FlickreviewR, Jarble, Kersti Nebelsiek, Mariomassone, Morning Sunshine, OgreBot 2 62
Figure 35 *Source:* https://en.wikipedia.org/w/index.php?title=File:Cuon.alpinus-cut.jpg *License:* GNU Free Documentation License *Contributors:* en:User:Kalyanvarma (?) 63
Figure 36 *Source:* https://en.wikipedia.org/w/index.php?title=File:Black_tailed_fox_(Bengal_Fox)_at_Desert_NP_(cropped).jpg *License:* Creative Commons Attribution-Sharealike 3.0 *Contributors:* User:Chinmayisk 63

469

Image *Source:* https://en.wikipedia.org/w/index.php?title=File:Portrait_of_a_Stallion,_mid_19th_century.jpg *Contributors:* Msanitam, OgreBot 2, Rilegator, Warburg1866, 1 anonymous edits 264
Figure 167 *Source:* https://en.wikipedia.org/w/index.php?title=File:Thirthankara_Suparshvanath_Museum_Rietberg_RVI_306.jpg *License:* Public Domain *Contributors:* User:AndreasPraefcke 270
Figure 168 *Source:* https://en.wikipedia.org/w/index.php?title=File:Bronze_sculpt_NMND-5.JPG *License:* Public Domain *Contributors:* Daderot 270
Figure 169 *Source:* https://en.wikipedia.org/w/index.php?title=File:Gandhara_Buddha_(tnm).jpeg *License:* Public domain *Contributors:* User:World Imaging 271
Figure 170 *Source:* https://en.wikipedia.org/w/index.php?title=File:Konark_Sun_Temple_Front_view.jpg *License:* Public Domain *Contributors:* http://en.wikipedia.org/wiki/User_talk:Vinayreddym 271
Figure 171 *Source:* https//en.wikipedia.org *Contributors:* Achim55, Capankajsmilyo, Fæ, JMCC1, Redtigerxyz, 1 anonymous edits 272
Figure 172 *Source:* https://en.wikipedia.org/w/index.php?title=File:Elephanta_Caves_Trimurti.jpg *License:* Creative Commons Attribution 2.0 *Contributors:* Christian Haugen 272
Figure 173 *Source:* https://en.wikipedia.org/w/index.php?title=File:Bahubali_Shravana_Belagola.jpg *License:* Creative Commons Attribution-Sharealike 3.0 *Contributors:* User:AJ.iitm 273
Figure 174 *Source:* https://en.wikipedia.org/w/index.php?title=File:Dancing_Girl_of_Mohenjo-daro.jpg *License:* Creative Commons Attribution-Sharealike 3.0 *Contributors:* Joe Ravi 273
Figure 175 *Source:* https://en.wikipedia.org/w/index.php?title=File:Asokanpillar-crop.jpg *License:* Creative Commons Attribution-Sharealike 2.5 *Contributors:* mself 274
Figure 176 *Source:* https://en.wikipedia.org/w/index.php?title=File:Column,_Sanchi.jpg *License:* Creative Commons Attribution-Share Alike *Contributors:* Yann (talk) 274
Figure 177 *Source:* https://en.wikipedia.org/w/index.php?title=File:Krishna_Killing_the_Horse_Demon_Keshi.jpg *License:* Creative Commons Attribution-Sharealike 2.0 *Contributors:* Claire H. 275
Figure 178 *Source:* https://en.wikipedia.org/w/index.php?title=File:Buddha_from_Sarnath.jpg *License:* Creative Commons Attribution-Sharealike 2.0 *Contributors:* Chaoborus, Ddalbiez, Ekabhishek, Gryffindor, Ismoon, Martin H., Mhss, Underwaterbuffalo 275
Figure 179 *Source:* https://en.wikipedia.org/w/index.php?title=File:Seated_Ganesha,_India,_Rajasthan,_9th_century,_sandstone,_Honolulu_Academy_of_Arts.jpg *License:* Public Domain *Contributors:* Hiart 276
Figure 180 *Source:* https://en.wikipedia.org/w/index.php?title=File:NatarajaMET.JPG *License:* Creative Commons Attribution-Sharealike 2.5 *Contributors:* User Kaysov on en.wikipedia 277
Figure 181 *Source:* https//en.wikipedia.org *License:* Creative Commons Zero *Contributors:* Hiart 277
Figure 182 *Source:* https://en.wikipedia.org/w/index.php?title=File:WLA_lacma_Celestial_Nymph_ca_1450_Rajasthan.jpg *License:* Creative Commons Attribution-Sharealike 2.5 *Contributors:* Wikipedia Loves Art participant " ARTiFACTS" 278
Figure 183 *Source:* https://en.wikipedia.org/w/index.php?title=File:Natarajartemple1.jpg *License:* Creative Commons Attribution-Sharealike 3.0 *Contributors:* Lakshmanan (talk) 278
Figure 184 *Source:* https://en.wikipedia.org/w/index.php?title=File:GandharaDonorFrieze2.JPG *License:* Public Domain *Contributors:* BotAdventures, Johnbod, Jonathan Cardy, Ronaldino, Sailko, Talmoryair, World Imaging, Zaccarias, 2 anonymous edits 279
Figure 185 *Source:* https://en.wikipedia.org/w/index.php?title=File:Muktesvara_deula.jpg *License:* Creative Commons Attribution-Sharealike 3.0 *Contributors:* Cpt.a.haddock, Oo91, Psubhashish, Tangopaso, Vivek Sarje 280
Figure 186 *Source:* https://en.wikipedia.org/w/index.php?title=File:WindGod2.JPG *License:* Creative Commons Attribution-ShareAlike 3.0 Unported *Contributors:* Original uploader was Per Honor et Gloria at en.wikipedia 280
Figure 187 *Source:* https://en.wikipedia.org/w/index.php?title=File:Demetrius_I_MET_coin.jpg *License:* Creative Commons Attribution-Sharealike 3.0 *Contributors:* Uploadalt 280
Figure 188 *Source:* https://en.wikipedia.org/w/index.php?title=File:Bouddha_Hadda_Guimet_181171.jpg *License:* Public Domain *Contributors:* Rama, Sailko, Vassil 281
Figure 189 *Source:* https://en.wikipedia.org/w/index.php?title=File:PoseidonGandhara.JPG *License:* Creative Commons Attribution-ShareAlike 3.0 Unported *Contributors:* User:World Imaging 282
Figure 190 *Source:* https://en.wikipedia.org/w/index.php?title=File:PharroAndArdoxsho.jpg *License:* Public Domain *Contributors:* Common Good, Daderot, Funfood, Ismoon, Itu, Jarekt, Johnbod, Kilom691, Kresspahl, Sailko, Scientia.asiae, Siebrand, World Imaging 282
Figure 191 *Source:* https://en.wikipedia.org/w/index.php?title=File:Taller_Buddha_of_Bamiyan_before_and_after_destruction.jpg *License:* Creative Commons Attribution-Sharealike 3.0 *Contributors:* Buddha_Bamiyan_1963.jpg: UNESCO/A Lezine; Original uploader was Tsui at de.wikipedia. Later version(s) were uploaded by 283
Figure 192 *Source:* https://en.wikipedia.org/w/index.php?title=File:Konark_Sun_Temple_Front_view.jpg *License:* Public Domain *Contributors:* http://en.wikipedia.org/wiki/User_talk:Vinayreddym 283
Figure 193 *Source:* https://en.wikipedia.org/w/index.php?title=File:GBA1(trimmed).jpg *License:* Public Domain *Contributors:* User:OrphanBot 284
Figure 194 *Source:* https://en.wikipedia.org/w/index.php?title=File:Didarganj-Yakshi-3bc-Patna.jpg *License:* Creative Commons Attribution 3.0 *Contributors:* User:Anandajoti 284
Figure 195 *Source:* https://en.wikipedia.org/w/index.php?title=File:Bronzes-Chola-2.jpg *License:* Creative Commons Attribution-ShareAlike 1.0 Generic *Contributors:* Gryffindor, HenkvD, Johnbod, Nataraja~commonswiki, Redtigerxyz, Roland zh, Tangopaso 285
Figure 196 *Source:* https://en.wikipedia.org/w/index.php?title=File:Bronzes-Chola-background_retouch.jpg *License:* Creative Commons Attribution-ShareAlike 1.0 Generic *Contributors:* Jdcollins13, Johnbod 285
Figure 197 *Source:* https://en.wikipedia.org/w/index.php?title=File:Ellora_Kailash_temple_Shiva_panel.jpg *License:* Creative Commons Attribution 2.5 *Contributors:* User:QuartierLatin1968, User:QuartierLatin1968 285
Figure 198 *Source:* https://en.wikipedia.org/w/index.php?title=File:Jaisalmer_Jain_Temple_6.jpg *License:* Creative Commons Attribution-Sharealike 3.0 *Contributors:* Ingo Mehling 286
Figure 199 *Source:* https://en.wikipedia.org/w/index.php?title=File:13th_century_Ganesha_statue.jpg *License:* Creative Commons Attribution-ShareAlike 3.0 Unported *Contributors:* Quadell 286
Figure 200 *Source:* https://en.wikipedia.org/w/index.php?title=File:Shiva_and_Uma_14th_century.jpg *License:* Creative Commons Attribution-ShareAlike 3.0 Unported *Contributors:* User:Quadell 287
Figure 201 *Source:* https://en.wikipedia.org/w/index.php?title=File:Bhudevi.jpg *License:* Creative Commons ShareAlike 1.0 Generic *Contributors:* Eternal-Entropy, Foroa, Jastrow, Ranveig, Roland zh, Stefan2, 1 anonymous edits 287
Figure 202 *Source:* https://en.wikipedia.org/w/index.php?title=File:Stone_Inscription_at_ASI_Museum,_Amaravathi.jpg *Contributors:* User:Krishna Chaitanya Velaga 288
Figure 203 *Source:* https://en.wikipedia.org/w/index.php?title=File:Secular_Scenes_Stone_at_ASI_Museum,_Amaravathi.jpg *Contributors:* User:Krishna Chaitanya Velaga 288
Figure 204 *Source:* https://en.wikipedia.org/w/index.php?title=File:Lintel_Beam_Model_at_ASI_Museum,_Amaravathi.jpg *Contributors:* User:Krishna Chaitanya Velaga 289
Figure 205 *Source:* https://en.wikipedia.org/w/index.php?title=File:Hindu_Goddess_Statue_at_ASI_Museum,_Amaravathi.jpg *Contributors:* User:Krishna Chaitanya Velaga 289
Figure 206 *Source:* https://en.wikipedia.org/w/index.php?title=File:TajMahalbyAmalMongia.jpg *License:* Creative Commons Attribution-Sharealike 2.0 *Contributors:* amaldla from san francisco 292
Figure 207 *Source:* https://en.wikipedia.org/w/index.php?title=File:DHOLAVIRA_SITE_(24).jpg *Contributors:* User:Lalit Gajjer 292
Image *Source:* https//en.wikipedia.org *License:* Public Domain *Contributors:* Rahul Bott, पाटलिपुत्र 293
Image *Source:* https//en.wikipedia.org *License:* Creative Commons Attribution-Sharealike 3.0 *Contributors:* User:Asitjain 293
Figure 208 *Source:* https://en.wikipedia.org/w/index.php?title=File:Jetavana_of_Sravasti_Sanchi_Stupa_1_Northern_Gateway.jpg *License:* Creative Commons Attribution 2.0 *Contributors:* पाटलिपुत्र 294
Figure 209 *Source:* https://en.wikipedia.org/w/index.php?title=File:Jivakarama_oblong_communal_hall.jpg *License:* Creative Commons Attribution 2.0 *Contributors:* पाटलिपुत्र 295
Figure 210 *Source:* https://en.wikipedia.org/w/index.php?title=File:Stupas-Original-00020.jpg *License:* Creative Commons Attribution-Sharealike 3.0 *Contributors:* JimRenge, पाटलिपुत्र 296
Figure 211 *Source:* https://en.wikipedia.org/w/index.php?title=File:Pataliputra_capital_front.jpg *Contributors:* Wienerbund, पाटलिपुत्र 297
Figure 212 *Source:* https://en.wikipedia.org/w/index.php?title=File:Ashoka_pillar_at_Vaishali,_Bihar,_India.jpg *License:* Creative Commons Attribution-Sharealike 2.5 *Contributors:* Bpilgrim, Ekabhishek, Ellywa, JMCC1, Pebble101, Tulsi Bhagat, Wiki-uk, पाटलिपुत्र, 4 anonymous edits ... 297
Figure 213 *Source:* https://en.wikipedia.org/w/index.php?title=File:Early_stupa_6_meters_in_diameter_with_fallen_umbrella_on_side_in_Chakpat_near_Chakdara.jpg *Contributors:* Beads and reels, JMCC1 298
Figure 214 *Source:* https://en.wikipedia.org/w/index.php?title=File:Mauryan_ruins_of_pillared_hall_at_Kumrahar_site_of_Pataliputra_ASIEC_1912-13.jpg *License:* Public Domain *Contributors:* 神风 298

Figure 215 *Source:* https://en.wikipedia.org/w/index.php?title=File:Mauryan_Hall_pillar.jpg *License:* Public Domain *Contributors:* Bukk, Ellywa, Roland zh, Zunkir, पाटलिपुत्र ... 299

Figure 216 *Source:* https://en.wikipedia.org/w/index.php?title=File:Sarnath_capital.jpg *Contributors:* Happyseeu, पाटलिपुत्र ... 299

Image *Source:* https://en.wikipedia.org/w/index.php?title=File:Lomas_Rishi_entrance.jpg *License:* Creative Commons Attribution 2.0 *Contributors:* पाटलिपुत्र ... 300

Image *Source:* https://en.wikipedia.org/w/index.php?title=File:Sudama_cave_mirror-polished_walls.jpg *License:* Creative Commons Attribution 2.0 *Contributors:* Marcus Cyron, पाटलिपुत्र ... 300

Figure 217 *Source:* https://en.wikipedia.org/w/index.php?title=File:Sanchi_Stupa_number_2_KSP_3660.jpg *Contributors:* पाटलिपुत्र ... 302

Figure 218 *Source:* https://en.wikipedia.org/w/index.php?title=File:Sanchi1_N-MP-220.jpg *License:* Creative Commons Attribution-Sharealike 3.0 *Contributors:* User:Asitjain ... 302

Figure 219 *Source:* https://en.wikipedia.org/w/index.php?title=File:Adoration_of_the_Diamond_Throne_and_the_Bodhi_Tree_Bharhut_relief.jpg *Contributors:* Bodhisattwa, पाटलिपुत्र ... 303

Figure 220 *Source:* https://en.wikipedia.org/w/index.php?title=File:Remnants_of_Stupa.jpg *License:* Creative Commons Attribution-Sharealike 3.0 *Contributors:* User:Giridharmamidi ... 304

Figure 221 *Source:* https://en.wikipedia.org/w/index.php?title=File:Bharhut_circular_Temple.jpg *License:* Public Domain *Contributors:* पाटलिपुत्र 304

Figure 222 *Source:* https://en.wikipedia.org/w/index.php?title=File:Andhra_pradesh,_santuario_a_più_piani,_da_ghantasala,_90-110_ca..JPG *License:* GNU Free Documentation License *Contributors:* [[user:sailko]] ... 304

Figure 223 *Source:* https://en.wikipedia.org/w/index.php?title=File:IA_Temple_40_Sanchi.jpg *License:* Public Domain *Contributors:* पाटलिपुत्र 305

Figure 224 *Source:* https://en.wikipedia.org/w/index.php?title=File:Trivikram_Temple_Ter_1.jpg *License:* Creative Commons Attribution-Sharealike 3.0 *Contributors:* User:संतोष दहिवळ ... 306

Figure 225 *Source:* https://en.wikipedia.org/w/index.php?title=File:Amvar_Chejerla_Kapoteswara_temple_in_guntur_district.jpg *License:* Creative Commons Attribution-Sharealike 3.0 *Contributors:* Adityamadhav83 ... 306

Image *Source:* https://en.wikipedia.org/w/index.php?title=File:Kumrahar_Mahabodhi_plaque.jpg *License:* Public Domain *Contributors:* पाटलिपुत्र 306

Image *Source:* https://en.wikipedia.org/w/index.php?title=File:Top_of_Temple.jpg *License:* Creative Commons Attribution-Sharealike 3.0 *Contributors:* User:Shahakshay58 ... 307

Figure 226 *Source:* https://en.wikipedia.org/w/index.php?title=File:Sanchi_temple_17.jpg *License:* Creative Commons Attribution 2.0 *Contributors:* Nagarjun Kandukuru ... 308

Figure 227 *Source:* https://en.wikipedia.org/w/index.php?title=File:Ellora_Cave_16_si0308.jpg *Contributors:* User:G41rn8 ... 309

Figure 228 *Source:* https://en.wikipedia.org/w/index.php?title=File:An_aerial_view_of_Madurai_city_from_atop_of_Meenakshi_Amman_temple.jpg *License:* Creative Commons Attribution 3.0 *Contributors:* எஸ்ஸார் ... 310

Figure 229 *Source:* https://en.wikipedia.org/w/index.php?title=File:Qutb_Minar_tower.jpg *License:* Creative Commons Attribution 2.5 *Contributors:* Ondřej Žváček ... 311

Figure 230 *Source:* https://en.wikipedia.org/w/index.php?title=File:Ladakh_Monastery.jpg *License:* Creative Commons Attribution 2.0 *Contributors:* File Upload Bot (Magnus Manske), FlickreviewR, Jacopo Werther, OgreBot 2, Roland zh, Snotch, 2 anonymous edits ... 312

Figure 231 *Source:* https://en.wikipedia.org/w/index.php?title=File:Tawang_Monastery_(Tibetan_Buddhist).jpg *Contributors:* User:Donvikro 313

Figure 232 *Source:* https://en.wikipedia.org/w/index.php?title=File:Vikramjit-Kakati-Rumtek.jpg *License:* Creative Commons Attribution-Sharealike 3.0 *Contributors:* User:Donvikro ... 313

Figure 233 *Source:* https://en.wikipedia.org/w/index.php?title=File:Humayun_Tomb_in_Delhi-Front_view.JPG *License:* Creative Commons Attribution-Sharealike 3.0 *Contributors:* User:Onlineolddelhi ... 314

Figure 234 *Source:* https://en.wikipedia.org/w/index.php?title=File:Fatehput_Sikiri_Buland_Darwaza_gate_2010.jpg *License:* GNU Free Documentation License *Contributors:* Marcin Białek ... 315

Figure 235 *Source:* https://en.wikipedia.org/w/index.php?title=File:Red_Fort_in_Delhi_03-2016_img3.jpg *Contributors:* A.Savin ... 316

Figure 236 *Source:* https://en.wikipedia.org/w/index.php?title=File:GolGumbaz2.jpg *License:* Public Domain *Contributors:* Jungpionier, OgreBot 2, Ppntori, Roland zh, Shizhao, Thuresson, 2 anonymous edits ... 316

Figure 237 *Source:* https://en.wikipedia.org/w/index.php?title=File:Charminar-Pride_of_Hyderabad.jpg *License:* Creative Commons Attribution-Sharealike 3.0 *Contributors:* User:Krishnagopi06 ... 316

Figure 238 *Source:* https://en.wikipedia.org/w/index.php?title=File:Malda_~_Adina_Mosque_5.JPG *License:* Creative Commons Attribution-Sharealike 3.0 *Contributors:* User:B.saptarshi1984 ... 317

Image *Source:* https://en.wikipedia.org/w/index.php?title=File:Shaniwarwada_gate.JPG *License:* Creative Commons Attribution-Sharealike 3.0 *Contributors:* User:Ashok Bagade ... 318

Image *Source:* https://en.wikipedia.org/w/index.php?title=File:Thanjavur_Maratha_Palace_Darbar_Hall.jpg *License:* Creative Commons Attribution-Sharealike 3.0 *Contributors:* User:Kalanidhi ... 318

Image *Source:* https://en.wikipedia.org/w/index.php?title=File:Sarovar_and_the_Golden_Temple.jpg *License:* Creative Commons Attribution-Sharealike 2.0 *Contributors:* Ken Wieland ... 319

Image *Source:* https://en.wikipedia.org/w/index.php?title=File:Akal_takhat_amritsar.jpg *License:* GNU Free Documentation License *Contributors:* Ekabhishek, Ggia, Havang(nl), MGA73bot2, Magog the Ogre, Roland zh, Tonkawa68, Wst ... 319

Image *Source:* https://en.wikipedia.org/w/index.php?title=File:Asian_Games_logo.svg *License:* Public Domain *Contributors:* Olympic Council of Asia ... 328

Image *Source:* https://en.wikipedia.org/w/index.php?title=File:Table_tennis_pictogram.svg *License:* Public Domain *Contributors:* Aspargos, Bearas, Bvs-aca, Cmapm, Ha98574, Mohsen1248, Parutakupiu, Quibik, Thadius856, 1 anonymous edits ... 328

Image *Source:* https://en.wikipedia.org/w/index.php?title=File:Cue_sports_pictogram.svg *License:* Public Domain *Contributors:* Billard_pictogram.jpg: Sports9494 derivative work: Edwod2001 (talk) ... 328

Image *Source:* https://en.wikipedia.org/w/index.php?title=File:Wrestling_pictogram.svg *License:* Public Domain *Contributors:* Thadius856 (SVG conversion) & Parutakupiu (original image) ... 329

Image *Source:* https://en.wikipedia.org/w/index.php?title=File:Boxing_pictogram.svg *License:* Public Domain *Contributors:* Thadius856 (SVG conversion) & Parutakupiu (original image) ... 329

Image *Source:* https://en.wikipedia.org/w/index.php?title=File:Archery_pictogram.svg *License:* Public Domain *Contributors:* User:Parutakupiu, User:Thadius856 ... 329

Image *Source:* https://en.wikipedia.org/w/index.php?title=File:Basketball_pictogram.svg *License:* Public Domain *Contributors:* Citius Altius Fortius, Cmapm, Delfort, Donz007, Ha98574, Hedavid, Herbythyme, Look2See1, Mohsen1248, Orrling, Parutakupiu, Rocket000, Sarang, TFCforever, Thadius856, The Evil IP address, Thomas Linard, 8 anonymous edits ... 329

Image *Source:* https://en.wikipedia.org/w/index.php?title=File:Field_hockey_pictogram.svg *License:* Public Domain *Contributors:* Thadius856 (SVG conversion) & Parutakupiu (original image) ... 329

Image *Source:* https://en.wikipedia.org/w/index.php?title=File:Cricket_pictogram.svg *License:* Public Domain *Contributors:* User:Parutakupiu, User:Thadius856 ... 329

Image *Source:* https://en.wikipedia.org/w/index.php?title=File:Cycling_pictogram.svg *Contributors:* - ... 329

Image *Source:* https://en.wikipedia.org/w/index.php?title=File:Rowing_pictogram.svg *License:* Public Domain *Contributors:* Thadius856 (SVG conversion) & Parutakupiu (original image) ... 329

Image *Source:* https://en.wikipedia.org/w/index.php?title=File:Athletics_pictogram.svg *License:* Public Domain *Contributors:* User:Thadius856 329

Image *Source:* https://en.wikipedia.org/w/index.php?title=File:Judo_pictogram.svg *License:* Public Domain *Contributors:* Thadius856 (SVG conversion) & Parutakupiu (original image) ... 330

Image *Source:* https://en.wikipedia.org/w/index.php?title=File:Tennis_pictogram.svg *License:* Public Domain *Contributors:* Thadius856 (SVG conversion) & Parutakupiu (original image) ... 330

Image *Source:* https://en.wikipedia.org/w/index.php?title=File:Canoeing_pictogram.svg *Contributors:* - ... 330

Image *Source:* https://en.wikipedia.org/w/index.php?title=File:Kabaddi_pictogram.svg *License:* Creative Commons Attribution-Sharealike 3.0 *Contributors:* User:Mohsen1248 ... 330

Image *Source:* https://en.wikipedia.org/w/index.php?title=File:Sailing_pictogram.svg *License:* Public Domain *Contributors:* Thadius856 (SVG conversion) & Parutakupiu (original image) ... 330

Image *Source:* https://en.wikipedia.org/w/index.php?title=File:Gymnastics_pictogram.svg *Contributors:* - ... 330

Image *Source:* https://en.wikipedia.org/w/index.php?title=File:Volleyball_(beach)_pictogram.svg *License:* Public Domain *Contributors:* Thadius856 (SVG conversion) & Parutakupiu (original image) ... 331

Figure 277 *Source:* https://en.wikipedia.org/w/index.php?title=File:Dena_paona_1931.jpg *License:* Public Domain *Contributors:* calcuttaweb.com 425

Figure 278 *Source:* https://en.wikipedia.org/w/index.php?title=File:BACHCHAN_Amitabh_03-24x30-2009b.jpg *License:* Creative Commons Attribution 3.0 *Contributors:* BACHCHAN_Amitabh_03-24x30-2009.jpg: Studio Harcourt derivative work: Materialscientist (talk) 428

Figure 279 *Source:* https://en.wikipedia.org/w/index.php?title=File:Vigathakumaran.jpg *License:* Public Domain *Contributors:* Joy Varghese 430

Figure 280 *Source:* https://en.wikipedia.org/w/index.php?title=File:Balan_1938.jpg *License:* Public Domain *Contributors:* Kailash29792, Roland zh, 1 anonymous edits 431

Figure 281 *Source:* https://en.wikipedia.org/w/index.php?title=File:Kalidas(1931).jpg *License:* Public Domain *Contributors:* Deanlaw, Kailash29792, Roland zh, Sodabottle, SpacemanSpiff, Vensatry 434

Figure 282 *Source:* https://en.wikipedia.org/w/index.php?title=File:Raghupati_Venkayya.jpg *License:* Creative Commons Attribution-Sharealike 3.0 *Contributors:* User:రహ్మానుద్దీన్ 436

License

Creative Commons Attribution-Share Alike 3.0
//creativecommons.org/licenses/by-sa/3.0/

Index

477

Ajñana, 36, 39
Akal Takht, 319
Akananuru, 371
Akbar, 374, 461
Akbarnama, 461
Akbar Padamsee, 262
Akbar the Great, 315
A. K. Hangal, 220
Akhara, 142, 369, 373, 375
Akhil Kumar, 344
Akho, 165
Akira Kurosawa, 418
Akkadian literature, 154
Akka Mahadevi, 167
Akkineni Kutumba Rao, 437
Akkineni Nageswara Rao, 437
Akki rotti, 96
A. K. Lohithadas, 431
A. K. Ramanujan, 164
Akshay Kumar, 346
A la carte cable television, 394
Alai Minar of Khalji, 312
Alam Ara, 197, 409
Alankar, 227
Alapana, 228
Alathur Brothers, 228
Alauddin Khalji, 312
Alchon Huns, 308
Alcohol by volume, 121
Alcoholic beverage, 89
Ali Akbar Khan, 234, 235
Aligarh, 426
Alisha Chinai, 234, 236
Alka Yagnik, 235
Allakappa, 295
Allama Prabhu, 167
Allan Octavian Hume, 52, 53
All England Open Badminton Championships, 340
All India Chess Federation, 352
All India Football Federation, 338
All India Radio, 393
All India & South Asia Rugby Tournament, 365
Almond, 119
Almond milk, 121
Alok Nath, 220
Ama Lai Shraddhanjali, 229
Amar, 354
Amar Akbar Anthony, 415
Amaravathi Mahachaitya, 296, 301
Amaravathi (village), Guntur district, 143
Amaravati, 301
Amar Prem, 414
Ambalappuzha, 98
Ambarish, 429

Ambedkar Stadium, 331
Ameer Sultan, 415
American football, 357, 365
Americanization, 127
American literature, 157
Amir Khusro, 174
Amitabh Bacchan, 428
Amitabh Bachchan, 412, 414
Amitav Ghosh, 164
Amoghavarsha, 166
Amrita-Sher-Gil, 265
Amrithapura, 311
Amritsar, 393, 439
Amulya Barua, 161
An Advanced History of India, 30
Analytic philosophy, 34
Anand (1971 film), 414
Ananda Coomaraswamy, 22
Ananda K. Coomaraswamy, 266, 323
Ananda Kentish Coomaraswamy, 221
Anand Krishna, 262
Anant Balani, 427
Ananth Nag, 219
Anant Nag, 429
Anargharāghava, 461
Anathapindika, 294
Anatta, 36, 41
Ancient Egyptian literature, 154, 157
Ancient Greece, 269, 279
Ancient Greek literature, 154
Ancient India, 35
Ancient literature, 157
Ancient Orient Museum, 282
Ancient philosophy, 35
Ancient Tamil music, 225
Andaman and Nicobar Islands, 85
Andamanese, 85
Andaman Islands, 50
Andhra dynasty, 301
Andhra Pradesh, 86, 185, 188, 435, 439
Andre de Quadros, 240
Anekantavada, 40, 44
Angarkha, 142, 146
Angkor, 6, 14, 21
Angkor Wat, 14, 24
Anglo-Indian cuisine, 107, 118
Aniconic, 307
Aniket Gupta, 355
Anil Kapoor, 417
Anil Srinivasan, 240
Anirban Lahiri, 343
Anita Desai, 164
Añjali Mudrā, 24
Anjan Srivastav, 212
Anju Bobby George, 349
Anju Makhija, 165

Egyptian literature, 157
Eight Miles High, 237
Ekalavya, 382
Ek Duuje Ke Liye, 417
Eknath, 168
Electrical engineering, 393
Elephanta Caves, 272, 273
Elippathayam, 416
Elite Football League of India, 357, 365
Ellora, 286
Ellora Caves, 131, 248, 273, 301, 312
Elphinstone Bioscope Company, 409
Embroidery, 145
Embroidery of India, 130
Empathy, 421
Empire of Japan, 418
Enclave and exclave, 357
Endemism, 49
En:Digital object identifier, 29, 30, 200
Endurance riding, 348
England, 127
England national cricket team, 352
English language, 206
En:JSTOR, 29, 30, 200
En:OCLC, 442
Entertainment, 204
Enthiran, 418
Epic film, 412
Epic poetry, 157
Epic Sanskrit, 461
Epigraphy, 6, 7, 15
Epistemology, 35, 36, 43
Equestrian sports, 348
Erawan Shrine, 25
Erick Sermon, 236
Ernest Binfield Havel, 258
Eromba, 103
Eros Films, 406
Eros International, 438
ESPN, 395
ESPN Asia, 364, 402
Ethanol fermentation, 99
Ethics, 35
Ethnic groups in India, 81, 129, 153, 181, 203, 225, 245, 325, 391, 405
Ethnic Malay, 17
ETV Network, 394, 396
Eunice De Souza, 165
Euphoria (Indian band), 235
Eurasian Plate, 9
Europe, 82, 235, 406
European cinema, 422
European literature, 157
European Tour, 343
Eventing, 348
Excavations, 130

Existentialism, 34
Exonym, 15
Exploitation film, 422
Extant literature, 166
Extinction, 48

F2000 Championship Series, 354
Fads and trends, 204
Fahadh Faasil, 431
Fakir Mohan Senapati, 171
Fasting, 91
Fatehpur Sikri, 314
Federation Cup (India), 338
Fédération Internationale de Hockey, 337
Federation of International Bandy, 360
Feni (liquor), 121
Fennel, 94
Fenugreek, 85, 115
Fermentation (food), 86
Fernao Nunes, 373
FIBA, 342
FIBA Asia Championship for Women, 331
FIBA Asia Cup, 329
FIBA Asia Under-16 Championship for Women, 333
FIBA Asia Under-18 Championship, 330
FIBA Asia Womens Cup, 333
Fiddlehead fern, 94
FIDE World Chess Championship 2000, 330
Field Hockey, 325, 326, 328–334, 365, 367
Field hockey at the 1980 Summer Olympics, 336
Field hockey at the 1980 Summer Olympics – Womens tournament, 336
Field hockey at the 1982 Asian Games, 336
Field hockey at the 2014 Asian Games, 336
Field hockey at the 2016 Summer Olympics, 336
Field hockey at the 2016 Summer Olympics – Womens tournament, 336
Field Hockey World Cup, 329, 331, 333
FIFA, 338
FIFA rankings, 337
FIFA U-17 World Cup, 333, 338
FIFA World Cup, 337
Fighter kite, 326
FIH Hockey World League, 332, 333
FIH World Rankings, 336, 337
Fijian cuisine, 82
File:Adoration of the Diamond Throne and the Bodhi Tree Bharhut relief.jpg, 303
File:Bharhut Jetavana Jataka.jpg, 294
File:Royal cortege leaving Rajagriha.jpg, 293
File:War over the Buddha%27s Relics, South Gate, Stupa no. 1, Sanchi.jpg, 293
Filipino cuisine, 125

Jackie Chan, 435
Jadunath Sarkar, 447
Jagadish Mohanty, 171
Jagannath, 189, 256, 257
Jaggery, 100
Jahangir, 253
Jahar Dasgupta, 262, 265
Jain, 39, 172, 269
Jain Agamas, 43
Jainism, 36, 39, 41, 124, 159, 167, 270
Jain philosophy, 34, 36
Jain Prakrit, 159
Jaintia Hills district, 103
Jainul Abedin, 265
Jain vegetarianism, 124
Jaipur, 187, 357, 439
Jaisalmer, 286, 439
Jai Santoshi Ma, 414
Jaishankar Bhojak, 211
Jaishankar Prasad, 165, 211
Jait Re Jait, 432
Jakarta, 28
Jalachhayam, 431
Jalandhar, 329
Jalebi, 99, 107, 118
Jallikattu, 361
Jalsaghar, 413
Jama (coat), 146
Jama costume, 142
Jamaican literature, 157
Jamai Shashthi, 425
Jamatia, 113
Jamavar, 134
Jambavan, 368, 370
Jamdani, 133
James Ivory (director), 418
James Matisoff, 3
Jamini Roy, 256, 262, 265
Jammu and Kashmir, 193, 360
Jammu dress, 139
Jammu & Kashmir, 439
Jamshedji Framji Madan, 409
Jamuna Kinare, 426
Jana Gana Mana, 224, 240
Janakpur, 125
Jan Natya Manch, 216
Japan, 7
Japanese literature, 158
Japanese New Wave, 438
Japanese occupation of Burma, 418
Japan Golf Tour, 343
Jarasandha, 344, 368, 370, 383
Jasmine, 133
Jataka tales, 159, 248
Jatayu, 24
Jatin Lalit, 234

Jatra (Bengal), 214
Jaulian, 307
Java, 4, 22, 23
Javanese dance, 199
Javanese language, 4, 26, 27
Javanese people, 18
Javed Akhtar, 414
Javed Siddiqui, 214, 216
Jawaharlal Nehru, 21, 149
Jawahar Wattal, 237
Jayadeva, 159, 257
Jayalalithaa, 413, 435
Jayamala (actress), 429
Jayan, 416
Jayanta Mahapatra, 164
Jayanthi (actress), 429
Jayapura, 28
Jayaram, 431
Jayasurya, 431
Jayavarman II, 16
Jayawijaya Mountains, 28
Jay Sean, 237
Jay-Z, 236
Jazz, 235
Jazz in India, 224
Jazzy B, 237
J. C. Daniel, 430
Jean-Loup Passek, 442
Jean Renoir, 422
Jeet Thayil, 165
Jeevana Nataka, 428
Jeev Milkha Singh, 342, 343
Jeff Beck, 237
Jerry Pinto, 165
Jetavana, 294
Jewish philosophy, 34
Jharkhand, 94, 386
Jhumair, 195
Jhumpa Lahiri, 164
Jibanananda Das, 162
Jijo Punnoose, 431
Jimmy R. Jagtiani, 346
Jitender Kumar (flyweight boxer), 344
Jivakarama vihara, 295
Jnanpith, 168
Jnanpith Award, 156, 165, 167, 168, 173, 179
Jodhpur, 230, 439
Jodhpur State, 145
Jogesh Das, 161
Jogi, 234
Johann Wolfgang von Goethe, 207
John Boardman (art historian), 290
John Coltrane, 235
John Keay, 321
John Marshall (archaeologist), 298
John Wilkins (Indian artist), 262, 265

Peruvian literature, 157
Petroglyph, 246
Petticoat, 136
PGA Tour, 343
Phanindranath Bose, 21
Phijigee Mani, 432
Philalethes, 35
Philippine languages, 26
Philippine mythology, 24
Philippines, 4, 6, 8, 22, 23
Philippines mens national basketball team, 341
Philomath, 35
Philosopher, 35
Philosophical skepticism, 42
Philosophy, 34
Philosophy of law, 35
Phiran, 139
Phirni, 118
Phoenix dactylifera, 99
Phulka, 109
Pietro Della Valle, 373
Pigeon pea, 84
Pilaf, 82, 99
Pillar of Ashoka, 300
Pillars of Ashoka, 269, 274, 296–298
Pineapple, 121
Pink-headed duck, 52
Piprahwa, 295, 296
Piquance, 112
Pirate television, 397
Piravi, 416
Pitcher, 358
Pittsburgh Pirates, 358
Piyush Mishra, 213, 220
Pizza, 124
P. Lal, 164, 165
Plantain (cooking), 279
Plate tectonic, 9
Plate tectonics, 48
Platform for Action in Creative Theater, 218
Plato, 34
Platonism, 34
Playback singer, 234, 436
Playback theatre, 210, 211
Playing card, 327
Playout, 364
P. L. Narayana, 437
Pnar language, 424
Poetic realism, 422
Poetry, 157
Poha (rice), 99, 102
Political philosophy, 35, 44
Polo, 326, 357
Polynesia, 103
Polysyllabic, 4
Pomfret, 90

Pongal, 111, 361
Poori, 113
Popular music, 234
Population, 49, 52
Porbandar, 121
Poriyal, 111
Portal:Food, 81
Portal:India, 81, 82, 129, 153, 181, 203, 225, 245, 325, 391, 405
Portal:Indian wildlife, 47
Portal:Literature, 156, 158
Portal:Philosophy, 35
Portuguese cuisine, 89
Portuguese Empire, 91
Portuguese language, 7
Portuguese people, 82
Poseidon, 282
Postcolonial, 260
Post-colonialism, 157
Postmodernism, 157
Poststructuralism, 157
Potala Palace, 313
Potato, 82
Potatoes, 103
Pound sterling, 127
Prabhakar, 429
Prabhat Film Company, 410
Prabhat Films, 432
Prabir Roy, 394
Prabodh Chandra Bagchi, 9, 21
Prag Cine Awards, 440
Pragmatism, 34
Prakash Padukone, 339
Prakash Raj, 429
Prakrit, 159, 205, 381
Prakrit literature, 154
Pramana, 36, 43
Prambanan, 8, 17, 18, 24
P. Ramdas, 431
Prannoy Kumar, 340
Prasads IMAX, 420
Prasad Studios, 406
Prasad Vara Potluri, 406
Prasanna, 212
Prasar Bharati, 393, 395
Pratidwandi, 412
Pratyabhijna, 38
Pravara art studio, 219
Prawn, 90
Pre-historic, 246
Prema Karanth, 429
Premanand Bhatt, 165
Premier Badminton League, 326, 365
Premier Futsal, 365
Premier Hockey League, 367
Premier League, 338

Salim-Javed, 414
Salim Khan, 414
Salim-Sulaiman, 234
Salman Khan, 417
Salman Rushdie, 164, 165
Salt Lake City, 334
Salt Lake Stadium, 338
Saltwater crocodile, 73
Salwar kameez, 134, 135
Samahaara, 218
Samarth Ramdas, 168
Samaveda, 184, 226
Sambalpuri Dance, 193
Sambalpuri Saree, 136
Sambar deer, 58
Sambar (dish), 98, 110, 111
Samgha, 295
Samkhya, 36, 37
Samosa, 82, 113
Sampeah, 24
Samsara, 37, 41, 42
Saṃsāra (Jainism), 40
Samskara (film), 415, 429
Sanam (band), 237
Sanchi, 269, 275, 293, 294, 296, 301–303,
    305, 307, 308, 312
Sanchi Stupa No.2, 301, 302
Sandalwood, 121, 428
Sandesh (confectionery), 116
Sandip Ray, 426
Sandstone, 303
Sangam literature, 155, 156, 172, 371
Sangam period, 361
Sangeet Natak Akademi, 185, 199
Sangeet Natak Akademi Award, 208, 218, 224
Sania Mirza, 339
Sanjay Subrahmanyan, 228
Sanjeevani, 354
Sankarabharanam, 415
Sankaracharya, 375
Sankar Venkateswaran, 213
Sannyasa, 42
Sannyasi, 375
Sanober, 237
Sanskrit, 4, 6, 15, 26, 27, 146, 156, 159, 174,
    187, 256, 344, 369, 408
Sanskrit cinema, 405, 423
Sanskrit-derived names, 27
Sanskrit drama, 204–206, 421
Sanskritization, 22
Sanskrit language, 165, 205
Sanskrit literature, 154, 156, 158, 206, 372
Santali cinema, 405, 423
Santhal people, 261
Santoor, 227
Santosh Sivan, 435

Sant Tukaram, 432
Sant Tukaram (film), 410
Sapadalaksha, 309
Sapera, 234
Saptakanda Ramayana, 227
Saptak Annual Festival of Music, 224
Saptaparni Cave, 294
Sarala Dasa, 170
Sarangi, 234
Saraswati Samman, 179
Sarayu, 27
Saree, 130, 137
Saregama, 438
Sari, 131, 134, 135
Sarnath, 276, 300
Sarojini Naidu, 164
Sarojini Sahoo, 171
Sarong, 144
Sarson da saag, 88, 107
Sarvepalli Radhakrishnan, 45
Sarveshwar Dayal Saxena, 213
Sasanian, 315
Sash, 132
Sasthi Brata, 164
Satellite Instructional Television Experiment,
    393
Sathish Kalathil, 431
Sathyan Anthikad, 430, 431
Satish Alekar, 213
Satish Kaushik, 219
Satnam Singh Bhamara, 341
Satra, 161
Satriya, 161
Sattra, 190
Sattriya, 185, 454
Satvic, 83
Satwiksairaj Rankireddy, 340
Satya (1998 film), 417
Satyadev Dubey, 212
Satyagraha, 44
Satyajit Ray, 411, 412
Satyajit Ray Film and Television Institute, 441
Satyawadi Raja Harishchandra, 409
Saurabh Srivastava, 210
Savitri (1933 film), 410
Savitri (actress), 437
Scale (music), 227
Screen Awards, 440
Screenwriter, 414
Sculpture in the Indian subcontinent, **269**
Sculptures, 310
SDAT Tennis Stadium, 330
S. D. Batish, 234
S. D. Burman, 234
Seafood, 85
Second Opium War, 117

512

www.ingramcontent.com/pod-product-compliance
Lightning Source LLC
Chambersburg PA
CBHW030728280326
41926CB00086B/512

* 9 7 8 9 3 5 2 9 7 9 7 3 8 *